This is
The 1
fourth
filmin
of twe
within
divers
as suc
Edge
progr
of int
well a

British Television
Drama in the 1980s

British Television Drama in the 1980s

Edited and introduced by

GEORGE W. BRANDT

CAMBRIDGE
UNIVERSITY PRESS

Published by the Press Syndicate of the University of Cambridge
The Pitt Building, Trumpington Street, Cambridge CB2 1RP
40 West 20th Street, New York, NY 10011-4211, USA
10 Stamford Road, Oakleigh, Victoria 3166, Australia

First published 1993

Printed in Great Britain at the University Press, Cambridge

A catalogue record for this book is available from the British Library

Library of Congress cataloguing in publication data
British television drama in the 1980s / edited and introduced by
George W. Brandt.
p.   cm.
Videography: p.
Includes bibliographical references (p. 00) and index.
ISBN 0 521 41726 0 (hc). – ISBN 0 521 42723 1 (pb)
1. Television plays, English – History and criticism.
2. Television programmes – Great Britain. I. Brandt, George W.
PN1992.65.B682 1993
822'.025090914 – dc20   92-41630   CIP

ISBN 0 521 41726 0 hardback
ISBN 0 521 42723 1 paperback

Contents

Illustrations

Notes on the contributors

JOHN ADAMS is Director of Film and Television Studies in the Drama Department of the University of Bristol, where he has taught since 1979. He has special interests in a range of cross-disciplinary approaches to the subject and to the development of practical studies. He has worked professionally as a writer, director and producer, and publishes and broadcasts on media issues.

ELIZABETH BIRD, the Head of the Department for Continuing Education at the University of Bristol, has taught many courses on film and media studies. A member of the editorial collective which produced *Half the Sky* (Virago, 1979), she presently co-ordinates the MSc in Gender & Social Policy at Bristol University. She has published in the field of cultural studies and on women returning to the labour market.

GEORGE BRANDT, Professor Emeritus in Radio, Film and Television Studies in the Drama Department of the University of Bristol, worked for the National Film Board of Canada before becoming a university teacher in 1951. He created the first practical postgraduate media course at a British university and regularly produced student-made TV documentaries for the BBC from 1970 to 1986. He edited *British Television Drama* (Cambridge University Press, 1981) and *German and Dutch Theatre, 1600–1848* (Cambridge University Press, 1993), translated plays from German and Spanish, and contributed essays to several dictionaries of the theatre as well as articles to theatre and media publications. He has taught in the Netherlands as well as Japan.

PAUL CLEMENTS is Director of the School of Drama at the Welsh College of Music and Drama in Cardiff. He trained and worked as a teacher in Birmingham before joining the staff of the Midlands Arts Centre. He was one of the founder directors of the Contact Theatre Company in

Manchester and has taught drama at the University of British Columbia and at Simon Fraser University in Canada.

JO ELIOT originally trained as a drama teacher; after teaching in inner-city primary schools and lecturing in Drama at St Martin's College, Lancaster, she took an M. Ed. at Bristol University. Now a Senior Lecturer in Education at the University of the West of England at Bristol, she helped to develop the interdisciplinary MA in Women's Studies in 1991. She has also been involved with the Open University's Women's Studies programmes since their inception.

VERA GOTTLIEB is Professor of Drama at Goldsmiths' College, University of London, and co-director of a theatre company, Magna Carta Productions. Publications include *Chekhov and the Vaudeville* (Cambridge University Press, 1982), *Chekhov in Performance in Russia and Soviet Russia* (Chadwyck-Healey, 1984), as well as articles for *Themes in Drama*, *New Theatre Quarterly* and other periodicals. Translator, adaptor and director of *A Chekhov Quartet* (performed in London, Yalta and Moscow, 1987). Directed *Red Earth* (1985) and *Waterloo Road* (Young Vic Studio, 1987).

HUGH HEBERT is a television critic and feature writer for *The Guardian*, where he worked mainly on profiles and coverage of the arts and publishing before the expansion of small-screen output took over most of his time. He has also written extensively on the social services, and before joining *The Guardian* he was on the staff of *The Times* and *The Financial Times*.

JOOST HUNNINGHER is Principal Lecturer in Film and Television Production at the University of Westminster (formerly the Polytechnic of Central London) and course leader of the BA (Hons) Course in Film, Video and Photographic Arts and of the Joint Board for Film Industry Training courses. He has a wide range of professional production experience as a producer, director, writer, lighting cameraman and editor. Film credits include *Playing, Play Music, Turning South, Days of the Commune* (for the Royal Shakespeare Company), and *Settling Scores*. Theatre work includes directing plays for the Soho Poly Theatre.

ALBERT HUNT was born in Burnley, went to Balliol, and has been based in West Yorkshire since 1965. He has written widely about theatre and popular entertainment. Work with the Bradford Art College Theatre Group included *John Ford's Cuban Missile Crisis* and *The Destruction of Dresden*. Television documentaries include *Spring Fever in Melbourne* (about Australian Rules football), *Pakistan in Yorkshire* and *From Learie to Viv* (both about cricket in the North of England). Currently involved with work in Poland, Derry, and the West Yorkshire Playhouse.

ANDREW LAVENDER lectures part-time at Goldsmiths' College, University of London, on Television, Film and Theatre, and takes seminar courses on British Television, Film and Theatre at Birkbeck College for the British Universities Summer Schools programme. Formerly the editor of *City Limits*, he writes on arts and the media for publications including *The Guardian, New Statesman and Society* and *The Times*.

BOB MILLINGTON lectures in Drama, Film and Television in the School of Community Studies at the Liverpool John Moores University. Together with Robin Nelson he was responsible for the book on the production of *Boys from the Blackstuff*, based largely on interviews with the writer, director and BBC production staff. His current interests include community theatre, video production practice and images of Liverpool in contemporary culture.

GEOFFREY REEVES has directed plays at the National, for the Royal Shakespeare Company, at the Royal Court and the Sunderland Empire, as well as in Denmark, Sweden, Germany, Holland, Switzerland, Portugal, France, Israel, the United States and Japan. He has run theatres in Exeter, Nottingham and Atlanta, Georgia, has taught drama at universities in Stanford, Warwick and St Etienne, and currently works at LAMDA and the National Film and Television School.

DAVID ROSE has been in television since 1954, when he joined the BBC, becoming the Head of Television Training in 1969 and working as Head of Regional Television Drama from 1971 to 1981. When Channel 4 was founded he became the Senior Commissioning Editor for Fiction, continuing in this post until 1990. Numerous awards include the Prix Italia, 1959, several BAFTA awards, the Prix Rossellini, 1987, and the RTS Gold Medal, 1988.

RICHARD SPARKS teaches Criminology at Keele University. He has previously worked at the University of Cambridge and for the Open University. Outside his work on crime and mass media his academic interests are mainly in the sociology of imprisonment. Recent publications include *Imprisonment: European Perspectives* (editor with John Muncie, Harvester Wheatsheaf, 1991) and *Television and the Drama of Crime* (Open University Press, 1992).

Foreword

DAVID ROSE

The eighties saw perhaps the most radical changes in British television drama since the advent of colour and the ability to record and edit tape. These changes, combined with the fact that television audiences engage in their millions nightly to enjoy drama, make this book both timely and welcome. The period starts with the most influential event of the decade – the setting in motion of a new channel in 1980 which was to come 'on air' in 1982: Channel 4.

Amid the flurry of new recording and editing technology the 'single camera' operation had the greatest impact on drama. This saw the demise of multi-camera studio production which had allowed the actor to perform scenes lasting minutes at a time. The vision mixer became superfluous, short filmic takes were in. The writers – and all drama starts with them – were able to think in terms of cinema. Scripts became screenplays. *Play for Today* and *Thirty Minute Theatre* became *Film on Four* and *Screen One* and *Two*.

The addition of satellite and cable to the existing four channels, the uncertainty caused by the new commercial franchises and the coming debate over the BBC Charter all heightened the ratings war. It became a schedulers' heyday. Their strong cards were 'soaps': twice-weekly – later extended to thrice-weekly – serials with omnibus repeats were in demand. In fulfilling its remit and seeking a 10 per cent share of the audience, Channel 4 anticipated small audiences for its programmes. It needed its soap: *Brookside*, from the first night on air, delivering a satisfactory audience rating throughout the eighties. ITV's *The Bill* and the BBC's *EastEnders* followed, together with overseas acquisitions like *Neighbours*. These additional hours were mainly at the expense of the television play. The demise of the single play was hotly debated and in my view so much hot air. Plays were still produced – but they came in two, three, four and six episodes.

One of the many requirements of the Broadcasting Act which brought Channel 4 into being was the engagement of 'a substantial number of independent film and programme-makers'. Among the many benefits this brought was the opportunity to establish a partnership with the old enemy, cinema. Work originated by television could now be released theatrically before television transmission. With feature films this brought serious consideration by film critics, recognition at film festivals in the five continents – and subsequent sales opportunities. The free passage of writers, directors and technicians between the two industries was both welcome and healthy.

The closer ties with Europe have already signalled benefits – and dangers. Co-production is essential for the survival of broadcast drama. But quality will only be maintained in Europe by a generous editorial approach recognising and respecting language – and the many diverse and rich cultures that make up our dramatic traditions.

Acknowledgements

As tends to be the case in a work by various hands, what appears between the covers of the book is merely the tip of the iceberg. Not only has there been a long and I trust mutually stimulating prior exchange of ideas between the editor and the writers of the various essays in the volume: a great many people outside the enterprise itself, including some of the authors of the plays under discussion, have made vital (though not always immediately visible) contributions to it.

I have been helped in writing the Introduction by the information and advice given me by, among others, Richard MacDonnell, for many years a Regional Officer of the IBA; by Barrie MacDonald, Head of the ITC Library; by Charles Elton, of First Choice, and Archie Tait, Head of Development of Zenith Productions Limited, as well as by Tim Preece, actor and playwright. For all the help, counsel and support received by the various contributors to the volume in preparing the essays collected here, I should like to express sincere thanks on their behalf and join my appreciation to theirs. Albert Hunt was given a most illuminating interview by Alan Bennett. Vera Gottlieb was supplied by London Weekend Television, through the good offices of Michael Small, with the post-production script of the *South Bank Show* of 13 April 1986: *Brookside* (edited and presented by Melvyn Bragg, produced and directed by Jill Freeman) and given permission by Mr Bragg to quote from it; she was also supplied with the script of *Brookside Episode 355* by Merseyside Television, through the good offices of Philip Reevell, Head of Corporate Affairs, and Ian Vasey, *Brookside* Location Manager. John Adams was granted an interview by Sir Antony Jay and obtained some additional insights into *Yes, Prime Minister* from correspondence with Jonathan Lynn and from information supplied by BBC Enterprises. Geoffrey Reeves had a long and productive interview with Charles Wood and had additional information kindly supplied by Ian Curteis. Paul Clements was able to interview Mike Leigh about *Four Days in July*. Hugh Hebert's interview with Bill Bryden and correspondence with John Byrne, as well as information given by Norman McCandlish (BBC Scotland) and, incidentally, Emma Thompson, provided valuable background to his essay. Liz Bird and Jo Eliot gratefully acknowledge that their interview with Fay Weldon yielded fresh insights into that writer's work; both co-authors of the essay on *The Life and Loves of a She-Devil* are also indebted to Jane Wyborn for providing a tape of this, and to the Women's Committee of the Writers' Guild of Great Britain for their comments. Joost Hunningher benefited from extensive interviews with Jon Amiel, Jim Clay, Kenith Trodd and Frances Hannon, which enabled him to gain a rounded overview of the making of *The Singing Detective*. Speaking for myself as the writer of the piece on *The Jewel in the Crown*, I should like to thank Sir Denis Forman and Tim Piggott-Smith for supplying some background information, as well as Diane Cooke, *Coronation Street* publicist, for answering several questions.

I have pleasure in acknowledging the substantial help I have been given in compiling the bibliographical information, both the brief listings attached to individual essays and the more comprehensive compilation at the end of the book, by Pat Perilli, then the Information Officer of the BFI Library, and Phil Wickham, BFI Library Services; by the staff of the Main Library of the University of Bristol; by Chris Weller, Director of BBC Books at BBC Enterprises, and by Caroline Pitt, of the Longman Group UK. I am particularly grateful to Elaine Sinclair and Susan Tattersall of the Media Research Centre, BBC Bristol, whose exertions in ferreting out dates and facts for me proved quite invaluable. I should also like to thank Dr Mallory Wober, Deputy Head of Research at the ITC, for data on IBA/ITC research papers (Appendix 2), and Ross McGinley, Assistant Producer BBC Video, for information concerning the availability of videotapes of BBC plays.

I wish to give my sincere thanks to Clive James and Messrs Peters, Fraser and Dunlop for permission to quote from his 1991 address to the Royal Television Society; to Brookside Productions Ltd, especially its Legal Assistant Stephen Byrne, as well as author Barry Woodward for permission to quote scenes 7 and 10 of *Brookside Episode 355:* 'Damon's YTS Comes to an End'; to Colin Dexter, the format owner and creator of Inspector Morse as well as Mr Dexter's agent, and to Central Independent Television, especially Deborah Waight, Ancillary Rights Manager, for permission to quote from 'The Last Enemy', written by Peter Buckman; to Charles Wood and Penguin Books Ltd for permission to quote from *Tumbledown*; to Mike Leigh for permission to quote from *Four Days in July*; to Penguin Books Ltd for permission to quote from John Byrne's *The*

Slab Boys Trilogy; to Messrs William Heinemann Ltd, the Octopus Publishing Group Library and David Higham Associates for permission to quote from Paul Scott's Raj Quartet and *My Appointment with Muse*; and to Messrs Faber and Faber for permission to quote from Dennis Potter's *The Singing Detective*. The quotations from *The Proceedings of the Royal Institution* in the essay on *Yes, Prime Minister* are by courtesy of the Royal Institution and Sir Antony Jay.

Thanks are also due to the BBC Photographic Library for permission to reproduce nine stills from BBC drama productions; I am particularly grateful to Bobbie Mitchell for her help and advice in selecting these. I am indebted to Julie Hearn and Jane Friggins of the Channel 4 Stills Library for the *Brookside* still, to Barry Ledingham, Picture Desk at Central Broadcasting Ltd, for the still from 'The Last Enemy', and to Dominique Faure of Granada Television for the still from *The Jewel in the Crown* (and for video information as well).

Every effort has been made to secure the consent of each artiste whose picture appears in the book, and I am happy to thank the following agents who have agreed to do so on behalf of their clients: Emma Bibby (ICM) for Maggie Smith; Ken McReddie Ltd for Nigel Hawthorne; Markham and Froggatt Ltd for Bob Peck; London Management for Michael Angelis; Annette Stone Associates for Simon O'Brien and Julie T. Wallace; Julian Belfrage Associates for Colin Firth; and CDA for Robbie Coltrane. I also gratefully acknowledge Mike Leigh's and Tim Piggott-Smith's kind permission to use their pictures.

Much of the quality of *British Television Drama in the Eighties* is due not only to the actual panel of contributors but also the less visible informants listed above. The book's shortcomings, on the other hand, are entirely in the editor's court – who, if he has inadvertently overlooked anybody or any institution that has helped it on its way, craves their forgiveness in advance.

G.W.B.

1   Introduction

GEORGE W. BRANDT

> A television programme is not a commodity. It might become one, but it begins as a labour of love. To make money in television you must first make things, and the things you make are things of the spirit.
>
> Clive James[1]

This volume is a follow-up to my earlier *British Television Drama* (Cambridge University Press, 1981) – but with a difference. In editing that book my aim had basically been a simple one: it was to argue the case for television playwriting as a legitimate form of drama, deserving of respect as much as any other form of playwriting and hence worthy of study. The overall pattern of *British Television Drama* – that is, each of its chapters being devoted to the work of one playwright – was not intended to imply any auteurist delusion either on my part or on that of the contributors to the volume. Yes, the author was and is at the heart of the playmaking process. But to say that is not tantamount to putting him or her on a pedestal as a solitary genius. We were not ignorant of the real world of TV, with its pressures of time slots, scheduling for specific audiences and the tyranny of ratings. But even if a writer is commissioned to produce some episodes of a soap opera originated by someone else, and thus obliged to work with pre-established characters and within situations leaving little space for self-expression, he or she still has to *write*. No matter whether the script arises out of what we might call primary or secondary creativity: without the act of writing there simply wouldn't be any programme.

That said, I was of course perfectly well aware of the massive input in the final product of countless workers other than the writer. Just to take producers: key people like Kenith Trodd, long-time associate of Dennis Potter; like Michael Wearing, responsible for some of the outstanding productions of the eighties, including two dealt with in this book (*Boys from the Blackstuff* and *Edge of Darkness*); like the late Innes Lloyd, who produced more than sixty films, dramas and series for the BBC, particularly promoting the plays of Alan Bennett;[2] like the formidable Verity Lambert, a powerful influence in countless productions at the BBC from *Doctor Who* onward, later the Controller of Drama at Thames TV and a director of that company's subsidiary Euston Films;[3] like Betty Willingale, who nursed along writers of the stature of Dennis Potter, Arthur Hopcraft, Ken Taylor, Troy Kennedy Martin and John Hopkins[4] – such individuals have always mattered enormously in the making of what is arguably still, at least at the time of writing, the best television drama in the world. They and their colleagues must be included in the overall evaluation of any programme – as must the directors, actors, composers, musicians, set/costume/lighting designers, cameramen, make-up artistes, and indeed all the other collaborators in the collective enterprise that is TV drama.

But the emphasis on the *writer* in a book written in the late seventies made sense. It was a strategy dictated by the academic prejudice still current at the time against what had already by then become a significant art form – but one lacking the sanction of literary esteem.

The need for arguing such a case no longer exists. The favourable reception of *British Television Drama* and later books on the subject suggests that the climate has changed. The exponential growth in recent years of TV studies, admittedly often more sociologically than aesthetically orientated, at universities in the English-speaking world shows that television, including its drama, has come to be recognised as an important factor in contemporary culture. In view of this, the present book's format differs somewhat from that of its predecessor. Apart from the fact that it takes for its theme a much more limited time span – only one decade: the eighties – it has adopted the *programme* rather than the playwright as its organising principle. This has allowed the contributors to look at a great many aspects other than, or rather in addition to, the written text.

Nevertheless the present volume, too, is concerned with the aesthetic response to given programmes. Admittedly there must be a subjective (which is not to say an arbitrary) element in such a response. This book does not set out to deny any other ways of looking at television drama in committing itself to a felt rather than a purely cerebral response. But it asserts that aesthetics, and hence value judgements, are a key function of the critic, as indeed they must be by definition. The direction taken by media and cultural studies in recent years makes it clear that this is not altogether an unproblematical attitude.

Let us take an example of what might be termed the New Establishment point of view. In the introduction to his *Television Drama*, published in

1990, John Tulloch devotes several pages to a critique of *British Television Drama* – which he sees as (unhappily) embedded in the liberal/critical discourse shared by many television practitioners. Tulloch says of the book that

the social location is the alliance between a liberal academia and a 'critical' media practice which allows the 'ventilation' of public issues; and the ideological work of the discourse is in promoting 'creativity' (though occasionally 'politics') to a 'mass audience' by way of, primarily, public service television.[5]

Having noted all the quotation marks raised like so many quizzical eyebrows, one might ask whether from a progressive point of view (which is that taken by Tulloch) it would be better *not* to ventilate any public issues, better *not* to present any politics to a mass audience. Or indeed not to value creativity, however defined. One notes the implied attack on a supposedly elitist stance – the programme-maker (or the academic) talking down to the 'mass audience' from a superior, class-based point of vantage. Paradoxically, Tulloch makes it clear that he prizes many authors – Griffiths, Potter, Bleasdale, McGrath – who would fit into the (as he might see it) liberal-humanist canon easily enough. So to take the argument beyond this particular instance: one cannot help wondering at the position of quite a few radical scholars who, in their eagerness to attack the 'liberal-critical' consensus in the matter of 'quality' drama, risk ending up, in effect if not in intention, close to a rightwing populism that Rupert Murdoch might well, and indeed does, endorse vociferously.

Let me state my own stance right from the start. The pattern of the present book may differ from that of its predecessor, but the underlying editorial attitude is much as it was before. That attitude no doubt runs counter to a good deal of the work done in cultural studies during the eighties. To quote Paul Kerr: 'These days it is unfashionable on the left to talk about "quality". It is an evaluative term – and evaluation has been out of intellectual favour for some time in cultural criticism.'[6] I am content to go against the fashion. This collection of essays, admittedly an incomplete and selective overview of the eighties, sets out to deal with critical – and that must include judgemental – issues. No attempt has been made to deal with television in value-free, merely 'ethnographic' or sociological terms.

The question of quality is central here. In an essay, 'Problems with Quality', Charlotte Brunsdon, the well-known contributor to *Screen*, has sought to unravel the distinguishing features of high-prestige drama productions. Taking Granada's *Bridehead Revisited* and *The Jewel in the Crown* as the paradigms, she has singled out the factors that appear to make these epics 'uncontroversial signifiers of quality'. According to her list, which I summarise, they are the following:

1 *Literary source.* British culture having a predominantly literary bias, middle-brow literature legitimates the 'vulgar' medium of television (whereas high literature might offend as being too good for TV). Adaptations gain prestige from their literariness.

2 *The best of British acting.* Prestigious actors with a theatrical pedigree give 'class' to quality productions – a notion supported by international opinion (i.e. the foreign market).

3 *Money.* Such programmes are distinguished by high (meaning high-cost) production values. Tastefully deployed, these tend to underwrite upper middle-class lifestyles. Ms Brunsdon reminds us that Rupert Murdoch asserted as much in an 'anti-elitist' diatribe in his MacTaggart Memorial Lecture at Edinburgh in 1988.

4 *Heritage aspect.* Classy serials tend to project a National Trust image of England and Englishness (though not necessarily of the rest of Britain).[7]

Touché! – the heritage thrust is a palpable hit. A largely idealised past which panders to nostalgia for a never-never-land of social harmony *is* a pitfall for 'quality' productions.[8]

The other arguments are more questionable.

For a start, throwing together the two ideologically very different Granada blockbusters, *Brideshead Revisited* and *The Jewel in the Crown*, muddies the waters. As for the literary aspect of drama (plotting, characterisation, dialogue), this is as much or nearly as much part of the television play as is the visual input – and that is true not only of adaptations, which are the point at issue here, but more generally. Whether literariness is commendable or otherwise depends entirely on the context. It would be as absurd to say dogmatically: 'Literary = bad' as it would be to assert the contrary.

And why on earth should outstanding performances, even by stage actors, be seen as irrelevant to 'quality'? British actors fortunately cross over from one medium to another quite freely. This would be reprehensible only if the skills on display were somehow inappropriate to the medium; which is not the case as a rule.

The money argument has some validity – but not much. A telefilm like *The Far Pavilions* sank without a trace in spite of its having a budget considerably larger than *The Jewel in the Crown*. It embodied the romance of empire in precisely the way that *Jewel* did not. Ms Brunsdon's case against prestige productions is not strengthened by her invoking Rupert Murdoch to prop it up. The pseudo-radicalism of that latter-day Citizen Kane is rightly suspect; it is the radicalism of the right, populism from the top down.

But perhaps the anti-evaluative stance of eighties radicalism is beginning to lose some of its gloss. To quote Ms Brunsdon again, who has written in (at least partial) revision of an earlier position:

Although frequently informed by a desire to investigate, rather than judge, other people's pleasures, this very avoidance of judgement seems somehow to recreate the old patterns of aesthetic domination and subordination, and to pathologize the audience. Because issues of judgement are never brought out into the open, but always kept, as it were, under the seminar table, criteria involved can never be interrogated ... I do not wish to argue that television studies should be devoted to discriminating between 'good' and 'bad' programs [*Why on earth not?* GB], but I do want to insist that most academics in television studies are using qualitative criteria, however expressed or repressed, and that the constitution of the criteria involved should be the subject of explicit debate ... 'What are we going to do about bad television?' Nothing, if we're not prepared to admit it exists.[9]

What then is quality? Far be it from me to lay down any a priori, once-and-for-all ground rules for defining that elusive beast. But the assessment of TV drama cannot be totally isolated from the criteria applied to other narrative and dramatic forms. The television play may be *sui generis* (though even that is questionable); it certainly does not exist in an aesthetic vacuum. Drama as a mirror of life (which may well be a distorting mirror: naturalism is no longer seen as the 'natural' language of TV); as a reflection of real human concerns (which are not necessarily just topical ones); able to relate individual experiences to an implicit moral structure and scale of values; able to broaden the viewers' sympathies beyond their normal confines, to lead them to a greater insight into interpersonal and social relationships, to educate their feelings (at all levels) through laughter, suspense, empathy or whatever, by means of images as well as words, and to do this in a form with a palpable beginning, middle and end – these aims are as valid for drama watched over a TV dinner as they are for its counterpart on the stage or the cinema screen. (Except that the Aristotelian insistence on an end as a necessary formal element doesn't apply to the closure-less continuous serial.)

As in *British Television Drama*, the contributors to this volume come from a variety of backgrounds. I negotiated with them as to which particular programmes they would be writing about, and we achieved a meeting of minds concerning the importance, however defined, of their chosen topics. The programmes discussed in the book represent highlights of the decade's TV drama on all four channels – which is not to say that there weren't a good many other outstanding plays which might alternatively have been selected. In any case, each of the productions chosen was interesting in its own right; each one commented directly or indirectly on the times we live in, either in affirmation or in dissent; and it is by these programmes and others like them that the small-screen drama of the eighties is going to be remembered.

In contrast to the plays examined in *British Television Drama*, they are not predominantly single plays but either serials or series. This reflects the actual change in the balance of TV drama programming during the eighties. All the plays raise a number of critical issues, both in themselves and in their historical, institutional or generic context. Many of them 'ventilate' public issues – and are none the worse for that (nor necessarily any the better either). Most of them pay at least a nodding tribute to genre conventions, but as often as not it's precisely their breaking through these conventions that gives them their distinctive character.

The hope of confining the topics to plays available on video, which would enable the interested reader to pursue the subject further, could unfortunately not be realised entirely. Nevertheless, a number of plays *can* be bought or rented for home viewing in the UK, so that the arguments advanced here are capable of being either verified or confuted (and the plays enjoyed all over again).[10] Though the essays all express personal points of view, differing from each other in approach as well as in style, they are so arranged as to offer something in the nature of an internal dialogue.

Albert Hunt opens with an examination of one of the monologues from Alan Bennett's *Talking Heads*. In this series, the six episodes of which had several directors, Bennett pared the form down to its barest essentials. All the dramatic communication is in the actor's hands, or rather in the actor's face. Here television shows its affinity not only with the stage – the monologue is after all a well-established minor theatrical form – but with the short story as well. This is TV drama at its most literary.

By way of contrast, Vera Gottlieb presents the opposite end of the spectrum in the second essay; she sets episode 355 of *Brookside* ('Damon's YTS Comes to an End') in the context of the soap opera form. The continuous serial has been flourishing mightily during the decade, and there is a growing volume of literature – academic, polemical or adulatory – covering this area. The episode in question, written by Barry Woodward, describes an all-too-typical event in the life of a young man during a period of high unemployment.

John Adams, in the third essay, uses an episode from the extremely successful series, *Yes, Prime Minister*, by Antony Jay and Jonathan Lynn, as a springboard for wide-ranging reflections on the nature of TV comedy.

In the fourth essay, Richard Sparks locates an episode from the Inspector Morse series, 'The Last Enemy', within a definite genre convention; and he shows that it runs counter to some of these conventions. That exceptionally popular series, built around the character first created by Colin Dexter in his nine Morse novels, has been served by writers as accomplished and diverse as Anthony Minghella, Julian Mitchell, Charles Wood and Peter Nichols.

Troy Kennedy Martin's mini-series, *Edge of Darkness*, is the subject of the fifth essay. In a detailed analysis, Andrew Lavender makes clear that this suspenseful story of nuclear skulduggery blends symbolism with realism and increasingly locates a politically inflected thriller in the realm of metaphor.

The writer of the sixth essay, Bob Millington, is well known as the co-author of a book on his chosen subject:[11] this is Alan Bleasdale's *Boys from the Blackstuff*, another treatment of political issues – but seen in essentially personal terms. This series of five self-contained but interlocking stories, with their X-ray vision of Liverpool working-class life in a period of recession, appears in retrospect to have been one of the representative statements of the decade.

Geoffrey Reeves presents in the seventh essay the history of the production as well as the reception in the press and the country at large of Charles Wood's Falklands drama, *Tumbledown*. He draws a parallel with the fate of Ian Curteis's *Falklands Play*, which failed to achieve production, and he raises questions of the public response to that ever-contentious genre, docu-drama.

Four Days in July – the only single play in this volume apart from *Tumbledown* – is writer-director Mike Leigh's study of the Ulster 'situation' as experienced in everyday life. In the eighth essay of the book Paul Clements, an acknowledged expert on Leigh's highly personal working methods,[12] examines this film which was shot on location in Northern Ireland.

The next essay – Hugh Hebert's piece on John Byrne's mini-series *Tutti Frutti* – also considers aspects of British life from a perspective other than that of the Home Counties. Scotland has during the decade been developing a more distinctive accent in TV drama, in which John Byrne's unmistakably Scottish tone of voice stands out.

In dealing in the tenth essay with *The Jewel in the Crown*, Ken Taylor's dramatisation of Paul Scott's Raj Quartet, I have engaged with some of the problems of adapting novels for television, a sore point with many critics who deplore this as an inherently second-rate form of writing.

The question of adaptation comes up again, together with problems of feminist representation on television, in the eleventh essay, Liz Bird and Jo Eliot's piece on Fay Weldon's *The Life and Loves of a She-Devil* as dramatised by Ted Whitehead. The writers relate the highly acclaimed serial to a number of current theoretical issues.

The last essay, Joost Hunningher's sleuthlike investigation of Dennis

Potter's *The Singing Detective*, arguably the most complex TV drama of the decade, uncovers some little-known details of its production history.

This listing of essays (which incidentally confirms the BBC's continuing place as the leader in the field) suffices to demonstrate that the eighties were a fertile period for television drama – *malgré tout*. Rather than attempt to give an exhaustive account of all the major plays of the period, let me sketch in the background against which this drama was written and produced.

Many of the previous decade's familiar landmarks – people as well as programmes – were, of course, still part of the scene. Thus, Alan Plater was in constant demand; he adapted Trollope in his *Barchester Chronicles* (BBC 1982) and Olivia Manning's Balkan and Levant trilogies under the title of *Fortunes of War* (BBC 1987), epics on a par with the Granada blockbusters; and he contributed many original stories such as *Thank you, Mrs. Clinkscales* (Yorkshire 1983) and *The Beiderbecke Trilogy* (Yorkshire 1984–6).

Alan Bennett went from strength to strength.[13] John Mortimer supplied a new stack of briefs to his crusty legal hero, Rumpole of the Bailey, who had first laid down the law for Thames TV as long ago as 1978. If Mortimer's dramatisation of Waugh's *Brideshead Revisited* (Granada 1981) was a nostalgia trip for some, his serial *Paradise Postponed* (Thames 1986) reported on the state of the nation between 1948 and 1985 from the perspective of disappointed postwar idealism.

Some writers of that sometimes underrated but perennially popular genre, sitcom, also proved to have enviable staying power. In the BBC stable there were Carla Lane, allegedly the highest-paid comedy writer of them all (*Bread*), John Sullivan (*Only Fools and Horses...*) as well as Roy Clarke (*Last of the Summer Wine*). At Central TV, the old team of Dick Clement and Ian La Frenais launched *Auf Wiedersehen, Pet* in 1983; it staged a comeback in 1986.

Some soap operas seemed to go on for ever – like *Coronation Street*. Though sometimes accused of living in a cosy Northern timewarp, The Street has been able to retain its dedicated following. Yorkshire TV's *Emmerdale Farm* carried on a bucolic career begun in 1982; the village where its exteriors are filmed has become a tourist trap, complete with Emmerdale rock, mugs and tea-towels.

A number of changes did take place though, in soaps as elsewhere. Scottish Television joined the chorus with *Take the High Road* at the beginning of the decade, whilst Central TV's *Crossroads* did not long survive the attempts in 1985 to beef up its anaemic, much maligned but passionately defended existence. Phil Redmond's *Brookside*, launched on Channel 4 in 1982, set out to break new ground. Its situation in a *real* housing estate updated the concept of location shooting, with sound and vision control placed in a technical block right among the actual houses. Eclipsing them all, Julia Smith and Tony Holland's *East Enders* managed to make Albert Square as familiar a place as The Rovers Return. In the year of its launch, 1985, the new soap reached an audience of 22.15 million in the week ending 14 December. The actor Leslie Grantham, with a real-life conviction for murder behind him, made Dirty Den an inexhaustible story for the tabloids.

If the eighties – like all decades – were a transitional period, they did have a distinctive character of their own. In the age of Thatcherism the postwar consensus screeched to a halt. The government hammered the public with the message that there was no alternative to its measures, however painful. The new ideology employed the language of libertarianism as a cover for reversing the social gains taken for granted for over three decades. Henceforward the free market was to be equated with freedom as such. To quote Howard Brenton:

Thatcherism, like all authoritarian dogmas, was brightly coloured. Writers were trying to get at the darkness, the social cruelty and suffering behind the numbingly neo-bright phrases – 'the right to choose', 'freedom under the law', 'rolling back the state'.[14]

According to Mrs Thatcher, there was no such thing as society. The Good Samaritan was merely a man with enough money in his pocket to be Good. The new rugged individualism aimed to undermine the public-service ideal which hitherto had informed many areas of life, notably broadcasting, and to substitute undiluted market principles – although historically dubious 'Victorian values' were also invoked from time to time. In the terminology that came to dominate public discourse, the citizen (an adult person possessed of certain inalienable rights irrespective of wealth) was to be replaced by the consumer (whose clout would vary according to purchasing power). The catchword used *ad nauseam* was that of 'choice'. What was ignored was the fact that in many fields, certainly in broadcasting, a greater multiplicity of goods in the shop window didn't necessarily spell greater variety. It might simply mean more of the same, with no *meaningful* widening of choice at all. American television, the free-market ideal towards which most Thatcherite thinking appeared to be tending, was a case in point. The approximately forty channels on tap in New York merely offered a choice of similar material greatly inferior on the whole to what was available to the British viewer on four.

Opposition among writers and broadcasters to such a philosophy couldn't be snuffed out overnight, but dissidents were to come under steadily growing, though often unacknowledged, pressure during the decade. The fact that Mrs Whitehouse maintained her old campaign to clean up the airwaves was only a minor irritant; the old campaigner's Punch-and-Judy show had almost become an endearing national institution. True, she sometimes went too far. There was, for instance, the radio interview in 1989 when she suggested that, if *The Singing Detective* was anything to go by, the cause of Dennis Potter's well-known psoriasis must have been the childhood trauma of seeing his mother being seduced in the woods. Mrs Potter senior was not amused, sued and received an apology. Mrs Whitehouse claimed she'd blacked out halfway through the interview and hadn't really meant what she'd said.

More serious was the relentlessly tightening government pressure on the BBC. One way of hobbling the Corporation was to question the licence fee – always a good populist ploy – and look to commercial ways of funding the Corporation. The Committee on Financing the BBC, set up in 1985 under the chairmanship of Alan Peacock, was charged with the task of assessing the effects of advertising or sponsorship for BBC programmes; in fact, its investigations covered the whole field of broadcasting. Its findings, published on 3 July 1986, didn't quite live up to what the government had obviously expected: the Committee's advice was *against* advertising. Some of its other recommendations were not so good. The policy, adopted in April 1988, of index-linking the licence fee failed to take into account the fact that TV production costs (not only for the BBC, of course) were rising faster than inflation. The recommendations that (a) a quota of airtime be reserved for independent producers, not only in BBC but also in ITV programming, and (b) the Independent Broadcasting Authority (IBA) should in future be guided by strictly commercial criteria in awarding ITV franchises, were later picked up with questionable results by the Home Affairs Committee on Broadcasting, in a report submitted on 22 June 1988.

Indeed, Independent Television wasn't safe in its commercial corner either, since the IBA was also committed to a public-service concept. There were repeated attacks in parliament and in the press not only on the BBC but on certain ITV programmes as well – controversial documentaries such as Thames TV's *Death on the Rock* (28 April 1988) stirring up even more of a hornet's nest than the broadcasting of mere plays.

Not that drama was immune. Some plays were red rags to the bulls of reaction – particularly if produced by the BBC. Trevor Griffiths, an enthusiastic and effective contributor to TV drama in the seventies, ran into a lot of flak with his less than idolatrous portrait of Scott of the Antarctic in *The Last Place on Earth* (BBC 1985) – after which, passively or even actively discouraged, no more of his work was seen on the small screen for the rest of the decade.[15] Another red rag was Alan Bleasdale's mini-series *The Monocled Mutineer* (BBC1, 1986), the fictionalised story of a real squaddie, Percy Toplis, who impersonated an officer during the First

World War. Both in its disenchanted portrayal of the Army and in the violent reaction this broadcast unleashed, *The Mutineer* was an uncanny replay of Jim Allen's *Days of Hope* back in 1975.[16] The episode that aroused the greatest passion was that of the mutiny in a British Army training camp at Etaples in 1917, during which the officers were temporarily held at bay by a rebellious soldiery. Immediately, indignant voices were raised in the House of Commons, questioning whether these events of long ago had been depicted with all due historical accuracy. (The attempt by Julian Critchley MP to get the Ministry of Defence to settle the matter by opening up its records on the mutiny proved fruitless.) The press, too, was in full cry. The *Daily Mail* suggested in a biting editorial that *The Monocled Mutineer* was yet further evidence of sinister leftwing bias at the BBC; and it recommended that whoever was to be appointed as the new Chairman of the Board of Governors (after the impending retirement of the incumbent, Stuart Young) should clean out these Augean stables.[17]

In fact the appointment went to Marmaduke Hussey, former chief executive of *The Times*, soon after the *Mutineer* brouhaha. Within four months the new chairman showed his teeth by firing Alasdair Milne, the BBC's Director-General. This unprecedented event took place in the course of a banquet – an elegant bit of stiletto-work of which Machiavelli might have approved. Such a *coup de théâtre* was not necessarily prompted just by *The Monocled Mutineer*: there had also been a good deal of argy-bargy about Ian Curteis' unproduced *Falklands Play*,[18] and further non-drama-related issues were undoubtedly involved as well, such as rows over the Zircon and the *Secret Society* broadcasts which the government was unhappy about. In any case, the Corporation had been served notice not to step too far out of line henceforward.

However, the overall picture was not without its contradictions. Another potentially provocative mini-series didn't stir up nearly the same shock-horror reflex; admittedly it was shown on Channel 4, not by the BBC. Whereas *The Monocled Mutineer* had highlighted a black spot in past military history, *A Very British Coup* (1988), Alan Plater's adaptation of a novel by Labour MP Chris Mullin, peered into the politics of the near future. *A Very British Coup* showed the Establishment alive and well, ready to throttle any policies, however democratically voted for, that might weaken existing power structures. True, Mick Jackson's direction of the three-episode story was magisterial; the late Ray McAnally's playing of Labour leader Harry Perkins, outmanoeuvred by a crafty Establishment, brilliantly combined wit and authority; but production quality as such has never yet been a guarantee against politically motivated attacks. Why then was there no storm like that aroused by *The Monocled Mutineer*? Perhaps Plater's occasionally jokey treatment disarmed subversion-sniffers; perhaps it was difficult to relate North Country working-class hero Harry Perkins to any Labour leader actually on offer. The fact remains that *A Very British Coup*, far from triggering the usual outcry, went on to win three BAFTA awards – and acclaim in the US to boot.

During the eighties, the existing pattern of TV broadcasting was increasingly overshadowed by technological portents of the future. The video revolution was in full swing, but this by itself did not automatically reduce the importance of terrestrially transmitted drama. Cable TV spread in the eighties without initially fulfilling some of the more extravagant hopes placed in it. Satellite broadcasting, ultimately no doubt destined to open the British domestic screen to foreign penetration, had a more significant potential. The long-term consequences of all these developments were not easy to assess, although many observers perceived the threat of falling standards in days to come. Broadcasting by satellite and by cable respectively were placed under supervisory authorities by the Cable and Broadcasting Act 1984.

Much of the sniping during the decade against the existing broadcasting duopoly came from the Murdoch press. This was not an entirely disinterested defence of the public good. Rupert Murdoch was anxious to break into broadcasting himself in order to consolidate his transnational multi-media empire. He and his spokesmen kept accusing broadcasters – the BBC in particular – of cultural elitism. He did finally manage to add broadcasting to his other opinion-moulding media: his Sky Channel started transmitting by satellite on 16 January 1984. But even when, at the end of our period (on 2 November 1990 to be precise), Sky merged with its rival British Satellite Broadcasting to form BSkyB, this channel had no significance whatever in terms of originating any drama.

One important change in production method, well under way before the eighties, was to gain considerable momentum. Multi-camera shooting, which had been the early way of doing TV drama (whether transmitted live or recorded on tape), gave way increasingly to single-camera production.[19] The old-style studio with four or more cameras on the floor may have had some advantages, such as operational speed and enabling the actor to give a (more or less) continuous performance. Against that, the rather general-purpose, never quite satisfactory, lighting, not to mention the often slightly hit-and-miss framing and editing, made it a less subtle and precise technique than that of traditional film-making. The general though not universal switch-over to single-camera work was to move TV drama largely out of the studio and bring it closer to the cinema. (The video camera, which some predicted would presently oust the cine-camera, did not in fact eclipse it altogether. But whether this single camera runs videotape or film is a secondary consideration: there are advocates of electronic, as there are of photographic, recording. The two methods have their somewhat distinct applications, depending on circumstances.)

In addition to technological changes, there were a number of institutional shake-ups. Commercial television was not to emerge entirely unscathed. When the Independent Broadcasting Authority awarded new franchises to run from 1 January 1982, Southern Television and Westward Television gave way to TVS and TSW. More significant from our point of view was the replacement of Associated Television (ATV), a great producer of plays, by Central Independent Television: this was to be more firmly Midlands-based than its predecessor. Fortunately, Central TV's first Controller of Drama, Margaret Matheson, laid down a lively production policy, kicking off with the satirical six-part serial *Muck and Brass* by Tom Clarke, in which Mel Smith positively glistened in the role of a sleazy property developer. During the eighties, Central was to join Granada, Yorkshire, Thames and LWT as a main provider of networked drama for the whole of Channel 3, followed at some distance by Anglia, STV and HTV.

But quite the most important institutional breakthrough was the creation of Channel 4, after years of vigorous debate. The Chief Executive of the new channel, which began broadcasting on 2 November 1982, was the dynamic Jeremy Isaacs, formerly Programme Controller at Thames TV. Its remit was to provide programmes to appeal to tastes not generally catered for by ITV and to encourage innovation in form and content. (By way of contrast, SC4 – Sianel Pedwar Cymru: Welsh Channel 4 – which was set up at the same time, was designed to serve as a mainstream, rather than an experimental, channel for Welsh-language programmes.)

The importance of Channel 4 in generating drama cannot be overestimated. Since its setup precluded in-house production, it was to commission programmes, including drama, from outside sources. Usually the ideas for projects did not originate from Channel 4 itself: there were over 2,000 submissions pouring in every year from which to choose. The new channel was massively committed to film from the very beginning. *Film on Four* was devised by Jeremy Isaacs and David Rose, C4's Senior Commissioning Editor for Fiction, as a bridge between cinema and television. Rose, who came to the job with a vast amount of experience in TV play production at the BBC behind him, became a major influence on the drama not only of the small but also the large screen.[20] The playwright-director David Hare, to whom he had given the first chance to direct his own script, *Licking Hitler* (BBC 1978), and whose later films *Wetherby* (1985) and *Paris by Night* (1988) were to have a considerable financial input from C4, has said of him: 'In David Rose I found a producer whose allegiance to the film maker is absolute.'[21]

The feature-length films commissioned for *Film on Four* were frequently intended to be seen both in the cinema and on the domestic screen. In its first year C4 funded or co-funded as many as twenty such films, including Peter Greenaway's *The Draughtsman's Contract*, the first of that idiosyncratic film-maker's full-length pictures, as well as *The Ploughman's Lunch*, an acid study of Thatcherite Britain scripted by Ian McEwan and directed by Richard Eyre. The 'First Love' anthology, for which David Puttnam served as Executive Producer, included such delightful items as June Roberts' *Experience Preferred, but not Essential*; Noella Smith's *Secrets* and Julia Welsh's *Those Glory, Glory Days*. If C4 gave an opportunity to a young film-maker, Michael Radford, to write and direct *Another Time, Another Place* (1983), it was also to provide work for such veteran directors as Stephen Frears, Mike Leigh, Jack Gold, Ken Loach, Mike Newell and Nicolas Roeg.

During the eighties, the boundary line between film for TV and the cinema became increasingly blurred. (Actually, the question of what makes a telefilm distinct from a cinema film is still far from decided. According to David Rose, any film that works in the cinema will also work on the small screen – whereas the reverse is not necessarily true.)[22] The final destination of a C4-sponsored film occasionally surprised even the commissioning editors. When Stephen Frears directed Hanif Kureishi's *My Beautiful Laundrette* (1986), he made it on 16 mm instead of 35 mm because no one envisaged anything other than a television showing. But the film's reception was so favourable that it had a successful run in the cinema as well.

By the end of the decade, *Film on Four* had been involved in more than 150 feature films, including co-production deals. Some people claim that this hasn't been altogether a good thing, that it has taught the British cinema to think small. But that's hardly fair. Channel 4 has not muscled in on a flourishing domestic film industry; on the contrary, it has helped to keep it afloat in very choppy waters.

All these new production opportunities fostered the growth of an independent production sector. Many new companies sprang up during the eighties; to name but a few (in alphabetical rather than in order of importance): Chatsworth Television, Cinema Verity (the punning title of the company run by Verity Lambert), First Choice, Greenpoint Films, Jim Henson Productions, Little Bird Co., Mersey Television (the producers of *Brookside*), Pennies from Heaven (run by the veteran producer Kenith Trodd), Picture Partnership Productions, Red Rooster Films, Skreba Films, Warner Sisters, Witzend Productions and Zenith Productions. The last named, established in October 1984 to produce both cinema films and television programmes, including drama, is a market leader in the independent field. The jewel in Zenith's telefilm crown is the *Inspector Morse* series, which enjoyed a regular UK audience of 15 million and a worldwide audience of 75 million viewers. *Morse* had 'become a cult – and a cult which crosses socio-economic boundaries. While the chattering classes stay at home in London to get their two-hour fix, so do the serious drinkers of the North.'[23] The role of the eponymous hero fitted John Thaw, previously well known from *The Sweeney* and other series, like a glove. He has said of the character he embodies, 'I think Morse is so popular because people don't know what makes him tick ... I like him because he's not a "cliché copper".'[24]

It was not only the sponsorship of Channel 4 that stimulated the growth of the independent production sector. In 1988 the government commanded that by 1993, 25 per cent of BBC's as well as ITV's own production (other than news and news magazines) should be commissioned from outside providers. Soon space in the schedules began to be created for independent programme-makers. However, this seemingly liberalising measure was not guaranteed to open all that many doors to fresh talents: the gatekeepers granting access to airtime would still be largely the same companies as before. Furthermore, the independent programme-makers would often not be newcomers at all but ex-BBC or ex-ITV personnel who had decided to launch out on their own, or had actually been made redundant in the drastic 'slimming-down' operations of the late eighties and early nineties. What the 25 per cent rule was sure to accomplish was to weaken both the BBC and the ITV companies by dispersing their personnel and facilities.

The more and more commercially orientated, competitive climate of the eighties made all broadcasters, including the BBC, highly conscious of ratings and costs.[25] The latter had a way of escalating relentlessly – not least because viewer expectations were rising with regard to production values (which is not quite the same thing as quality). By the end of the decade, one hour of 'quality' drama could easily cost around £450,000. A way of sharing the burden of this budgetary inflation was to enter into co-production arrangements with overseas broadcasting organisations. This was not necessarily a bad thing: it would help towards meeting costs and might even bring about a less parochial approach to drama. But there was always the danger of a regional or national tone of voice turning fuzzy and becoming mid-Atlantic or mid-Channel. The foreign presales on which big-budget productions have more and more come to depend give overseas buyers substantial influence on what is (or is not) to be shown on British television.

The decline of the single play, a frequent cause for lament during the seventies, accelerated during the eighties. Since the single play is less subject to management interference, it has conventionally been seen as the best vehicle for asking awkward social questions. Was that the reason for its diminution during the Thatcher era? Perhaps in part; but it was due at least as much to the ratings battle. It is obviously easier to build up audience loyalty over time for a series or a serial than for a one-off drama slot. There are also quite straightforward cost factors working against the single play. In ongoing drama, sets and costumes will be used in more than one episode, and the cast, increasingly familiar with their characters, will need less rehearsal time.

It would be false to sentimentalise the single play of the sixties. Distinguished examples were few and far between at the best of times. Even some of the classics of the golden age sometimes prove disappointing when revived. Perhaps the very success of the plays of the era of *Armchair Theatre* or the *Wednesday Play* whetted the appetite for the more expansive development of dramatic ideas: in other words, for serials. If at one time the latter tended to run to thirteen episodes, in the eighties a shorter format – somewhat loosely called the 'mini-series' and consisting of anything from three to six episodes – was to gain ground.

But, inevitable or not, the dwindling away of single plays did have one detrimental effect. As Alan Plater put it:

in the early Sixties when we were all young and innocent, there were 300 plays a year on the two channels. Today, it is doubtful whether we have 100 on four channels... It is six times as difficult for a new writer to find a way into television, and once he or she finds a space, it is quite likely to be on a long-running soap opera.[26]

It was natural for him to conclude that

We must battle for original work, for the single play, for the preservation of a solid middle-ground in television drama where new writers can learn the trade and discover the sound of their own voices.[27]

To conclude: British television drama flourished in the eighties and many outstanding productions reached the small screen, sometimes in the teeth of financial and political pressures. But these pressures kept building up during the decade and left much of the creative talent exhausted, in writing as well as in production. The end of the decade saw the skies darkening even further. On 1 November 1990 the Broadcasting Bill received the Royal Assent after many amendments in its passage through the House. Among other changes it introduced a new licensing authority, the Independent Television Commission (ITC) in place of the IBA, with far less of an interventionist role than that of its quality-conscious predecessor. It also brought in a new competitive tendering for ITV franchises. This was, to quote Clive James, an ideologically inspired measure:

Bedazzled by elementary notions about the supposed benefits of deregulation in America, the Thatcher Government's target was public-service broadcasting. The BBC and ITV were thought of, correctly, as a single institution insufficiently responsive to Downing Street.[28]

A needlessly opaque system which involved sealed bids and vague commitments to programme quality resulted in sensational decisions by the ITC on 16 October 1991. Four companies lost their franchise: TVS, TSW, TV-am and Thames TV. (It was noted that the last named had attracted official displeasure with *Death on the Rock*.) Thames was the only company among the losers that mattered from the drama point of view. This, the biggest shake-up in commercial television's history, was to bring in its wake considerable job losses and uncertainty about future programming. Anthony Smith, President of Magdalen College, Oxford, called the whole exercise a 'story of subtle political revenge and blind ideological commit-ment'.[29] Even Mrs Thatcher, herself out of office by then, expressed herself 'mystified' as well as 'heart-broken' at the way deregulation had careered out of control, in a letter of condolence to the chief executive of TV-am (where incidentally her daughter was working as a journalist).

When David Plowright was abruptly dismissed from the chairmanship of Granada Television in February 1992, many saw this as a further straw in a chilly wind. Plowright had been with Granada since 1957, and he – together with his predecessor in the post, Denis Forman – had turned the company into 'the BBC of ITV', that is, a bastion of quality. The fact that such a man could be replaced at short notice by a newcomer to the company suggested that a steelier ethos was being laid down for the nineties.

I regret having to end on a note of foreboding as I gaze into a clouded crystal ball. British television drama will not disappear, nor will its quality decline overnight. But if some of the omens at the end of the decade are anything to go by, its brightest moments of glory in the eighties may prove to have been the golden glow of a setting sun. When Ludovic Kennedy was asked what was his one wish for television, he replied, 'My only wish is that standards of British broadcasting are not diminished – as I feel they may be.' And Jonathan Dimbleby's answer to the same question was simple: 'I wish that television will survive the market.'[30]

To which, looking back over a remarkable, stormy and ambiguous decade, one can only add: Amen!

Notes

1 In a speech to the Royal Television Society in May 1991.
2 See Reg Gadney's obituary of Lloyd in *The Guardian*, 26 August 1991.
3 See Suzie Mackenzie's portrait of Verity Lambert, 'Her brilliant career', *The Guardian*, 31 October 1990, 19.
4 For a brief tribute to Betty Willingale, see Alan Plater, 'Langham Diary', *Listener*, 17/24 December 1987, 48.
5 John Tulloch, *Television Drama: Agency, Audience and Myth* (London: Routledge, 1990), 4.

6 'Quality control', *New Statesman and Society*, 21 July 1989, 37.
7 *Screen* 31, spring 1990, 85–6.
8 See Brandt, *British Television Drama* (Cambridge University Press, 1981), 21–2.
9 'Television/aesthetics and audiences', in Patricia Mellencamp (ed.), *Logics of Television* (Bloomington and Indianapolis: Indiana University Press and BFI, 1990, 69–70).
10 See Appendix 1.
11 Bob Millington and Robin Nelson, *'Boys from the Blackstuff': The Making of a TV Drama* (London: Comedia, 1986).
12 See Paul Clements, *The Improvised Play: the Work of Mike Leigh* (London: Methuen, 1983).
13 See pp. 19–24.
14 'The art of survival', *The Guardian*, 29 November 1990, 25.
15 For Griffiths' earlier work for television, see Edward Braun's chapter in Brandt, *British Television Drama*, 56–81 and Mike Poole and John Wyver, *Powerplay: Trevor Griffiths in Television* (London: BFI, 1984). For a detailed discussion of *The Last Place on Earth*, see Tulloch, *Television Drama*.
16 For *Days of Hope*, see Brandt, *British Television Drama*, 26, 28, 48–52. For the theoretical controversy over this serial in *Screen*, see Tony Bennett, Susan Boyd-Bowman *et al.* (eds.), *Popular Television and Film* (London: BFI Publishing, 1981), 302–52.
17 See Julian Petley, 'Over the top', *Sight and Sound* 56, 2 (spring 1987), 126–31, for a discussion of *The Monocled Mutineer*.
18 See pp. 141–5, 156–7.
19 See Brandt, *British Television Drama*, 18–19, and David Rose's Foreword to this book.
20 For a brief CV of David Rose, see p. xiii.
21 In Frank Pike, *Ah! Mischief: The Role of Public Broadcasting* (London: Faber & Faber, 1982), 49.
22 David Rose in an interview with the author, 5 February 1992.
23 Richard Brooks, 'Morose Morse, a TV hero for the nineties', *Observer*, 17 February 1991, 69.
24 Geoff Tibballs, *TV Detectives* (London: Boxtree, 1992), 197–8.
25 In 1981 the BBC and ITCA (the body representing all the ITV companies) jointly set up the Broadcasters' Audience Research Board (BARB) whose authoritative audience surveys were to avoid the two rival systems making statistically questionable ratings claims. BARB data are derived from computer-linked electronics in 3,000 survey homes – a system further refined by including such factors as guests, multiple sets, VCRs and timeshifting. In addition to ratings, BARB also supplies a qualitative assessment, the Appreciation Index (AI) which works on a six-point scale.
26 'Langham Diary', *The Listener*, 17/24 December 1987, 48.
27 *The Listener*, 2 March 1989, 7.
28 See note 1.
29 *The Observer*, 20 October 1991.
30 'What is your one wish for television?', *New Statesman and Society*, 25 August 1989, 32–3.

Talking Heads: 'Bed Among the Lentils'
(Alan Bennett)

ALBERT HUNT

'Geoffrey's bad enough, but' – Maggie Smith pauses – 'I'm glad I'm not
married to Jesus.'

It's the opening line of 'Bed Among the Lentils', one of six plays by Alan
Bennett, written and recorded for BBC television in 1987, under the title of
Talking Heads. Each play involved only one performer talking directly to
camera. It would be difficult to imagine a more basic form of television
drama.

As a successful playwright, Bennett had come to television comparatively late. He had made his name in the theatre in the sixties, first as a
performer in *Beyond the Fringe*, then as a writer and performer, alongside
John Gielgud, in *Forty Years On*. But he scripted his first play for television
in 1972. It was called *A Day Out*, and he has published a hilarious account
of the first ten days' filming in May that year in and around Halifax. 'What
was intended as an Edwardian idyll', he writes, was turned by the weather
into 'an altogether brisker piece'.[1]

The 1980s, though, saw him writing frequently for television. In the
autumn of 1982, the BBC screened five of his plays – he grouped them
together under the title, *Objects of Affection*. Other TV plays included the
prize-winning *An Englishman Abroad* (1983) about an encounter in
Moscow between the Old Vic actress, Coral Browne, and the defector, Guy
Burgess; and an extraordinary play about an episode in the life of Kafka,
The Insurance Man (1985). Directed by Richard Eyre, this latter play is,
formally, extremely complex. It is told in the form of a flashback from the
Czechoslovakia of 1945 to a period before the First World War. In a huge
building, where the victims of industrial injury come looking for compensa-
tion, Kafka works as an insurance man. Bennett and Eyre create the Kafka
world in a labyrinth of offices, endless corridors and staircases and
fragments of overheard conversation. In its complexity, *The Insurance Man*

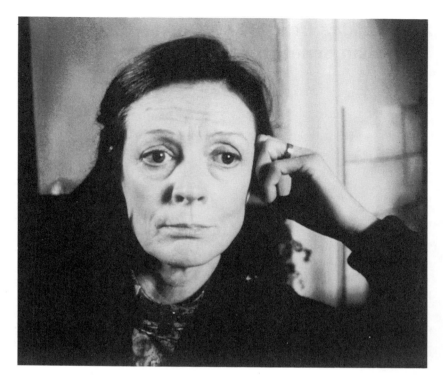

1 A Talking Head: *Maggie Smith as Susan, the trendy vicar's alcoholic wife, in Alan Bennett's 'Bed Among the Lentils'. BBC 1987*

seems at the other end of formal exploration from *Talking Heads*. But the urge to experiment revealed in *The Insurance Man* also informs Bennett's engagement with a form that he himself has called 'a synonym in television for boredom'.[2]

Bennett had first arrived at the form in 1982 with one of the *Objects of Affection, A Woman of No Importance*. In his published introduction to the play, he says, modestly, that he wrote it 'thinking I might direct it myself'. He had never directed before, either for stage or television, and 'the possibility of having to do so accounts for the simplicity (not to say crudity) of the form'. He goes on: 'Thinking I would be able to manage at the least two cameras, I planned the play as a series of midshots with the camera tracking in very slowly to a close-up, holding the close-up for a while then, just as slowly, coming out again.'[3] He didn't intend to make any cuts within scenes, which, he was to find, placed a heavy burden on the performer – the opening scene lasted twelve minutes.

The performer was Patricia Routledge, an actress who was still to be associated with *Talking Heads* ten years later. As well as playing Miss Schofield in *A Woman of No Importance*, she was to perform Miss Ruddock in the third of the *Talking Heads*, 'A Lady of Letters'. Even more significantly, she was to appear with Alan Bennett when he put some of the *Talking Heads* on stage in the Comedy Theatre in London early in 1992 – a highly successful venture which, incidentally, puts into question some of the preconceptions that have grown up over the years about 'television drama'.

In the early days, TV drama had been conceived as a form that was shot live in a studio (for decades, *Crossroads* was shot and screened without the benefit of post-production editing). The form created its own tension – the demands made on all involved, actors and TV crews, were considerable and made for a particular kind of immediacy. But in general both writers and directors found the form limiting. They reached out towards the more flexible (and more expensive) form of film: the makers of *Coronation Street*, for example, used film to shoot outdoor links between scenes shot on the studio set, and they looked like film sequences. Bennett conceived much of *A Day Out* in terms of film form, and *The Insurance Man* has the feel of a film. *Talking Heads*, on the other hand, relates directly back to a form of television that gives us someone reading the news or describing an incident in an interview. But this, paradoxically, reveals itself as theatrical, if theatre is seen, not as something that happens between the actors in a set separated from the audience by an imaginary fourth wall, but as something that involves direct communication between actors and audience. In this sense, *Talking Heads* can be seen as a reassertion of theatricality in a TV form. Although each play was recorded on video, the demands made on the performers – on Patricia Routledge, for example, in the shooting of the opening twelve-minute scene of *A Woman of No Importance* – brought back a theatrical quality of immediacy, which created its own tension on the screen.

This kind of tension might not have been uppermost in Bennett's mind when he scripted *A Woman of No Importance* as a 'talking head' – if we are to believe him he was thinking primarily of keeping the form simple because he thought he was going to direct. But he also says that he was influenced by childhood memories of one of his aunts. 'My mother,' he told me (in an informal interview without which the writing of this chapter would have been impossible), 'had two sisters and one of them used to tell you everything that happened to her in Proustian detail. She worked in a shoe shop in Leeds, and she used to come up after work and tell you everything. And when she'd gone, my dad used to say, "I wouldn't care but you're no further on when she's finished."'

Miss Schofield, in *A Woman of No Importance*, is like Bennett's aunt: she has to 'tell everything'. Not only is the 'talking head' a synonym for boredom: she herself is also a bore. But, writes Bennett, 'to have her in full close-up, retailing in unremitting detail how she borrowed the salt in the canteen takes one, I hope, beyond tedium'.[4] (Only it was, of course, the highly professional Patricia Routledge telling in 'unremitting detail' a story that had been crafted by the highly professional Alan Bennett.)

There was yet another impulse, though, which pushed Bennett towards the 'talking head' form. Thinking about Miss Schofield, he recognised that she resembled a character he had written about before, in a 30-minute two-hander for television called *A Visit from Miss Prothero* (1978). Miss Prothero, like Miss Schofield, works in an office. She has been the personal assistant of a man who has retired and she goes to visit him. Like Bennett's aunt, she has to 'tell everything'. She tells him how 'they' have reorganised the office. Until then, her former boss has been happily retired. But in effect her story means that his life's work has been destroyed. 'It's quite funny,' says Bennett, 'but she's a really unpleasant person. Anyway, when I started thinking about doing another one, I thought, Well, it's the same sort of person, and then I thought, Well, the more you know about her the more you perhaps come to understand a person like that.' To allow her to tell her story in her own words from her own point of view would be 'somehow to redeem her'. The talking-head form would insist (to paraphrase Arthur Miller) that 'attention must be paid'.

All Bennett's stated reasons for inventing *Talking Heads* were personal: he wanted to direct, he remembered his auntie, he wanted to 'redeem' a character. But it would be possible to argue, quite logically, that completely impersonal social forces were driving towards the form. In the Thatcher years, the BBC, like other institutions, was being urged to 'slim down'. It would be impossible to conceive of a 'slimmer' form of drama than the talking head: each play involved only one performer, two weeks' rehearsal and six hours of studio time with only two cameras. In theory, the BBC should have welcomed Bennett's series with open arms. But this isn't how Bennett remembers it (when I made the suggestion, he was wryly amused).

He sent the scripts, he says, to his producer, Innes Lloyd. He was always mildly surprised that Lloyd supported his work: 'Proust, Kafka – they weren't really up his street. He liked doing films about heroes like Donald Campbell. But once he'd committed himself to you he kept to it.'

Innes Lloyd, he says, 'made a space in which you could work. His opinion was always worth having, but he wouldn't over-rule you.' And he trusted you. 'He felt you were going through whatever developments as a writer you had to go through.'

Innes Lloyd wanted to do the plays. And Michael Grade was head of the

BBC at the time – 'He'd always liked my stuff.' Grade read the scripts, says Bennett, liked them and was going to schedule them for 9.0 p.m. on Sunday evenings. But then Grade left the BBC and went to Channel 4. *Talking Heads*, Bennett thinks, was seen by the BBC bureaucracy as one of Grade's babies and the plays were put on the shelf for several months.

'I don't think the BBC ever really liked them,' says Bennett. 'It's a funny thing about working for a bureaucracy – they think that the longer you've worked for them and the better you've done the less credit you have.' Someone suggested putting on the plays at 10.20 p.m. on Tuesdays – 'They said I would pick up the audience for the third repeat of *Reginald Perrin*.' Bennett, as he puts it, 'dug his heels in'. After months of delay, he was finally given a Sunday night slot.

Maggie Smith hadn't worked for television for fifteen years. Sounding like one of the characters in *Talking Heads*, Bennett says, 'I wasn't bothered about the publicity for myself. But I thought she should be on the front cover of *Radio Times*.' *Radio Times* obviously didn't. Bennett feels that the plays finally went out 'slightly hole-in-corner'.

Logically, the BBC might have seen *Talking Heads* as a form which would enable them to make prestige dramas cheaply. But the ideology of the laws of the market doesn't seem to have influenced the BBC's response to *Talking Heads* – if what Bennett has to say about it several years later is accurate.

What Bennett has to say is, of course, gossip. It's what he remembers of what he experienced at the time, told in an informal conversation. But gossip is a central feature of his writing anyway – which is why *Talking Heads* seems to have been a form waiting to be discovered by him. *Talking Heads* is gossip turned into drama.

Even when Bennett is apparently handling Grand Themes – like patriotism and treachery in *An Englishman Abroad* – he does so in the form of gossip. His published account of the origins of *An Englishman Abroad* is pure gossip. He had this play, *The Old Country*, running in the West End. And Alec Guinness was playing the part of a former Foreign Office official who had defected and who was now, we're surprised to discover, living in the Russian countryside. And people thought he was Philby, only of course he wasn't – when Philby heard about the play, in Moscow, he said it didn't sound like him at all. But admirers of Guinness used to come back-stage after the performances and tell stories about Philby and Burgess and Maclean. And one night Coral Browne came to see the show, and Guinness took her and Bennett for supper at The Mirabelle: 'I mention the restaurant only because the mixture of Moscow drabness and London luxe was a part of the telling of the tale, as it is a part of the tale told.'[5] And Coral Browne told this story of how, when she was playing Gertrude in the Old Vic's

Hamlet in Moscow, Burgess invited her round to his flat and asked her to bring a tape measure so that she could measure him for a suit and take the measurements back to his tailor in London. And she and Burgess spent a long afternoon listening to a record of Jack Buchanan singing, 'Who stole my heart away?' – Bennett found the image 'funny and sad'. And years later, when he started to write the play, Bennett found that Coral Brown had not only some letters from Burgess, but a cheque, uncashed, for £6, which he'd given her to treat herself and a friend to lunch at the Caprice.

In the play, Bennett has Burgess say to Coral Browne, 'Now, tell me all the gossip. Do you know Harold Nicholson?... Nice man, nice man... What about Cyril Connolly? He's everywhere... Auden, do you know him? Pope-Hennessy?' Later, she asks him, 'What do you miss most?' and he replies: 'Apart from the Reform Club, the streets of London, and occasionally the English countryside, the only thing I really miss is gossip.' And he adds, 'The comrades, though splendid in every other respect, don't gossip quite the way we do.'

In the play, Coral Browne does have lunch with 'Claudius' at the Caprice – on Guy Burgess's cheque. Burgess has sent her a letter, asking her to order some pyjamas. 'Claudius' tries to read it: 'Then at last my outfit will be complete and I shall look like a real agent again.' Coral Browne corrects him: 'Then I shall look like a real gent again.'

To say that Bennett's work is built around gossip is not in any way to disparage that work. The comrades don't gossip – and neither do the people and institutions in our society who are in the business of inventing and upholding what the film-maker Luis Buñuel called 'official reality'. Gossip, in the way Bennett uses it, is an antidote to 'official reality'. It confronts the grand and the abstract with the particular. The Susan of 'Bed Among the Lentils' wages war with her husband Geoffrey's version of 'official reality'. Her principal weapon is her own form of gossip – ironic, sceptical, deconstructing.

'The lesson this morning was the business in the Garden of Gethsemane when Jesus prays and the disciples keep falling asleep. He wakes them up and says' – Maggie Smith allows her voice to take on the mildest suggestion of reproach – '"Could you not watch with me one hour?" It's my mother', she adds. She goes on, 'I overslept this morning, flung on a cardigan and got there just as everybody was standing up. It was Holy Communion so the militants were out in force.'

Geoffrey, we quickly learn, is a vicar. He does an 'underneath this cassock I am but a man like anybody else' act. The bishop who comes to the vicarage for lunch with Susan and Geoffrey calls her Mrs Vicar. Susan says, 'Asks Geoff how outgoing I am. Actually says that: "How outgoing is Mrs

Vicar"?' She puts the question in verbal quotation marks: the verbal quotation marks have the effect of calling our attention to the outrageousness of the bishop's apparent bonhomie.

Susan speaks the unspeakable questions: 'One of the unsolved mysteries of life, or the unsolved mysteries of my life, is why the vicar's wife is expected to go to church at all. A barrister's wife doesn't have to go to court, an actor's wife isn't at every performance, so why have I always got to be on display?'

'Not to mention the larger question of whether one believes in God in the first place.' She's always longed to ask Geoffrey if he believes in God, 'only God never seems to crop up. "Geoffrey," I'd say. "Yes, Susan?" "Do you really believe in God? I mean, cards on the table, you don't honestly, do you? God's just a job like any other. You've got to bring home the bacon somehow." But no. Not a word. The subject's never discussed.'

The language of gossip – 'cards on the table', 'bring home the bacon' – brings God down to earth with a bump. Later, she will refer to him as 'The God. The definite article' – in contrast to the many thousands of the 'jolly little gods, doing everything under the sun to each other', of Mr Ramesh, the Indian owner of a grocer's shop she discovers in Leeds.

During the lunch at the vicarage, Geoffrey and the bishop are setting up their own version of 'official reality'. Susan demolishes it by her gossip. 'We were discussing the ordination of women. The bishop asked me what I thought. Should women take the services? So long as it doesn't have to be me, I wanted to say, they can be taken by a trained gorilla. "Oh, yes," Geoffrey chips in. "Susan's all in favour, aren't you, darling?" "More sprouts anybody?" I said.' What Susan really thinks isn't part of the men's 'official reality', and neither is the fact that she's acting as a domestic servant while they are upholding women's rights – in the abstract, of course. Gossip belongs to the concrete, the particular and the everyday. 'It's Mary Magdalen and the Nivea cream all over again,' she says when the bishop gives her a 'funny look' after a jug of 'decanted' Carnation milk gets knocked over, 'possibly by me'. The reference to Nivea cream puts Mary Magdalen's precious ointment firmly and irreverently in the everyday world.

When Bennett has Susan put the down-to-earth questions, he reveals a startling resemblance to a writer we wouldn't normally associate with him – Bertolt Brecht. 'Closely observe the behaviour of these people', wrote Brecht. 'Consider it strange, although familiar.'[6] Susan closely observes the familiar behaviour of the people around her and considers it strange indeed. Geoffrey is white-faced and practically in tears when he discovers, just before Holy Communion, that 'somebody has drunk' all the communion wine. How strange! 'It's on the tip of my tongue to say that if Jesus is all he's cracked up to be, why doesn't he use tap water?' 'You never see pictures of Jesus smiling, do you?' says Susan, and the question startles. When Geoffrey says she should think of Our Lord as having an inward smile, because as a man he smiled, laughed 'and did everything just like the rest of us,' she says, 'Do you think he ever smirked?' (Geoffrey suddenly remembers he is burying somebody in five minutes.)

Susan lists the skills necessary to be seen as a 'wonderful woman' – 'How to produce jam which, after reaching a good, rolling boil, successfully coats the spoon; how to whip up a Victoria sponge that just gives to the finger-tips; how to plan, execute and carry through a successful garden fete.' 'If you think squash is a competitive activity, try flower-arrangement,' she tells us. As she describes it, the familiar world in which she lives becomes very strange. Conversely, when the Indian grocer invites her to take off her clothes in the back room of his shop in Leeds, this scarcely seems strange at all. Maggie Smith has Mrs Vicar pause briefly before she simply tells us, 'And I did.'

Did Alan Bennett, I ask, write the script for Maggie Smith? He didn't begin it with her in mind, he says, but as he was writing it, he began to see her in the part. 'I didn't dare think she would do it – she's very choosy.' But he'd worked with her before and they'd got on well, so he by-passed her agent and sent her the script direct. And, to his surprise, she'd liked it: 'She can be quite difficult.'

He'd written *A Woman of No Importance* with the thought that he might direct it, but in fact he hadn't done so, he'd been busy with other plays. So this was to be his first experience of directing: he was, he says, 'petrified'.

'Fortunately, I'd acted in the one before' – he plays the part of Graham in 'A Chip in the Sugar' – 'and we had the same camera crew throughout. So they knew I could do it at the other end. I'd been through it and so I think they forgave me some of my bumbling.'

Giles Foster, who did direct *A Woman of No Importance*, had at first, according to Bennett, found the restrictions of the form irksome. 'He began by moving the play around, with Miss Schofield traversing the studio to match the movements described in the text.' The process of rehearsal had been one of simplification: the movements were 'taken back inside the character, who ended up static in front of the camera as I had originally imagined'.[7]

Stuart Burge directed Bennett in 'A Chip in the Sugar'. 'He made me sit facing him with less than a foot between us, so I had to look into his face. And he's odd in one of his eyes.' (Bennett, himself now the gossip, has his own eye for the particular.) 'So there was the additional complication of which eye to look at. I am very shy and it was such an intimate relationship.' (In the early sequences of 'Bed Among the Lentils', Maggie

Smith sometimes seems to be avoiding our eye. Our eye? The camera's? Bennett's? She keeps flicking her eyes to a point somewhere off-screen over her right shoulder.) 'But once you got used to having someone so close,' says Bennett, 'then, when he withdrew and sat at the other side of the rehearsal room, you felt bereft. You had actually become dependent on his being there.'

'Once the camera came in,' Bennett adds, 'it was a kind of comfort. It was a kind of confessional thing. It was almost a screen between you and the world.'

'It was a kind of human experience, not a theatrical one. It wasn't like performing, because you couldn't perform at such close range. Mine was the first to be done, and I did Maggie in the same way.'

Before she made 'Bed Among the Lentils', says Bennett, Maggie Smith had been shooting a film with Jack Clayton. And the film had overshot. She'd been intending to have a holiday before she came to work with Bennett, but she hadn't had the time. She finished shooting the film one day, took one day off, 'and then started rehearsing with us'.

She didn't know the words. So the first week I didn't really see her – she was just learning the words. And so then we started rehearsing at the beginning of the second week. And the thing I think with her is that she's so clever she gets bored very easily. When she gets bored, she starts over-ornamenting – she can do exactly what she wants, she can turn on a sixpence. And I didn't want her to ornament, so circumstances were in our favour in a way. She just really had time to master it, and so she did it in a very plain way.

Bennett, as a writer who sometimes acts, may have felt that 'it wasn't like performing'. Maggie Smith clearly is performing, in a very selective way. The writing in a talking head, says Bennett, in his introduction to the published scripts, has to be austere, stripped-down: ' "Said" or "says" is generally all that is required to introduce reported speech ... Adverbs too ... seem to over-egg the pudding.'[8] Maggie Smith's acting is equally 'stripped-down'. Her gestures and changes of facial and vocal expression are minimal: but when she makes them, she makes them tell.

Sometimes, she plays on the contradiction between what we can see on the screen and the image she is creating in words. 'Amazing scenes at the church door', she says, in a carefully unamazed voice ... 'Geoffrey stands there, the wind billowing out his surplice and ruffling his hair, what "Who's Who in the Diocese of Ripon" calls "his schoolboy good looks." ' She's sitting in a bare wooden chair at a bare wooden table in a gloomy kitchen. She's wearing an old black coat, her hair is straight and straggling and she has no make-up. Her face is flat and tired. She's at the other extreme from 'schoolboy good looks'. When she says, 'I helped put the books away while he did his "underneath this cassock I am but a man like anybody else" act', her refusal to act out his performance shows Geoffrey as the ham. Similarly, when later she reports that the bishop 'claps his hand to his temple because he's suddenly remembered he's supposed to be in Keighley blessing a steam-engine', the fact that she doesn't illustrate the gesture calls attention to the bishop's amateur dramatics.

When she's describing for us Geoffrey's female 'fan club', she allows herself the luxury of a strangled smile and a syrupy tone of voice. She takes on the style of a sit-down television comic – Mrs Belcher and Mrs Shrubsole become a double-act. '"Such a live wire,"' says Mrs Belcher of Geoffrey, "really putting the parish on the map." "That's right," burbles Mrs Shrubsole, looking at me. "We must cherish him." We came back and I cherished him with some chicken wings in a tuna sauce. He said, "That went down well." I said, "The chicken wings?" He said, 'My sermon. I felt it hit the nail on the head."' Maggie Smith brings her clenched hand slowly down on to the bare wooden table: the gesture is exactly enough to give us what we need to see of Geoffrey.

Later, she describes an encounter between her and Mrs Belcher, Mrs Shrubsole and Miss Frobisher, when they're doing flower-arranging in the church. Bennett has invented a form which allows her to operate on three levels: she speaks directly to us, telling us what she is thinking; she gives us the three women, all smiles and slightly raised eyes; and she gives us herself talking to the women.

'I wander over to the church with a few dog-eared chrysanthemums. They look as though they could do with an immediate drink, so I call in at the vestry and root out a vase or two from the cupboard where Geoffrey keeps his communion wine...' When she comes out, Mrs Shrubsole is working on the altar. 'I said, "I thought I was doing the altar." She said, "No. I think Mrs Belcher will bear me out. I'm down to do the altar. You are doing the lectern. Why?" She smiled sweetly.' Maggie Smith smiles sweetly. '"Do you have a preference?"' Maggie Smith says to the camera, 'The only preference I have is to shove my chrysanthemums up her nose but instead I practise a bit of Christian forbearance and go stick them in a vase by the lectern.' She tries to borrow 'a bit of backing' from Mrs Belcher. '"Are you using this?" I say, picking up a bit of mouldy fern. "I certainly am. I need every bit of my spiraea. It gives it body."' Maggie Smith imitates Mrs Belcher's rejoinder.

Rebuffed by Mrs Belcher and Miss Frobisher (who's 'doing some Japanese number ... in which she's throttling a lone carnation'), Susan retires to the vestry for a bit 'to calm my shattered nerves'. When she comes out, her conversation with the women has acquired an added edge. Inspecting Mrs Shrubsole's Forest Murmurs ('it's a brown job, beech leaves, teazles, grass, that school of thought'), she tells her, 'Mrs. Shrubsole. This is the altar of St Michael and All Angels. It is not The Wind in the Willows.' Maggie Smith puts on a sickly smile and becomes Mrs Belcher.

Mrs Belcher said, 'I think we ought to sit down.' I said, 'We do not want to sit down.' I said, 'It's all very well to transform the altar into something out of Bambi but do not forget that for the vicar the altar is his working surface. Furthermore,' I added, 'should the vicar sink to his knees in prayer, which since this is the altar he is wont to do, he is quite likely to get one of these teazle things in his eye. This is not a flower arrangement. It is a booby trap.' And I begin getting down on my knees just to prove how lethal her bloody Forest Murmurs is. Only I must have slipped because next thing I know I'm rolling down the altar steps and end up banging my head on the communion rail.

The image Maggie Smith creates for us in her narrative is of Susan lying down in a semi-conscious state on the church floor. But what we see is her sitting in the kitchen with her elbow on the Aga cooker. She gives us the double-act which is supposed to be taking place above her prone body.

'Leave them lying down,' says Mrs Belcher, 'and they inhale their own vomit . . .' 'Only,' says Mrs Shrubsole, 'when they have vomited. She hasn't vomited.' 'No,' I say, 'but I will if I have to listen to any more of this drivel,' and begin to get up. 'Is that blood, Veronica?' says Mrs Belcher pointing to my head.'

The performance is straight out of stand-up (or rather sit-down) comedy.

The scene ends with Susan laid out on the sofa in the vicarage in a light doze – only we see her still sitting by the Aga. Maggie Smith now has her eyes closed. 'I come round to hear Geoffrey saying, "Mrs Shrubsole's going now, darling." I don't get up. I never even open my eyes.' Maggie Smith keeps her eyes closed. 'I just wave and say, "Goodbye, Mrs Shrubsole."' Maggie Smith doesn't wave. 'Only thinking about it as I drift off again I think I may have said, "Goodbye, Mrs Subsoil."' It's the punch-line at the end of a highly professional comic turn.

Alan Bennett says of Susan, 'I slightly don't know how much she knows. It's almost as if she's smarter than I am. But that may be me projecting Maggie on to her.'

Bennett describes the narrators in *Talking Heads* as 'artless'. He writes: 'They didn't quite know what they are saying and are telling a story to the meaning of which they are not entirely privy.'[9]

This is certainly true of Miss Schofield in Bennett's first experiment in the form, *A Woman of No Importance*. The play works precisely because Miss Schofield never knows as much as we know. As she describes 'the happy family' which she gathers around herself at her table in the canteen – 'what Mrs Brunskill calls "our little backwater"' – we know she's the kind of person whose table everyone would like to avoid. But she regards herself as the life and soul of everyone's party. 'My secret,' she assures us, talking endlessly about herself, 'is, I don't talk about myself.'

Later, in hospital, she tells us 'Nurse Trickett says I'm their star patient.' When she tells the nurse that the patient opposite, Mrs Maudsley, says she needs her toenails cutting, she reports the nurse as saying to her, 'I don't know how we managed before you came, Miss Schofield, I honestly don't.' ('Actually,' she tells us disarmingly in the next sentence, 'I found out later her toenails had been cut. Apparently Nurse Conkie must have cut them the same day as she cut mine ... only Mrs Maudsley wouldn't know because she's no feeling in her feet.') 'If they just left me alone, I should be all right,' she says towards the end of the play. In the final shot, we see her empty bed with the mattress folded back and know that she's died.

The irony in the play springs from the fact that we, the viewers, can see more than Miss Schofield sees. The talking-head form means that we are allowed to share her point of view ('Attention must be paid') and, therefore, as Bennett puts it, to 'understand' her. But we can also see that her point of view is based on her own lack of awareness. At first, we laugh at this, but the laughter gradually becomes painful. We experience the pain, but from a position of comparative comfort, because we're allowed to feel superior to her. And this feeling of superiority is embedded in the form.

This applies to most of the *Talking Heads*. In 'A Lady of Letters', for example, Patricia Routledge plays the part of Irene Ruddock ('an ordinary middle-aged woman', Bennett calls her), who also turns out to be a compulsive letter-writer. She herself believes that she writes letters from high-mindedness, as a public-spirited guardian of morals. In the very first paragraph of the play, she tells us that she is writing to the crematorium to complain of hearse-drivers outside the Chapel of Rest, 'skulking in the rhododendrons with tab-ends on their mouths'. She writes to the Queen about dog-dirt outside Buckingham Palace; to the makers of pork sausage because she finds a black hair in the packet; to the newspaper about the length of the Archbishop of Canterbury's hair. She is very concerned that a couple in the house opposite hers seem to be neglecting their child – they go out and leave it every night.

But gradually we become aware that she has previously written other letters which have caused her difficulties with the law – she has written to a chemist telling him that his wife is a prostitute, has caused a lollipop man to have a nervous breakdown by accusing him of interfering with children. And the couple across the way? A policeman and a policewoman come to the house to tell her that the couple have been visiting their kiddy every night in hospital in Bradford and the kiddy has just died: 'I said, "What of? Neglect?" She said, "No. Leukemia." He said, "You'd better get your hat and coat on."'

Bennett reveals Miss Ruddock as a woman driven, not by high-mindedness, but by her own frustrations and loneliness – in the end, ironically, she feels herself free in prison because she's part of a community. But we're the ones who are 'privy' to the 'meaning' of the story: Miss Ruddock certainly doesn't understand what she's telling us.

This is even more true of Lesley, played by Julie Walters, in 'Her Big Chance'. The play is very funny, cruelly so, because the comedy springs from the gap between the way Lesley sees herself and the way we see her. She sees herself as a 'serious' actress, with a lot of ideas, which she is always eager to feed to producers, writers, and directors, and with a need to understand the motives of the characters she is playing. ('What would help your character,' Nigel, the first assistant on the film she is making tells her, 'is if you took your bikini top off . . . Gunther wants to see your knockers' – Gunther is the director). Lesley says, 'People who know me tell me I'm a very serious person, only it's funny, I never get to do serious parts. The parts I get offered tend to be fun-loving girls who take life as it comes and aren't afraid of a good time should the opportunity arise-type-thing.' Lesley goes to bed with virtually every man in the crew, though she insists that they value her for her 'serious' qualities, even when she's describing picking a man up in a bar:

I sat in the bar for a bit. Just one fellow in there. I said, 'My hobby is people, what do you do?' Lo and behold, he's on the film too, the animal handler, Kenny. In charge of the cat. I said, 'That's interesting, Kenny, I didn't know there was going to be a cat. I love cats . . .' He said, 'Would you care to see her? She's asleep on my bed.' I said, 'That's convenient.' He said, 'Lesley, don't run away with that idea. I am wedded to my small charges.' So I go up and pal on a bit with the cat and Kenny tells me about all the animals he's handled . . . He has a trout there too in a tank. It was going to be caught later on in the film . . . I sat on the bed and listened to him talk about animal behaviour. I said, 'Kenny, this is the kind of evening I like, two people just talking about something interesting.' I woke up in the night and couldn't remember where I was. Then I saw the cat sitting there, watching the trout.

Bennett writes of Lesley that she 'thinks she has a great deal to offer both as an actress and a person',[10] with the implication that we can see she hasn't. And he also writes of Susan, in 'Bed Among the Lentils', that she 'doesn't realise it's not just the woman in the off-licence but the whole parish that knows she's on the drink'.[11] He implies that Susan, like the other *Talking Heads* characters, isn't fully 'privy' to the 'meaning' of her story.

Now it would be possible, simply by reading Bennett's original script, to see this lack of awareness in the Susan he has created. But it's difficult to see it in the Susan created by Maggie Smith.

One reason why the play is so successful is that it teases the viewer. Looking back on it, we find it hard to say at what point we discovered that this Mrs Vicar was an alcoholic. 'I'm so bad at plots', says Bennett, but in fact this salient feature of 'Bed Among the Lentils' is extremely skilfully plotted. We're given the first hint in the last sentences of the opening scene, after Geoffrey has gone off alone to Evensong: 'I discovered we were out of sherry so I've just been round to the off-licence. The woman served me. Didn't smile. I can't think why. I spend enough.'

In the next scene, the one with the bishop, Susan remarks in passing that the bishop 'wants beer with his lunch and Geoffrey says he'll join him so this leaves me with the wine'. When 'disaster strikes' with the tinned peaches and the knocked-over jug of 'decanted' Carnation milk, 'Geoffrey, for whom turning the other cheek is part of the job, claims it caught his elbow.' But as Susan sponges off the bishop's gaiters, she catches the bishop giving her 'a funny look' (it's just after this that he suddenly remembers he ought to be in Keighley blessing the steam-engine). Susan dozes off and wakes to find a note from Geoffrey saying he's gone to talk to the Ladies' Bright Hour and telling her to go to bed: 'I'm not sleepy,' she tells us, 'and anyway we're running low on sherry so I drive into Leeds. I've stopped going to the shop round the corner now as I owe them a bit on the side and she's always so surly. There's a little Indian shop behind the Infirmary I've found. It's a newsagent's basically but it sells drink and anything really, the way they do. Open last thing at night, Sundays included, my ideal.'

It's in the next scene that we find her taking the dog-eared chrysanthemums for a drink from vases in the cupboard 'where Geoffrey keeps his communion wine', retiring again to the vestry 'for a bit of quiet to calm my shattered nerves', and slipping as she tries to kneel at the altar. By the time Geoffrey, white-faced, is shouting, 'The communion wine ... We haven't run out ... Somebody has drunk it', we're completely in the know – we know who the somebody is.

But as Maggie Smith plays these carefully plotted scenes, there's no sense that we (or, for that matter, the 'fan club') know something she doesn't know. She plays the lines with the knowing innocence of a good soldier Schweyk. 'What me', she implies, 'a drunk?', as she describes herself slipping down the altar steps. And that bottle of communion wine, still full on Friday! Who could possibly have drunk that? Luckily, there's the choirmaster's cough-mixture – 'It's red and sweet ...' Maggie Smith the minimalist doesn't offer us anything so overt as a wink. But there's an implied wink in the way she talks to us. She invites our collusion. We don't find her funny because we know more than she does, but because she's letting us in on a joke – 'Only thinking about it as I drift off again I think I may have said, "Goodbye, Mrs Subsoil." Anyway, I meant the other.' (No, honestly – I did.) 'Shrubsoil.'

The irony in 'Bed Among the Lentils' doesn't spring from the fact that we know more than Susan does, but from what Maggie Smith shows us to be Susan's own attitude – towards the people around her and towards herself. 'Once upon a time I had my life planned out . . . or half of it at any rate. I wasn't clear about the first part, but at the stroke of fifty I was all set to turn into a wonderful woman.' Bennett provides the lines: Maggie Smith brings to them her own sharp sense of irony.

'She's so self-aware and that's where the irony comes from', says Bennett. 'Maggie is witty and self-aware and ironic in herself. She lifts it off the ground. And that's why the ending is so upsetting, because, with all this self-awareness, she's still in this trap. I felt that all the self-awareness in the world doesn't get her away from her own predicament in the finish.'

The final scene of 'Bed Among the Lentils' lasts eleven and a half minutes. It's been shot in one uninterrupted take. Throughout the take, Maggie Smith stares, almost without moving, directly at the camera. She's in a fairly close midshot – we can see the edge of a picture frame behind her head, curtains to her left. After about nine minutes the camera begins its only movement in the scene – it moves very slowly, almost imperceptibly, towards her. By the time it has finished its movement, roughly half a minute later, her talking head is close enough to cut the picture frame out.

'Why have I always got to be on parade?' Susan has asked in the first scene. Here she's ultimately 'on parade', herself, in Brecht's words, 'closely observed' by the unremitting camera.

She's physically changed. She wears a neat yellow cardigan, and a smart white blouse with a brooch at the neck. Her hair is no longer straight and straggling – it's been cut, gathered neatly on top of her head. She looks at the camera, her head slightly tilted to one side.

She begins, 'I stand up and say, "My name is Susan. I am a vicar's wife and I am an alcoholic." Then I tell my story.'

In his introduction to *A Woman of No Importance*, Bennett has referred to 'the simplicity (not to say crudity)' of the talking-head form. But in this final scene his text piles narrative complexity on narrative complexity. He creates story-telling within story-telling.

'It was a kind of confessional thing', he says of his own experience in front of the *Talking Heads* camera and, 'It wasn't like performing, because you couldn't perform at such close range.' But here he asks Maggie Smith to perform confessional within confessional.

Susan begins by telling us how she confesses to the Alcoholics Anonymous that she is an alcoholic. Then she confesses to us that she hasn't confessed everything. 'Don't pull any punches,' she has Clem, her counsellor say – Maggie Smith makes him sound very like Geoffrey – 'Nobody's going to be shocked, believe me, love, we've all been there.'

Only, she tells us – not the Alcoholics Anonymous – 'I don't tell them about Mr Ramesh because they haven't been there.' Then she performs what she might have told them: 'Listen, people. I was so drunk that I used to go and sleep with an Asian grocer. Dear oh dear,' she comments to the camera – to us. 'This was a real drunken lady.'

Later, Bennett has her add yet more levels of story within story. She tells us that she told Geoffrey that she'd told the AA the story of the flower-arranging (which, of course, she's already told us). 'Result: he starts telling it all over the diocese.' She offers us two versions of Geoffrey's storytelling.

'The first time was at a conference on The Supportive Church. Gales of deep, liberated' – Maggie Smith pauses, giving a slight, ironic emphasis to the next word – 'caring laughter.' In the absence of the comedian's studio audience, Bennett has her add the canned audience response as a stage direction. Then she gives us the second version.

'He's now given it a new twist and tells the story as if he's talking about a parishioner, then at the end he says, "Friends, I want to tell you something." (Deep hush). "That drunken flower-arranger was my wife."' (The description is brutally crude.) 'Silence . . . then the applause. Terrific.'

The writing is extremely complex, but Maggie Smith's performance throughout the scene is, in Bennett's words, 'very plain'. She allows the ironies to speak for themselves. '"So how did you come to the AA?" they ask. "My husband," I say. "The vicar. He persuaded me." But I lie.' It was 'the exquisitely delicate and polite Mr Ramesh' who asked her one Sunday night 'if he might take the bull by the horns and enquire if intoxication was a prerequisite for sexual intercourse . . .?' Or was it only with him that she had to be inebriated? 'Because if not he would like to float the suggestion that sober might be even nicer. So the credit for the road to Damascus goes to Mr Ramesh – whose first name also turns out to be Ramesh. Ramesh Ramesh,' Maggie Smith briefly savours the name then adds, 'a member of the community council and the Leeds Federation of Trade.' (The Leeds Federation of Trade momentarily sounds like somewhere over the rainbow.) 'But none of this I say . . .' (Not to Alcoholics Anonymous, anyway – she says it to us.) So who gets the credit? 'It's full marks to Geoffrey's chum, the Deity, moving in his well-known mysterious way.' Maggie Smith quotes Geoffrey and now the quote too sounds brutal: 'My wife's an alcoholic, you know. Yes, it's a great challenge to me – and to the parish as extended family.'

'The extended family', he reveals, has been praying for her – he includes the revelation in a sermon on Prayers Answered. 'It practically sends me racing back to the Tio Pepe to think of it', Maggie Smith/Susan comments, in her direct, irreverent mode to us. 'The fans, of course, never dreaming that their prayers would be answered, are furious.' She goes on to describe, caustically, how Geoffrey 'at some doleful diocesan jamboree – I'm stuck there clutching my grapefruit juice' is 'telling the tale to some bearded cleric. Suddenly,' she says, 'he seizes my hand. "We met it with love," he cries, as if love were some all-purpose antibiotic, which to Geoffrey it probably is.'

Talking about Maggie Smith's performance in this scene, Alan Bennett refers to 'the way she doesn't quite break down when she's talking about the grocer in the end'. It's during this speech that the camera does its one almost imperceptible movement. Mr Ramesh, Susan tells us, has gone back to India to fetch his wife – 'She's old enough now apparently.' She finds a boy writing 'Under New Management' on the shop window: 'Spelled wrongly. And something underneath in Hindu, spelled right probably.' The boy thinks Mr Ramesh will be getting another shop, 'only in Preston'. Susan comments, 'They do that, of course, Asians, build something up, get it going nicely, then take the profit and move on. It's a good thing. We ought to be more like that, more enterprising.'

There's a catch in Maggie Smith's voice. The camera, now closer, scrutinises her eyes for tears. Is she really on the edge? If she is, she rapidly re-imposes her mask. 'My group members meet twice a week and I go. Religiously. And that's what it is, of course. That's what Geoffrey would call the wonderful mystery of God. I never liked going to one church and I end up going to two.' She pauses. Then, 'I call it bad taste,' she says. 'And I wouldn't do it to a dog. But that's the thing nobody ever says about God.' She pauses for one last time. 'He has no taste at all.'

'One thing that happened with Maggie', says Alan Bennett, 'was that the whole of the last section she did in a perfect first take. And then she slightly muffed the words at the end. It wasn't obvious – she just got the sentences the wrong way round.'

What Bennett had written was: 'I never liked going to one church so I end up going to two. Geoffrey would call that the wonderful mystery of God. I call it bad taste . . .' – the word 'call' is passed from one sentence to the next. Maggie Smith transposes the first two sentences, putting the sentence about going to two churches between 'Geoffrey would call . . .' and 'I call . . .' and losing the logic.

It's the kind of transposition that a writer would be very conscious of, particularly, coming as it does, at the end of such a carefully worked play. Bennett says, 'I was in despair because I thought she'd done it so beautifully and I had to go down and say, Can we do it again? And when you're doing a long take like that, the tension by the time you get to the end of it is unbearable. Anyway, she did do it again. But we looked at it and we thought we'd rather live with the one with the mistake in than the second one.'

Nobody watching the television version, without consciously referring to the published version, would notice that there'd been a mistake at all – the text as Maggie Smith speaks it makes complete sense. But Bennett's reference to the tension as 'unbearable' adds a dimension to our understanding of the form – and raises questions as irreverent as the text of the play. Like: to what extent did the tension towards the end of the long take affect the catch in Maggie Smith's voice? Did the longish pause after Geoffrey's final reference to 'the wonderful mystery of God' happen, not because Maggie Smith was letting the mystery sink in, but because she was having to re-organise in her mind the sentences she had transposed?

When Bennett first explored the form in *A Woman of No Importance*, he had been thinking of simplifying the job of the director. But he hadn't realised that while simplifying the job of the director he was putting 'unbearable' pressure on the performer, and that this would produce its own tension – a tension that communicates itself in the finished product.

With the camera so close that, in Bennett's words, 'It wasn't like performing because you couldn't perform at such close range', the performer was also required not to make the slightest fluff or stumble, or to give the slightest hint of a wrong emphasis because there was nowhere to hide (on stage, at a distance, finding cover would have been comparatively easy). Performing becomes a bit like going for a walk on a tightrope.

In Maggie Smith's case, there was added tension because she'd had to learn her lines in a comparatively short time. And one reason why her performance is such a *tour de force* is that she comes across as a performer who is, triumphantly, thinking on her feet.

In the decoration of the altar scene, for example, Bennett has written at one point, 'Gert and Daisy are of course speechless with admiration.' Maggie Smith says, 'Gert and Daisy are of course speechless.' Then, apparently as an afterthought, she adds, 'With admiration.' But then she gathers up the next sentence and makes it part of a changed rhythm, which itself, as she speaks it, becomes exactly right.

The effect of this successful struggle with the form is exhilarating. The talking head, says Bennett, is a synonym in television for boredom. But real television boredom happens (often in programmes that seem to be visually rich) when the word becomes a written lecture that carries the content and the pictures become no more than illustration.

Bennett's experiments with *Talking Heads* stripped down the medium to its simplest element. But at the same time they opened up new possibilities of immediacy and directness. Instead of illustrating the action, what we see adds a dimension, creating a tension between the word and the image. The word is describing actions that are past, completed and unchangeable. The visuals show the narrator in a present disassociated from the actions described. Bennett talks of 'over-egging the pudding' with adverbs, and the cooking metaphor is apt. The two elements – narrative in the past being reported by a performer we see in the present – can be mixed in a rich variety of ways, as Maggie Smith's performance of this particular text, itself complex, demonstrates.

And the tension between the fixed word (fixed in the past by a writer who has carefully composed it) and the re-creation of that word in a present scrutinised by a camera from which it is impossible to hide creates something of the excitement of a sporting event televised live. The performer walking on the tightrope offers the possibility of falling off. When the performer is as skilful as Maggie Smith, the skill of the performance leaves us with a sense of elation at the end.

Alan Bennett finds the ending of 'Bed Among the Lentils' 'upsetting'. Maggie Smith, he says, has given us a character who is witty, self-aware and ironic, but who, with all her self-awareness, is still trapped in the end, unable to escape from her predicament.

But the play, as performed by Maggie Smith, can be read in a very different way, as a blueprint for survival. Maggie Smith shows us a Mrs Vicar who is deeply subversive of the values her husband and his disciples pretend to live by. Caught in a world for which she has no respect, she uses her own weapons – wit, vulgarity (the services could be taken by a 'trained gorilla'), irony ("'We're a team," Geoffrey cries'), cunning (she can get drunk on the communion wine while feigning innocence), impropriety (going to bed with a married Indian grocer and enjoying it). 'For the moment,' she tells us in the final scene, 'I am a new woman and Geoffrey is a new man' – but that 'For the moment' has mischievous implications.

'There's no stopping Geoffrey now,' Susan says. But the cleverness of Maggie Smith's performance, and the knowingness she has brought to the character, contradict the fatalism. The Mrs Vicar of Maggie Smith has demonstrated her survival skills. Once Susan has got over the catch in her throat that the defection of the 'beautiful Mr Ramesh with wonderful legs' has left her with, there will surely be more jugs of 'decanted' Carnation milk to spill on the bishop's trousers, more bottles of communion wine to drink when there's no Tio Pepe, more irreverent and sceptical questions to put with subversive curiosity, more joyfully outrageous stories to tell. Resilience is implicit in Maggie Smith's performance.

Mrs Vicar's parting declaration that Geoffrey's God has 'no taste at all' – or, as Alan Bennett's mother would have said, is 'common' – needn't be read as a despairing last word. Its lack of respect contains the seeds of renewed resistance. It doesn't suggest that Geoffrey's future as a rural dean, or even 'on the bench', will turn out to be a synonym for boredom.

Talking Heads: 'Bed Among the Lentils'

Transmission date: 3 May 1988 (BBC1)   Repeated 19 July 1992 (BBC2)

Cast

Susan   Maggie Smith

Technical and production

Production Associate	Ralph Wilton
Production Manager	Paul Judges
Vision Mixer	Valerie Simmonds
Camera Supervisor	Rodney Taylor
Make-Up Designer	Jean Speak
Videotape Editor	Phil Southby
Sound	Richard Partridge
Lighting Director	Harry Bradley
Designer	Tony Burroughs
Music by	George Fenton
Produced by	Innes Lloyd
Directed by	Alan Bennett

Notes

The author wishes to express his gratitude to Alan Bennett for his help, given in an informal interview in December 1991. Any quotations that are not given a specific reference are taken from this interview.

1 *Objects of Affection and Other Plays for Television* (London: BBC Publications, 1982).
2 *Ibid.*, 34.
3 *Ibid.*
4 *Ibid.*
5 *Ibid.*, 217.
6 Brecht, *The Exception and the Rule*, cited by Michael Kustow, 'To hell with the pearl', *Encore*, 7, 3 (May–June, 1960) 19.
7 *Objects of Affection*, 34.
8 *Talking Heads* (BBC Books, 1988).
9 *Ibid.*
10 *Ibid.*, 8.
11 *Ibid.*

Select bibliography

Published plays by Bennett:

Office Suite: Two One-Act Plays (London: Faber, 1981). Includes *Doris and Doreen*

Objects of Affection and Other Plays for Television (London: BBC Publications, 1982)

The Writer in Disguise (London: Faber, 1985). Contents: *Me, I'm Afraid of Virginia Woolf, All Day on the Sands, One Fine Day, The Old Crowd, Afternoon Off*

Two Kafka Plays (London: Faber, 1987). Contents: *Kafka's Dick* and *The Insurance Man*

Talking Heads (London: BBC Books, 1988). Contents: 'A Chip in the Sugar', 'Bed Among the Lentils', 'A Lady of Letters', 'Her Big Chance', 'Soldiering On', and 'A Cream Cracker under the Settee'

Single Spies (London: Faber, 1989). Contents: *An Englishman Abroad* and *A Question of Attribution*

Bennett, Alan and others, *Intensive Care and Other TV Plays* (London: Longman, 1989)

Articles

Auty, Martyn, 'A Yorkshireman abroad', *Time Out*, 13–19 September 1984, 13

Bennett, Alan, 'Six of one' (*Talking Heads*), *Radio Times*, 16–22 April 1988, 9

Kingsley, Madeleine, 'Under observation' (Interview with Alan Bennett), *Radio Times*, 6–12 November 1982, 7–9

'Mr Bennett is a gentleman', *Radio Times*, 6–12 August 1988, 82–3

Lennon, Peter, 'Alan Bennett's "quaint" talking heads', *The Listener*, 28 April 1988, 46

Pym, John, 'Older women: *Talking Heads*', *Sight and Sound*, 57, 3 (summer 1988), 214

Tayor, Paul, 'Small talk, grand feelings', *The Independent*, 11 April 1988, 14

See also:

Broadcast, 21 February 1986, 22 (Bennett on his TV drama work and viewing preferences)

City Limits 11–18 September 1986, 22 (Bennett about his writing career)

3   *Brookside*: 'Damon's YTS Comes to an End' (Barry Woodward)

Paradoxes and contradictions

VERA GOTTLIEB

We believe that *Dallas* came just at the right time. It started in 1978, at the time of the second Arab oil embargo when Texas oilmen were being regarded with interest. The time had also come to show rich people. The economy was starting to be shaky. What happened was something like what happened in the 30s with the Fred Astaire and Ginger Rogers movies, those marvellous fairy stories in which a poor young girl is discovered by a very rich man, and people went to the cinema and, for two hours, forgot they didn't have enough to eat at home.[1]

The motivation behind *Dallas*, expressed here by its scriptwriters, is very different from that expressed by the creator of *Brookside*, Phil Redmond:

by the late 1970s I think a lot of the steam had gone out of these early efforts [*Coronation Street*], and I wanted to use the twice-weekly form to explore social issues, and, hopefully, contribute to any continuing social debate... From the outset one of my main aims was to try and reflect Britain in the 1980s... In 1982 I wanted to tackle the relevant social issues. Things like long-term unemployment, women's position in society, the black economy, the micro-electronic technological revolution and its impact on both management and union structures within industry. Five years on, these issues are still a major concern to us, but the perspective has shifted slightly from the post-socialist society of the 1970s to the capitalist entrepreneurial ethic of the 1980s.[2]

Both *Dallas* and *Brookside* are generically 'soap operas' – serial television dramas without narrative closure; both, according to their creators, arose quite explicitly from the economic, social and political climate of their times, one in the United States and the other in Britain, and both were intended to serve a particular function for their audience. It is in that function that the major difference appears: *Dallas* was intended as a 'fairy story' and to provide escape; *Brookside* was motivated from its inception by the wish to reflect and confront social issues. This essential difference of intention and philosophy dictates, in turn, the very different treatment of content and form within the 'soap' format. The eighties, however, seem to have provided a fertile context for both kinds of 'soap opera': they were, in fact, the *decade* of soap operas, whether of the escapist or of the socially reflective kind.

The increase of soap operas transmitted in Britain in the eighties, whether imported or domestic, is in itself characteristic of the decade. The main American products shown in Britain were *Dallas*, 1978–91; *Knots Landing*, 1980; *Dynasty*, 1982–91, and *The Colbys*, 1986–7,[3] all of which may be termed 'escapist' or 'fairy story' drama serials. The eighties also witnessed an explosion of Australian 'soaps' which found a new market in the United Kingdom for what had initially been designed as domestic products: *Sons and Daughters*, 1982–6; *Neighbours*, 1986– ; *A Country Practice*, 1981– ; *Home and Away*; *The Young Doctors*, 1976 ; and *Prisoner: Cell Block H*, 1987– . Of these, only *Prisoner: Cell Block H* challenged conventional expectations (in its treatment of lesbianism, for instance), whilst the others, particularly *Neighbours*, effectively increased the number of emigration applications received at Australia House in London by projecting a cosy image of 'neat houses, quickly tidied problems, strong young bodies, strong old biddies, token grown men and a hint of sex'.[4] Both the American and Australian soaps demonstrate, as Hilary Kingsley put it, 'that lather lasts longer if there's never any dirt'.[5] In contrast, *Prisoner: Cell Block H*, which was intended to be more serious in its confrontation of social realities in a women's prison, has had 'the dirt washed out of it'. To this highly selective list of English-language soaps must be added the relatively short-lived French ('Dallas-sur-Loire') response to American 'cultural imperialism': *Chateauvallon*, 1987, shown on Channel 4 in a late slot, given female nudity; and the West German *Black Forest Clinic*, shown on Channel 4 from January to March, 1988. Both were extremely popular within their domestic markets, both were rendered absurd in the UK by poor translation and even worse lip-sync, but neither was motivated by the confrontation of social issues any further than their American or Australian counterparts.

That confrontation with social reality within the soap format started when the home-produced British soaps, *Coronation Street*, 1960– , *Emmerdale Farm*, 1972– , and *Crossroads*, 1964–88, were joined by the newcomers *Brookside*, 1982 (Channel 4), and *EastEnders*, 1985 (BBC1).

From the outset, the intention of *Brookside* was to challenge the traditional soap-opera format by introducing 'issues' drama – a brief which is inseparable from the original remit of Channel 4. At the Edinburgh International TV Festival in 1979, Jeremy Isaacs (appointed Chief Executive of the Channel in 1980) referred to the need for 'actuality programmes which would embrace a complete spectrum of political attitude and opinion;'[6] while David Rose, Commissioning Editor of

Brookside, makes a different point: 'Clearly with all the minority programmes we were going to be producing, commissioning and transmitting,
we also needed to build an audience.'⁷ The twin – and sometimes
contradictory – motives of market and 'minority' resulted in the particular
'mix' of *Brookside*: a challenge to tradition, but one which would also sell in
the increasingly competitive market of commercial television. Or, as Peter
Ansorge put it positively: 'I would have thought that from the beginning
Brookside has helped to bring people's awareness to the channel and an
audience to the channel that might not otherwise have come to it.'⁸ But it is
exactly the duality of motives which *Brookside* demonstrates. In a *South
Bank Show* on *Brookside* in 1986, Melvyn Bragg commented:

In commissioning *Brookside*, Channel 4 recognised the potential of soap operas to
hook an audience at the start of an evening's viewing. *Coronation Street* which in
1982 was the unchallenged brand leader of British soaps brings over 20 million
people to ITV's first channel. But a visit to Brookside Close was never intended to
be as comfortable as an evening at the Rovers Return.⁹

The 'discomfort' arises exactly from the confrontation with social reality
on a private housing estate in eighties Liverpool – from the reflection of
current social issues. Over the ten years of its existence, *Brookside* has
'dealt' with attempted rape (of a schoolgirl); actual rape (of Sheila Grant);
with the problems of DHSS claimants; union–management conflicts
including lockouts, pickets and strikes; with issues of the NHS and the
ethics of nursing in the private sector; with homosexuality and Aids; with
redundancy and unemployment; the black economy; issues about community care; the tension between the priesthood and sexual attraction; with
criminality and justice, death, divorce, violence – both domestic and public
– and, in an episode shown in 1986, with the government's Youth Training
Scheme (YTS).¹⁰

This episode, written by Barry Woodward (transmitted on 24 March
1986), demonstrates the contemporary issue-led format which has made
Brookside significantly different from traditional soaps, and for that reason
it is important to sketch in the actual context in which the fictional drama
occurs. The YTS, introduced by the Conservative government in April 1985,
swallowed up previous schemes – such as the Youth Opportunities
Programme (YOP) – and was intended to bridge school and work as a
one-year scheme aimed primarily at unemployed 16-year-olds. The problem
– as the episode illustrates – was that at the end of the year's training, there
was rarely any employment for the trainee. In 1986, the government
extended the scheme to two years (for 16-year-olds) – an extension which
simply kept young people off the streets for a further year.¹¹

2 *Damon Grant (Simon O'Brien) has high hopes that his training as a decorator will actually lead to a job. Episode 355 of* Brookside: *'Damon's YTS Comes to an End'. Merseyside Television for Channel 4, 1986*

In the episode, 16-year-old Damon Grant (son of Sheila and Bobby Grant) has come to the end of his YTS year, and is expecting to be taken on by the decorating and building firm with which he has done his training. This, one of several narratives in the episode called 'Damon's YTS Comes to an End' (episode 355), follows Damon from youthful optimism and hope to a profound sense of injustice and rejection. The narrative is initiated (Scene 2) over breakfast in the Grants' kitchen on Bobby Grant's birthday when Damon, apologising for not getting his father a present, makes the promise that he'll be able to get his father something when he's 'in the money'. The scene builds from that assumption, and Damon ignores Bobby's warning: 'Yeah, well you wanna see how it's goin' before you start talking money.' The narrative, centred on the breakfast table, is filmed by a single video camera, and consists solely of 2-shots and, with Damon's entrance, 3-shots. When Damon leaves, he simply walks out of camera, leaving Sheila and Bobby where they were. The movement, constricted by the use of one camera, is static, yet puts the emphasis on dialogue, subtext and character rather than action. It is significant that the viewer knows what will happen – the title of the episode makes the ending clear – so the emphasis is on *how* the narrative is developed, rather than on 'cliff-hangers'. In this sense, in its avoidance of 'high drama' in locations and settings, dialogue, characterisation and climaxes, the episode is typical of *Brookside*'s refusal to follow the melodramatic plot-lines and violent action and climaxes of *Dallas* or *Dynasty*. The emphasis is on process – on how such things happen – and not on 'what will happen next' or suspense. But it is Damon's optimism which carries the viewer's interest into the scene (Scene 7) in the boss's office.

Sc.355.07 (INT) Halligan's office day 11.15 a.m.
Halligan moves round to his desk and waves Damon to a seat.

DAMON: Alright?
HALLIGAN: Oh, hi there. Sit down, Damon. Sorry to keep you hanging about.
DAMON: That's alright.
HALLIGAN   (*sitting, taking out some papers*): I've just been looking at some of your handiwork.
DAMON: Yeah.
HALLIGAN   (*smile*): Yeah. That job at the old swimming baths. You were on that, weren't you?
DAMON: Finished last Friday.
HALLIGAN: Yeah ... It's a nice job. Difficult, but well done ... (*pause*) You like the work, do you?
DAMON: Yeah.
HALLIGAN: Twelve months, eh? It's flown by, hasn't it?
DAMON   (*smiles*): It seems it, yeah.

HALLIGAN: They go by a damn sight faster and all when you get to my age. (*beat*) Still, I suppose it's better than going to school, though, eh?

DAMON: Yeah, well anything's better than that ... No, what I mean ... Well, I didn't mean that, you know what I mean.

HALLIGAN: I know what you mean, son. (*Picks up folded sheet of paper*) Ted tells me you get on pretty well with the other blokes. I'm pleased about that. The lumber I've had over the years with fellers always at each other's throats. A bit of harmony makes all the difference in a small outfit like this. In fact, Ted doesn't seem to have a word to say against you. He's written this. It's a reference. We have to do this for all you *YTS* lads. It's a good one. Listen.
Damon's pleased reaction.

HALLIGAN (*reading*): 'To whom it may concern ... blah, blah, blah ... Damon Grant has worked under my supervision for the past twelve months. In that time I have found him keen and willing to learn. His work has been of very high standard for a young man and I have found him to be punctual, honest and polite at all times. I would recommend him to any employer as an apprentice painter.'
Damon beaming.

HALLIGAN (*not reading*): Told you it was a good one, didn't I? I don't see many like that. Thanks for not letting us down, son.
Damon nods diffidently

HALLIGAN: Yeah, it's always a risk taking on you YTS lads, but I had a feeling when I first met you, you'd do alright. (*He stands up, offers his hand*) Well, Damon, congratulations, and thank you. (*Damon shakes his hand*) You'd better hang onto this reference. It puts you ahead of the rest ...
Damon now a little puzzled

HALLIGAN: Well, son, there's work to be done, people to see ... I'll just wish you the best and say goodbye ...
Damon's shocked reaction

HALLIGAN: ... It's been a pleasure to know you ...

DAMON: You're not taking me on?

HALLIGAN (*a short laugh*): Oh, I've no money for that, son. No, you YTS lads, you come for a year and that's it ...
He moves round and puts an arm on Damon's shoulder

HALLIGAN: Apply to a bigger firm. Show them that reference ... I'll see you.
Damon gapes in shock and disbelief. Looks at the folded reference. He turns and leaves the office hurriedly.
Halligan shrugs.

In real time, the scene takes 3 minutes in which Damon's world, sense of self, and sense of justice come crashing down – but with an almost casual normality which renders it all the more painful. Halligan confides in him, flatters him and congratulates him until the viewer, like Damon, starts to respond positively. Halligan avoids spelling out the reality until Damon's direct question forces a direct response. The scene, shot as always with a single video camera, is again carried largely by Medium Close Up 2-shot framing: a Medium Long Shot when Damon comes into the store/office (shot on location), but then for the rest of the scene either the 2-shot MCU with Damon and Halligan on either side of the desk, or MCU of Halligan with MCU reaction shots of Damon, and then returning to MCU 2-shots. Not only are there none of the BCU's so frequently used in American soaps, but here there is not even a close-up on Damon. The viewer is kept at a distance. The lighting – motivated by the office window – is subdued, with colour becoming almost monochrome, while the office is shabby and purely functional. After Damon's entrance, the only movement within the scene is when Halligan stands up at the end of the interview – a position of dominance and control heightened by Damon's incomprehension – and when he comes round the desk and puts an arm on Damon's shoulder. Both the tension and the subtext of the scene rely on dramatic irony in which Halligan knows something which Damon does not. Unlike the American soap format, there is no music, no villain (Halligan is not good at firing people) – and no climax. The sense of both anti-climax *and* a 'generalised' situation is heightened by the following scene (8) in the yard outside the office when Damon bumps into another 16-year-old boy – a new YTS trainee: 'Whatever he says in there about being kept on after . . . don't you believe a word.'[13] Clearly the point has wider social significance and is not only personal and individual.

The personal effect, however, is demonstrated in Part 2, scene 10.

Sc.355.10 (INT) Grants' living room day 12.30 p.m.
Where Damon is sitting on the settee with his head in his hands
Sheila straight in to him. He shakes his head.
SHEILA   (*She realises, flatly*): Damon, Damon, love. What's up, love? Damon, what is it? Oh God. It's your job, isn't it?
DAMON   (*Very upset*): They sacked me. He give (*pushing reference at her*) me that and he sacked me!
SHEILA: Sacked you?
DAMON: I thought I was gonna get it, thought I was going to be okay.
He tails off in despair, rubbing his face
Sheila reads the reference
SHEILA: You didn't do anything wrong, did you, love?
DAMON   (*Anger*): What d'yeh mean? Read that, will yeh? How can I have done anything wrong? They just wouldn't take me on!
SHEILA: But this says you're good. One of the best . . .
DAMON   (*Hiding his upset, hands to face*): That doesn't matter. They don't care. They just want that twelve months out of you, then they couldn't care less!
He shakes his head in misery
She puts her hands on his shoulders. Tries to comfort him
SHEILA: I know it seems . . . rotten, but you can't go getting y'self like this.
He pulls away

DAMON: I've worked like mad for them. Days I didn't have to do overtime. I didn't get a penny for it! I just wanted a job!
He puts his head in his hands again, forcing back tears
SHEILA   (*Just open hand on his shoulder*): I know love. But . . . you could still get a job . . .
DAMON   (*Not looking at her*): Where?
SHEILA: Well this is a good reference. It is love, it's good.
DAMON: It's not worth nothin' off them! I might as well have stayed on the dole!
He puts his head in his hands
SHEILA   (*Upset herself now*): I'm sorry, love . . . I'm sorry.[14]

The tone, pace and rhythm of the scene is summed up by the word 'flatly': the single static camera frames Sheila and Damon in an MCU 2-shot, and the strength of the scene lies in the credibility of the acting and the reality of situation. There is no music to provide emotional colouring, and the viewer is again placed in an objective – documentary – relation to the action. The action itself consists entirely of the personal effect of a social issue; the political implications remain unspoken.

In a subsequent episode, the mood and hence the seriousness of the issue is qualified: Sheila encourages Damon to apply for jobs and in a scene which ends on an 'upbeat', Damon regains his optimism with 'Look out, Liverpool, here I come!'

Several viewers, interviewed in the *South Bank Show*'s *Brookside*,[15] argued that the treatment of unemployment in *Brookside* has not truthfully represented the reality in which the unemployed in Liverpool have, by and large, stayed unemployed. The difficulty, of course, is that the soap (dubbed by Hilary Kingsley as 'the soap to commit suicide to') would not retain audience ratings if it were to deal unremittingly with social reality – and with documentary fidelity. As Laurie Taylor put it: 'There really is no need for people involved to go around apologising for the fact that it's not a major social documentary all the time. It's a soap opera.'[16]

Nonetheless, both the content *and* the treatment raise expectations of 'fidelity', 'credibility' and 'social reality' which are not always realised – and perhaps cannot be, given that the very format militates against narrative closure or resolution. But the contradiction between the soap-opera format and the intention of 'social debate' or 'social reflection' is increased by the technological and production values of the serial: innovatory as they were in the eighties, these values impose their own limitations.

In 1982, the use of *real* houses in a *real* close as the setting for a drama serial was new: *Coronation Street* had a 'purpose-built' street with studio interiors, and a multi-camera studio set-up. Part of the innovatory nature of Redmond's conception was that it should be shot in real houses in a real street on a private housing estate located outside Liverpool city centre – in fact, across the road from a tower block of a run-down council estate. As one critic put it, *Brookside*: 'blew away the tired conventions and flimsy stucco sets of the soap opera genre'.[17]

Redmond bought six houses which:

follow the typical specification of neighbouring private estates, although the density of housing is a little lower to allow wider camera angles and movement. Each house has running water, electricity, somewhat adapted to the householders' requirements. But nevertheless reality does stop here. The Grants can't park their car in their garage [filled with equipment], and the next door house only looks vacant. Upstairs in the master bedroom one million pounds worth of video tape machinery is in residence. Back downstairs the reception room holds the wardrobe store. Brookside Close is home to a fully equipped, self-sufficient TV production company, Mersey Television.[18]

Each house was adapted for filming with some walls knocked down to make room for lighting and camera set-ups. This approach to settings, however, created its own technical problems: links to the camera-chain had to be looped to keep them out of shot; three houses were joined together to provide a technical block for monitoring sound and picture, and an editing suite; additional power was needed for sound and lighting – both of which, given the 'studio-on-location' set-up, are more complex than within a purpose-built and controlled studio. Sound recording (with cables looped to the technical block, as well as the camera and lighting cables) is at the mercy of external and extraneous noise; lighting is potentially at the mercy of the weather. The technical problems for both light and sound are, in fact, 'real ones' – but the solutions, whilst innovatory and ingenious, actually militate against a 'documentary feel':

External lighting is provided by 2.5 KW lamps placed on hydraulic lifts to simulate daylight either downstairs or raised for use in bedroom scenes . . . Inside the house . . . will be two electricians who will arrange the hardware of the external and internal lighting in a lighting plot worked out by the lighting cameraman to simulate the most favourable realistic light.[19]

Similarly, the 'hollow' sound of the houses had to be counteracted by fixing sound-absorbent tiles to ceilings, and using sound panels. Recording stops when a plane flies over or there is other extraneous noise. Thus the technological innovations and the production values lie in the *simulation* of reality or 'the natural'.

Equally, the use of the single video camera, whilst 'more real' or even 'documentary' than the multi-camera studio set-up with mixing from one camera to another, creates different problems of 'naturalism'. First, video is more light-sensitive; second, the same scene has to be shot again from a different position and/or angle to get, for example, reaction shots. It is for this reason that one of the characteristics *and* limitations of *Brookside* is the rather static camera and MCU 2-shot or 3-shot formula. The very realism or naturalism becomes, in fact, visually boring and repetitive. Thus while the production team believe that the flexibility of the single video camera technique *increases* the realism, it also creates limitations for a drama serial which actual documentary may either ignore – or exploit.

The credibility of the drama, however, is carried by the quality of the acting: low-key, three-dimensional and 'felt' in a way which is radically different from the heightened melodramatic (though enjoyable) two-dimensional style of *Dallas* or *Dynasty*. A contrasting study of the acting style of Joan Collins (Alexis in *Dynasty*) with Sue Johnston (Sheila Grant) would make the differences in production values and characterisation immediately apparent. Alexis exercises her power in a way which renders inseparable her economic and sexual domination. The heightened and 'melodramatic' performance style is accompanied by the visual images of the power and wealth of her business empire: clothes, jewellery, cars, telephones, baths and caviar. She is what she owns. In contrast, Sheila is representational of the (probably equally mythical) 'ordinary housewife': trying to better herself (like Rita in *Educating Rita*) by going to literature classes, but at the mercy of men and social realities over which she has little control because she has no economic power. The acting style is correspondingly low-key, subtextual and expressive of pain and impotence, although strong. Alexis is brought down and humbled; Sheila fights simply to keep herself and her family afloat. To add fantasy to fiction by imagining a hypothetical meeting between the two women, it seems likely that Alexis would either fail to notice Sheila – or treat her with contempt.

The gender representation is radically different and inseparable from the representation of class in both 'soaps'. Given that 'soap' is historically viewed as 'women's fiction' (arising from day-time drama serials aimed at women in the home), the differences are significant and seemingly contradictory. Alexis has the economic power to function as an independent and professional woman; Sheila has none of the independence which economic security brings, and in her struggle to educate herself comes into conflict with the insecurity, jealousy and chauvinism of her husband Bobby. The women in American soaps like *Dallas* and *Dynasty* are highly competitive with each other – a rivalry which has climaxed in physical fights between, for instance, Alexis and Krystle Carrington – and invariably fight over a man (in this instance, over Blake Carrington). The female discourse in *Brookside*, on the other hand, demonstrates the depth and value of women's friendships (as between, for example, Sheila and Kathy when they have a night out on the town together), and a sense of solidarity against their men. Comparing the conflict between Alexis and Krystle over Blake with that between Sheila and Doreen over Billy Corkhill (with whom Sheila falls in love) reveals many of the differences in gender representation: Sheila and Doreen begin the confrontation over the washing-line in the Corkhills' back garden; the narrative is carried by the dialogue, and not physical conflict, and there is no sense of male sexual voyeurism as there is in *Dynasty* when two beautiful and elegant women get down in the mud to slug each other.

The representation of women in *Brookside* may, therefore, be seen as more 'real' than in American soaps, but it may also be argued that the emphasis on family and the home – whether in *Brookside* or *Coronation Street* – in fact reinforces gender assumptions or stereotypes. Again, 'difference' does not in itself result in fidelity to reality. Thus:

The women handle the complex web of relationships that make up a soap opera with a care and intensity which recognises the importance of close relationships and celebrates the undervalued skills of women in handling them. *Brookside*, because of its other concerns, has never had this full-blooded commitment to its women characters. It does take on women's issues – infertility, pregnancy, low pay – but the way in which it represents women seems to reinforce sexual stereotyping rather than to challenge it. Whereas most serials concentrate on the personal world, *Brookside* also tries to operate in the public arena and gives more attention to what are defined as public problems. Women are almost always excluded from these activities ... there is no attempt to represent women working in the factory or organising in the unions. It is Bobby Grant who is the shop steward; his wife, Sheila, one of the strongest women characters, is not even a union member. The norm is relentlessly that of a married couple, with or without children, with the women taking on the traditional roles of cleaning, cooking and maintaining the family relationships. The public world of work and unions is represented as being exclusively male and the women are presented as supporting their men rather than challenging them.[20]

In the same article, written in 1984, Christine Geraghty also makes the point that one of the intentions behind *Brookside* was to widen the representation of groups which had not hitherto been given much space or sympathy in soaps: men and adolescents. Since 1984, both 'groups' have increasingly been catered for – whether in *Brookside*, *Neighbours*, or *Coronation Street* where a whole younger generation has been written in – but paradoxically this subverts balanced gender representation: in order to attract male and younger viewers to a genre traditionally considered 'women's fiction', the balance shifted towards 'male concerns'. 'Social issues' seem to be confronted largely by men: picket lines, management and police, for example, maintain the stereotypic assumption in the serial that confrontation or opposition in the public arena is almost exclusively male-dominated.

The 'contradictions' surrounding *Brookside* partly arise from the tension between commercial ratings – and yet satisfying Channel 4's minority remit. Contradictions also arise from the very differences of *Brookside* to other soaps (apart from *EastEnders*) in that differing expectations cannot all be rewarded – and may well cancel each other out. But other contradictions arise from the decade in which *Brookside* developed: it both maintains and subverts some of the issues and values of the eighties. For this reason, critical responses to the serial have been overtly contradictory: one 'school' of thought has accused *Brookside* of 'left-wing bias' while another has accused it of 'going soft on Socialism'. Again, this disparity seems to arise from the expectations created by realism and social-issue drama. But if the gender representation in the serial has not, until recently, challenged the status quo, the class representation *has* actually subverted some of the values of eighties Britain.

The reality of cars which don't start, clothes which don't fit, furniture which is shabby, and people who are too fat or too thin, actually did undermine the 'aspirational' images of American soap, Reagan's America, and Thatcher's Britain. As Michael Bywater put it: 'The belief that it's what you are which counts, not what you've got, though perhaps inimical to the present government, is deeply embedded in our national nature.' Part of the escapist value and appeal of the American 'fairy-story' soap lies in the aspirations of wealth and power – and in watching the wealthy and powerful brought down: 'The American misery is Biblical, visited on the rich.'[21] In *Brookside*, the 'aspirations, like the rooms and the clothes, are shabby and small'.[22] Survival is not a matter of big business corporations like Ewing Oil in *Dallas*, but of simply getting and retaining a job – and paying the bills. Misery is visited, in both *Brookside* and *EastEnders*, on the already disadvantaged, whether women, the elderly, the unemployed, ethnic minorities, or the sick.

An expectation of explanation, however, is rarely rewarded: we are given the effect, but rarely an analysis of cause. The problem, again, is that of genre versus content. As Chris Dunkley put it:

If you approach soap opera which is after all drama, with politics, economics and social matters in line, you're in danger of ending up with the kind of drama that looks as though that is how you set out. And whereas *EastEnders*, for example, grows out of its characters, I think it really does, like classic drama, emerge from the reality of specific people . . . the plot and the little bits of narrative emerge from what feel like real people. *Brookside* feels to me too often as though it is people being put on social or economic theories. So it begins to look rather like a kind of London School of Economics lesson about Sociology rather than a drama.[23]

Brookside's distinctive use of the soap-opera genre, however, is social – and not political. Phil Redmond articulated it clearly:

It never was a socialist soap – only a social soap. It reflected what was happening, how people felt in 1982. In 1987 it's a Tory society of conspicuous consumption with a sharp North–South divide. We must reflect that.[24]

This reflection of contemporary reality, however, was sufficient to get

Brookside into trouble – and formed part of a concerted attack not only on the serial itself, but on Channel 4. Under the terms of the Broadcast Act, Channel 4 (as ITV) had to ensure that it did not offend 'good taste' or 'decency'. *Brookside*'s realism extended to the use of dialect, slang – and swear words. This immediately allowed Mary Whitehouse, the Honorary President of the National Viewers' and Listeners' Association, to go on the attack:

Unless something is done and done quickly, we'll have four-letter words littering our programmes in future, just as 'bloody' does now. What we're talking about is the crudeness and craziness and innate vulgarity of these words. They tend to destroy the nuance of feeling which language exists to express. They reduce sexual experience to a harsh and cruel act. They're destructive to our culture and destructive to relationships. People, ordinary people, are concerned, and frustrated beyond measure.[25]

Phil Redmond, describing the conception of *Brookside*, stated that: 'I wanted to be honest about swearing. Everyone swears in some form, even vicars. Jeremy [Isaacs] agreed.'[26] But the furore about the language actually masked a much deeper reaction against the programme – and the channel. The right-wing press, and in particular the *Daily Express*, accused the serial of 'left-wing propaganda' and demanded the resignation of Isaacs; *Private Eye* started a strip cartoon called *Bogside*, and complaints issued from Conservative Party Central Office about an episode dealing with the NHS. This reaction is also symptomatic of another feature of the eighties: the osmosis between the tabloid press and television soap operas in which the one often helped to sell the other. Tabloid headlines have variously 'reported' on 'soap narratives' as if they were real.

Thus the 'soap decade' effectively started when in March 1980 tabloid newspapers carried the headline: 'Who Shot J.R.?' – reporting on the assassination attempt on J. R. Ewing in *Dallas* (an item also reported on the BBC's 9 o'clock News). This provided a cliff-hanger across fifty-six countries involving an estimated 300 million viewers, and only resolved in November of the same year in an episode that reputedly brought 27.3 million viewers in the United Kingdom alone.[27]

In a more 'localised' context, and more recently, British tabloids have sold on the headline: 'Will Deirdre Leave Ken?' – a story about the deteriorating marriage of Deirdre and Ken Barlow in *Coronation Street*. *EastEnders* has regularly provided tabloid copy – such as 'TV Soap "Too Sexy for Kids"' (*The Sun*, 3 September 1985), or 'EastEnders "Strip or Whip" Rumpus' (*The Mirror*, 4 November 1985).[28] Much of this was motivated by the circulation wars which, in turn, manufactured a 'soap war', but there has also been a particular relationship between Mary Whitehouse and the *Daily Express* and the *Daily Mail*, both of which supported her criticisms not only in the news section but in editorials. As with *Brookside* and Channel 4, so the attacks on *EastEnders* involved a deeper attack on the BBC for 'left-wing bias'. For the right-wing critics of *Brookside* and *EastEnders*, being 'social' and 'realistic' meant being 'political' – and being 'political' meant 'left-wing'. The thinking is evident in one of the Conservative Party's election posters for the general election of 11 June 1987: 'Take the politics out of education – vote Conservative.' The assumption is that the traditional soaps like *Dallas* or *Coronation Street* are untainted by a value system – and separable from the times and society which produced them, and in which they were produced. This political dimension to soap opera surfaced with Mark Lawson's TV programme: *J'Accuse: 'Coronation Street'*, and a subsequent response from Andy Mayer in *The Guardian*, 30 September 1991. Lawson's 'chief grouse was that unlike *Brookside* and *EastEnders*, the Street evaded current issues of concern. He felt that any drama which pretends to be contemporary has a responsibility to reflect social developments. Deirdre Barlow's sex life put her at risk of Aids but the series continued to treat adultery as mere plot twist.' Mayer quotes the longest-serving producer of *Coronation Street*, Bill Podmore: 'I never allowed the programme to become a platform for debate, moral or otherwise. I regard that as the province of documentary, not light entertainment', but Roy Hattersley (one of many fans including Harold Wilson, Margaret Thatcher, Mary Whitehouse and Sir John Betjeman) views the programme as a major social document. Hattersley stated that *Coronation Street* 'now reflects the complicated class and racial structure which characterises British society' – and – 'It is a chronicle of our times and future historians will find no better way of learning about the way we live now.'[29] It would seem that the resolutely 'non-social' *Coronation Street* does have political ramifications – even if those consist of the sparse representation of ethnic groups and contemporary women, but most particularly in what Mayer called the 'depressingly negative philosophy' of Billy Liar: 'If you want to be happy, stay where you are. Know your place.' *Coronation Street* is 'status quo' drama with neither the aspirational images and values of *Dallas* or *Dynasty*, nor the reflection of actual social reality attempted by *Brookside* and *EastEnders*.

The creators of *EastEnders* – Julia Smith and Tony Holland – hit back at their critics in general, and Mary Whitehouse in particular,[30] and, crucially, had the protection of the BBC. Phil Redmond, however, had earlier responded to the attacks by changing course: soon after the opening of *Brookside*, and when viewing figures had dropped to 250,000, Redmond framed the famous *Daily Express* front page, put it up on his office wall – and adopted a new relationship with the press. He set out to use the press instead of being used.

The approach to the media – formerly cautious and wary – changed. Story-lines were suddenly mysteriously leaked. A hype – using other soap operas – began. A 'Brookside' camera crew turned up outside Granada studios to film as part of a story-line. Some characters wanted to take back 'Coronation Street' souvenirs to their Liverpool home. Granada executives were not amused, and said so. As the hype grew, so the story-lines became more daring.[31]

The hype, or orchestrated media campaign, was also used successfully with the 'writing out' of two *Brookside* characters: Petra Taylor, whose planned disappearance resulted in 'sightings' all over the country – and a jump in viewing figures; and the 'Free George Jackson' campaign when the character was sent to jail as a result of the actor leaving the programme – a media campaign involving posters, T-shirts, recordings, and 'graffiti'. The viewing figures rose to 4 million. In the meantime, the language of *Brookside* was modified: the swearing stopped. It would seem that Redmond decided to 'play the system' rather than to buck it.

This element of 'playing the system' is, in itself, symptomatic of the commercial ethics of the eighties. Redmond set himself up as an entrepreneur, running Mersey Television in a way which, with hindsight, seems characteristic of the 'market forces' philosophy of the decade – and Channel 4. The originator of the highly successful children's series, *Grange Hill*, Redmond decided to go independent with a new soap. As he put it: 'The BBC had shut the door, ITV had *Coronation Street* and *Crossroads*.'[32] And:

I set out to ... do two things with Mersey Television when Channel 4 came along with Independent Production and that is to gain more creative control over my own work, secondly to provide a kind of more secure future for myself, you know, like any kind of business entrepreneur would want to do.[33]

Redmond went to the Department of Trade and Industry for a grant:

I didn't qualify, because I wasn't a manufacturer, but they gave me £195,000 over three years as an assistance grant because I was setting up in Liverpool creating seventy jobs. They took £100,000 back in tax later, but that was another matter. I decided to keep all costs capital – not running. I decided to buy all the equipment and thirteen houses. Since then I've bought a further seven flats, another house and two Portakabins.[34]

With this independent financial arrangement, Isaacs agreed to back the project, Redmond borrowed £1 million, and Mersey Television opened for business. As Melvyn Bragg put it in his *South Bank Show* on *Brookside*: 'Behind the scenes lies a considerable business success, its Chairman, who owns property now worth a quarter of a million pounds, is once again Phil Redmond.'[35] And what Bragg called 'a shrewd investment if the series fails' was, in fact, an investment in the property market: the real houses have a real value on the open market.

Phil Redmond is now, according to Hilary Kingsley, a very rich man – but Mersey Television had also, by 1988, brought £17 million to the Liverpool economy. The relationship between market economy, investment, ratings and 'soap' is as evident in the development of *Brookside* from 1982 in the United Kingdom as it is in the production and marketing of *Dallas* or *Dynasty* in the United States. Even the launch of *EastEnders*, within the licensed and thus protected context of the BBC, was couched in terms of 'the launch of a new brand into a difficult market' in a paper delivered to the Market Research Society.[36] Arguments about the contradictions of *Brookside* must be placed in the real world of the independent television industry. A one-off drama which seriously questions the status quo *may* get sponsorship and advertising revenue (though this is increasingly rare); a drama serial which consistently challenges the society from which it is produced is at the mercy of that society for its means of production.

The contradictions which make up *Brookside* are evident also in Mersey Television's working methods. Redmond 'is seen more as the tyrannical tight-fisted tycoon than as the boy-wonder of teenage drama', and Hilary Kingsley continues:

His actors and technicians work long and hard and, they claim, on minimum rates and miserly allowances. Unlike other television studios, 'Brookside' is 'dry': alcohol is banned. The soapsters' perks – fees of £2000 and more to attend the openings of shops – are allowed only if it suits the boss. Personnel are contracted to share fees with the company, Mersey Television, which regulates and vets the engagements. Redmond believes he has the right to his 'cut': he created the characters.[37]

The business ethic bears some comparison with the old Hollywood Studio system – and partly explains the high turnover of managers and actors: 'It is partly because some cannot stomach the dictatorial regime', and partly because 'many of the stars have been openly political – something most mealy-mouthed management hate'.[38] Sue Johnston, who left the serial in 1986, campaigned vigorously on behalf of the Miners' Strike in 1985, as did Ricky Tomlinson. The production staff are known as the 601 club – deriving from the meal allowance for overtime: £6.01; while the *per diem* for a location trip to Rome was £4.85 for each crew member, including meals and board.[39]

A different contradiction – indicative also, perhaps, of unease with the programme values – was articulated by one of the twelve series writers, Jimmy McGovern: 'What I want to see on *Brookside* is the flexibility whereby we can slot episodes in. On burning issues – slot them in somehow, find space in the system to do that.'[40] The production system itself, however, militates against topicality. 'We work so far ahead where we're writing March and April episodes to take place April, May, June, July, August, September. We cannot be sure when our stories hit the screen.'[41] The production process, with story-lines written five months in advance, two weeks in which to write an episode, with two episodes filmed each week (10 minutes of each programme shot every day), carries its own realistic limitations. But as Laurie Taylor put it:

> When in fact the Heysel Stadium and Hatton are sitting around the corner it does look a bit perverse of Brookside not to incorporate it. I suppose that all you can say is that if Brookside didn't take any notice of such major events occurring on its own doorstep, then probably no soap opera ever will.[42]

The Miners' Strike was only briefly mentioned, the bankruptcy of Liverpool Council and the political row surrounding Council Leader Derek Hatton were ignored; the Toxteth and Croxteth riots were never included. The limitations relate not only to topicality, but also to locality. 'Issues' are evidently and inevitably selected and edited. Again, a contradiction arises between potential and realisation, but this particular contradiction would only be resolved by the kind of 'politicisation' which was never intended by *Brookside*'s creator – and which could not have survived the pressures on broadcasting in the eighties.

Two other aspects of *Brookside*, however, may also be seen as characteristic of the eighties: the locating of the serial on a private estate, and the 'privatisation' of the families on the estate. Both resulted from Redmond's refusal to follow the structural device of traditional British soaps: a communal meeting-place, whether a pub, a café, a launderette or a shop, which allowed for the 'natural' intermingling of the characters. This lack of a central focus or meeting-point, although motivated by 'realism' in its rejection of a dramatic device, has in turn created the dramatic problem of how the characters can meet and interact (subsequently at the famous post-box and, more recently, in a shop). More significantly, it reflected the increase in the eighties of 'separate individualised units': one of the Thatcherite values of the eighties was a rejection of 'society' in favour of 'the family'. *Brookside* has both reflected this and, in fact, propagated this view. In this sense, *EastEnders* (and even the historically anachronistic *Coronation Street*) have kept alive the idea of social interaction and 'community'. The artifice of the dramatic and structural device of pubs like the Queen Vic or the Rovers' Return, the use of the market stalls, café, shop and launderette have enabled the characters to interrelate in a 'natural' context, *and* have also qualified the 'privatised' and 'individualised' values of the decade.

The choice of a private estate, Brookside Close, was explained by Redmond in these terms:

At the time, in the early 1980s, approximately 58 per cent of homes were owner-occupied, approximately 15 per cent were private rented accommodation and the rest was council-owned accommodation. In the mid to late 1980s the owner-occupying percentage has risen to about 62. Therefore it seemed more realistic and more logical to have a residential drama serial reflecting such owner-occupation. However, one of the ironies of producing the programme in Liverpool is that Liverpool has one of the highest instances of council property with approximately 40 per cent of the city living in council accommodation. Still, as we are often reminding people, 'Brookside' is not about Liverpool and Merseyside in particular but about Britain – it just happens to be set in Liverpool![43]

Redmond's aim in reflecting the apparent social mobility in eighties Britain, the values of home-ownership, changes in the building trade, and sale of council property was also, however, motivated by the much less 'realistic' dramatic device of 'the triangle' of management, union, and black economy – a representation offering the potential for debate or what Redmond called 'an arena'. In effect, however, as one viewer pointed out on *The South Bank Show*: 'It's artificial to have that cross-section of society all placed in one particular Close.'[44]

Paradoxically, the social and dramatic device of 'the triangle' has resulted in more artifice than the structural and community-based devices of *EastEnders*, or even the old-fashioned *Coronation Street*. The reflection of 'new' or contemporary values need not in itself be either 'realistic' or necessarily 'progressive'.

Some of the contradictions of *Brookside*, however, must also be seen in the context of Channel 4: both were launched together in November 1982, and there are important parallels in their development throughout the eighties. Channel 4 opened in 1982 with the remit of 'distinctiveness': (1) it was to be used by smaller interest groups; (2) the channel was to be used more by independent producers, and (3) it was to have a distinctive approach to content and form. Its remit derived from the previous decade, and by 1982 it was already becoming an historical anachronism – and certainly a political one. In October 1983, it became clear that Thatcher wished the channel to justify itself in commercial terms, 'as it slowly dawned on her that to a considerable extent the channel was in effect being subsidised by the Treasury. The problem was then, as now, that to move in that direction would almost certainly mean the end of the mission implicit within the mandate.'[45]

The contradictions are manifold: free market – but creeping censorship; removal of subsidy – yet the requirement of 'risk-taking' innovation in content and form; and, most important, deregulation, competition and the ratings wars – and yet the protection of minority interests.

In this context, it is not surprising that *EastEnders*, produced within the structure of the BBC, has been able to take more risks than *Brookside* – a drift articulated by Andy Lavender in relation to overall programming. Lavender argues that BBC2 has now taken over Channel 4's role as the initiator of 'difference':

> Under Michael Grade and Liz Forgan, C4 has found itself fighting on two fronts: working towards convincing advertisers that it offers something attractive and different to their clients but at the same time trying to convince the industry, and in particular suspicious independents, that in preparing to sell that advertising it has not lost its programming edge.[46]

As it developed over the decade, *Brookside* illustrates some of the contradictions of its own channel; the pressure on broadcasting in the eighties; some of the contradictions within British society in that decade, and the contradictions between control over production and the means of production. But it also demonstrates a contradiction between its own genre and format – and its wider aspirations to 'social drama'. As Chris Dunkley put it in *The South Bank Show*:

> While sympathising with it personally and understanding the desire [to deal with large issues] . . . I think it's extremely difficult to do it successfully in soap opera, and I think *Brookside* itself proves that that's difficult. I don't suggest that the way it's been done is putting people off, I think obviously it's not. It's getting Channel 4's biggest audience after all, and I believe it would get an even bigger, much bigger audience again if it were ever shown on BBC1, or much more likely on ITV, because I think that the sheer hunger, desire for soap opera is such that you could do remarkably difficult things and still get an audience.[47]

Brookside: 'Damon's YTS Comes to an End'

Transmission date: 24 March 1986 (C4)

Cast

Bobby Grant	Ricky Tomlinson
Sheila Grant	Sue Johnston
Karen Grant	Shelagh O'Hara
Damon Grant	Simon O'Brien
Pat Hancock	David Easter
Sandra Maghie	Sheila Grier
Derek Halligan	Brian Abbott
Guy Willis	Ian Michie
Matty Nolan	Tony Scoggo

Technical and production

Devised by	Phil Redmond
Written by	Barry Woodward
Lighting Cameraman	Tony Caveen
Dubbing Mixer	John McNabb
Vision Engineer	Duncan Goodard
Editor	Mark Doran
Lighting Electrician	Paul Taylor
Script Assistant	Elizabeth Malpas
Casting	Dorothy Andrew
Make Up	Maggie Magee
Wardrobe	Gillion Ion
Design	Carol Sheeran
Music	Steve Wright
Title Music	Steve Wright & Dave Roylance
Location Manager	Ian Vasey
Production Manager	Sally Morgan
Executive Producer	Phil Redmond
Director	Eszter Nordin
Producer	Stuart Doughty

Notes

1 Quoted in Alessandro Silj *et al.*, *East of Dallas: The European Challenge to American Television* (BFI Publishing, London, 1988), 21.

2 *Phil Redmond's Brookside: The Official Companion* (Weidenfeld and Nicolson Ltd, London, 1987), 5–6.

3 The dates given are of first transmission in the UK.

4 Hilary Kingsley, *Soap Box: The Papermac Guide to Soap Opera*, (Macmillan Publishers Ltd, London, 1988), 360.

5 *Ibid.*

6 David Docherty, David Morrison, Michael Tracey, *Keeping Faith?*, *Channel Four and Its Audience*, Broadcasting Research Unit Monograph (John Libbey & Company Ltd, London and Paris, 1988), 5.

7 Quoted in *ibid.* 65–6.

8 *Ibid.*

9 Broadcast by London Weekend Television on 13 April 1986: Editor/Presenter Melvyn Bragg; Producer/Director Jill Freeman. All quotations are from the post-production script and are the copyright of London Weekend Television. This quotation is from pp. 11–12.

10 This episode was commercially available from Channel 4 Television: Phil Redmond's *Brookside Classics*, vol. 2: *The Sheila Grant Years*, Mersey Television Company, in *The Video Collection*, but distribution has been discontinued.

11 See Jo Roll, *Young People: Growing up in the Welfare State* (Family Policy Studies Centre, Occasional Paper Number 10, London, 1990), and 'Ensuing changes to the social security rules in September 1988 introduced a note of

compulsion into the scheme as it became the only way for unemployed 16 and 17 year olds to receive government assistance', 33.

12 Quotations from this episode come from the transmission script, Copyright 1985 Brookside Productions Ltd. This scene is pp. 21–5 of the transmission script.

13 *Ibid.*, 26.

14 *Ibid.*, 30–2.

15 Post-production script, *The South Bank Show*, 35.

16 *Ibid.*, 54.

17 Chris Stacey and Darcy Sullivan, *Supersoaps* (London: Boxtree Ltd, published in association with Independent Television Publications Ltd, 1988), 83.

18 Post-production script, *The South Bank Show*, 9.

19 *Phil Redmond's Brookside*, 13–14.

20 Christine Geraghty, *Brookside, Marxism Today* (February 1984), 38. Since her article appeared, *Brookside* has presented unmarried couples, and both heterosexual and homosexual relationships.

21 Michael Bywater, 'Tastes Like Soap', *The Listener*, 21 April 1988, 4.

22 *Ibid.*

23 Post-production script, *The South Bank Show*, 30.

24 Quoted in Hilary Kingsley, *Soap Box*, 49.

25 Quoted in Docherty, Morrison, Tracey, *Keeping Faith?*, 25.

26 Quoted in Hilary Kingsley, *Soap Box*, 48.

27 *Ibid.*, 184.

28 For a full discussion of the publicity afforded *EastEnders*, see David Buckingham, *Public Secrets: EastEnders & Its Audience* (BFI Publishing, London, 1987), 124–7.

29 Quoted in *The Guardian*, 30 September 1991, 23.

30 See Buckingham, *Public Secrets*, 146–52.

31 Hilary Kingsley, *Soap Box*, 46.

32 Quoted in *ibid.*, 47–8.

33 Post-production script, *The South Bank Show*, 10.

34 Quoted in Hilary Kingsley, *Soap Box*, 48.

35 Post-production script, *The South Bank Show*, 9.

36 Quoted in Buckingham, *Public Secrets*, 23.

37 Hilary Kingsley, *Soap Box*, 49.

38 *Ibid.*

39 Stacey and Sullivan, *Supersoaps*, 88.

40 Post-production script, *The South Bank Show*, 39.

41 *Ibid.*, 37.

42 *Ibid.*, 36.

43 *Phil Redmond's Brookside*, 6.

44 Post-production script, *The South Bank Show*, 17.

45 Docherty, Morrison, Tracey, *Keeping Faith?*, 23.

46 Andrew Lavender, 'Channel Crossings', *The Guardian*, 23 December 1991.

47 Post-production script, *The South Bank Show*, 51.

Select bibliography

Books

Ang, Ien, *Watching Dallas: Soap Opera and the Melodramatic Imagination* (London: Methuen, 1985)

Collins, Richard, *Television: Policy and Culture* (London: Unwin Hyman Ltd, 1990)

Docherty, David, David E. Morrison, Michael Tracey, *Keeping Faith? Channel Four and its Audience*, Broadcasting Research Monograph (London and Paris: John Libbey & Company, 1988)

Dyer, Richard, *Light Entertainment*, BFI Television Monograph (London: BFI, 1973)

Gledhill, Christine (ed.), *Home is Where the Heart is: Studies in Melodrama and the Woman's Film* (London: BFI Publishing, 1987)

Roll, Jo, *Young People: Growing up in the Welfare State*, Occasional Paper no. 10 (London: Family Policies Study Centre, 1990)

Silj, Alessandro, with Alvarado *et al.*, *East of Dallas: The European Challenge to American Television* (London: BFI Publishing, 1988)

Tibbals, Geoff, *Brookside: The First Ten Years* (London: Boxtree, 1992)

Articles

Bywater, Michael, 'Tastes like soap', *The Listener*, 21 April 1988

Geraghty, Christine, '*Brookside* – No common ground', *Screen*, 24, 4–5 (1983), 137–41

'Brookside', *Marxism Today*, February 1984

'East Enders', *Marxism Today*, August 1985

Lavender, Andrew, 'Channel crossing', *The Guardian*, 23 December 1991

Mayer, Andy, 'Funny side of the Street', *The Guardian*, 30 September 1991

Root, Jane, 'Unsuitable case for treatment?' (Rape in *Brookside*), *The Listener*, 7 August 1986, 28–9

4   *Yes, Prime Minister*: 'The Ministerial Broadcast' (Jonathan Lynn and Antony Jay)
Social reality and comic realism in popular television drama

JOHN ADAMS

Introduction

The television series,[1] as a product of popular culture, is not necessarily amenable to evaluation by the same methods or criteria as those of high culture; questions of context and intent are usually of a different kind, and need to be inflected in different ways. The intention of this essay is not therefore to identify meaning in *Yes, Prime Minister*, but to locate the series in a tradition of comedy with reference to some conventions of verisimilitude through which audiences of television sitcoms make sense of what they know to be non-sense.

Yes, Prime Minister is the only sitcom considered in this collection of essays. However, it cannot be seen as representative of a notional genre; from the outset it is necessary to acknowledge the complexity of 'sitcom' as a generic classification, ranging through farce and fantasy to comedies located in a tradition of social realism from *Hancock's Half Hour* (first transmitted in 1956), through *Steptoe and Son* (1964–73) and *Dad's Army* (1968–77) to contemporary programmes, with many hybrids in between.[2] In this context, *Yes, Minister* and *Yes, Prime Minister* are firmly located towards the 'social realist' end of the spectrum. However, a number of features distinguish this series as atypical, and it is precisely these differences which bring into focus some important characteristics of sitcom (and implications of such generic classification) that will be discussed later.

The idea for *Yes, Minister* was originally submitted to the BBC in 1977, having been conceived by Jonathan Lynn and Antony Jay. Jay had been a senior producer on the *Tonight* programme, a role that had given him extensive experience of politicians during the 1960s; Jonathan Lynn was an experienced actor, writer and director in both theatre and television. They worked closely together during the 1970s as creators of the Video Arts training films with John Cleese.[3] However, the BBC delayed production of the series for the best part of three years until the general election question, an ongoing possibility during the period, was resolved in 1979 with a new government and a secure majority in the House of Commons.[4]

Institutional ambitions for the programme were high, but the success of the series was by no means a foregone conclusion; early reviews were distinctly mixed,[5] and the writers were themselves uncertain about the comic potential: 'we took great trouble to make the actual story as interesting and realistic as we could. This was originally an insurance policy. We were frightened that people would not laugh. But we felt that if we failed to make it funny, at least people would be held and interested.'[6] In the event, the series rapidly established a regular place near the top of the BBC2 ratings[7] and critical opinion settled in its favour, with the second and third series drawing almost unanimous praise. On the basis of its apparent authenticity, the series also generated press coverage well beyond the columns of the television critics and drew enthusiastic endorsement across the political spectrum from, amongst others, Roy Hattersley, Gerald Kaufmann, Paul Channon and, in due course, Margaret Thatcher. (Labour 'support' appears to have waned after a while, with Paul Eddington reporting that 'whenever I meet a [Conservative] Cabinet Minister I get treated as a colleague, while the [Labour] opposition regard me with suspicion'.)[8]

However, the formal and generic lineage of *Yes, Minister* and *Yes, Prime Minister* is securely rooted in a tradition of satiric political drama dating back through the Atellan farce of early Roman times to the Attic comedy of Aristophanes in the fifth century BC.[9] This contextualisation is not a banal attempt to canonise the series; rather, it is necessary to locate dominant conventions of the series in this way in order to explore relations between such conventions and the codes of social realism through which the recurrently emphasised 'authenticity' is constructed. I will approach these questions of genre, convention and codes with reference to three kinds of verisimilitude, which are closely aligned with what may be termed different *registers* of knowledge.[10]

Steve Neale has usefully referred to Tzvetan Todorov's distinction between generic verisimilitude and social or cultural verisimilitude: 'the field of knowledge, opinion, and belief as a whole can be divided into the broadly socio-cultural, the specifically aesthetic and the even more specifically generic, thus giving rise to at least two kinds of verisimilitude'.[11] A third kind of verisimilitude is located in internal narrative plausibility, where 'pseudo-logical liaisons', to use Roland Barthes' term, keep the viewer locked into the internal narrative logic of the comic world.[12] This essay will draw on these 'registers of verisimilitude' as the basis for a textual critique of *Yes, Prime Minister*, with main reference to the 'Ministerial Broadcast' episode.

The socio-historical context

The economy

The 1970s had seen major developments in the breakdown of the manufacturing base in the UK; the economic slow-down of 1973–9 was followed by the deep recession of 1979–81; it was a critical period of 'deindustrialisation', the beginnings of reversal of a process that had started with the industrial revolution. In the eyes of one analyst, the main features of the industrial crisis of the 1970s could be identified as:

the combination of stagnant output, negligible productivity growth, acute balance of payments problems, escalating wage inflation, and a major wave of industrial unrest . . . In the 1970s Keynesianism seemed unable either to promote industrial and economic recovery or to reduce endemic inflation. In contrast to the buoyant 'swinging sixties', an atmosphere of disillusionment and discontent pervaded the 'stagnant seventies': the economy was in decline, there seemed no cure for the British disease and the country appeared to have become ungovernable.[13]

In this context, Roy Jenkins rather understated the case when he summarised this period of crisis for Labour: 'the years 1976–79 contributed practically nothing to the achievements of Labour as a party of government'.[14] This *zeitgeist* seeped into press reaction to the series; for example, reviewing the first episode of *Yes, Prime Minister*, the television correspondent of the *Daily Mail* could write that the programme symptomised 'a new national awareness that Britain doesn't amount to much in the world any more . . . *Yes, Prime Minister* could only happen in a country which had stopped taking itself seriously';[15] *Variety* offered a succinct transatlantic perspective: '. . . this is a pretty cynical view of politics. But it's one that seems to have struck a chord in Britain, where the program is popularly regarded as being accurate.'[16]

The media

It is important to remember that the media, and television in particular, were becoming increasingly confident and persistent in their role of watch-dogs of the public interest. The patrician image of politicians, and indeed of government itself, continued to crumble in the face of evidence of complacence, incompetence and even deception on the part of those invested with political power and responsibility; socio-economic conditions, aggravated by factors such as a series of political scandals, were exploited by a viciously competitive right-wing press; and increasing signs of governmental paranoia were evident in the depressingly frequent deployment of the Official Secrets Act of 1911.[17]

In the realm of television comedy, such iconoclastic confidence was reflected in the advent of *That Was the Week That Was* (*TW3*) in 1963, with Willie Rushton's bare-knuckled caricatures of the Home Secretary, Henry Brooke, and the milder lampooning of Harold Macmillan contributing a healthy corrective to hitherto servile television representations of the world of politics.

Increasingly aware of the need for a 'counter-offensive', politicians and their advisers began to look more closely at the possibilities of image manipulation through a commercially sensitised broadcast system and avaricious print media. In particular there was a growing understanding that television, especially, required issues mediated by personalities (a basic theme of 'The Ministerial Broadcast'). More formal recognition of the potential of the systematic creation of images came with the Conservative response to the precarious position of the Labour government in early 1978 when it awarded a contract for the pending election campaign to an advertising agency, Saatchi and Saatchi. This was the first time that an advertising agency had been employed by any political party in the United Kingdom, and led to the carefully targeted 'Labour isn't Working' campaign that dominated the contest in 1979; it also ushered in the new era of slogan politics, in which television played a central role in developing the audio-visual rhetoric of the sound-bite and the photo-opportunity.

Government and the civil service

If representations and public perceptions of the political world at large were in a state of flux, the groundwork for the over-arching issue ('Who governs Britain?') in *Yes, Minister* and *Yes, Prime Minister* had been laid by two reports on the civil service.

In 1968, the Fulton Report proposed wide-ranging changes in structure and organisation (especially in the areas of recruitment, training and pay). Many of the recommendations were ignored, but one relevant to this discussion was the subsequent setting up of a new Civil Service Department (CSD). This was the inspiration for the Department of Administrative Affairs over which the Hacker/Appleby team presided in such a singular fashion. Paul Channon, the minister responsible for the new department, was reported to be an avid viewer of *Yes, Minister*;[18] of greater relevance, the CSD was commonly perceived to be manned by 'civil servants steeped in those very traditions which Fulton wanted to replace and was well placed to frustrate the Fulton reforms'.[19] In fact, the first Permanent Secretary at the CSD, Lord Armstrong, admitted in retirement that he had managed to deflect many of the proposed changes. The Civil Service Department, after a short and undistinguished life, was abolished in 1981.

Further controversy in the late seventies centred on the English Report, the first investigation of the civil service by MPs since 1873, and its powerful confrontation of the question of the extent to which the civil service was in fact controlled by elected politicians. Brian Sedgemore MP, a member of the English Committee who had once been a civil servant, asserted that:

> most of the problems of the civil service stem from the fact that top civil servants misconceive their role in society. The role they have invented for themselves is that of governing the country . . . They seek to govern . . . according to their own narrow, well-defined interests, tastes, education and background . . . They can and do relegate ministers to the second division through a variety of devices.[20]

Much of the criticism came from the left wing of the Labour Party, but an anonymous minister in Mrs Thatcher's new government in 1979 was quoted in the following terms:

> Unless we break out of the civil service strait-jacket now, we'll never get another chance to rule. It is beginning to look to many of us that civil servants are a breed who really believe they run the country, and that all they've got to do is knock new ministers into shape.[21]

In sum, political systems and institutions of government were caught astride a widening credibility gap in terms of the ability of any government to control the destiny of the nation; and the potent mix of conflict, cynicism and incompetence in *Yes, Minister* caught the spirit of the time, playing precisely and knowingly on audience sensibilities only too ready to accept this image of government.

'The Ministerial Broadcast'

The episode entitled 'The Ministerial Broadcast', which provides the main textual reference for this essay, was transmitted on 16 January 1986, the second episode in the first series of *Yes, Prime Minister*.[22]

The episode opens with Hacker's return from America. Following his meeting with the President, he announces his intention to introduce the 'Grand Design' during his first prime-ministerial broadcast.[23] Sir Humphrey takes the line that the introduction of new ideas sets a dangerous precedent.[24] Hacker nevertheless goes ahead with the rehearsal for the broadcast (a sequence which provides an extended lampoon of the systems, language and conventions deployed to construct an iconography of political leadership).

Following the rehearsal, Sir Humphrey develops a strategy for bringing forward the date of the broadcast, thus preventing Hacker from clearing the idea with the Cabinet. Hacker sees the 'Grand Design' as a vote-winner, a view based on a Party opinion poll showing a majority of voters in favour of re-introducing conscription. Sir Humphrey demonstrates the fallibility of opinion polls to Bernard,[25] then convenes a meeting of senior civil servants to co-ordinate appropriate 'briefings' for their political masters; as he points out to Bernard, the fact that Hacker is 'very keen' to discuss the Grand Design on television is neither here nor there: 'things don't happen just because Prime Ministers are keen on them. Neville Chamberlain was very keen on peace.'[26] He also suggests that the Ministry of Defence should commission another poll on the subject of conscription.

The Cabinet reacts as Sir Humphrey intended, and Hacker is forced to drop his plan to feature the 'Grand Design' in the broadcast. He also receives the results of the Ministry of Defence opinion poll showing that 73 per cent of the public are against conscription.[27] As the episode ends, Hacker decides that the decor for the broadcast should be contemporary and innovative in order to conceal the absence of new ideas.

Genre verisimilitude

Critical notions of television genre turn on ways in which viewers engage with content, style and modes of address in a given programme. Through a complex frame of generic references, each programme proposes, or allows recognition of, what *kind* of comedy is being presented. Such a process of recognition is essential for the operations of generic verisimilitude, providing criteria through which to gauge the internal dynamics, coherence and plausibility of the comic world. These frames of reference include familiarity with actors, types, relationships, narrative parameters and form, gestural conventions, and iconography. Similarly, institutional imperatives to maximise audiences for popular programmes require that public consciousness be raised and viewer expectation shaped through a range of promotional strategies – features in television listings, preview spots, interviews with actors and creative talent, editorial comment in the press and so on. Finally, the style of the opening titles and credits provides a significant generic key; in *Yes, Prime Minister* an emphatic intertextuality is created through the use of Gerald Scarfe as designer of the title sequences.

A regular viewer will, therefore, as a natural consequence of such commitment, possess a powerful body of accumulated knowledge of content and convention that renders even small narrative detail significant and gestural nuances highly legible.

Many kinds of comic revelry are permissible on television, as long as any perceived transgression of taste may be attributed to its retinue of licensed fools – the television comics. It may be noted that most of the more 'dangerous' forms of comedy keep the personality of the performer to the fore; the more anonymous forms of comedy – especially the fictions of comic drama – operate under a tighter set of constraints, since the public perception is that they are 'author-ised', so to speak, by the broadcast institution itself. The sites for comedy on television are therefore carefully segmented, appearing in a number of generic guises: the topical review (*That Was the Week That Was, Who Dares Wins . . ., Spitting Image*), the variety sketch (Benny Hill, *Monty Python*), the personality routine (Dave Allen, Jasper Carrott, Ben Elton), combinations of these (Morecambe and Wise, the Two Ronnies), the comedy serial (*Tutti Frutti*), and the comedy series – a form of comic drama virtually monopolised by the ubiquitous and enduring sitcom.

Sitcom as a genre is demonstrably successful in attracting viewers. It is especially attractive to broadcasters since factors such as the (usually) small number of characters, limited number of settings and sets, and committed production teams offer an economic use of resources and facilities over a period. Sitcoms have also consistently shown a capacity to transcend their immediate social and cultural frames of reference – a fact most clearly demonstrated in terms of overseas sales in the case of *Yes, Minister* and *Yes, Prime Minister*.[28] Therefore, from an institutional perspective, it is not a genre where undue risks may be taken in terms of deviation from generic norms.

In the early episodes, generic antecedents for *Yes, Minister* were comparatively remote. One possible precedent may be identified in *If It Moves, File It* (1970), a short-lived series with a civil service setting. Aside from this, fictional representations of the worlds of politics, government and state in television drama were comparatively rare before the 1980s. As if to compensate for this perceived generic fragility, the first series of *Yes, Minister* was heavily promoted on content, with particular emphasis on its 'authenticity'; such promotional activities play a central part in defining elements of generic lineage and shaping viewer expectations.[29]

Perhaps because of a limited internal frame of reference, where the play of difference inevitably becomes routine and repetitive in the long run, the comic drama seems particularly vulnerable to exhaustion. Following transmission and regular repeats of *Yes, Minister* across the previous five years, situation and character had become vividly established in the public mind. In 1985, with some press reviews indicating that *Yes, Minister* appeared to be running out of steam, the writers decided that political elevation for Hacker would allow significant scope for development of the drama:

We decided to make Hacker P.M. because that office opened up all sorts of fun areas that were not available to a Departmental minister: nuclear defence, espionage, foreign policy, the creation of bishops . . .[30]

The first episode of *Yes, Prime Minister* was transmitted in January 1986. Following Margaret Thatcher's endorsement of the programme, when she participated in a short sketch at the NVLA awards in 1984,[31] the press colluded with a postmodern zest in the game of blurring distinctions between fiction and reality to the point of treating the actors as if they were the genuine politicians.[32] The initial success of the new, slightly differentiated series provided ample illustration of ways in which the play of difference may work within a framework of established generic verisimilitude.

Narrative

Structure

Stories in comic drama are essentially about failure, ineptitude and frustration; however, neither content nor structure are in themselves comic, and the main function of narrative structure is to deliver to us a calculated degree of knowledge of a given situation or event. Once 'in place', comedy is developed in two basic ways. First, through what is usually termed narrative 'excess', a site is created for jokes and gags (verbal and physical humour respectively) that function outside the requirements of narrative development; sources of humour may stem from the immediate situation – the genuine 'situation comedy' – or be extraneous to the situation and funny in their own right. Second, through visual humour frequently linked with a playful use of the formal limitations of the medium itself, such as the play with camera position and framing which position and reposition the viewer in the television studio sequence in 'The Ministerial Broadcast'.

Each programme in the series consists of a simple but formally liberating dual story structure, one story strand usually lying with Hacker, the other with Humphrey. Antony Jay has outlined the approach the writers took to developing each episode; once the conflict at the heart of the relationship in every episode had been established:

we had to find a theme – an issue which divides politicians from civil servants: secrecy, publicity, civil service pay, civil service honours, the use of government authority and resources for party political advantage and so on. Then we had to invent a story, and it was a requirement of the story that it should land one or other of the two principals, or preferably both, in a ghastly predicament, or preferably several ghastly predicaments.[33]

Characteristically, episodes are structured in seven or eight scenes, with a maximum of three (fixed) front sets and two (variable) back sets, each scene usually lasting between 2 and 4 minutes. As in 'The Ministerial Broadcast', an episode starts with a scene that contains an articulation of intent – an impetus for change – usually initiated by Hacker in the broader context of an element of the 'Grand Design' (hatched in the eponymous episode). This challenge to the equilibrium of the status quo demands an equal or greater effort from Sir Humphrey in order to neutralise the threat. Then follows a tortuously negotiated battle of wits, usually developed across both story lines, and characteristically resolved in such a way as to leave the status quo broadly as it was at the start of the programme. In *Yes, Minister*, Humphrey was almost invariably victorious; in *Yes, Prime Minister* Hacker not infrequently gains a minor victory, but always in terms of winning the battle, never the war.

Address

As in most sitcoms, the narrative structure of *Yes, Minister* and *Yes, Prime Minister* positions the audience in ironic mode, in possession of a greater knowledge of the situation than any single character – particularly in terms of knowledge of other characters' motives, actions and feelings.[34] The plots centre on plays of power and protocol, with both Appleby and Hacker involved in multi-layered schemes of manipulation and deception, each occupying positions of relative knowledge or ignorance articulated through structures of suspense and surprise, and only the spectator able to map their relative positions.[35] In terms of narrative address, this carefully designed comic structure rigorously maintains a position for the audience apart from the characters, allowing only a certain degree of sympathy rather than any sentiment approaching empathy.

In terms of the narrative design, it is worth noting that consistent references across episodes (for example, to the 'Grand Design' and social actualities) serve to confirm the authenticity of the comic world, constructing an exterior frame of reference which increases the plausibility and coherence of events within each episode. This also allows the characters to demonstrate a capacity for memory of events (in previous episodes) and, indeed, an apparent sense of history that is unusual in sitcom. Such epistemic devices play on, and simultaneously enhance, the pleasures of familiarity and play of knowledge that lie at the heart of the genre.

Narrative groupings

Yes, Minister and *Yes, Prime Minister* are only incidentally about *politics* or the operations of *state*; in essence, the series is dedicated to a set of basic propositions about *government*: that Britain is largely governed by a manipulative and devious bureaucracy; that political decisions are dictated by the self-seeking motives and incompetence of politicians; and that the electorate is hideously incompetent to participate in the democratic process. These propositions provide the basic groupings within the narrative design.

It is a critical orthodoxy that the narratives of comic drama are fuelled by the dynamics of disruption of the status quo, typically caused by an intrusion which has to be dealt with in order for the status quo to be re-established. The tight dramatic economy of the sitcom usually shapes this dynamic in terms of a dichotomy between insiders and outsiders. In *Yes, Prime Minister* this basic dynamic is slightly modified. Underpinning each episode is the opposition between the centrifugal force of change, of which Hacker is the agent, and the centripetal resistance represented by Sir Humphrey Appleby. The 'insiders' are constantly in conflict, but equally each needs the other as the absolute condition of their own existence: 'that conflict at the heart of the relationship ... was the foundation on which we built every episode'.[36] The 'outsiders' are, of, course the electorate – the ultimate arbiters of power – invariably constructed as the paradigm of gullibility. Sir Humphrey, in one of many such utterances, articulates a characteristic attitude when he refers to a defence policy which is 'designed to impress all those simple ignorant British citizens who shuffle in and out of houses, buses, pubs and factories'.[37]

In this context of groupings, it is worth noting the role of the media, which function as a kind of ever-present off-stage chorus. Driven by a political instinct infinitely more developed than his intellect, Hacker intuitively focuses on the dual power of the media: the ability to write the first draft of history, linked with the power to destroy. Armed with this insight, his overwhelming concern in the public arena is the construction of his image. In 'The Ministerial Broadcast', for example, his obsessive concern is with news television coverage of himself with the US President on the Washington trip: 'shots of me and the President alone together ... hopefully grasping my elbow with his left hand'.[38] Sir Humphrey is equally aware of the second function: 'Open Government, Prime Minister, Freedom of Information. We should always tell the press, freely and frankly, *anything* that they can easily find out some other way.'[39]

In the light of the way each of these groups (politicians, civil servants, the electorate) is constructed, it is hardly surprising that for Paul Eddington the series 'reached such depths of cynicism that it gave me vertigo'.[40] In fact, much of the pleasure of the series comes from such privileged 'insights' into the ethos of this closed world; and it is of course this very distance between the viewer's experience and the fixed and confident representation of the electorate as awesomely gullible that reifies these characters in the comic mode.

Character

Character groupings and types

Underpinning the basic propositions of the series, and locating it firmly in the comic mode, is the traditional comic relationship between servant and master, formally acknowledged at every turn and equally consistently observed in the breach. Key elements of the relationship between Hacker and Sir Humphrey were consciously modelled on the Wooster–Jeeves relationship created by P. G. Wodehouse;[41] however, as noted earlier, antecedents for such relationships and types stretch back via the *commedia dell'arte* to traditions of political comedy rooted in Atellan farce and Attic comedy. In this comic tradition we encounter a set of recognisable personae locked in a closed world, responsive to situations constructed primarily to allow them to embody 'type' characteristics, driven by fixed compulsions and desires, unchanged by experience.

Hacker

The Hacker of *Yes, Minister* is the self-seeking innocent abroad, and the dupe of the Machiavellian Humphrey. Constructed from the common foibles of vanity, ambition and high anxiety (essentially about the discovery of his ignorance and incompetence), he is 'deeply confused for most of his time in office'.[42] Some critics saw this innocence as a potential dramatic weakness[43] – as did the authors who, having originally envisaged the series as illustrating the triumph of the civil service over the politicians, rapidly readjusted the dramatic balance so that a Humphrey victory did not become inevitable:

as Hacker spent more time in government it became impossible for him to continue in the ignorance and naivety that had provided so much scope for comedy when he first arrived [in office as a minister]... We were compelled to construct more sophisticated errors and traps for him to fall into.[44]

Despite this he remains, in terms of comic structure, the underdog, the dupe.

However, in empathetic terms, his shortcomings have been seen as an attraction: 'one of the essential parts of Jim's appeal apart from pomposity, low cunning, self-regard and general inadequacy is his unashamed

3 *Left to right: Prime Minister Jim Hacker (Paul Eddington) being advised – or is he? – by Bernard Woolley (Derek Fowlds) and Sir Humphrey Appleby (Nigel Hawthorne): a recurrent situation in* Yes, Prime Minister. *BBC*

cowardice'.[45] By comparison with Sir Humphrey he appears vulnerable and deserving of sympathy, a human by-product of the democratic process, exposed to the whims of a grotesquely caricatured electorate.

On a formal level, we should note that Hacker occupies a rather greater amount of screen time than the other characters, both within and across scenes.[46] This is in line with the referential role of the character (i.e. a Prime Minister) as initiator of events; however, the central structural role of dupe also requires that the character spends much time *reacting* to information and events – and the heart of screen comedy is found in the reaction shot. Such shots, which follow the comic incident (a joke, gag, moment of revelation and so on) ground us in the moment of change, where the character's ability to comprehend (a person, situation, event) is in some way tested.

Sir Humphrey and Bernard

Sir Humphrey is a pure incarnation of the spirit of intrigue and self-interest – determined to maintain the status quo which guarantees his power, professional status and, not least, material comfort and personal wealth (a theme explored in detail when civil service pay becomes an issue in 'A Real Partnership'). In terms of lineage, the character had been conceived as a Cecil Parker type, 'a neurotic Butler, very proper, with suppressed passions';[48] moving further back, the model was Malvolio, 'overweening, the cloak of subservience frequently slipping to reveal the inner anger and frustration'.[49] The character had a less prominent part in the first series of *Yes, Minister*. However, the importance of the role was increased after the first series as the structural strength of the triumvirate was better understood by the authors, together with an increased appreciation of the qualities Nigel Hawthorne brought to the part[50] (the early episodes of the first series of *Yes, Minister* having been written before the part was cast).[51]

It is worth noting that Bernard's *raison d'être* owes as much to dramatic as comic necessity; the comic potential of his wretched position and impossible allegiance as a servant of two masters is frequently exploited (at length, for example, in 'A Victory for Democracy'), and strengthened by his characterisation as a well-meaning but obsessive pedant whose logic is both impeccable and irrelevant. However, in dramatic terms he serves the same essential role as all confidants: allowing the exposition of ideas, attitudes and motives by the principals.

Such conventional origins for characters and relationships provide an important key to the way in which the verisimilitude of comedy overlays the referential realities. The setting allows a clear (comic) play to develop between the two superimposed frames of reference, as the referential reality is colonised by types whose origins are rooted in comic tradition – the clown (foolish master variant), the rogue (scheming servant variant) and so on. In character terms, the pleasure comes not from a satire of political personalities and institutions but from the manner in which efficiently constructed comic types ruthlessly appropriate the elevated roles and settings of state at every turn of language, action and gesture as the sole condition of their existence. There are no heroes in comedy.

Performance

Once character is determined in comic drama, particularly in the series context of sitcom, actions tend to confirm known, fixed qualities, providing an exact measure of the nature of the type. The challenge for the actor is, first, to conform to expectation whilst maintaining a sense of immediacy in performance; second, to identify that which prevents us from taking a serious action seriously, thus ensuring we remain in the realm of comedy.

As already noted, the values and practices of different belief systems have little relevance; in every sense, *Yes, Prime Minister* constructs a world of *gesture*. In the realm of social events, little happens to disrupt the established processes of state and government. The drama is played out in the arena of personal conflict, where political policy, questions of state and the rhetoric of public service are simply grist to the mill of self-interest; few consequences from decisions taken under Hacker's regime impinge on the flow of public events.

The implications for performance of the gestural culture and aesthetic of comic drama are central to the comic dynamic, where gesture must take precedence over action. Bergson offers a precise formulation: 'instead of concentrating our attention on actions, comedy directs it rather to gestures'.[52] In this formulation, action is voluntary, or conscious, whilst the gesture is automatic; moreover, action is exactly proportionate to the sentiment that inspires it, whilst there is something explosive about the gesture that breaks our empathy. Antony Jay gives the pragmatic view: 'given a theme and a plot, how do you set about constructing scenes that will make people laugh? . . . The first condition is that someone should be in a highly tense or emotional state about something he is trying to achieve or avert. There is no comedy if everyone is relaxed and reasonable.'[53] One of the main performance challenges is therefore to judge precisely the degree of intensity with which to inflect a particular reaction, physically and vocally; and one of the advantages of a long-running series is the increasing confidence with which actors can make such judgements.[54]

A key element of comic performance obviously centres on the question of the actor's timing. During the performance, much of the comic dynamic hinges on the positioning and re-positioning of what may be termed the viewer's 'imaginative focus': that constant movement between people/ objects/events constructed in language, and therefore in the imagination of the viewer, and the physical events or gestures on screen. In 'The Ministerial Broadcast' we need look no further than the linguistic referencing of the various media personality interviewers – Robin Day, Brian Walden, Terry Wogan, Jimmy Young.[55]

In addition, there are significant shifts in imaginative focus between the two basic components of character – the *persona* (the scripted entity) and the *player* (the actor embodying the part). For example, in a characteristic set-piece, the bounds of realist convention are perilously tested when Humphrey takes language into realms where it is detached from meaning; as we the audience become aware that he has embarked on a lengthy sentence of bureaucratic unintelligibility, the performance skills of the actor become part of the pleasure, taking us close to the point where the actor's linguistic dexterity is foregrounded. The oration over, Hawthorne 'freezes', and at that moment the frame of reference changes again; without dropping the mask of the persona, the player pauses for appreciation of his skills, creating one of those vital moments that suture the audience into the comic drama *as event* through a shared recognition of its fundamental artifice. As Bergson concludes, 'as soon as our attention is fixed on gesture and not on action, we are in the realm of comedy'.[56]

Language

The real world of objects and events enters the comic world of *Yes, Minister* and *Yes, Prime Minister* almost exclusively by way of language; and social and political issues are instantly annexed into the comic mode through a battery of well-established comic conventions and devices of linguistic style, of which the most insistent – and the essence of character typage in the series – is an appropriation of the language of public-spiritedness to mask self-serving motives.

It is worth exploring this use of language in more detail. First, it is commonplace to assert that comedy revels the inadequacies of language: it frequently fails when confronted with the unusual and unexpected; it falters under the pressures of social decorum; above all, it is always on hand to betray the characters when they lapse into meaning what they say.

The distance between intention and expression is the site for a good deal of humour; for example, Bernard evokes a complete culture with his questioning of the wisdom of one element of the Grand Design: 'Isn't conscription a rather courageous policy, Prime Minister?'[57] The important factor for the comedy is that we are able to gauge this distance precisely. A similar site of humour is the 'self-conscious' awareness of the characters that the function of political language is not to reveal or articulate intent, but to conceal – a culture revealed again by the ingenuous Bernard:

HACKER: Bernard, that doesn't say anything.
BERNARD: Thank you, Prime Minister.
HACKER: Totally devoid of impact.
BERNARD: You're too kind.[58]

A consistent source of comedy derives from the restrictions placed on the way characters use language. Language systems revolve around the basic supposition, indeed fundamental belief, that articulation is synonymous with meaning and truth; however, when individuals with different language sets are drawn into the site of conflict between points of view, beliefs or value judgements, then language will continually break down.[59] In discussion of language functions, Mikhail Bakhtin makes the case that 'plot itself is subordinated to the task of co-ordinating and exposing languages to each other'.[60] He develops the notion of language 'sets' – ways of talking that mark the character as a member of a group – and proposes that much speech consists of quotations, or ready-made packages of 'thought-speech'.[61]

In this context, Sir Humphrey is both enabled and constrained by the obfuscating conventions of bureaucratic expression, where language functions through allusion, inference and innuendo, and where meaning is construed rather than constructed. On the one hand, he deftly and routinely empties language of meaning in order to deflect or defer action,[62] or to translate Hacker's whims into parodies of the sophisticated casuistries of governance; on the other hand, Hacker's linguistic insouciance demands a directness of response which Humphrey's 'language set', and the formal demands of deference and decorum with his political master, render almost impossible. This frequently results in a litany of increasingly desperate prefatory phrases: 'with respect ... with the *greatest* respect'.[63]

In fact, the comic power of Humphrey's discourse lies not so much in accuracy of observation, but in the precision with which the script parodies popular notions of bureaucratic discourse; as Bakhtin points out, in order to be effective, a parodic stylisation must 'recreate the parodied language as an authentic whole, giving it its due as a language possessing its own internal logic and one capable of revealing its own world'.[64] Indeed, the powerful closure achieved by the concluding phrase 'Yes, Prime Minister' at the end of each episode may be attributed to the fact that this is one of the few points where situation, feelings and language achieve a degree of congruence.

Mise-en-scène

It is frequently asserted that sitcom is an essentially verbal form, dealing in comedies of character and language. However, in close shot, a grimace may have all the force of an event; physiognomy, facial expression and the power of the gesture both orchestrate and are orchestrated by language, particularly in allowing the rapid movement of the imaginative focus between (linguistic) image and (staged) event. The comic potential of the grimace is well illustrated in the studio sequence in 'The Ministerial Broadcast', where Hacker's professional *gravitas* and sense of personal esteem – and consequently the body itself as a *locus* of human dignity – are constructed (and deconstructed) by the television production team.

It is also worth remembering that action is not only contained in language but also constrained by language: in the dual sense, language *contains* the impulse to action, and so provides the force of reaction, of inertia. When Hacker outlines his outrageous intention of taking action, Humphrey cries in panic, 'But you can't *do* that'; the conflict is essentially acted out on a terrain of intention far removed from real-world consequence – the terrain of language, and one well suited to the physical constraints placed on sitcoms by the conditions of production.

Setting and artefacts

The settings of *Yes, Prime Minister* are both realistic and authentic, replicating actual locations as far as possible. In line with the generic constraints, the world of *Yes, Prime Minister* is a world of interiors and encounters, of people sitting and talking; the table in the cabinet room is simply an elaborate variation on the central object of the domestic sitcom – the settee.[65] The occasional exteriors simply function to locate the action and provide an added sense of authenticity to the subsequent interior action.

As noted, there is comparatively little physical comedy, although occasionally the action moves towards farce in the rhythms and deployment of space; for example, Sir Humphrey's attempts to remedy his exclusion from Downing Street in 'The Key', the comedy of doors in the cabinet room towards the end of 'The Smokescreen', the intrusion of the security guard in 'The Grand Design'. There is no comic conspiracy of objects to match the mooseheads, clocks, kitchen implements and other animated artefacts of *Fawlty Towers*; only occasionally does something show anthropomorphic tendencies, such as the studio teleprompter in 'The Ministerial Broadcast'.[66] The community of objects act primarily as synecdoches for the rigid systems and operations of government and state – for example, the comic disproportion between the artefact and its potential effect in the case of the nuclear button in 'The Grand Design'.[67]

Costume is strictly in the realist mode and conventionally functions as an index of character; for example, questioning whether the shirt, tie and pinstripe suit of his character suggested a Tory minister, Paul Eddington was assured by presenter Robert McKenzie that they were 'the badge of rising Labour politicians'[68]. Other elements relating to the semiotics of political presentation are of course given a thorough-going treatment in 'The Ministerial Broadcast'.

A note on form

The series was recorded in front of a live audience[69] and shot strictly in accordance with dominant generic conventions of the realist comedy text, usually with three cameras for a given scene, allowing for both action and reaction shots. However, it is worth noting two ways in which these conventions are deployed in a rather more subtle way than simply recording events. For example, in terms of formal address, the camera position, framing and editing complement the script and performance dynamic in terms of constructing an audience position: in 'The Ministerial Broadcast', as Sir Humphrey sketches out the techniques of the pollster, the formal construction of the short sequence first positions the viewer with Bernard, as the *subject* of Humphrey's discourse, a coincidental frame of reference; as the pay-off is reached, the viewer is returned to the position of omniscience to observe the reaction of Bernard.[70] In the same episode, some significant deconstructivist play is achieved through the coincidence of the viewer's screen frame with that of the monitor in the television studio; in addition, the varying ways Hacker is framed within the studio television monitor invite reflection on the conventions of such broadcasts.

Conclusion

The intention of this essay has been to explore some ways in which apparently authentic representations of a particular world are largely colonised and animated by the dynamics of comic drama and conventions of television sitcom, with reference to *Yes, Prime Minister* as an exemplar of a sitcom generically located within the spectrum of social realism. Again, as a product of a particular historical moment the series, like most of the more effective examples of the genre, gains much of its force through provision of a site in which to rehearse powerful and potentially troubling issues. In comedies set in a domestic environment, such issues will centre on questions of family relationships, gender, sexuality, class, race, age difference and so on. Where *Yes, Minister* and *Yes, Prime Minister* depart from type is in the relentless focus on issues in the public domain.

This returns us finally to the question of audience address in the series,[71] brought into particular focus if we consider some implications of the fundamental decision not to identify Hacker's party affiliation or political persuasion. The omission places a stringent qualification on a basic dynamic of drama – that the audience should perceive 'the gap between what [a man (*sic*)] says he is and what we see him to be'.[72] It also precisely locates the series in the realm of comedy: without attribution of 'real' public motives to characters, events in *Yes, Prime Minister* are necessarily enacted within the register of generic verisimilitude rather than that of social realism. The comedy arises from – and is defined by – a structure of displacement; in place of public motives we are given a play of dissimulation centred exclusively on motives of self-interest and aggrandisement, articulated through an array of comic motifs and devices, which drive the system of narrative enigmas.[73]

The extent to which these 'subversive playlets'[74] retain their comic potential across the years may well provide an index of the extent to which imperatives of media representation cause integrity and authenticity in the political arena to yield to the demands of their simulation. In any event, it is currently difficult to disagree with Christopher Norris that there is a sense in which history – or the history of the 'free world' democracies – has entered a phase of absurd self-parody.[75]

Yes, Prime Minister: 'The Ministerial Broadcast'

Transmission date (tx): 16 January 1986 (BBC2)

Cast

Jim Hacker	Paul Eddington
Sir Humphrey Appleby	Nigel Hawthorne
Bernard Woolley	Derek Fowlds
Television Producer	John Wells
Malcolm Warren	Barry Stanton
Television Technician	Brian Gwaspari
Fiona	Carolyn Lyster

Production and technical

Title Sequence	Gerald Scarfe
Music	Ronnie Hazelhurst
Costume Designer	Richard Winter
Makeup Designer	Cheryl Wright
Properties Buyer	Francis Smith
Camera Supervisor	John Dailley
Technical Co-Ordinator	Reg Poulter
Sound	Peter Barville
Vision Mixer	Angela Beveridge
Production Asst.	Judy Loe
V/T Editor	Chris Wadsworth
Lighting Director	Ron Bristow
Production Manager	Brian Jones
Design	Gloria Clayton
Produced and directed by	Sydney Lotterby

Transmission history

The first episode of *Yes, Minister*, entitled 'Open Government', was transmitted on the BBC2 channel on 25 February 1980, followed by a further six episodes and two further series, each of seven episodes, running until 'The Middle Class Rip-off' (tx: 23 December 1982). With repeats, transmissions continued until December 1985, together with a one-hour special episode 'Party Games' (tx: 17 December 1984).

The first episode of *Yes, Prime Minister*, 'The Grand Design', was transmitted on BBC2 on 9 January 1986; 'The Ministerial Broadcast' was first transmitted 16 January 1986, and first repeated on BBC1 21 October 1986, followed by the remaining episodes of the first series, ending with 'One of Us' (tx: 27 February 1987). The second and final series followed in 1987, starting with 'Man Overboard' (tx: 3 December 1987) and ending with 'The Tangled Web' (tx: 28 January 1988).

Formal recognitions included the Broadcast Press Guild award for 'Best Comedy', 1980; 'Best Comedy Programme' award, National Viewers and Listeners Association, 1984. Paul Eddington and Nigel Hawthorne were both awarded CBEs in the 1986 New Year's Honours. Antony Jay was knighted in 1988.

Notes

References in the text are to the programme as transmitted; however, in the absence of a published script, sources for citations (unless otherwise indicated) refer to the equivalent passage in the novelised forms of the scripts published as *The Complete Yes Minister* [*YM*] and *The Complete Yes Prime Minister* [*YPM*]. Main reference is to the episode entitled 'The Ministerial Broadcast' [MB]; other episodes are designated by their full title.

1 *Series* form, as distinct from *serial* form, refers to programmes in which the major narrative expectations are resolved within, rather than across, individual episodes. The television comedy series has become virtually synonymous with 'situation comedy' in current usage.
2 For a useful discussion of sitcom and genre, see Terry Lovell, 'A genre of social disruption?', *BFI Dossier 17: Television Sitcom* (London, 1982), 21–4.
3 For an account of this background, see Antony Jay, 'Understanding laughter', *Proceedings of the Royal Institution*, 62, no. 99 (1990), 103–4.
4 *The Times*, 18 February 1980.
5 Critical comments ranged from 'very, very funny' (*Morning Star*, 1 March 1980) to 'predictable and uninteresting' (John Wain, *The Times Educational Supplement*, 11 April 1980).
6 Jay, *Proceedings*, 106.
7 During the first run, the series consistently topped the BBC2 Broadcast Audience Research Bureau (BARB) audience ratings, averaging close on 7 million viewers.
8 Paul Eddington, quoted in *Daily Telegraph*, 21 January 1984.
9 In fact the demise of Atellan farce has been attributed to 'a perennial and often fatal interest in politics'. *The Oxford Companion to the Theatre* (Oxford, 1972).
10 Such epistemological categories have been proposed with different inflections by many theorists – Barthes's 'codes' and Lyotard's 'phrase-regimes' to give but two random examples.
11 S. Neale and F. Krutnik, *Popular Film and Television Comedy* (London, 1990), 84; see also Steve Neale, 'Questions of genre', *Screen*, 31, 1 (1990), 45–66.

'Verisimilitude', is defined by Todorov as 'the individual text's conformity to a textual norm external to it ... [that] produces the *illusion* of realism' (quoted in John Caughie's challenging questioning of assumptions about television genre in 'Adorno's reproach: repetition, difference and television genre', *Screen*, 32, 2 (1991), 127–53).

12 The general operations of comedy within this register have been explored in detail by Jerry Palmer in *The Logic of the Absurd* (London, 1987), 146–53, and *passim.*

13 R. Martin, 'Deindustrialisation and state intervention: Keynesianism, Thatcherism and the regions' in J. Mohan (ed.), *The Political Geography of Contemporary Britain* (London, 1989), 92. Key economic indicators for the period 1973–81 give a clear economic picture: manufacturing output fell by 22%, productivity growth ceased, pre-tax corporate profits fell from 10% to 4%, investment fell by 23%, 89.

14 Roy Jenkins, *A Life at the Centre* (London, 1991), quoted in *The Observer*, 8 September 1991, 47.

15 Herbert Kretzmer, *Daily Mail*, 10 January 1986, 23.

16 Review of 'The Smokescreen' [*YPM*], *Variety*, 21 May 1986.

17 One strand of the new 'investigative' journalism exploited the public appetite for political scandal. Whetted by the Profumo affair in 1963, other personal indiscretions by political figures followed at gratifyingly regular intervals: Reginald Maudling's resignation in the wake of the Poulson corruption scandal (1972), Lords Lampton and Jellicoe and the call-girls (1973), John Stonehouse (1974), Jeremy Thorpe's resignation (1976) and trial for 'conspiracy to incite murder' (1978), continued in fine style with Cecil Parkinson's resignation over Sarah Keays (1983). The patrician typification of the politician in the popular imagination was permanently revised.

18 'London Diary', *The Times*, 18 March 1980.

19 Editorial in *The Guardian*, 13 November 1981, quoted in P. Gabriel and A. Masler, *British Politics* (Harlow, 1986), 96.

20 *Ibid.*, 99.

21 *Ibid.*

22 Tx: 16 January 1986. Available on video; see Appendix 1.

23 The 'Grand Design' refers to Hacker's new policy platform, based on cancellation of the Trident missile system and the introduction of conscription. See 'The Grand Design', *YPM*, 68–9.

24 MB, *YPM*, 88.

25 *Ibid.*, 106.

26 *Ibid.*, 104.

27 *Ibid.*, 112.

28 At the time of writing, in early 1992, the series had sold to fifty-seven countries in all five continents (information supplied by BBC Enterprises).

29 In the event, *Yes, Minister* and *Yes, Prime Minister* became something of a phenomenon, generating more press coverage than almost any other (non-serial) programme in the history of broadcast television.

30 Antony Jay, letter to author, 10 February 1992.

31 '*Yes, Minister* is my favourite programme ... Its closely observed portrayal of what goes on in the corridors of power has given me pure joy.' Mrs Thatcher, quoted in *The Scotsman*, 21 January 1984, 2. This comment was made on the

occasion of the 1984 National Viewers and Listeners Association Awards Ceremony.

32 Nancy Banks-Smith reports that the press showing of *Yes, Prime Minister* was attended 'by journalists I had never seen in my life ... Political correspondents, war correspondents ... they asked him [Paul Eddington] serious political questions, to which he replied with a non-committal slipperiness which commanded universal admiration.' *The Guardian*, 10 January 1986, 12.

33 Jay, *Proceedings*, 106.

34 One of Jay's 'essential conditions' for comedy is that a character 'must be unaware of something the audience knows' (*Proceedings*, 107).

35 In fact, Jay was much impressed by John Cleese's structuring of *Fawlty Towers*, and particularly Cleese's view that 'the whole secret of comedy is the order in which you give information to the audience' (Jay, interview, 4 December 1991).

36 Jay, *Proceedings*, 106.

37 MB, *YPM*, 88.

38 'The Grand Design', *YPM*, 83.

39 *Ibid.*, 76.

40 *Evening Standard*, 25 February 1980, 14.

41 Jay, interview with author, 4 December 1991.

42 'Editor's Note', *YM*, 8.

43 Mervyn Jones, *The Listener*, 24 April 1980, 550.

44 Jay, letter to author, 10 February 1992.

45 Richard Last, *Daily Telegraph*, 10 January 1985, 11.

46 See Deborah Klika's quantification of close shots and medium shots on Hacker in the *YM* episode 'Doing the Honours' in 'A note on textual analysis', *BFI Dossier 17*, 83–4.

47 *YPM*, 143.

48 Jay, interview with author, 4 December 1991.

49 *Ibid.*

50 Such as a particular style of giving a 'performance within a performance' (Russell Davies, *Sunday Times*, 2 March 1980).

51 Jay, interview, 4 December 1991.

52 Henri Bergson, 'Laughter', in Wylie Sypher (ed.), *Comedy* (New York, 1956; 1980), 153.

53 Jay, *Proceedings*, 107.

54 The change in writing and acting style in the later series, once the actors have established the characters, is quite pronounced. Jay, interview with author, 4 December 1991.

55 MB, *YPM*, 89–90.

56 Bergson, 'Laughter', 154.

57 'Grand Design', *YPM*, 69.

58 MB, *YPM*, 96; the early Hacker viewed language 'not as a window into the mind but as a curtain to draw across it'. *YPM*, 8.

59 At this point, language is revealed as 'conventional, false, maliciously inadequate to reality'; incorporated languages are unmasked and self-interest revealed, 'truth is only restored by reducing the lie to an absurdity'. Mikhail Bakhtin, *The Dialogic Imagination*, ed. Michael Holquist; trans. C. Emerson and M. Holquist (Austin and London, 1981), 309.

60 *Ibid.*, 365.

61 *Ibid.*, 338.
62 For example, the classic 168-word sentence at the end of 'The Ministerial Broadcast', reproduced as a memo in MB, *YPM*, 112.
63 MB, *YPM*, 94.
64 Bakhtin, *Dialogic Imagination*, 364.
65 According to Antony Jay, the interior of 10 Downing Street was designed on the same principles as the stage set for a farce – to allow various options on entrances and exits in order to accommodate the various secret comings and goings required by the intrigues of government. Jay, interview with author, 4 December, 1991.
66 MB, *YPM*, 96–7.
67 'Grand Design', *YPM*, 60.
68 *Evening Standard*, 25 February 1980, 10.
69 See Jay, *Proceedings*, 103–5 for the importance of a live audience at the recordings.
70 MB, *YPM*, 106.
71 Defined by Barry Curtis simply as a position from which operations of the narrative and the points of the jokes make sense: 'such a position offers confirmation of a community identity and solidarity, a "common sense" of shared perceptions'. Curtis, 'Aspects of sitcom', *BFI Dossier 17*, 9.
72 David Hare, 'A lecture given at King's College, Cambridge', in *Licking Hitler* (London, 1978), 59.
73 This narrative strategy has been seen both as a fundamental flaw and as a liberating device: '*Yes, Minister* is deprived of its best source of drama and humour: the contrast between supposed principles and actions (since Hacker's party is not attributed)' *The Listener*, 20 March 1980, 550; '*Yes, Prime Minister* is even better than *Spitting Image*, because it is non-specific and can suggest everything while actually saying nothing.' *Daily Express*, 10 January 1986, 23.
74 Lucy Hughes-Hallett, *London Standard*, 10 January 1986, 30.
75 C. Norris, *What's Wrong with Postmodernism: Critical Theory and the Ends of Philosophy* (New York, 1990), 36.

Select bibliography

There has been extensive press coverage of the series, far too much to include here, but little serious critical analysis. The programme scripts have not been published, but the adaptations (in the form of pastiche diary entries, correspondence and memos; see * below) follow the scripts with minimal variation, with dialogue rendered in various forms of reported speech.

Jay, Antony, 'Understanding laughter', *Proceedings of the Royal Institution*, 62 (1990), 106
*Lynn, Jonathan, and Antony Jay, *The Complete Yes Minister* (London: BBC, 1981; rev. 1984: Pb 1989)
    The Complete Yes Prime Minister (London: BBC, 1986; 1989)
Oakley, Giles, 'Yes Minister', *BFI Dossier 17: Television Sitcom* (London: BFI, 1982)

Articles and books about comedy, with substantial sections on television sitcom, include:

Eaton, Mick, 'Television situation comedy', *Screen*, 19, 4 (1978–9)
'Laughter in the dark', *Screen*, 22, 2 (1981)
Horton, A. S. (ed.), *Comedy/Cinema/Theory* (London: University of California Press, 1991)
MacCabe, Colin (ed.), *High Theory/Low Culture: Analysing Popular Television and Film* (Manchester University Press, 1986)
Neale, Steve, and Frank Krutnik, *Popular Film and Television Comedy* (London: Routledge, 1990)
Palmer, Jerry, *The Logic of the Absurd: On Film and Television Comedy* (London: BFI, 1987)
Woollacott, Jane, 'Class, sex and the family in situation comedy', *Politics, Ideology and Popular Culture 2* (Milton Keynes: Open University, 1982)

Articles on Yes, Prime Minister

Broadcast, 17 January 1986, 42; 28 February 1986, 27; 9 May 1986, 17 (Antony Jay and Jonathan Lynn discuss the series)
The Guardian, 6 January 1986, 11 (Peter Fiddick interviews Antony Jay)
The Listener, 2 January 1986, 27–8; 16 January 1986, 38; 30 January 1986, 34; 10 December 1987, 43
The Observer, 2 February 1986, 60 (Miriam Gross, 'The secret life of Jim Hacker')
The Radio Times, 4–10 January 1986, 3, 5; 28 November – 4 December 1987, 98.
Time Out, 2–9 December 1987, 26 (Article on the truthfulness of the programme's depiction of life in the Cabinet)
Variety, 21 May 1986, 78

5   *Inspector Morse*: 'The Last Enemy' (Peter Buckman)

RICHARD SPARKS

It is at least arguable that of all fictional forms it is in the crime story that the boundary between literary 'high' culture and vulgar 'popular' tastes is messiest and most blurred. T. S. Eliot remarked upon this when he noted the 'thriller interest' in Shakespearian tragedy; and he went on to probe the capacity of the Elizabethans to create poetry out of 'the equivalent of the *News of the World* murder report'.[1] Part of what Eliot seems to have meant is that some things that are often called sensational and exploitative, and others that are canonised as being archetypal and profound, share their subject-matter. However else they may be distinguished, it is often not in the basic stories that they tell. Indeed, Eliot inferred that 'melodrama is perennial and ... the craving for it is perennial and must be satisfied. If we cannot get this satisfaction from what the publishers present as literature, then we will read – with less and less pretence of concealment – what we call thrillers.' Eliot viewed the topics of crime fiction (principally on his interpretation sin and death) as being the stuff of life, and hence the preserve not only of a morbidly interested mass audience. Interestingly – and in common with other commentators, notably W. H. Auden[2] – he also went further and claimed to detect a particular affinity between the stuffy civility of English 'high' culture and nasty murder stories. He writes feelingly of 'the ferocious comedy of England whose special mark is violence' – a theme to which I shall return in discussing the particular charms and unpleasantnesses of *Inspector Morse*.

If Eliot is right in this then it should hardly surprise us not only that crime stories are abidingly popular but also that they are capable of many inflections of topic and mood. It may well be that some of their basic narrative elements and sequences – transgression, pursuit, capture, retribution – survive across large spans of time and cultural difference. But it is also clear that these fundamental forms (the 'mythic' dimensions of the crime story if you will) are capable of being variously reworked and reinterpreted, occasionally subversively, to suit the particular demands of the medium, the moment, and their shifting construction of the audiences they presume to address. Crime stories can touch their audiences at some of their tenderest points. They fold together the satisfaction of some rather deeply embedded desires and the invocation of some of our most unsettling anxieties.[3]

Crime stories can therefore speak to us on a number of levels at once. Often they begin from a premise of a relatively ordered world suddenly disrupted by a crime. In such cases the narrative unravels towards a conclusive resolution, and the detective's solution of the crime suggests a reordering of the world. In the simplest and most wish-fulfilling cases this is virtually all there is. As Oscar Wilde has it in *The Importance of Being Earnest*: 'The good end happily, the bad unhappily. That is what fiction is for.' Thought of in this way, crime stories call upon that implicit and sometimes unacknowledged desire to see punishment done which philosophers and social theorists have variously celebrated and despaired of. As Durkheim commented, however complex and technical the secular institutions of justice may become, there remains a sense in which 'passion is the soul of punishment'.[4] Perhaps, too, the very messy complexity of the way that the real institutions of justice go about their business is part of what impels us to seek the satisfaction of our punitive passions in the consoling simplicity of stories. Yet such wish-fulfilment rarely goes untempered and unalloyed. Even where the basic components of the story in some way partake of this 'mythic' dimension, the world against which they are enacted must bear some relation, however distant and transformative, to the one we inhabit. In this sense the details of crimes and criminals, of detectives and police forces, of modes of detection and their settings (the discursive aspects of story-telling) tend to bring us down from the folkloric plane and ground the story in ways that respond to our own more immediate, contingent concerns. Crime stories can thereby speak not only of fulfilled wishes but simultaneously of urban disorder, of violence and drug-taking, of corruption in high places, of the sources of risk and threat, and of our disrupted sense of trust in the safety and habitability of our surroundings.

Such tensions between fantasy and gritty realism can be glossed in a host of ways, and the different weights which particular stories attach to each demarcate the subdivisions within the basic genre. Crime stories are always, in varying ways, *both* reassuring *and* unnerving. Perhaps, then, it is here that the key to the special affinity between television, as the dominant mode of story-telling in our times, and the crime story is to be found. For television seems peculiarly capable both of fitting stories into familiar and relatively highly conventionalised formats and at the same time of tracking the contours of a changing social world with particular contemporaneity and immediacy. Television thus delivers both 'formulae' (which of their nature are reassuring because routinised) and commentary, sometimes quite alarming in its implications. Television writes the mythologies of our age in real time, co-ordinating its generic fictions and its reality claims in supple and labile combinations.

In its short history, broadcast television has provided us with a variety of ways of looking at crime, law enforcement and punishment, which have both followed and helped to construct our changing structures of feeling about those matters. The appearance and demise of particular shows may serve as points of reference which help briefly to illustrate this argument. During the 1960s British television drama developed a powerful strain of ostensive realism in its depictions of policing and law enforcement. In *Dixon of Dock Green* this took a strongly communitarian and normative form. George Dixon arguably encapsulated a preferred self-image of British policing – known to be an ideal type, it was yet one whose grounding in reality was held by many almost as an article of faith. Dixon's screen persona outlived its real-world referents (such as they ever were) by perhaps a decade: he did not leave the screen until 1976, and in his final appearances he must already have seemed to speak from another age. His direct successors in *Z Cars* and *Softly, Softly* related in fictive form the shift away from the bobby on his manor and towards a different conception of the police role: motorised, relatively distant, increasingly reliant on technology, marked by the development of specialist squads and functions, with police–public encounters often overtly antagonistic. The development of the depiction of police in British television suggests a society less at ease with its own received ideas. The police officer becomes displaced from his organic relation to a settled community. The force stands a little to one side, stoically resisting the rising tide of crime and sustaining its humane commitments with deepening difficulty.

By the middle of the 1970s the projection of the police officer as heroically alienated had become a key trope of television crime drama. Inspector Jack Regan in *The Sweeney* (John Thaw's first popular screen incarnation in a detective role) is abrupt, cynical, insubordinate, workaholic, hard-drinking, scruffy and primed to resort to force. He confronts a city peopled by gangsters, narks, fences, spivs, molls and scrubbers. In bringing this demotic vocabulary into the common currency of television entertainment *The Sweeney* proposes short shrift with legal niceties and imputes to the audience a desire for strong measures.[5] At the same time an increasing number of American series began to appear on British screens. Taking up a bundle of themes first enunciated in the cinema (most especially in a succession of films starring Clint Eastwood: *Dirty Harry, Magnum Force, Coogan's Bluff*) they tended to depict both the police and the private eye in activist, masculine mode. In *Starsky and Hutch, Hawaii Five-O, The Streets of San Francisco* and elsewhere the police genre solidified into a format. The variations played around a restricted set of themes and plots: the crime story became the 'cop show'.

A number of authors have noted the implicit authoritarianism of the seventies cop show.[6] They point to its tight narrative closure, its permission of force on the part of the hero, its resort to extra-legal methods. Cop shows set the apparent optimism of the heroic intervention from without, the means whereby the happy ending is magically secured, against a premise of a violent, corrupt and disintegrative social world. Nor is it accidental, given our tendency to read television fictions as documents which 'express' or 'reflect' aspects of the world to which they claim to allude, that the heyday of the tough cop coincides with the high point of social concern with the effects of 'violence on TV'.[7] Yet, interestingly, it is perhaps the very simplicities of the cop show formula which has provoked a more various and at times consciously divergent set of responses in both British and American television depictions of crime and law enforcement during the 1980s. Even while the tough cops (*Dempsey and Makepeace, Hunter*) continued to ply their rough trade, they were answered by a varied and sophisticated inflection of the genre. In the United States this included both the self-conscious artifice and pathos of *Miami Vice* and the documentary feel and deliberate inconclusiveness of *Hill Street Blues*. In Britain it incorporated the soap-operatic realism of *The Bill* and *Rockliffe's Babies*, as well as a return towards more cerebral 'classic detection', in *Bulman*, for example. There were, too, a number of expensive and much discussed British set-pieces which explored themes of corporate and governmental wrong-doing (*Out, Edge of Darkness, The Detective*) which posed the problems of crime, law and justice in increasingly sophisticated and problematic form.

Inspector Morse clearly belongs to this later family of stories. From the moment that Chief Inspector Morse's immaculately preserved crimson Jaguar first purred across our screens, few viewers can have failed to remark that *Inspector Morse* intended consciously to stand somewhat apart from the erstwhile conventions governing the depiction of the police and detectives on television. In television detective stories, vehicles bespeak their owners. Starsky and Hutch's aggressively striped coupé was a public display of youth and prowess (and easily imitated by anyone with a Ford Capri). Crockett and Tubbs in *Miami Vice* generally cruise in a dandyish Porsche (less easily imitated), photographed either from above or from the level of its potent wide rear wheels and growling exhaust. Rockford's car is quick but not new. Being unobtrusive it goes with his several disguises. Poirot does not drive but is transported by Hastings in a Lagonda. Poirot is not capable of mundane activity; he becomes a mind on wheels. Miss Marple sensibly and discreetly goes by train. Morse's Jaguar, however, suggests taste and good judgement rather than wealth; a concern, perhaps nostalgic, with craftsmanship; and the preoccupation of English gentility with nice things that last well. It is consciously and carefully stylish but in a slightly fogeyish way, mildly self-indulgent – a bachelor's car.

The attention which is devoted to the implications of each detail of Morse's environment and possessions indicates just what an artful construction *Inspector Morse* is. The whole *mise-en-scène* – the daring length at two hours per episode, the use of 'name' authors such as Julian Mitchell and Peter Nichols, the brilliant pastiche operatic and baroque incidental music by Barrington Pheloung, the languid panning shots of Oxford (where it is always summer), the use of prestigious actors, the very scarcity of episodes – announces that this is quality television. Having been made with evident, patient and expensive care, *Inspector Morse* invites patient and involved viewing. As long and at least as complex as most feature films, *Morse* is at times quite cinematic in its pleasures, especially in its sheer visual and aural richness and the rather un-televisually relaxed pace of its narrative development. Yet it also exploits in full aspects both of story-telling and discursive contemplation which television has made particularly its own – notably the reiteration of a basic and familiar situation, and the exploration of character in and through domestic and work settings. This conjunction of styles seems unusual (when I try to think of comparisons which similarly spin sundry stories from a fixed initial premise my mind keeps turning improbably to *Star Trek*!) and has been unusually successful. If the investment of effort and expense which *Morse* represents ever was a gamble it has paid off handsomely. As the 1980s ended *Inspector Morse* was perhaps (with the partial exception of the institutional soap operas) the most popular drama on British television, with audiences that were not only exceptionally large, at times topping 15 million for a first run, but also unusually affluent and highly educated. For advertisers a *Morse* episode became two of the most desirable and costly hours of television time. For audiences it broke free of the suspicion that most television programmes are little more than items of domestic routine, looked upon with mild fondness, and assumed the status of minor public event.

Inspector Morse is thus arguably about as far from being a run-of-the-mill 'cop show' as a cop's show can be. Yet Morse's particular variation on the theme of the policeman as hero is nevertheless part of an identifiable tradition. The character and complexities of Morse himself are central to the show's success, as heroes are always pivotal in detective fiction. Indeed, as Orrin Klapp once argued,[8] if such stories have any public significance in the affirmation of certain moral stances and the censure of others, then at times the events of any particular plot may be incidental to the depiction of the heroic agent. Similarly, whilst Morse is scarcely a typical policeman (even amongst fictional police heroes) he has a number of *confrères* within the traditions of classic detection. He has contemporary kin too. Morse refers us back to Sherlock Holmes (at least in that he is a substance-abusing, musical bachelor), but differs from him in that he is fallible, capable of prejudice and humanly vulnerable. At the same time he shares some of his lonely and curmudgeonly probity with Ruth Rendell's Chief Inspector Wexford and P. D. James's Commander Adam Dalgliesh. Morse's family resemblance to these other police heroes of the 1980s seems to me to be of considerable interest, for reasons which I hope to make apparent below. Not least they seem to betoken a revival of interest in the detective story both in terms of popularity and as a distinctly *literary* form. If, as I believe, such stories presuppose that some vexing and enigmatic features of our current mores have a special affinity for the crime story, then it is intriguing to look at them with some care, in order to question their relation to the mood and temper of the times.

In common with Wexford's stories and those of Dalgliesh, *Inspector Morse* signals the return of mystery and uncertainty as key dimensions of police fictions. As I have already suggested, in the so-called 'action series' of the 1970s (notably *Starsky and Hutch* or for that matter in John Thaw's earlier incarnation as Inspector Jack Regan in *The Sweeney*) puzzling over the identity of the villain was not usually much at issue. The entrapment, pursuit, capture or death of known villains was more central. Even the ingenious *Columbo* typically knew or suspected the guilty party from an early point, though he might go to intricate lengths to demonstrate it. For all his vaunted brilliance, Morse spends much of his time in the dark, pursuing misleading lines of enquiry and harrying innocent (though dislikeable and morally compromised) people. He achieves enlightenment late and sometimes fortuitously. In this he is equally unlike Miss Marple or Hercule Poirot, who are unerringly deductive. Morse is intuitive. His distinction lies in his privileged insight into human motivation, especially in its more recondite byways, rather than in unusual forensic skill. In this sense the greater part of an episode of *Inspector Morse* is passed in a mood of perplexity, in apparent denial of what we also know, namely that the narrative is unravelling towards some form of resolution. But such resolution in *Morse* is often incomplete, or at least emotionally unsatisfying to Morse. It simply confirms his dark view of human nature, and leaves him alone again in his romantic *tristesse*. Often there is more than one killer.

Often, too, at least one of the guilty is someone with whom Morse has a degree of personal involvement. Sometimes the crimes are misleadingly unconnected. Sometimes they are surprisingly connected. Sometimes they seem to cancel (or compound) one another. In the latter case, whilst there may be some sort of moral or providential symmetry at work, it is a long way from the geometric closure of an Agatha Christie.

These perplexities and indirections allow particular scope for the development of Morse's problematic character and his uneasy relations with others. Unlike the lonesome drifter of Clint Eastwood's early Westerns, Morse presumably has a first name but he will never say what it is. Viewed from a naturalistic perspective this conceit is enormously implausible. In the episode discussed below at least two of the characters have known Morse since his student days – do they not know his name either? In fact, of course, this literal-mindedness is inappropriate. Morse's want of a first name is a distancing device. It sets him slightly apart from conventional society. Even if other characters have to answer demands of naturalistic plausibility, Morse himself is hedged about with this part-mythic, part-comic protection: he is exotic. His namelessness emphasises his intensely private nature and emotional defensiveness. Similarly, Morse is not usually seen to eat. He lives on beer, whisky and sweetened black coffee. He is also an aesthete. At home alone he listens only to Wagner, Mozart, Puccini and Beethoven late quartets (or perhaps Beethoven pastiche by Pheloung). He is generally gloomy and grouchy (conditions in this kind of story which suggest absolute integrity). He dislikes intellectuals, of whom he is one, and ostensibly Oxford, which is his natural habitat. His only continuing relationships are with Sergeant Lewis, his down-to-earth Geordie assistant on whom he is at times pathetically reliant, Chief Superintendent Strange whom he exasperates and Doctor Russell, the gauchely attractive pathologist with whom he repeatedly fails to begin an affair. All three relationships have a comedic tension. In each episode a considerable time is spent in conversations between Morse and these or other characters which abruptly break off from the plot (as for example when Morse and Doctor Russell interrupt the discussion of the cadaver's cause of death to discuss their shared preference for fountain pens over word processors). Morse is old-fashioned, sexist, chivalric (he cannot stop calling Russell 'my dear') and acutely susceptible to the beauty of women.

Let us consider these tropes, and their relation to the characterisation of Morse and the world he inhabits, in more detail via a discussion of one Morse story. In *The Last Enemy* Morse has toothache. This accentuates his usual grumpiness. It also allows Lewis and Doctor Russell ample opportunity to demonstrate their affectionate indulgence of his eccentricity, and for Morse to disregard the sensible advice of his officious dentist.

At the same time the episode condenses a number of characteristic *Morse* themes: the intensity of academic and sexual rivalries in Oxford colleges; the diverse and arcane forms of both instrumentality and passion which generate murder, and their eruption from within outwardly placid and privileged circumstances; the untrustworthiness of the powerful.

The plotting is also characteristically convoluted. The story opens with an attractive young couple languidly drifting down a sun-dappled canal on a barge. The pastoralism (we know) cannot last. The barge drifts off course, the music shifts towards an unsettling minor key. In the rushes floats a headless, limbless torso. The body (which Morse is always too queasy to examine) wears the suit of a missing don. (Such details are discovered by Lewis, acting on Morse's instructions, whilst our hero himself sits in his office reading *Gramophone*.) Yet the suspected victim is found to be alive and well, only to be done to death later in the story. Meanwhile, Morse receives a telephone call from the Master of Beaumont College, an acquaintance from Morse's own student days.

The college, its Master and his antagonistic relationship with Morse turn out to be the connecting threads of the story and its three eventual murders. The principal dramatic irony is provided by the fact that the Master calls upon Morse to make discreet enquiries into the whereabouts of the missing don on the strength of their former acquaintance and of Morse's understanding of the university and its mores. Yet Morse demonstrates no affection for either, and it is his foreknowledge of each which enables him to delve the more deeply, inculpating the Master in the process. The biographical and personal symmetry of oppositions between Morse and the Master is established with deft compression and allowed to unravel as the narrative itself unwinds. As Morse enters the Master's Lodgings for the first time a young woman storms out, weeping. The Master shrugs with callous urbanity. 'Over-educated women!' he explains. Morse's ambivalence is already apparent. The camera closes in on their conversation. Nose to nose, in silhouette they look remarkably alike, growling at one another with gradually more visible hostility. Finally Morse enquires, 'Why should I help *you*, Alex?' 'Professional pride,' the Master replies, thereby striking Morse at what is simultaneously his strongest and weakest point. Later, needling Morse, the Master asks casually, 'What *was* the name of that girl we both knew?' Here a whole history is suddenly sketched in. In their youthful rivalry Alex won, but cared too little. Morse the true lover remembers everything with perfect clarity and can still feel a pang which Alex exploits. Morse does not forgive.

Morse rather quickly comes to regard the Master as his prime suspect. In the moral universe of *Inspector Morse*, however, things necessarily turn out to be more complicated than this. The murders result from a quadrangular

set of enmities between four senior members of Beaumont College. These
are: (1) Sir Nicholas Ballarat, Honorary Fellow and senior government
economic adviser (first victim), (2) Dr David Kerridge (second victim),
Vice-Master, known intellectual enemy of Ballarat and personal foe of (3)
Arthur Drysedale, Morse's former tutor, on leave of absence suffering from
a terminal illness and (4) Sir Alexander Reece, Master of the college.
Reece's overweening ambition makes him beloved of no one. Morse
discovers that Ballarat has not recommended Reece for the Chair of a
Royal Commission on which his hopes are pinned. Meanwhile, both
Kerridge and Drysedale are capable of exposing Reece's plagiarism. The
latter issue arises most acutely within Reece's relationship with his student
Deborah Burns, whom he also exploits sexually. This whole little
intramural war of each against all packs the narrative with a distracting
number of possible motives for murder. Thus what Umberto Eco has called
the 'game space' of the tale[9] is pregnant with possible 'moves' and false
trails, which in turn provide for the perplexity and misapprehension in
which both Morse and the audience pass the greater part of the story.

Morse's 'method', arguably both irrational and vindictive, is to seek
evidence to corroborate his suspicions against Reece. Along the way he
thereby enters into two significant conflicts. The first is with Mr Collins, a
supercilious civil servant (an 'arrogant pillock' according to Lewis) who
seeks to evade Morse's questions about Ballarat and Reece. Collins has
only one function in the plot, namely to reveal that Reece is not going to
chair the Royal Commission. The lengthy scene devoted to exchanges
between him and Morse and Lewis is pursued for the sake of its own
dramatic tension and to juxtapose the moral numbness of the powerful
against the probity of Morse and Lewis. Morse's second conflict is with
Chief Superintendent Strange. It follows directly from the first in that
Strange carpets Morse for having tried to bully Collins. Strange is outraged
both by Morse's indiscretion and by his purely conjectural case against
Reece. Again the ensuing exchange exceeds the simple demands of plotting:

STRANGE: You must be getting even more insensitive in your old age.
MORSE: Look sir, I was at Oxford with half the senior ranks of the civil
service...
STRANGE: That's where you learned to behave so badly I suppose. Thank God
my daughters went red brick!
MORSE: Civil servants respect a bit of effortless superiority. It's what they're
always trying on the rest of the world.

I shall consider some of the implications of Morse's ambivalent stance
towards Oxford and his antagonism to power more fully below. Here it is
worth noting that Strange is of course correct in identifying the weakness of
Morse's case against Reece. Morse acknowledges this only when Reece

himself is killed. From this moment on the story unwinds of its own accord. Of the four contending members of Beaumont only Drysedale is still alive. The others have been eliminated from the enquiry by death. Morse has achieved little in terms of strict detection. Yet, though he may be mistaken at the level of fact, Morse is vindicated in his judgement of character.

It is Drysedale, then, who is the killer of Ballarat and Reece, though not of Kerridge. Reece did that after Drysedale had first failed and then allowed Kerridge to plead for his life. We are invited to dwell on the irony that in the midst of the sundry kinds of sleaze, envy and self-aggrandisement abroad in and around Beaumont College, and which looked to provide the motives for murder, in fact it is Drysedale's absolutist morality and righteous desire for vengeance which have impelled his actions. Indeed, Morse's searching out of base motives has led him to entirely the wrong conclusions: the suspects are in fact the victims. Once Drysedale has been revealed as the murderer, Morse grasps his motivation completely, indeed empathically (as Lewis does not). Morse understands that Drysedale's conception of himself as a man of virtue righting ancient wrongs done to him by his victims has been exacerbated by his illness. He now lives through and enacts the moral categories of classical mythology, and these final valiant vengeful deeds are a bid for Olympian heroic status.

From this point on Drysedale and Morse are involved in a private communication, from which others are entirely excluded. Even in the bathetic moment of his capture (he is knocked down by a bicycle) Drysedale murmurs 'Like Laius on the road to Thebes, eh Morse?', to which Morse (as if back in an undergraduate supervision) responds, 'Where Oedipus killed his father.' Finally in hospital, with Drysedale on his deathbed, they exchange confidences and classical allusions. Drysedale shows no contrition. He likens his disposal of Ballarat's remains using bin-bag and J-cloth to Hercules cleansing the Augean stable. When he begins to recite a poem (Francis Thompson's *The Hound of Heaven*) Morse takes it up and continues. They discuss Morse's failings as a student, and the academic career that might have been his had he not flunked his exams because of a romantic disappointment. At last Drysedale whispers 'My days have crackled and gone up in smoke...' and dies.

Although executed with enormous style this scene is almost too arch and too pretentious for credence, even given the very willing suspension of disbelief which we offer *Inspector Morse*. If considered as self-parodic then it strikes an incongruous note; if portentous, then it is so to a risible degree. Moreover, viewed strictly from within the genre rules of classic detection, the whole story is slackly plotted. To introduce the killer only in the final reel is an odd (perhaps an illegitimate) trick. But this recognition only emphasises what we already know, namely that *Inspector Morse* is not

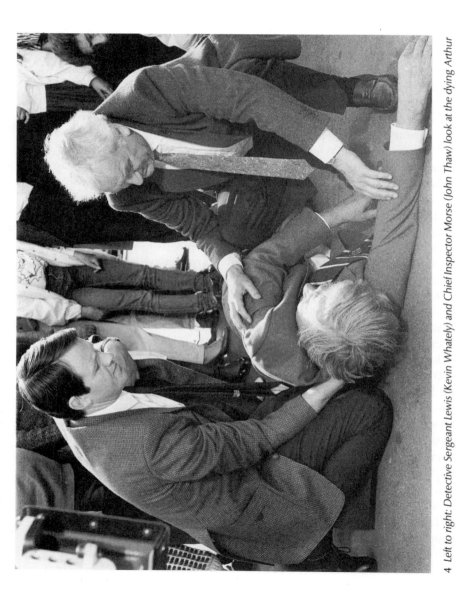

4 *Left to right: Detective Sergeant Lewis (Kevin Whately) and Chief Inspector Morse (John Thaw) look at the dying Arthur Drysedale (Michael Aldridge), at the end of Inspector Morse: 'The Last Enemy' (written by Peter Buckman, directed by James Scott). Zenith Productions for Central Television, 1989*

really a classic detective series. It is not mainly about 'games of deductive intelligence',[10] though it includes them. Rather, it is much more centrally interested in mood, atmosphere, sense of place, character and pathos – the pathos of Morse's return to loneliness at the story's end on the one hand, and of the troubled human situations which generate murder on the other. By the same token, it matters little that secular justice is not served in this story. Drysedale's history mimics that of his beloved classical tragedies. Having avenged himself he is free to die. In *Inspector Morse* it is poetic justice that counts. The narrative seeks moral symmetry rather than a trial and conviction. Often there must be punishment, though it gives Morse no pleasure to deliver it. Simply, where murder is almost always a crime of passion, that is how stories end.

Let us then consider some of these dimensions of *Inspector Morse* a little more closely. That the show projects a strong sense of place hardly needs emphasising. Morse is as organically connected with Oxford as Kojak is with New York or Maigret with Paris. Similarly, just as Morse himself is an exotic character, so Oxford in *Inspector Morse* is an exotic location (and in both senses it is far from being a straightforwardly 'realist' show). In the first place the camera dwells on Oxford with lingering pleasure. It enjoys its honey sandstone walls and gateways, college lawns, golden youth playing croquet, jumbled roofscape and so forth. In this respect *Inspector Morse* is at least part travelogue, in a way that cannot hinder its marketability, for example in the United States. At the same time, Morse's enquiries take him on journeys of exploration behind the tourist façades and into the cloisters and gardens and fellows' sets and combination rooms which are usually closed to the visitor. There, rather like William of Baskerville in Eco's *The Name of the Rose*, he discovers a whole inner world of intrigue, ambition, jealousy, and a heady intellectualism which, within the introspective confines of the college, makes academic principles into motives for murder. Exactly why the rest of us should apparently prove so interested in this rather particular social sphere is itself somewhat puzzling. In part it must relate to its very privacy and the consequent sense that behind the closed doors something momentous is at stake. In this sense the college politics rather resemble another topic of marked public curiosity during the 1980s, namely the boardroom struggles of *Capital City* and its ilk. At the same time the confined purlieu of the college works for the story in the same way as the country house, or the train, or the Nile river-boat work in other murder mysteries, pitting a finite number of characters against one another in a claustrophobic and intense setting. Thirdly, the conjunction of passion and restraint which *Inspector Morse* attributes to the colleges looks like a highly focused version of an English archetype, in which the repression of the passions both conceals and engenders violence. By extension, one should not ignore the place which Oxbridge occupies in English cultural life, ambivalently regarded both as an icon of the national heritage and as the hiding-place of privileged, self-serving and egotistical drones. *Inspector Morse* plays cleverly upon this cocktail of mixed feelings. At one point in *The Last Enemy* Morse chances upon Deborah Burns, Reece's aggrieved student and lover, in a pub. His real identity still unknown to her, they fall to talking about Oxford, and her bitterness pours forth:

BURNS: Are you anything to do with Oxford, Mr Morse?
MORSE: In a way...
BURNS: A vicious, back-biting, petty-minded, parochial little town that thinks it's the centre of the universe...
MORSE: Pretty though, for a city.
BURNS: It's the people that spoil it.

We know of course that she will go to extraordinary lengths to achieve recognition within this reviled place. Morse himself embodies a deep ambivalence towards Oxford. He has been an Oxford student, yet mysteriously underachieved. He has never left Oxford. His own tastes and interests are those of the high cultural elite (though he prefers pubs to high table), yet he carries with him our *ressentiment* and suspicion of the colleges' denizens. Morse understands that academic vanity is a powerful force. As he and Lewis stroll through Oxford they pause outside the Sheldonian, site of the Sheldon Lectures for which Reece, Kerridge and Drysedale contended. 'Imagine being the centre of attention in such a place,' he murmurs wistfully. Morse's Oxford, like other cities in other crime stories, is a 'strange, sad city of the imagination'.[11] In it the murder rate is very high. Only Miss Marple's St Mary Mead is proportionally more deadly. Detroit is nowhere by comparison.

Morse's tense but intimate relation to Oxford is one of his defining characteristics. Another lies in his relations with women. Morse is both gruffly charming and easily charmed. But the women he meets are, almost by necessary implication, involved in his investigations – sometimes culpably so. The prospects for whatever relationship he undertakes are automatically delimited by the scope of each individual narrative (Morse could not form an attachment which would carry over into the next story). In *The Last Enemy* Morse gains the confidence both of Deborah Burns (the ill-used student) and the Master's secretary. Both are attached to Reece and injured by him. Morse is a chivalrous comforter, but hardly an alternative suitor. If he were less charming he would be a lesser policeman, and if he were not a policeman the relationship might turn out otherwise. The vulnerability of these women, which makes them turn to Morse, stems directly from their involvement in the events of the story, which prevents any further relationship. The only real exception to this pattern lies in Morse's relationship with Doctor Russell. But that too is tentative and unachieved. Even when they at last go for a drink together she meets an 'old friend' from medical school. As Morse turns to buy drinks for all and shambles away, shoulders down, the credits roll. We know of course that Morse is doomed to remain alone. An agent of providential justice must go unencumbered by worldly attachments. Morse both envies Lewis his domestic happiness and condescends to his wife and 'kiddies'. Morse's aloneness is inherent. By extension, his personal integrity at times brings him into conflict with his superiors and occasionally with the law itself. I have argued elsewhere[12] that in police fictions it is not the institution or the uniform that validates the hero, but vice versa, and that one of the morally troubling aspects of such heroic tales is how easily they sanction extra-legality. When the hero answers a higher calling he is not answerable, not accountable, and he must eventually be vindicated. *Morse* is much more sophisticated than most on this point, but I think less untypical than at first appears.

I began this essay by wondering in what ways detective fictions might be considered to be phenomena which bear the imprint of their times, and whether, by extension, *Inspector Morse* illuminates anything about our feelings towards crime and punishment in the 1980s. Let me therefore conclude by hazarding some tentative reflections on these points. It seems to me that there are two kinds of answer to such questions. Simply put, they concern what is included and what is left out.

What *Inspector Morse* includes is both complex and intriguing. In the first place *Inspector Morse* is highly self-consciously stylish. It is witty, sometimes playful, sometimes rather painful, but always artful. It draws attention to its own cleverness. In so doing it extends (even subverts) the earlier boundaries of the 'cop' format and invites a literate response from a knowledgeable audience. Albeit in varying ways, it arguably has this much in common not only with the television adaptations of stories by Ruth Rendell and P. D. James but also with *Miami Vice*. It also unexpectedly resembles the latter in its preoccupation with the loneliness and romantic disappointments of its central character. It has been argued[13] that *Miami Vice* chooses to project a tragic conception of crime and punishment, and that the liminality of its central characters is in part established by showing them to be almost constantly in states of mourning at the loss of beloved women. There are, however, no car chases to speak of in *Inspector Morse*, no hand grenades, no karate, no shoot-outs, no drug busts, no master criminals. Rather there is simply a detective, whose mode of investigation is intuitive and sometimes contorted and who has a privileged insight into the pity of crime and the pathos of punishment. This is in a strong sense a humane perspective and it credits its audience with a tolerance for a degree of irresolution at the story's end. But Morse's sad compassion stems from his pessimistic outlook on human nature and the ways of the world: it suggests a conservatism of human imperfection. Secondly, *Inspector Morse* is anxiously concerned with the crimes and misdemeanours of people in powerful and privileged positions. This suspicion seems to me to resonate rather clearly with a developing consciousness (or at least unease) on the part of many people throughout the 1980s. In *The Last Enemy* the two most unsympathetically drawn characters are (not to put too fine a point on it) a yuppie academic (Reece) and a yuppie civil servant (Collins). The corridors of power, whether academic or political, are dangerous and morally compromised places. That Morse himself is so evidently old-fashioned accentuates this sense that the times are decadent. Is the corrupt state of the Oxford college a metaphor for a larger political condition?

Yet what is left out in *Inspector Morse* is the other side of this coin. If crime is about power and passion and personal failings in Oxford colleges, it is equally not about many other things. It is not about poverty, nor resentment, nor thwarted opportunity. Morse's Oxford has no Blackbird Leys estate. Neither do Morse's 1980s show any sign of having included a Miners' Strike, a Broadwater Farm, nor any of the consequent queries about the roles and powers of the police. The 1980s have been by far the most troubled decade in British policing this century. That Dexter, Rendell, James and others have revived the literary centrality of the crime story and begun to explore some of its rich potentiality is indeed welcome. That this should have been so fruitfully registered in television drama has been both pleasurable and challenging. Yet the concentration of these writers on the metaphysics of murder is only partly satisfying. Indeed, in a succession of other cases (*Sherlock Holmes, Miss Marple, Poirot, Lord Peter Wimsey, Campion*) the revival of detection on television has been subsumed within a nostalgic interest in period and costume. They turn sharply away from the *vérité* tradition in British television depictions of the police. In this sense *Inspector Morse* is a *divertissement* in both possible meanings of that term – an entertainment and a diversion. Morse's Oxford presents a vision of the problems of policing which is beguilingly timeless, and upon which the impress of the 1980s and their troubles is denied.

Inspector Morse: 'The Last Enemy'

Transmission date: 11 January 1989 (ITV)   Repeated 5 October 1991 (C4)

Cast

John Thaw	Chief Inspector Morse
Kevin Whately	Sergeant Lewis

Barry Foster   Sir Alexander Reece
Michael Aldridge   Mr Arthur Drysedale
Tenniel Evans   Dr David Kerridge
Amanda Hillwood   Dr Grayling Russell
Beatie Edney   Deborah Burns
Sian Thomas   Carol Sharp
James Grout   Chief Superintendent Strange

Technical and production

Screenplay by   Peter Buckman (from a story by Colin Dexter)
Music by   Barrington Pheloung
Casting by   Marilyn Johnson
Art Director   Mark Ragget
Supervising Editor   Laurence Méry Clark
Production Designer   Rod Stratfold
Director of Photography Michael Davis
Directed by   James Scott
Original series
  developed by   Kenny McBain
Executive producer   Ted Childs.
Filmed on location and at Lee International Studios, Wembley by Zenith
  Productions for Central TV.

Notes

1 See the essay on Eliot's approach to the crime story by Eric Griffiths, 'The fine art of murder', *The Independent*, 24 September 1988, 30.
2 W. H. Auden, 'The guilty vicarage', in *The Dyer's Hand* (London: Faber, 1948).
3 This argument is developed more fully in J. R. Sparks, *Television and the Drama of Crime* (Buckingham, Open University Press, 1992).
4 Emile Durkheim, *The Division of Labour* (Glencoe, Ill.: The Free Press, 1964), 90–110. The best accounts of such views are those given by David Garland in his article 'Frameworks of inquiry in the sociology of punishment', *British Journal of Sociology*, 41, 1 (1990), 1–15, and his *Punishment and Modern Society*, (Oxford University Press, 1990). See also, amongst others, Susan Jacoby, *Wild Justice: The Evolution of Revenge* (London; Collins, 1985).
5 See the two papers by Alan Clarke, 'Holding the blue lamp: television and the police in Britain', *Crime and Social Justice*, 19 (1983), 44–51, and 'This is not the boy scouts: television police series and definitions of law and order', in T. Bennett, C. Mercer and J. Woollacott (eds.), *Popular Culture and Social Relations* (Milton Keynes: Open University Press, 1986).
6 See, on this theme, Todd Gitlin, *Inside Prime-Time* (New York: Pantheon, 1985) and Robert Reiner, *The Politics of the Police* (Brighton: Wheatsheaf Books, 1985), chapter 5.
7 The mid-1970s marked the high-watermark of the public prominence in Britain of the campaigning activities of Mrs Mary Whitehouse and in the United States of the like-minded Anita Bryant. The 1970s also saw major officially sponsored commissions of inquiry into 'TV violence' on both sides of the Atlantic,

especially in the US the mammoth report of the Surgeon-General's Scientific Advisory Committee, *Television and Growing Up* (Washington DC, US Government Printing Office, 1972). A decade later one informed source estimated that in the intervening time there had been some 2,500 published research reports and reviews of research on the topic, making 'TV violence' the most researched topic in the behavioural sciences at that period.

8 See O. Klapp, 'Heroes, villains and fools as agents of social control', *American Sociological Review* 19, 1 (1956), 56–62.

9 See Eco's classic essay, 'Narrative structures in Fleming', in Umberto Eco, *The Role of the Reader* (London: Hutchinson, 1979).

10 E. Mandel, *Delightful Murder* (London: Pluto Press, 1984), 24.

11 The phrase comes from Robert Warshow, cited by Dick Hebdige in his *The Kray Twins: a Study of a System of Closure* (Birmingham: Centre for Contemporary Cultural Studies, 1974).

12 Sparks, *Television and the Drama of Crime*, chapters 2, 6 and 7.

13 T. Grodal, *'Miami Vice*, melancholia and post-modernity'. Paper presented to the International Television Studies Conference, University of London, July 1988.

Select Bibliography

Auden, W. H., 'The guilty vicarage', in *The Dyer's Hand* (London, Faber, 1948)

Clarke, A., 'Holding the blue lamp', *Crime and Social Justice*, 19 (1983), 44–51
   'This is not the boy scouts' in T. Bennett, C. Mercer and J. Woollacott (eds.), *Popular Culture and Social Relations* (Milton Keynes: Open University Press, 1986)

Durkheim, E., *The Division of Labour* (Glencoe, Ill.: The Free Press, 1964)

Eco, U., *The Role of the Reader* (London: Hutchinson, 1979)

Garland, D., 'Frameworks of inquiry in the sociology of punishment', *British Journal of Sociology* 41 (1990), 1–15
   Punishment and Modern Society (Oxford University Press, 1990)

Gitlin, T., *Inside Prime-Time* (New York: Pantheon, 1985)

Jacoby, S., *Wild Justice* (London: Collins, 1985)

Klapp, O., 'Heroes, villains and fools as agents of social control', *American Sociological Review*, 1 (1956), 56–62

Mandel, E., *Delightful Murder* (London; Pluto Press, 1984)

Reiner, R., *The Politics of the Police* (Sussex: Wheatsheaf Books, 1985)

Sparks, J. R., *Television and the Drama of Crime* (Buckingham: Open University Press, 1992)

Tibballs, G., *TV Detectives* (London: Boxtree, 1992)

Articles

Brooks, R., 'Morose Morse, a TV hero for the nineties', *The Observer*, 17 February 1991, 69

Griffiths, E., 'The fine art of murder', *The Independent*, 24 September, 1988

White, Jim, 'We love him, grumpy old cuss', *The Independent*, 13 February 1991

6 *Edge of Darkness* (Troy Kennedy Martin)

ANDREW LAVENDER

I

On the face of it, the phenomenal success of *Edge of Darkness* might have been difficult to predict. A prolonged focus on a personal tragedy, a sinuously complex storyline and a persistent atmosphere of gloom and foreboding might not have seemed the most obvious tools with which to rivet the viewers' attention. But *Edge of Darkness* was a landmark. Transmitted halfway through the 1980s and halfway through the premiership of Margaret Thatcher, it captured the spirit of its age but went far beyond the drama of its time.

Edge of Darkness was generally described as a thriller, but this hardly begins to explain the programme's nature. Its effect lay partly in its volatility, flickering between the realistic and the improbable in a tone which was variously serious, wry and comic, sometimes all at once. It had an unorthodox tenderness, gently exploring the depth of one man's grief. At the same time it was insistently unsentimental. It pushed against expectations attaching to the thriller form, often transcending the limits of the genre. In part it was elegiac, an atmosphere supported by the plaintive music of Michael Kamen and Eric Clapton. Elsewhere it contained action sequences that reminded some critics of James Bond films. Its locations, variously shabby and salubrious, include the streets of Shepherd's Bush, committee rooms in the House of Commons, the interior of a disused mine and the Scottish countryside. Central to its effect was the way it connected the experiences of its central character with the politics of the time. It was precise in its attention to small contemporary details, but it addressed nothing less than the destruction of the planet. With such intense energy something had to give, arguably the conclusion: a valiant effort to throw a shaft of optimism over a resoundingly pessimistic narrative.

'*Edge of Darkness* is a masterpiece', wrote Sean Day-Lewis in the *Daily*

Telegraph. 'It is one of those very rare television creations so rich in form and content that the spectator wishes there was some way of prolonging it indefinitely.'[1] The critics were largely in agreement. Response to the programme in the press centred on two areas: the grand scale of its political themes, addressing nuclear technology and government secrecy; and the emotional depth of Bob Peck's performance as the central character Ronald Craven. Indeed, in Craven *Edge of Darkness* had one of the iconic figures of 1980s television drama: alienated, haunted, and driven by a search for truth in a disturbing world. 'What begins as a small provincial tragedy ends up encompassing issues of global and cosmic significance', said author Troy Kennedy Martin,[2] and viewers responded to such epic aspirations.

In December 1985, ten days after the last of six episodes was transmitted on BBC2, *Edge of Darkness* was repeated on BBC1 in three parts on consecutive nights: an unprecedented achievement for a drama serial. This latter showing gained an audience of roughly 8 million viewers for each night: double the average for the showing on BBC2. Even accounting for the fact that some viewers may have watched the programme twice, the aggregate of viewers was impressive for a serial which had an avowedly political theme and a social issues content.

With £400,000 of American money from Lionheart Television International, a significant part of the £2 million the programme cost, *Edge of Darkness* demonstrated that transatlantic co-production needn't lead to a bland and conformist product. The impact the programme made within the British television industry was signalled when it received six BAFTA awards for 1985, and it subsequently sold to nineteen countries abroad. Its success rejuvenated the reputation of Troy Kennedy Martin, who was invited to give the MacTaggart Lecture at the Edinburgh International Television Festival the following year.

Not that Kennedy Martin had slipped entirely from view. His work in establishing the newly realistic police series *Z Cars* (1962) marked him as one of the pioneers of television drama in the 1960s. He later moved further towards the mainstream, writing episodes of *The Sweeney* (1975–8) and the films *The Italian Job* (1969) and *Kelly's Heroes* (1970), which mixed tough action with amusing and sardonic dialogue. His style is not easily sketched, however. 'There is a mystical dimension to Troy's imagination. His instincts are visual and non-naturalistic',[3] observed Michael Wearing, the producer of *Edge of Darkness*, and although the programme belongs to a realist tradition, Kennedy Martin's renowned antipathy to naturalism[4] helps to account for its additional poetic qualities. Wearing's own credits include the much-respected *Boys From the Blackstuff* (1982), *Bird of Prey* (1982) and *Blind Justice* (1988), and *Edge of Darkness* fits comfortably in this stable of controversial contemporary realism. Wearing went on to become Head of Serials at the BBC in 1989.

II

In common with most drama on television *Edge of Darkness* is emphatically narrative-based. Its central character is Ronald Craven, a detective in the West Yorkshire police force. Craven collects his daughter, Emma, from a political meeting she is chairing at the college where she studies. On returning to their house in the country, Emma is shot by a gunman.

This is the plot-spring for an intensive focus on Craven's grief and his subsequent overriding desire to 'solve' the murder. But while Craven is indisputably the central focus, the dramatic texture is worked so that it subtly throws his isolation into bigger relief. This is partly achieved by an immediate sense of personality even in characters who only appear in a single scene. Craven has to retrieve Emma's belongings from the Teacher Training College. The caretaker who opens her locker for him complains about the complaints he gets: 'I open too late, the courts are not swept, the showers are cold...' There is a distinct trace of comic observation.

The grieving Craven undertakes his own enquiry into Emma's murder, travelling to London. He is partly aided in his endeavours by Pendleton and Harcourt, an enigmatic pair of civil servants working to the Cabinet Office; and Darius Jedburgh, an unconventional CIA operative and expert on nuclear technology. His investigations, it seems, are of considerable interest to both Whitehall and Washington. The characterisations are distinctive, as is the dialogue. Pendleton, for instance, is studiously urbane and is described to Craven as a man who 'drives a green Mercedes, and parks in other people's places'. Jedburgh, a larger-than-life Texan, drives a white Rolls Royce and wears a stetson, with the explanation, 'Now that Reagan's in the White House we get to keep a higher profile.'

If characters are finely observed, so are settings and situations. In episode 2, for instance, Craven enters a telephone box on Battersea Bridge. The camera views him through the window, on which is scrawled 'DEATH OR BONGO'. The telephone doesn't work, much to Craven's annoyance. Again there is a muted comic tone. It is a small and unimportant moment, but it contributes to the accumulating difficulties Craven is facing.

Up to this stage the programme appears to be a detective drama with a developed focus on its protagonist: Craven is a shrewd and experienced member of the CID and he is undertaking an investigation, albeit for personal reasons. The first half of the serial situates him in the context of routine police work. As Craven moves further into the narrative, however, the programme's identity shifts. The sardonic tone remains. 'We've no intention of putting you in the picture,' Harcourt tells Craven. 'That's what we're paid for.' But Craven makes headway and enters more explicitly political territory. He discovers that Emma had led an expedition into Northmoor, an underground facility for the storage of low-grade nuclear waste, in her capacity as a member of the ecological movement GAIA. He comes to suspect, as Emma had, that the plant is actually being used for the reprocessing of plutonium. Meanwhile an American company – a contender for contracts to develop President Reagan's Star Wars programme – is engaged in a takeover bid for the company which owns Northmoor.

Craven and Jedburgh break into Northmoor and discover that it does indeed contain a 'hot cell' for the reprocessing of plutonium. Despite the attentions of security staff, culminating in a gun battle, they manage to escape, now badly irradiated. Jedburgh takes the plutonium with him, and subsequently produces it at a NATO weapons conference, at which the delegates flee the hall. Jedburgh escapes and arms the plutonium so that it is capable of causing a nuclear explosion: the maverick has become a threat to life, and the programme brings the potential military application of nuclear material to the forefront.

Craven, now dying of radiation poisoning, tracks Jedburgh down to a Scottish guest house, where the latter is shot during a raid by security forces despatched by the government. The programme ends with Craven, alone on a hillside, watching security personnel recovering the stolen plutonium from a loch. The viewer has meanwhile discovered that members of the British government had authorised the reprocessing as part of an experimental military programme, hiding the fact not just from Britain's American allies but even from fellow members of the government.

There are two shoot-outs, then, which contribute most to the partial identity of *Edge of Darkness* as an action drama, with its polarised forces of good and evil, gun-fights and narrow escapes. Certainly the assailants in the shoot-outs are shadowily defined and depersonalised, very much in line with the expendable villains of conventional action dramas, and the slick directorial style of these scenes undoubtedly owes much to director Martin Campbell's work on a number of other action series, including *Shoestring* (1979–80), *The Professionals* (1977–80, 82–91) and *Bergerac* (1981–91). There are other simplifying tendencies. Bennett and Grogan, for instance, the British and American nuclear entrepreneurs, are pictured amid the trappings of wealth and power, and spend much of the programme exchanging veiled and secretive looks in accordance with their function as unequivocally the villains of the piece.

For *Edge of Darkness* clearly has a political agenda. It is about nuclear technology and its devastating military implications; it touches on the uneasy 'special relationship' which developed between the Thatcher and

Reagan administrations; and it makes connections between government secrecy and the international activities of the military–industrial private sector. The programme's most characteristic genre identity, of course, is as a political thriller, a form ideally suited to place existential anguish within a contemporary political setting. The genre flowered during the 1980s, with acclaimed serials like *A Very British Coup* (1988) and *Traffik* (1989), and a host of less impactful offerings including *Brond* (1987), *Thin Air* (1988), *Confessional* (1989) and *The Real Eddie English* (1989). Throughout the latter part of the decade the thriller was the most robust dramatic form on British television, able at least to address the unsettling nexus between public and private worlds.

The genre depends, by definition, on a narrative structure which depicts an initial threat which the protagonist(s) must escape, come to terms with, resolve or be defeated by. Eighties Thatcherism clearly marked a departure from the more comfortable certainties of the previous Welfare State era. 'One of the problems is that, to a certain extent, everyone who's writing about Thatcher's Britain . . . is unbelievably depressed about it',[5] suggested Kennedy Martin, and this pessimism takes an expansive turn in *Edge of Darkness*. Craven is embarked on a struggle for individual coherence; bereft not only of his family but eventually of his role in society as he discovers that the status quo he is defending is itself corrupt and life-threatening. A number of dramas of the period displayed similar anxieties.

Writing in *Sight and Sound* in 1988 Julian Petley noted that 'the last few years have seen a remarkable number of works which, in their various ways, have reflected doubts about the central institutions of the British state'.[6] The year 1985, when *Edge of Darkness* was transmitted, saw also the transmission of the BBC series *The Detective*, which partly dealt with government corruption and the growth of a centralist state; and the film *Defence of the Realm*, a taut political thriller focusing on government secrecy in the face of the expansion of nuclear military capacity. *Muck and Brass* (1982) had previously dealt with corruption in a satirical manner, while in 1987 the film *The Whistleblower* had as its backdrop the controversy surrounding the government's decision to remove trade union rights from civil service staff working at the Government Communications Headquarters.

Meanwhile, controversial documentaries centring on supposed abuses of power include Thames Television's *Death on the Rock* (1988), which suggested that the shooting of three IRA members in Gibraltar by members of the SAS had taken place unnecessarily; and Duncan Campbell's series *Secret Society* (1987), which examined information held by the state to which the public were routinely denied access. And 1990 saw the transmission of three related drama documentaries, *Who Bombed Birmingham?*,

Shoot to Kill and *Dear Sarah*, all of which had an Irish political reference, and addressed cases where the British government was alleged to have presided over miscarriages of justice. Some social commentators argue that the threat to civil liberties offered by succeeding Thatcher administrations could hardly be overstated, and had indeed reached a 'state of crisis'.[7]

Edge of Darkness, with its reference to the secretive operations of the state, addressed this context. 'What the serial does suggest', offered producer Michael Wearing, 'is that the nuclear state is a state-within-a-state, and has grown up without public debate or democratic control.'[8] As the serial progresses, the nuclear theme becomes more predominant, and this too relates to widespread social concern.

Mrs Thatcher's first Conservative government made a wholehearted commitment to the 'deterrent' defence argument, purchasing the costly American Trident system and agreeing that American Cruise missiles could be housed in England. Meanwhile, East–West detente seemed to be breaking down, and peace movements grew all over Europe. At its healthiest in 1984 the Campaign for Nuclear Disarmament could boast a membership of 110,000.

The connections between defence and the nuclear industry were given a new twist on 23 March 1983, when President Reagan gave his Star Wars speech outlining his Strategic Defence Initiative. It was possible, Reagan argued, to develop a system of high-intensity lasers powered by nuclear energy and operated from space. This caused consternation, not least among America's allies in the West. By any reckoning SDI would upset the delicate system of checks and balances upon which defence policies had been founded and open up the unquantifiable horror of militarising space.

A number of television dramas were produced in reaction to the implications of nuclear technology. Kennedy Martin himself adapted Angus Wilson's nuclear war novel, *The Old Men at the Zoo*, for transmission in 1982. *Defence of the Realm* (1985) focused on the growth of nuclear capacity; Mick Jackson's *Threads* (1984) graphically dramatised the predicted effect of a nuclear explosion over Sheffield; and the same director's *A Very British Coup* (1988) included a triumphalist sequence in which a nuclear warhead is dismantled, a symbolic event staged at the behest of the socialist Prime Minister who is the programme's central character.

III

Edge of Darkness belongs to a swathe of dramas and documentaries which reflected anxiety at the operations of both government and the nuclear industry, and its success doubtless owed much to this timely expression of current concerns. But the programme attained a unique intensity by showing how events in the public sphere impinged on the experiences of an individual. This necessitated a more tender and reflective mode, giving the abrasive political themes of *Edge of Darkness* an intensely emotional context.

The aesthetic consequences are significant, and can partly be addressed by considering a key passage early in the serial. Midway through episode 1, after Craven's police colleagues have left his house, he goes upstairs to Emma's bedroom. He is still wearing his mac, wet from the rain, and carrying a shotgun. Kamen and Clapton's evocative theme music is playing as this sequence begins.

Craven moves around the room, and the camera slowly pans over its details, a poster which has 'PEACE' written in capital letters above an image of poppies; a hanging rainbow mobile; a shelf cluttered with childish ephemera. The implication is that this is the first time Craven has really stopped to notice his daughter's effects. There is a record player, and Craven sets it going. The record on the turntable is Willie Nelson's plangent country ballad, 'The Time of the Preacher'.

Craven continues his exploration. He walks to a wardrobe, sorts through a couple of dresses, lifts one out towards him and smells it. He moves to a chest of drawers, and cursorily tidies the underwear in the open top drawer, which he then pushes closed. He pulls open the second drawer to reveal a pink-and-white box-file which has 'GAIA' written on it. Inside the box there is a map, a book with part of the title showing ('Mineral Identities') and another object, which we later learn is a geiger counter.

Craven then sits on the bed, and puts his head in his hand. He opens the drawer of a bedside cabinet, which is below the level of the shot, and thus out of view. Craven takes out a wallet and a passport. He then looks towards the drawer and gives an expression of surprise. He takes out a vibrator. He kisses it, and in putting it back into the drawer is surprised to notice another object. He lifts out a revolver, which he stares at perplexedly. The camera stays tight on Craven with the gun in front of him as he lies back on the bed. There is a teddy bear by his right shoulder. He pulls it up, looks at it and then at the gun as he lays the teddy on his left shoulder.

The last shot of the sequence is from overhead, and shows Craven lying on the bed, staring upwards as he rests the gun on his groin with the teddy still held on his left shoulder. The song finishes with the lines, 'Now the lesson is over / And the killin''s begun.'

It is a remarkable sequence, lasting for nine minutes and unfolding very slowly. During its course Craven's character and motivation are established, strands of the narrative are revealed, and a particular emotional context is created, which subsequently informs the whole programme.

The scene has a number of functions, the first of which lies in its intensely private aspect. The sense is of a man invading his daughter's privacy, but doing so in order to understand her the better. Craven pushes Emma's underwear down in its drawer, smells her dress and even kisses her vibrator. He is touching aspects of her life which would normally remain private. There is a sense of violation, but this is offset by the greater violation of her murder, which has brought him into the room in the first place in some kind of act of remembrance. There is an incestuous undercurrent. But Emma's ghost appears to Craven at various points throughout the programme, a device which depends on the viewer accepting the strength of the father–daughter relationship. The evocation of Craven's grief at Emma's death and the demonstration of his sense of intimacy justify the departure from the prosaic confines of realistic plausibility. This applies to the programme as a whole.

A second function concerns Craven's discovery of items which relate directly to elements of the narrative. He takes the GAIA file with him to London and discovers the extent of Emma's involvement in the ecological pressure group. The geiger counter is later used to motivate a section of the narrative, when Craven accidentally discovers that a lock of Emma's hair is highly radioactive. The revolver is more immediately interesting. It contradicts the other articles – toys, sea-shells and ornaments – which weave a sense of innocence and vulnerability into the scene and illustrate that this has been her bedroom since childhood. The revolver transgresses the image of a secure and domestic world and implies one which is dangerous, mysterious and ill-defined. There are aspects of Emma's life, then, which it will be essential for the programme, through Craven, to reveal.

This is the conventional placing of clues within the thriller mode, but it relates to a third function of the sequence: the displacement of Craven's values which occurs throughout the serial, and their replacement by an alternative set of values. Craven enters the room with a shotgun and ends the sequence with the smaller and more private weapon, and while this is a coincidental effect of the scene, it does represent the more emphatic development of Craven's pacifism through the programme. In the scene between Craven and Jedburgh in the Scottish guest house, Craven stops Jedburgh taking up his revolver at the arrival of the security forces, in order to continue their conversation about the ecological future of the planet. Jedburgh participates in the programme's final shoot-out, but Craven stays in his seat, by now confirmed in a position of radical pacifism which rejects the use of force altogether ('I don't see the point of moving from this spot').

The posters in Emma's bedroom indicate her pacifist beliefs. By the end of the programme, Craven has come round to his daughter's point of view. The sequence consists of alternating long pans and tight close-ups: a camera language which expresses in visual terms the dynamic between objective representation and subjective experience. This is an aesthetic mode evident throughout the programme, and its effect is contained in the overhead shot which closes the sequence. The image itself is complex: Craven is caught between conflicting worlds: a world of domestic comfort and security (the teddy bear nestling against his cheek), and a world of masculine threat and violence (the gun held against his groin).

But there is a further point. The composition of this particular shot is used at other significant moments in the programme. In episode 3, for instance, Craven has been talking to the ghost of Emma in London's Hyde Park. He looks round to discover that she is no longer there. Craven is framed in a big close-up. He cries 'Emma.' There is a cut to an overhead shot which shows him wheeling round, surrounded by scattered vacant deckchairs: a moment of sudden despair viewed with graphic precision, and the detail of the collapsed deckchairs itself reinforces the emotion of the moment, situating Craven within an environment which is both material and metaphysical.

This is similar to a moment which the critic Ruth Baumgarten noted, after the body of the murdered Emma has been carried away by the police: 'the camera slowly cranes upwards, gently pulling out from the frantic events and the fast sequence of tight close-ups. Like a narrator, simultaneously world-weary and pitying, it sets a mythic scene, laying out events in the human world with Olympian aloofness.'[9]

It is a telling technique, both subjective and detached. Looking down from a height, the viewer has a perspective of intensified objectivity, while the subject of the shot is framed in a moment of existential anguish. In any event, Craven's quest is profoundly disturbing.

IV

The cement which binds the divergent elements of *Edge of Darkness* is a form of scrupulous naturalism which, as Lez Cooke suggests, gives the serial 'a credibility lacking in other political thrillers and makes it hard to dismiss as "merely entertainment", a harmless piece of fiction'.[10]

Hence Craven watches the news on television, on which the newscaster Kenneth Kendall is reading a report on the growth of the Green movement. He watches a report on alleged police violence, which includes footage of fighting between the police and pickets (*Edge of Darkness* was shot during the Miners' Strike of 1984). He catches part of an edition of the current affairs programme *Panorama*, on which Margaret Thatcher, interviewed by Robin Day, declares that the nuclear deterrent has been effective in prolonging world peace. These pieces of actual programmes are woven as a 'natural' cultural backdrop to the story, but carefully chosen to express central themes which the programme develops, and the use of personalities playing themselves (Michael Meacher MP, and the broadcaster Sue Cook) also reinforces the intended authenticity and contemporaneity of the programme.

Despite this, the supposed plausibility of the programme hardly stands up to scrutiny. Why does Craven need to break into the MI5 computer, when Pendleton or Harcourt could presumably have obtained the information for him? How does Craven escape from Northmoor? Why is Jedburgh, irradiated and in possession of plutonium, allowed to attend a weapons technology conference?

But in an important respect these are secondary concerns, as Michael Wearing recognised. 'In an investigative journalism sense,' he said, 'it's not *meant* to be a plausible plot.'[11] Elsewhere he suggests that *Edge of Darkness* 'stops being a normal detective story, a who-dun-it, early on because by about the end of Episode 2 everyone knows who-dun-it and it becomes instead a kind of what-can-be-dun-about-it'.[12]

And it is here that *Edge of Darkness* departs most significantly from conventional genres to enter a more individualised mode. The programme identifies the nuclear threat, the anti-humanist effects of international business, and government secrecy as areas of concern. If individual parts of the story are improbable, it is suggested that they are part of a very plausible *context* for life in Britain in 1985. The forces ranged against the freedom and safety of the individual seem extensive and all-powerful. In order to achieve a narrative resolution which is not entirely pessimistic, there is a movement from the gritty realities of the political sphere to a more poetic sensibility. In *Edge of Darkness* fact is countered with the mythic and the mystical.

Emma's ghost is the most obvious element of the mystical dimension. She appears at intervals throughout the narrative to comfort, coax and chide her father. She is presented as 'real' to him, and her presence or absence is beyond his control. He cannot call her up whenever he desires, nor make her stay. Craven sees not only the 'contemporary' Emma, an adult woman. A number of flashbacks show that he remembers Emma as a young girl; but this is not presented simply as a trick of Craven's memory. In episode 4, for instance, Craven is surprised to hear the sound of the young Emma, in the kitchen, singing 'All I want is ratatouille' to the tune of the children's song 'Here we go round the mulberry bush'. This reminds him of the meal he was preparing on the eve of Emma's death, and compels him to look in a recipe book. Between its pages he finds a list of tube stations, which he subsequently discovers is a code which represents the route which Emma and her companions took into the Northmoor mines.

The coincidence is contrived in order to bind the supernatural element as an intrinsic part of the plot. If Craven is to make any progress, he *has* to be helped by the supernatural – a force beyond the jurisdiction of the 'real' political world. The existence of this mysterious other world is seemingly corroborated when Craven discovers that a stream has sprung up in his garden at the place where Emma was shot.

The mystical element connects to the mythic. In his 'Introduction' to the text of *Edge of Darkness* Kennedy Martin writes of his desire 'to make [Craven] the reincarnation of the original "green man", whose destiny was to confront and destroy in the name of the planet the free-market forces of modern entrepreneurial capitalism, as represented by the chairman of the Fusion Corporation of Kansas, Mr Jerry Grogan'.[13] Certainly, Craven's trajectory through the programme takes him from the urban world of police detective work to an exterior world where he is radically removed from his previous life and much closer to nature. The serial ends with him, alone and abandoned, on a hillside overlooking a Scottish loch.

Even so, Craven's 'green man' lineage is never developed enough in the programme to be comprehensible to the viewer, operating rather as a concept informing the writer's work. But it does have a subsidiary role in the development of an ecological theme in *Edge of Darkness*, partly expressed by an unorthodox use of tree imagery. In episode 3, Craven is wandering in Hyde Park, close to a nervous breakdown, when Emma again appears to him. 'This is no time to break down,' she tells her father. 'You've got to be strong – like a tree – don't break . . .'[14] Later in the same episode, when Craven rereads letters his daughter had sent him, we notice that there are trees drawn on all the envelopes. Kennedy Martin intended to end the serial by having Craven, alone on the Scottish hillside, turning into a tree. The idea was eventually rejected by the production team.[15]

Kennedy Martin did manage, however, to replace this crude transubstantiation with something more subtle. In one of her supernatural visits Emma tells her father that in a past ice age black flowers had grown through the ice to draw the sun's rays into the earth. In the guest house with Jedburgh, Craven retells the story. The programme ends with the image of black flowers growing on the hillside where Craven had, in the previous shot, been standing – a gesture of ecological hope in the face of the hero's abandonment and death.

It is an important final image: the 'solution' to the threat offered by nuclear technology is not found in any individual action, but in the regenerative properties of the planet itself. This, the central mythic theme of *Edge of Darkness*, derives from the writings of the NASA scientist J. D. Lovelock. Kennedy Martin acknowledged a debt to Lovelock's book *GAIA – A New Look at Life on Earth*, the basic premise of which, as developed in the programme, is that life-forms on earth exist to regulate optimum conditions for life on the planet; that man has the capacity, through nuclear technology, to fracture this equilibrium; but that within a larger time-span, the planet will operate as an integrated organism to defend itself from threats to its existence.

The final endorsement of the GAIA theory has profound ideological consequences. *Edge of Darkness* juxtaposes individual sensibility, as represented by Craven, with a broad raft of inhibiting agents – the British police, the civil service, the nuclear industry – whose final authority derives, within the programme, from central government.

'*Edge of Darkness* was produced in a far more reactionary climate than the earlier generation of BBC "social issue" dramas', writes Lez Cooke. 'The terms of debate under Mrs Thatcher are not so much about how socialism can be achieved but about how a total hegemony of right-wing ideology can be averted . . . In the context of a reactionary conjuncture, the act of confirming half-formed beliefs and suspicions which viewers might hold can be considered progressive, epecially if it serves to make those viewers question the ideology of "the dark forces that rule our planet".'[16]

This is an argument which suggests that *Edge of Darkness* is a 'progressive' television drama in the sense outlined by Millington and Nelson in *'Boys from the Blackstuff': The Making of TV Drama*: as a 'means of exposing and exploring contradictions in society in such a way as to produce a sense of contradiction in the audience that may in turn promote the will to create social change'.[17] But what new perception is the viewer of *Edge of Darkness* left with? Craven's adoption of Emma's eco-political beliefs is important, for it is the alternative ideology which *Edge of Darkness* proposes. As Craven is driving to seek out Jedburgh in the programme's dénouement, the car radio announces that Fusion Corporation is rumoured to be a strong contender for substantial contracts for the Star Wars programme. The image on screen is of Craven, dying of radiation sickness, sweating and coughing, signifying by implication the human cost of the pursuit of nuclear technology: a grim piece of irony. By the end of the programme he believes that the planet will win any battle between the planet and mankind: he is, as he tells Jedburgh, 'on the side of the planet'.[18]

Craven's rejection of the Establishment seems final. When he is captured, the security chief Nallers shines a torch in Craven's face (again the big close-up, viewing Craven from above, fixes him with disturbing intensity),

5 *Ronald Craven (Bob Peck) dying of radiation sickness, in the final episode of Troy Kennedy Martin's serial* Edge of Darkness. *BBC 1985*

and a gun is held to his face. 'Do it, do it,' he cries. 'No, no, old son. You're on our side,' comes the reply. '*I am not on your side,*' Craven screams, emphasising every word.[19]

But paradoxically Craven is still partly on 'their' side. He telephones Pendleton to notify the latter of the location of the hidden plutonium, and is present – at a distance – at its recovery. He is once again an agent for the re-establishment of social order, the role in which he was presented at the start of the programme.

This is an ambivalent position, and it is one which the narrative never quite resolves. The final image – the black flowers, with the slightest suggestion of a subsequent ice age – is both a vindication of Craven's radical isolationism, and a means of withdrawing from any final confrontation between the programme's contradictory social forces. *Edge of Darkness* eventually 'manages' contradiction by deferring it. The equilibrium it achieves at its resolution is an uneasy one, founded on a gesture of huge mythic faith, represented by the black flowers, in which the metaphorical foces of darkness remain firmly within this world.

The signal achievement here is that the operations of big business and international politics are seen to impinge so directly on the life of an individual. There is something existential in Craven's plight, not least in his primal scream of 'Emma' which closes the programme; but there is also something utterly contemporary about his devastation. He is driven to death *because* he moved too close to the insidious power structures which shape modern Britain. The status quo seems unshakeable. It is hardly surprising that the only solution should be located in a detached future, but it does mean that a drama rooted throughout in a political and social context ends by slipping into a mystical yonder.

Even so, the viewer is left with a profound sense of loss and violation. The tragedy is not only that a man has died, but that a system remains intact. The impact of *Edge of Darkness* was in part down to its potent mix of genres and styles; but its colourings of passion and emotion were surely most significant. You could argue that this places *Edge of Darkness* firmly in the stable of other paranoia dramas of the 1980s. It remains, by any estimation, a uniquely emblematic response to its time.

Edge of Darkness

Transmission dates: November 1985 (BBC2)   Repeated December 1985
(BBC1), May 1992 (BBC2)

Cast

Ronald Craven	Bob Peck
Darius Jedburgh	Joe Don Baker
Emma Craven	Joanne Whalley
James Godbolt	Jack Watson
Pendleton	Charles Kay
Harcourt	Ian McNeice
Jerry Grogan	Kenneth Nelson

Robert Bennett	Hugh Fraser
Clementine	Zoë Wanamaker
Assistant Chief Constable Ross	John Woodvine
Terry Shields	Tim McInnerny

Technical and production

Producer	Michael Wearing
Director	Martin Campbell
Make-up	Daphne Croker
Costume	Denver Hall
Sound	Dickie Bird
Photography	Andrew Dunn
Film Editors	Ardan Fisher
	Dan Rae
Designer	Graeme Thomson
Music	Eric Clapton
	Michael Kamen

Edge of Darkness won six BAFTA Awards in 1986. They were presented for Best Drama Series, Best Actor (Bob Peck), Best Music (Eric Clapton with Michael Kamen), Best Photography (Andrew Dunn), Best Editor (Andrew Fisher and others), and Best Sound (Dickie Bird and others).

Notes

1 Sean Day-Lewis, *Daily Telegraph*, 26 November 1985, 17.
2 *Television Today*, 24 October 1985, 19.
3 *City Limits*, 1–7 November 1985, 17.
4 See for instance Troy Kennedy Martin, 'nats go home'. *Encore*, 11, 2 (March–April 1964), 21–33, and 'Up the Junction and after', *Contrast*, 4, 5/6 (spring 1966).
5 *Morning Star*, 4 November 1985.
6 Julian Petley, 'A Very British Coup', *Sight and Sound* 57, 2 (spring 1988), 95.
7 K. D. Ewing and C. A. Gearty, *Freedom under Thatcher: Civil Liberties in Modern Britain* (Oxford University Press, 1990), 255.
8 *Daily Mail*, 2 November 1985.
9 Ruth Baumgarten, in *The Listener*, 31 October 1985, 36.
10 Lez Cooke, 'Edge of Darkness', *Movie* 33 (winter 1989), 45.
11 *City Limits*, 1–7 November 1985.
12 *The Guardian*, 4 November 1985, 11.
13 Troy Kennedy Martin, *Edge of Darkness* (London: Faber & Faber, 1990), x.
14 *Ibid.*, 75.
15 *Ibid.*, x–xi.
16 Lez Cooke, 'Edge of Darkness', 45.
17 Bob Millington and Robin Nelson, *'Boys from the Blackstuff': The Making of a TV Drama* (London: Comedia, 1986), 174.
18 Kennedy Martin, *Edge of Darkness*, 175.
19 *Ibid.*, 177.

Select bibliography

Books

Kennedy Martin, Troy, *Edge of Darkness* (London: Faber: 1990)

Articles

Baumgarten, Ruth, review of *Edge of Darkness*, *The Listener*, 31 October 1985, 36
Cooke, Lez, 'Edge of Darkness', *Movie* 33 (winter 1989), 45
Day-Lewis, Sean, review of *Edge of Darkness*, *Daily Telegraph*, 26 November 1992, 17
Kennedy Martin, Troy, 'nats go home', *Encore*, 11, 2 (March–April 1964), 21–33
   'Up the Junction and after', *Contrast*, 4, 5/6 (spring 1966)
Woolley, Benjamin, 'Power politics', *Radio Times*, 2–8 November 1985, 82–3, 5

See also:

Broadcast, 19 July 1985, 10; 15 November 1985, 43
City Limits, 1–7 November 1985, 17 (Background article)
The Listener, 14 November 1985, 43
Television Today, 18 April 1985, 18; 24 October 1985, 19 (Interview with Troy Kennedy Martin)
Televisual, November 1985, 29–30 (Analysis of the themes of *Edge of Darkness*)
Time Out, 31 October–7 November 1985, 17 (Background article)
Variety, 1 January 1986, 84

7   *Boys from the Blackstuff* (Alan Bleasdale)

BOB MILLINGTON

Boys from the Blackstuff may be claimed as the TV drama event of the eighties on the grounds of the exceptional intervention the programme made in British culture in the autumn of 1982. Rocketing unemployment was the burning social problem of the day, and the drama series' haunting tragi-comic images of life on the dole engaged the collective anxiety of the nation and fuelled the debate in the real world. As a result the programme was taken up by a popular audience extending well beyond what might be expected for a TV drama transmitted on BBC2 on a Sunday night.

The series' remarkable take-up was augmented still further when it was repeated with unprecedented speed on BBC1 in January 1983. Its impact is borne out in the superlatives lavished by press reviewers of both the political left and right, the string of academy awards made to programme-makers and, subsequently, the quantity of academic writing generated by the series. Several of the series' screen motifs were appropriated and reworked in popular culture and one of its characters, Yosser, became a considerable folk hero. There were Yosser look-alike competitions, Yosser posters, T-shirts and pop records. His catch-phrases 'Gizza job!' and 'I can do that!' were everywhere. Sometimes they provided slogans for dole claimants and 'Right to Work' campaigners. Less seriously, the phrases were briefly appropriated as chants on the Liverpool Kop to reward successful home play. More worryingly for the BBC, a rash of 'Yosser' head-butting broke out in playground scuffles among primary school children, most of whom can never have watched the programme at first hand.

This essay is devoted to examining the several production, textual and cultural factors that had a bearing on the creation of this remarkable television event. First, some consideration will be given to the authorship and production circumstances of *Boys from the Blackstuff*. Next the series will be examined with regard to genre, the sets of expectations that accompany the viewing of programmes of a similar type. Attention will then centre on the impact of the realist images of unemployment shown on screen, especially with regard to the construction of working-class masculinity.

Authorship and production

Pre-eminent in all discussions about *Boys from the Blackstuff* is the name of its writer, Alan Bleasdale. Following the success of this programme, and with three more series and a feature film/*Film on Four* to his credit subsequently,[1] Bleasdale is now acclaimed as a major 'author' of TV drama alongside Alan Bennett, Trevor Griffiths and Dennis Potter. TV drama production relies on industrial division of labour and many skills other than that of the writer, so it is somewhat anomalous to find single names dominating the way of thinking about programmes.[2] However, from the earliest days of television, production companies have chosen to distinguish their 'serious' or 'art' drama from their anonymous popular fiction by citing the name of the writer as 'author' of the TV play. In this respect, they are following the model of the British theatre, traditionally a writer-focused medium.

The practice of privileging the writer is not just working to enhance artistic reputation, of course, but is also serving the ends of the broadcasting institution. Authorship affords a neat mechanism around which programmes can be marketed to viewers. For instance, before its transmission, *Boys from the Blackstuff* was previewed in the *Radio Times* and national press via a series of interviews with Alan Bleasdale. More strategically, in the course of the long-running TV deregulation debate (1986–91), authored drama series like *Boys from the Blackstuff* have been claimed as 'quality television' and used retrospectively to defend the beleaguered reputation of the BBC and, indeed, the whole principle of public-service broadcasting.

In the earlier 'golden age' of television it was precisely the imperative of public-service broadcasting – the obligation to make programmes to educate, inform and entertain – that fostered the rise of original TV drama and placed its writers in a favoured position. Whereas for most 'outsiders' access to television was severely restricted, the doors were opened wide for the serious drama writer precisely because of his (or exceptionally her) ability to develop an independent viewpoint in an original way. Controversial and sometimes subversive ideas, untenable elsewhere in television, have been permitted and even welcomed in the name of art. While most programming reproduced the cultural norms of the Establishment and papered over the cracks and divisions that existed in society, the independent drama-writer offered an alternative perspective and was sometimes actively involved in exposing social divisions.

Alan Bleasdale's scripts for *Boys from the Blackstuff* can be viewed as a high water mark in this oppositional tradition, presenting viewers with images of a nation divided by the grille screen of the dole office. In determining to tackle the unemployment issue Bleasdale had found himself incensed by the moral panic sustained in the Tory press against 'dole scroungers',[3] and he wrote to the BBC in November 1978 proposing a series that would follow up the fortunes of the characters previously established in his successful film play, *The Black Stuff*.[4] In this earlier film a Liverpool tarmac gang, away on a job in Middlesborough, are tempted by the ever-ambitious Yosser to do a foreigner (i.e. take on illegal work using materials and labour already paid for by another contractor), but are caught in the act by their boss and sacked without any prospect but that of returning to Liverpool and joining the dole queue. That the idea for a series was not merely a derivative spin-off, but an opportunity for new committed drama is clear from the letter's tone:

I think it very important right now to write about the Dole as seen from the point of view of those who are on it, and to side with them against the people and papers who would like us to believe, despite the million and a half out of work and mass redundancies at every opportunity, that the majority of the unemployed are malingerers and rogues.[5]

By the time this proposal was made the space available for original TV drama of any description was rapidly evaporating across the industry, as increasing production effort was devoted to developing commercial products aimed at the international market. That *Boys from the Blackstuff* ever found its way onto the screen owes much to Bleasdale's letter being directed to English Regions drama, a production house whose interests and priorities clearly favoured his work. This small satellite of the BBC Drama group was set up in Birmingham in 1971, headed by David Rose, with the clear commitment to developing new work for television from the regional writers being taken up in the local repertory theatres. Alan Bleasdale was one of a number of up-and-coming writers English Regions Drama adopted, along with Willy Russell, Alan Plater, Peter Terson and Mike Leigh.

Despite Alan Bleasdale's unique importance to *Boys from the Blackstuff* as the creator of its scripts, there can be no single author of a TV drama, and the success of the production depended fundamentally on teamwork on several different levels.[6] It certainly gained from the rapport among technical, production and design staff facilitated by the small scale of operations at BBC, Birmingham. More visibly, it gained from the strength and commitment of the Liverpool acting contingent. Frequently Bleasdale was working with particular actors in mind for the various roles. In developing the Boys' characters Bleasdale wrote specifically to the strengths of his actors: Bernard Hill as Yosser, Tom Georgeson as Dixie, Alan Igbon as Loggo, Peter Kerrigan as George, Michael Angelis as Chrissie and Julie Walters as Angie, who in the course of the production became 'one of the Boys'.[7] The major decision-making for the production, however, relied on the successful collaboration between the writer, the director and the producer of the series. Although there were occasional clashes in personality, the relationship stimulated good work. As Alan Bleasdale was to comment, '... they were good battles. There wasn't petulance and jumping up and down. It was creative argument!'[8]

It was chiefly due to the tenacity of Michael Wearing, the series' producer, that *Blackstuff* was prevented from foundering in the face of inadequate budget resources. To keep costs down Wearing decided to record all but one episode on the cheaper OB (location video) format and to take advantage of recent technological advances in lightweight equipment and post-production editing. Because of the faster production turnover of OB compared to 16mm film, substantial savings were to be achieved with the system.[9]

The development of a drama series' project is a convoluted process at the best of times, normally taking two or three years to realise. *Boys from the Blackstuff* was to take four years from letter proposal to screen transmission. The problems Wearing faced in convincing management of the project's worth were also compounded by the late commissioning of Birmingham's new OB facility. By chance of fate, the delay in mustering the necessary resources was ultimately to contribute positively to the impact of the programme by holding back transmission to coincide with the peak of public concern surrounding unemployment – as the consequences of Tory monetarist economics began to take effect – and official statistics passed over the 3 million mark.

To maintain Bleasdale's interest during the protracted delay, Wearing proposed removing one of the submitted episodes from the series to make a separate film. The play concerning the fate of the middle-class boss of the tarmac firm (a spectacular bankruptcy set against Liverpool gangland machinations) was chosen because, as a self-contained episode, its loss would threaten less the viability of the rest of the series. *The Muscle Market*, as it was now named, was filmed and eventually transmitted in January 1981.[10] The removal of this episode had the effect of sharpening *Blackstuff*'s focus on the working-class response to unemployment.

The director of *Boys from the Blackstuff* was Philip Saville, a veteran of

TV drama production, whose career stretches back to ABC's *Armchair Theatre*.[11] Because of Saville's responsibility for the realisation of every image of the series, his contribution to its authorship was great.[12] Relatively unfamiliar with the Liverpool context himself, he brought to the production a greater detachment and helped to make it more meaningful to outsiders who, of course, constituted the vast majority of the programme's audience. In his work with the actors, for instance, Saville was to comment on the slowing-down of the pace of performance to let them 'sit in their own space, their own panic, their own predicament'.[13] In terms of visual style, on occasions he was to match the writer's verbal daring with cinematic pyrotechnics of his own. Undoubtedly Saville's single most important creative contribution to the production lay in his ideas for a new third episode to replace a rejected script. As Bleasdale himself acknowledges:

He was absolutely right! I think somebody like the person who made the original *Black Stuff* would have accepted it, because it was another man's tale. But Philip said to me, 'There are no women in this. You must have the woman's point of view.' And because I find it much easier to write about men than women, I'd dodged out of it!'[14]

The implementation of the director's proposal did go some way to correcting the programme's considerable gender imbalance.

The rewriting of this script was just one among many other rewriting tasks that Alan Bleasdale undertook before the script was ready for production. The example serves to illustrate the extent to which ideas for the series evolved and developed at every stage in the collaborative process of production. After all the discussions and changes a 5×60 min. play series was screened. The episodes were:

(1) 'Jobs for the Boys'
(2) 'Moonlighter'
(3) 'Shop Thy Neighbour'
(4) 'Yosser's Story'
(5) 'George's Last Ride'

Genre

TV dramas like *Boys from the Blackstuff* are neither produced nor viewed in isolation, and their meaning is shaped with reference to the assumptions and expectations prompted by their genre, or programme category, that are circulating in culture. Quite simply, one programme is read according to the rules of similar programmes that have preceded it.[15] The existence of genres is fundamental to the TV industry's method of maximising its audience and supplying it with recognisable products. Programmes are normally planned and marketed with regard to established programme categories or with regard to their place in a pre-existing series (an internal form of genre classification).

Though with serious TV drama emphasis is often placed on the work's artistic uniqueness or its realism in relation to a world 'out there', its meaning is ultimately anchored in generic similarities and conventions – indeed, its readability depends on these. *Boys from the Blackstuff* went through planning and production in the BBC with regard to the contractual obligations, resource provision, aesthetic approach and marketing strategy that had become custom and practice for single plays. Not surprisingly, then, when episodes of the drama went out on BBC2, each had the look of a BBC *Play for Today* and commanded the attention of an audience – to a greater or lesser extent – used to the intricacy of narration and the degree of ideological or aesthetic challenge that they had come to associate with serious TV drama. In point of fact, of course, *Boys from the Blackstuff* sits as something of a hybrid between the industrial categories of the single play and the series, as is clear even in the way it was promoted as a 'series of five new plays' in the *Radio Times*.[16] Though the narratives of each episode remain largely self-contained, at points they are interlinked and the programme draws on the series device of on-going characters as a mechanism for increasing audience size on a word-of-mouth basis from week to week.

While to stimulate the additional interest of viewers *Boys from the Blackstuff* intermittently engages in parody of a number of different genres (including the police thriller, the escape film and the science fiction series), its situation and characters are firmly embedded in Northern realism, an influential generic trend in British fiction that extends across print and screen media. Northern realism fulfils a significant and socially progressive role in TV by providing a space for the exploration of working-class life. It is conspicuous across the major industrial categories of TV fiction, offering acclaimed single plays such as *Our Day Out* and *Road*,[17] police series like *Z Cars* (BBC, 1962–78) and *Juliet Bravo* (BBC, 1980–5), situation comedies like *Liver Birds* (BBC, 1969–78) and *Watching* (Granada, 1987–) and *Coronation Street* (Granada, 1960–), the longest-running drama programme on British TV. The fictions characteristically focus on the day-to-day lives of individuals living in an industrial 'Northern' (or at least regional) setting and stress the resolution of social problems within narratives focused on personal events, such as the task of winning a suitable partner.[18]

From an anthropological perspective, fiction genres can be regarded as a form of modern myth enabling a culture to talk to itself and rehearse the resolution of fundamental contradictions.[19] Part of the pleasure of viewing Northern realist TV drama and films is derived from the way they address deep-seated anxieties surrounding modern urban life, especially with regard to gender and sexuality, relationships and self-fulfilment. In the Northern realism of the sixties, self-fulfilment is enmeshed with the concept of 'embourgeoisement', out of which the 'classless' social-democratic consensus of the Harold Wilson government emerged. The narrative trajectory of the Beatles' first feature film, *A Hard Day's Night* (1964), provides a simple paradigm for a process in which working-class individuals escape their origins to become absorbed by an affluent middle class.[20] Themes of upward mobility, self-betterment and affluence are widely taken up in Northern TV drama. For instance, in the very first episode of *Coronation Street* (Granada, 9 December 1960) a youthful and 'uppish' Ken Barlow, in the final year at university, has a row with his working-class father because of his scheme to take his middle-class girl-friend for a drink at the Imperial Hotel, where his mother works in the kitchens.

The individualistic inflection of Northern realism – suitably adapted to the bleaker economic times – remains to this day the dominant one, and *Boys from the Blackstuff* takes up a number of its conventions. The narrative is preoccupied with individuals and the exploration of the personal consequences of unemployment and, as with so many other Northern fictions, the action is frequently centred in domestic space. Moreover, the Boys' unemployment originates from a self-betterment story that goes disastrously wrong in the original *The Black Stuff* film when they try to get rich at their boss's expense, in the circumstances described earlier. However, in one important respect, the series is different from conventional Northern fictions in its complete lack of romantic or sexual intrigue.

Boys from the Blackstuff also takes up some of the conventions of the political inflection of Northern realism that arose in the seventies. In this period serious TV drama – reflecting the euphoria of the New Left after the student uprising in Paris, 1968 – entered a pronounced oppositional phase, and occasionally even rehearsed the socialist transformation of society. Though oppositional dramas form only a tiny part of the total output of TV fiction they are nevertheless influential, because of the controversies they provoke among the Establishment. The Northern documentary film dramas scripted by Jim Allen and directed by either Ken Loach or Roland Joffé are outspoken in their Marxist analysis of working-class life centring on political organisation, collective action and class struggle – activities neglected in the dominant inflection of the genre. The aura of veracity in *The Big Flame, The Rank and File, The Spongers* and *United Kingdom*[21] is achieved chiefly by the use of actor improvisation with the script and the appropriation of the production techniques associated with TV documentary programmes.[22] Though much less didactic and radical in its stance, *Boys from the Blackstuff* takes up something of the political initiative set in motion by these oppositional films, and a significant part of its action resides in the public space they characteristically occupy. The series also resorts, from time to time, to the same documentary techniques to produce a sense of unmediated truth, as will be further discussed below. Moreover, in the casting of Peter Kerrigan as its dying political activist, George Malone, *Blackstuff* happens to have adopted one of the most prominent actors in the Jim Allen films (whether the irony created was conscious or unconscious is unclear). The use of this actor provides one striking illustration of the way generic knowledge is mobilised in the series, as his screen persona provides an iconographic link with the earlier films and arouses expectations of class struggle and socialist activism.

Following its success on screen, *Boys from the Blackstuff* has itself become part of the repository of circulating genre knowledge, contributing an iconography of life on the dole. Through the influence of *Blackstuff*, the prospect of a Liverpool screen fiction automatically arouses expectations about unemployment, working-class resilience to social hardship and, above all, comedy in the face of adversity. Some, if not all, of these expectations are realised in the leading examples of Liverpool fictions, which in the eighties have proliferated in the wake of the programme's fame. Over the years the Channel 4 soap opera *Brookside* (2 November 1982–) has devoted a considerable number of story-lines to the problem of long-term unemployment.[23] Similarly, unemployment and social hardship have provided the starting-points for the interesting bunch of Liverpool feature films/*Films on Four* which include *Letter to Brezhnev, Business as Usual* and *No Surrender*.[24] Nearly all the screen fictions have also adopted *Blackstuff*'s socially progressive stance, but not the situation comedy *Bread* (BBC1, 1986–91) which turned *Blackstuff*'s iconography of deprivation on its head to sustain a long-running reactionary joke about swindling the benefits system. But it is time now to turn to an analysis of *Boys from the Blackstuff* itself.

Realism

TV drama normally works to engage our interest in the major characters and to create the impression that they are realistic or 'true to life'. To achieve this *Boys from the Blackstuff*, like all other mainstream screen fictions, deploys the time-honoured techniques of *mise-en-scène* (staging), camerawork and editing. So embedded in culture have these conventions become that they go unnoticed by the casual viewer. The title sequence of

'Jobs for the Boys' introduces each of the Boys – Chrissie, Loggo, Yosser, George and Dixie – signing on at the Department of Employment, in separate confrontations with their respective counter clerks. In the establishing (wide angle) shots the camera frames each of the Boys in relation to other claimants in a crowded dole office, so establishing for us a recognisable and coherent world. The camera then moves position and, in combination with editing, follows the dialogue to offer shot/reverse shots (alternating shots) of the speakers. This allows us to study character in detail and so be drawn emotionally into the Boys' problems and their common predicament: surviving on the dole.

In this way a basic sense of verisimilitude is created for us. However, like other TV dramas of the realist school, *Boys from the Blackstuff* adopts additional strategies to authenticate the narrative and create the illusion that it is not a fiction at all, but instead showing us 'how things really are'. One way this is done is by embellishing the image with a wealth of specific cultural references. For instance, quite soon into 'Jobs for the Boys' Snowy refers to the Toxteth riots. The allusion to a real event in Liverpool's recent past helps convince us that the drama too is 'real'. Realism is also claimed in the series by obliterating a conventional sense of performance from the *mise-en-scène*. In 'Jobs for the Boys' the impression is created of spontaneous unstaged action as the conversation is one moment cramped into the impossible space of a van interior and then, the next, allowed to range freely over the building-site. The acting of the characters veers towards an extreme naturalism, with lines being delivered with regard to 'real' tasks and behaviour. Yosser, for instance, argues almost incomprehensibly with the boss as his mouth is stuffed full of chips. Another way realism is enhanced occurs through use of camera work and editing. As noted above, *Blackstuff* adopts similar techniques to those used in the Jim Allen/Ken Loach films to overlay conventional drama rhetoric with devices drawn from documentary programme-making. 'Jobs for the Boys' opens, for instance, with a series of descriptive shots of the real community in the Liverpool street outside the DoE to impress on us the sense that the scene unfolding inside is also part of a wider social truth. In 'Yosser's Story' the method of claiming the real becomes still more ingenious as Yosser sits and talks with the instantly recognisable real-life football stars, Graeme Souness and Sammy Lee, who have been brought into the series to play themselves. These and other conventions all work in combination to create the impression that the unfolding character drama is 'the real thing'.

It should be acknowledged, at this stage, that *Blackstuff* embraces a far wider range of dramatic styles than is conventionally associated with TV realism. The unfolding narrative develops to encompass increasingly the expressionist, the surreal and the grotesquely comic. Such devices are gradually introduced, however, and are largely contained in a logical, coherent framework of reference – a realistic diegesis. Even Yosser's surreal dream sequence in episode 4 is explained in realist terms as soon as the character is shown waking up. In this way the viewer is able to accept the experimentation with dramatic style with some confidence and accept the surprises produced in the narrative as broadly representative of the vicissitudes of life itself.

Now although realism pretends to show an unmediated reality, it will be clear from what has been said already that it is as constructed and persuasive as any other style of artistic address. In the process of ordering and selecting content into a coherent narrative, realism actively makes sense of the world, and so works ideologically. In the opening scene of *Boys from the Blackstuff* the rhetoric of production works to position us in favour of the oppressed – the Boys – in their struggle against the bureaucracy of the benefits system. The imposition of the dole screen-grille in the *mise-en-scène* presents the Boys as trapped, like caged animals in a zoo, so inviting our sympathy. The witty/ironic rejoinders they utter to the counter clerks and the dominant status they are afforded in the camera frame empower them in the image and so work to enlist our support in their resistance. What the realist rhetoric of production is doing in more general terms, however, is to present unemployment from the perspective of male power.

In Cultural Studies, realism is viewed as working ideologically to naturalise as 'common sense' the discourses (interested utterances) of the dominant power groups in society. As a dramaturgical strategy *Blackstuff* takes up the dominant male-centred view of the world – it assumes that unemployment is a male problem and, as in the first scene where some women are placed in the dole queue in long shot, ensures that the female perspective on unemployment remains ancillary. In recent years cultural changes in Western society in relation to employment and the position of women have caused traditional views of masculinity to be challenged and redefined in culture.[25] Fictional representations have been actively engaged in this process of redefinition, not the least being Bleasdale's stage and TV plays in their preoccupation with male angst. So in *Boys from the Blackstuff* especially the discourse of masculinity is taken up to be deliberately undermined.[26]

Male behaviour is characteristically represented in terms of physical action and the successful performance of tasks – in the workplace, on the battlefield, at sport etc. By its very nature, unemployment denies physical action and consequently must put conventional constructions of masculinity in crisis. This problem is temporarily averted in *Boys from the Blackstuff*, and 'Jobs For the Boys' continues following Chrissie and Loggo

6 *Chrissie (Michael Angelis) runs away from the fraud section investigators ('sniffers') in 'Jobs for the Boys', the first episode of the Alan Bleasdale series,* Boys from the Blackstuff. *BBC 1982*

in physical action, 'moonlighting'. They take illegal work on a building site to supplement their dole, attempting to evade the surveillance of the DoE fraud 'sniffers'. Despite the subterfuge there are numerous signs of comradeship and the celebration of the common-sense values of the working man.

At the centre of the episode stands George's son, Snowy (played by Chris Darwin), confident in his masculinity as he finishes off the plastering of a wall. He is a 'whole man', filled with his sense of achievement in his work and secure in his revolutionary politics even if these are frequently the target of the Boys' jokes. But Snowy's pride is to be brief and he is summarily 'killed off' in a tragic accident when the sniffers raid the site to arrest dole-fiddlers. The raid is grotesquely bungled and some escape, but not Snowy, who falls to his death trying to abseil from an upstairs window on a rope fastened to a badly fitted banister rail. The camera cuts from a close shot of Chrissie grimly bending over the body to a shot from his point of view, that pans across Snowy's smashed head to the blood ebbing away in the dirt. There is grim irony in the way the master-craftsman, in the William Morris labour-activist tradition, is made the victim of contemporary shoddy workmanship.[27] Against the harsh realities of Thatcherist economics and enterprise, Snowy's model of masculinity is shown to be unworkable and obsolete.

In the first episode the human cost of unemployment is shown in terms of a sudden, capricious accident befalling a subordinate character. In subsequent episodes emphasis is placed on its psychological effects on the Boys themselves.

In 'Moonlighter', the life values of Dixie (Tom Georgeson) are brought into crisis. He, too, has been forced into the world of the black economy to survive and has taken on the passive task of night security guard on the docks, where his role is continually challenged by dockers. His problems spread equally to the home which has fallen under DoE surveillance because of his wife's part-time leafleting job. The ex-foreman of the tarmac gang exhibits a 'hard', reactionary masculinity; he is dour, closed and authoritarian in manner. He is shown in the *mise-en-scène* as a solitary figure, cutting himself off from the company of the Boys, sitting outside the dockers' community of theft, and walking back alone from the docks after his shift. The setting of Dixie as 'a man apart' might have been used in different circumstances to produce an ideal of heroic masculinity, but the character lacks the power of autonomy and he is here just an isolated figure brought to the edge of his own private despair.

As a working-class Tory, Dixie clings blindly to his belief in the seeming correspondence between success and individual effort. This he seeks to hand on to his children, if necessary enforcing his authority as father with physical force. However, he is infuriated to discover his youngest son 'sagging' school and the eldest lying in bed all day, having given up the idea of ever finding work. His authority has been challenged because the values on which it is based no longer deliver results:

DIXIE: What's wrong with qualifications?
DANNY: Y' need nuclear physics t'be a binman these days, dad.[28]

The values are equally useless on the docks, and the story reaches its climax with Dixie intimidated into being an accessory to a large-scale cargo robbery the last night the ship is in port. A futile effort to assert his own integrity produces a brutal tirade from the dockers' leader against all security men:

'Cos the likes of y'are shite, you're nothin. Y' the dregs, dragged here off the dole. Now stand there an' do what y'supposed to do – watch us work.[29]

Dixie's emotional life has hitherto been completely repressed, but the pressure here is too much. To prolong suspense the camera shows us first a shot of the gang filing past him, one by one. Then as the music rises we suddenly cut to a close-up of Dixie's face glistening with the 'soft' tears of humiliation. Dixie, as a 'hard' working-man, has been broken.

In 'Shop Thy Neighbour' the action focuses on the impact of male unemployment on marriage. Chrissie (Michael Angelis) and his wife, Angie (Julie Walters), are continually rowing because of the shortage of food and money. Chrissie is brought to the emotional brink because of his impending prosecution for dole fraud and his guilt over failing to provide for the family. He is, at once, a more affable and easy-going male type than Dixie, displaying sensitivity in the care of the family's animals and the handling of his daughters, and an ease in relationships demonstrated by his continual association with Loggo outside the home. But he is not the 'new man' of consumer culture, and his less dominant status in the image is created as much by making Angie correspondingly assertive and strong; she is even allowed witty repartee at Chrissie's expense. Though Angie is afforded equal status in the *mise-en-scène* to Chrissie, it still remains his story and the women's perspective on unemployment is subordinated to the male predicament.[30]

Chrissie's crisis of masculinity centres on his failure to be the breadwinner of the family. The relationship between his impotence in economic terms and his sexual identity are clear in the quarrel that follows the gas being cut off:

CHRISSIE: But they can't cut me off though, can they – that's your department!
    ANGIE: I can't cut off what you haven't got.[31]

Chrissie characteristically occupies a passive position in the narrative and is frequently the victim of events as, for instance, in the unexpected DoE raid on the house. He is equally passive in the fight scene when, after the clearing of the meal, Angie launches a surprisingly physical attack on him and he lets her use him as a kind of punch-bag. As at so many other points in the series, this last incident gains its realism and emotional conviction through the combination of skilful writing, integrity of performance and artistic deployment of camera/*mise-en-scène*. The choice of a long take, with a hand-held camera, to shoot the entire scene adds a documentary immediacy to the image as it simultaneously enables the actor's pace of performance to dominate the proceedings.[32]

The episode approaches its emotional climax when the couple come together and confide their troubles in the bedroom scene, which affords the series' clearest statement on the personal cost of unemployment. Chrissie, though, is once again overwhelmed by his guilt and attempts to laugh off the situation with another joke. This provokes an infuriated response from Angie in which he is pushed off the bed:

ANGIE: It's not funny, it's not friggin' funny – I've had enough of that – you've got to laugh or else you'll cry – I've heard it for years – this stupid soddin' city's full of it – well why don't you cry – why don't you scream – why don't you fight back, you bastard. Fight back. They're knockin' the shite an' stuffin' out of you, Chrissie Todd, and if you haven't had enough, I have.

CHRISSIE: And what do you think it's like for me? Hey? A second-class citizen. A second-rate man. With no money .. and no job ... and no ... no ... place![33]

However, Angie continues to press him to provide for the family, and in a massive reassertion of destructive machismo he does just this. He shoots the family geese to fill the larder, in a one-time gesture of impotent rage. Affable Chrissie has lost control of himself and resorted to the violence of the gun.

'Yosser's Story' charts the mental breakdown of the most fanatically ambitious of the Boys. The focus of the episode switches from Yosser's absurd demands on all and sundry to 'Gizza job,' to the problems of retaining custody of his children. The eventual loss of the children is prefigured in the dream sequence with which the story begins, and which at the same time serves to draw us subjectively into his disturbed state of mind. Yosser (Bernard Hill) walks into a lake with his children fully dressed and loses them one by one under the water.[34]

As befits his psychotic condition, Yosser displays a confused image of masculinity in the *mise-en-scène*, a bizarre amalgam of the extreme hard and soft types. In terms of his dress and behaviour, he displays a powerful and threatening machismo, yet always this is tempered by the softening effect of his children who accompany him in the scene. In action he cannot match up successfully to either type. He fails, for instance, to exact retribution on his unfaithful wife by choosing, at the last second, to butt a lamp-post rather than her head. Similarly, as the domesticated father, he dismally fails to cook the children's tea.

Yosser's psychosis is driven by his obsessive male ambition 'to be somebody', and his absurd faith in the significance of his own name in the overall scheme of things. To Yosser success has nothing to do with talent or effort, but just the power of personality. Hence his determination to be seen in the company of somebody famous, like Graeme Souness. His fixation to be 'noticed' as 'Yosser Hughes' also dominates the start of the scene with the Wino (James Ellis) at the Pier Head. Yosser is talking to himself, but then gets caught up in a crazy cross-talk with the tramp in which they exchange obsessions. The expressionistic camera-work reinforces our impression of his psychosis here, as a low-angle tracking shot is executed which, as it sweeps along a line of tramps to discover Yosser in front of the Liver Building, both disorientates and disturbs.

Physical violence, of course, is the likeliest outcome whenever Yosser's masculinity is challenged, as was shown in the first episode when he 'nutted' the builder for criticising his wall-building. In 'Yosser's Story' the character is seen being violent to himself and his violence to others is spoken of – it is threatened even – but, to maximise suspense, it is not actually shown on screen till later. In the scene on the Pier Head, our expectations of violence are aroused and played with as the Wino mistakes Yosser's advances and relations with his daughter as expressions of sexual deviance. Yosser does indeed shape up to revenge the last monstrous slur on his manhood as he grabs the tramp by the lapels. However, the urge falls away as, in a flash of insane illumination, he suddenly recognises the futility of his aspirations in his comment, 'I built sandcastles and sometimes I think that's all I've ever done.'[35]

The final test of Yosser's slender grip on reality centres on his determination as a father to retain custody of his children. Though his unstable case history renders him utterly unsuitable for this task, his attempt as a single parent to keep the family together nevertheless earns our respect. Yosser's efforts to assert his paternal rights, like everything else he does, are doomed to end in failure, and the care order is served in a scene where all the impending violence from earlier is allowed to erupt on screen. Yosser attempts to defend the home from invasion, masterfully swinging a baseball bat to extend his male power, but he is overwhelmed by the police and brutally beaten into submission. Rapid mental deterioration follows the loss of his children; there is nothing left to hold him together. He wanders the streets of Liverpool indistinguishable from its other vagrants, a disturbing and pathetic victim of the social system. Eventually overwhelmed by his situation he attempts unsuccessfully to commit suicide in the lake.

Boys from the Blackstuff's final episode deals with the death of George (Peter Kerrigan), the old-school Labour activist, and its consequences to the working-class community he has served. In 'George's Last Ride', the character is discharged from hospital to die quietly at home, but instead he fills his last hours helping people with their social problems. George is the complete man; he is centred in an extended family group and is the patriarch in the community. His presence offers an ideal model of working-class masculinity, assembled around a wealth of historical allusions to the labour movement, union organisation and lawful protest against exploitation.

George's values are celebrated emotionally in the nostalgic 'last ride' sequence in the wheelchair around the derelict docks, the decaying reminder of Liverpool's industrial past. George's aspirations are in marked contrast with the ruins surrounding him and finally, in close up, he steadfastly proclaims that his dreams from long ago 'still give me hope and faith in my class . . . I can't believe there is no hope, I can't'.[36] But then he dies, and the order he stood for passes too. Chrissie is left behind, an individual in solitary panic on the docks, running for help, as the camera zooms out on him to extreme wide-angle and reduces his image to insignificance in relation to the acres of mud and towering derelict ruins that surround him.

The killing off of both the activist characters in *Blackstuff* prompts further questions on the way realism is used to make sense of the world in political terms. The series seems to deny the possibility of effective collective action in response to unemployment (even George works on a one-to-one basis) and, working against the politicising process of the Jim Allen films, leaves agency solely in the hampered hands of politically agnostic individuals like Chrissie. It is all very well Angie demanding that Chrissie fight back, but how exactly can one individual make his protest felt? Chrissie does, of course, make a stand of sorts, when he interrupts the priest in the middle of his inappropriate funeral oration. The impact he makes, though, relies on the presence of a community that is there in tribute to the organising powers of George.

George's death in *Blackstuff*, and the political vacuum that is allowed to remain after it, have led some left critics to charge the series with fatalism.[37] In many respects, though, the programme catches the bleak mood of the times: the widespread disillusionment in socialism that accompanied the failure of the Labour government to arrest Britain's economic decline and that in turn enabled the authoritarian populism of Margaret Thatcher to take power in 1979. *Blackstuff*'s emphasis on individualism was also accurately reflecting the isolated predicament of people who were unemployed, and who would agree with Chrissie that 'beliefs go right out of the window when . . . debtors knock at your door'.[38] As will be clear from his later works, *No Surrender* and *GBH*, Alan Bleasdale has a marked aversion to polemics and rigid political dogma, and with *Blackstuff* there was a determination 'not to score easy political points where there's no easy answer'. So at the end of the series there was no attempt to resolve the problems that had been presented and, instead, viewers were left with an open question to draw their own conclusions, as Chrissie, Loggo and Yosser walked down the road to an uncertain future.

 Like most significant Western dramas before it, *Blackstuff* used empathy rather than argument to make an impact on its audience. It engaged the emotional experience of being unemployed, took the part of those that were dispossessed and provided, in John McGrath's phrase, a 'public pronouncement of a widespread private grief'.[39] The political significance of *Blackstuff* – to adopt John Caughie's definition of progressive TV drama – resides precisely in its ability 'to contest the dominant image with an alternative identity'.[40] Running against the overwhelmingly escapist/nostalgic trend of major drama series in the eighties – epitomised by *Brideshead Revisited* (Granada, 1981) – *Boys from the Blackstuff* addressed contemporary reality and in the autumn of 1982 succeeded in redirecting public consciousness back to Britain's problems at home when, all through that spring and summer, it had been distracted abroad by the spectacular colonial diversion provided by the Falklands War.

The success of *Boys from the Blackstuff* as progressive TV drama, though, hinged on its ability to entertain as well as inform. A striking feature of the series' appeal was the offsetting of emotional drama with verbal and visual comedy. Though sometimes surprising and extravagant in effect, the comedy is nevertheless rooted in a realism – the observable folk-humour of the Liverpool streets. On a straightforward level the use of repartee through the series works to display the resilience of the male community in the face of adversity. When used in the DoE by the Boys it becomes a deliberate form of effrontery, a ritual of resistance against the tyrannies of petty bureaucracy. Comedy also works throughout the series as an instrument of social justice, exacting retribution on all-comers for over-zealous application. The sniffers pursuing the Boys to the building site are booked by the police for speeding; the social worker who takes custody of Yosser's daughter from her father is 'nutted' by her in the course of the task, the police sergeant who uses undue violence on Yosser to enforce the child custody order is shot in the rump with an air rifle, and so on.

The use of comedy extends the emotional range of the series enormously, enabling the bleak, the pathetic and the tragic to be set in sharp relief, and vice versa. Conventionally, realist TV drama works within relatively narrow parameters, but in oscillating between comedic and tragic extremes *Blackstuff* attempts to comprehend the whole range of human emotion. Mere laughter in the face of life's tribulations presents a problem for comedy that Angie nicely encapsulates in her attack on the 'if you don't laugh you'll cry' mentality cited earlier. It can lead to trivialisation and losing sight of the pain that the comedy is attempting to mask over. Arguably in Bleasdale's later scripts, *No Surrender* and *GBH*, extravagant comic gags have become so much stylistic ends in their own right that on occasion they tend to obscure the truth they attempt to represent: sectarian Irish politics and totalitarian versus democratic roads to socialism. The balance is right, though, in *Blackstuff* and the black comedy serves to highlight the writer's view of life (and especially life on the dole) as an 'absurd, mad, black farce'.[41] Effective black comedy must do more than provoke laughter; it must simultaneously disturb. Yosser's famous unwitting gag – 'I'm desperate Dan' – in the confessional momentarily distances us from the character's sense of anguish, only to return us to a terrible recognition that the joke is mocking at the human condition itself. Similarly, the mad farce of the redundancy party in the pub at the end of 'George's Last Ride' may provoke our laughter and provide relief to the emotional tension provided in the scenes surrounding George's death. However, simultaneously it also disturbs us with its images of social and psychological breakdown, all brought about as the consequences of unemployment.

Blackstuff's comedy went a long way to make serious TV drama accessible to a popular audience. The range of comic invention shown on screen, and especially the shock of the transitions from high drama to black comedy, differentiated the series from conventional TV fictions and made it *worth talking about* in conversation, in all areas of society. The comedy and jokes were quoted first for their own sake, but then provided the stimulus for wider discussion of the characters and the experience of being unemployed. So the meanings of *Boys From the Blackstuff* were negotiated socially and conclusions drawn. This is the likeliest explanation of how the major TV drama event came to be.

Boys from the Blackstuff

For complete cast, production and technical credits, see *Boys from the Blackstuff: BFI Dossier 20*, 68–75

Notes

1 Alan Bleasdale's screen production credits, post-1982:
   - *Boys from the Blackstuff*, dir. Philip Saville, prod. Michael Wearing, five-part series (BBC2, transmission date (tx) 10 October 1982 – 7 November 1982) (BBC1, tx 13 January 1983 – 8 February 1983).
   - *Scully*, dir. Les Chatfield, prod. Steven Morrison, seven-part serial (Granada–Channel 4, tx 14 May 1984 – 26 June 1984).
   - *No Surrender*, dir. Peter Smith, prod. Mamoun Hassan, feature film *Film on Four* (UK Palace Pictures, 1986) (Channel 4, tx 19 March 1987).
   - *The Monocled Mutineer*, dir. Jim O'Brien, prod. Richard Broke, four-part serial (BBC1, tx 31 August 1986 – 21 September 1986).
   - *GBH*, dir. Robert Young, prod. David Jones Alan Bleasdale, seven-part serial (GBH (films)–Channel 4, tx 6 and 9 May 1991 – 18 and 21 July 1991).
2 For a theorised approach to the authorship of TV drama production, see Graham Murdock, 'Authorship and organization', *Screen Education*, 35 (1980), 19–34.

3 See Peter Golding and Sue Middleton, 'Why is the press so obsessed with welfare scroungers?', *New Society*, 26 October 1978, 195–7.

4 *The Black Stuff*, dir. Jim Goddard, prod. David Rose (BBC2, tx 2 January 1980).

5 Letter dated 22 November 1978 from Alan Bleasdale to David Rose and Michael Wearing, reproduced in *'Boys from the Blackstuff'*, *BFI Dossier No. 20* (London, BFI, 1984) 21–4, and Bob Millington and Robin Nelson, *'Boys from the Blackstuff': The Making of TV Drama* (London: Comedia, 1986), 179–83.

6 See Millington and Nelson, *ibid.*, for a detailed account of the series' evolution at each stage of production.

7 Unpublished interview with Michael Angelis (27 August 1984).

8 Cited in Millington, 'Making *Boys from the Blackstuff'* (*BFI Dossier 20*), 10.

9 The episode assigned to 16mm film was 'Yosser's Story'. For a comparison of OB recording and 16mm filming, see Millington and Nelson, *Making of TV Drama*, especially 110–14.

10 *The Muscle Market*, dir. Alan Dossor, prod. Michael Wearing (BBC1, tx. 13 January 1981).

11 For an overview of Philip Saville's career as a director of TV drama up to and including *Boys from the Blackstuff*, see 'A man for all seasons', *Stills*, 7 (July–Aug. 1983), 32–5.

12 For a humorous account of Saville's claim to authorship of *Boys from the Blackstuff*, see John Wyver, 'The great authorship mystery', *The Listener*, 14 April 1983.

13 Cited in Millington and Nelson, *Making of TV Drama*, 102.

14 *Ibid.*, 60.

15 For theorised accounts of the role of genre in reading TV, see John Fiske, *Television Culture* (London, Methuen, 1987), 108–16, and Jane Feuer, 'Genre', in Robert Allen (ed.), *Channels of Discourse* (London: Methuen, 1987), 13–33.

16 *Radio Times*, 9–15 October 1982, 19.

17 • *Our Day Out*, scri. Willy Russell, dir. Pedr James, prod. David Rose (BBC1, tx 28 December 1977).
   • *Road*, scri. Jim Cartwright, dir. Alan Clarke, prod. André Molyneux/David Thompson (BBC, tx 7 October 1989).

18 For a fuller examination of Northern realism (within the wider generic umbrella of social drama/realism), see Marion Jordan, 'Realism and convention', in Richard Dyer *et al.*, *'Coronation Street'*; *BFI Television Monograph* (London: BFI, 1981), 27–39, and Alan Lovell, 'The context of British social drama', in *'Boys from the Blackstuff'*, *BFI Dossier 20* (London: British Film Institute, 1984), 25–9.

19 See Jane Feuer, 'Genre', 119.

20 Stuart Laing, *Representations of Working Class Life, 1957–1964* (London: Macmillan, 1986), 220.

21 • *The Big Flame*, dir. Ken Loach, prod. Tony Garnett (BBC1, tx 19 February 1969)
   • *The Rank and File*, dir. Ken Loach, prod. Tony Garnett (BBC1, tx 2 May 1971)
   • *The Spongers*, dir. Roland Joffé, prod. Tony Garnett (BBC1, tx 24 January 1978)

- *United Kingdom*, dir. Roland Joffé, prod. Kenith Trodd (BBC1, tx 8 December 1981)

22 See Paul Madden, 'Jim Allen', in George W. Brandt (ed.), *British Television Drama* (Cambridge University Press, 1981), 36–55.

23 See pp. 40, 42–7.

24 - *Letter to Brezhnev*, scri. Frank Clarke, dir. Chris Bernard (UK, Palace Pictures, November 1985)
    - *No Surrender*, scri. Alan Bleasdale, dir. Peter Smith (UK, Palace Pictures, March 1986)
    - *Business as Usual*, dir. Lezli-An Barrett (UK, Cannon, 1987).

25 For an account of the conflicting representations of masculinity in popular culture in the eighties, see Jonathan Rutherford, 'Who's that man', in Rowena Chapman and Jonathan Rutherford (eds.), *Male Order: Unwrapping Masculinity* (London: Lawrence and Wishart, 1988), 1–67.

26 For a further account of masculinity in the series, which relates to melodramatic 'excess' and audience response, see Richard Paterson, 'Restyling masculinity: the impact of *Boys from the Blackstuff*', in James Curran, Anthony Smith and Pauline Wingate (eds.), *Impacts and Influences: Essays in Media Power in the Twentieth Century* (London, Methuen, 1987), 218–30.

27 David Lusted, 'What's left of *Blackstuff*: political meaning for a popular audience', in '*Boys from the Blackstuff* BFI Dossier 20*, 46.

28 *Boys from the Blackstuff*, Studio Scripts, episode 2, sc.14, 91.

29 *Ibid.*, episode 2, sc.39, 119.

30 For a feminist critique of the series see Ruth Smith, '*Boys from the Blackstuff*: a feminist view', *The Leveller*, February, 1983 (also *BFI Dossier 20*, 39–40).

31 Studio Scripts, episode 3, sc.18, 152.

32 For a production analysis of this scene, see Millington and Nelson, *Making of TV Drama*, 116.

33 Studio Scripts, episode 3, sc.40, 176–7. For a production analysis of the scene see Millington and Nelson, *Making of TV Drama*, 117–18.

34 For a production analysis, see Millington and Nelson, *ibid.*, 118–20.

35 Studio Scripts, episode 4, sc.24, 202.

36 *Ibid.*, episode 5, sc.22, 253.

37 See, for instance, David Lusted, 'What's left of *Blackstuff*', 46.

38 Studio Scripts, episode 1, sc.21, 48.

39 John McGrath, 'The boys are back', in *Boys from the Blackstuff*, *BFI Dossier 20* (London: British Film Institute, 1984), 64.

40 John Caughie, 'Progressive television and documentary drama', *Screen*, 21, 3 (1980), 350.

41 Cited in Millington and Nelson, *Making of TV Drama*, 21.

Select bibliography

Scripts

Alan Bleasdale, *Boys from the Blackstuff* (ed. D. Self) (Studio Scripts, London: Hutchinson, 1985)

Critical books

Millington, Bob, and Robin Nelson, *'Boys From the Blackstuff'*: *The Making of TV Drama* (London: Comedia, 1986)
Paterson, Richard (ed.) *'Boys From the Blackstuff' BFI Dossier 20* (London: British Film Institute)

Critical essays

Eaton, Gordon, *'Boys from the Blackstuff*: progressive television', in *BFI Dossier 20*, 1984, 30–4
Lovell, Alan, 'The context of British social drama', in *BFI Dossier 20*, 1984, 25–9
Lusted, David, 'What's left of Blackstuff: political meaning for a popular audience', *BFI Dossier 20*, 1984, 41–7
Millington, Bob, 'Making *Boys from the Blackstuff*: a production perspective', in *BFI Dossier 20*, 1984, 4–24
O'Sullivan, Kevin, 'A look at *Boys from the Blackstuff'*, *BFI Dossier 20*, 1984, 35–8
Paterson, Richard, 'Restyling masculinity: the impact of *Boys from the Blackstuff'*, in Curran, James, Anthony Smith and Pauline Wingate (eds.), *Impacts and Influences: Essays on Media Power in the Twentieth Century* (London: Methuen, 1987), 218–30

Reviews and journalism

Arden, John, 'Relevance is relative', *The Listener*, 18 August 1983, 29 (The impact of the series in Ireland)
Cormack, Bill, 'A man for all season', *Stills*, July/August 1983, 32–5 (On the work of director Philip Saville)
McGrath, John, 'The boys are back', *The Listener*, 13 January 1983, 28 (also *BFI Dossier 20*, 62–3)
du Noyer, Paul, 'England today, uglier by far', *New Musical Express*, 13 November 1982 (also *BFI Dossier 20*, 64–7)
Paterson, Richard, 'Contributions from the press – establishing a television event', *BFI Dossier 20*, 59–62
Smith, Ruth, *'Boys from the Blackstuff*: a feminist view', *The Leveller*, February 1983 (also *BFI Dossier 20*, 39–40)

See also:

Broadcast, 1 November 1982, 14–15
Drama 163 (1987), 45
The Listener, 21 October 1982, 25; 20 January 1983, 16 (Summary of a discussion of the series on *Did You See . . .*)
Monthly Film Bulletin 602 (March 1984), 92–4
Television Today, 30 July 1981, 16; 27 May 1982, 23
Time Out, 8–14 October 1982, 68

8 *Tumbledown* (Charles Wood) and *The Falklands Play* (Ian Curteis)

The Falklands faction

GEOFFREY REEVES

The run-up

In August 1984 Mark Burns, an actor and close friend of the author Charles Wood, sent him a cutting from *The Guardian* about the 'Falklands victims the army tried to forget':

> Lt Robert Lawrence was a 21-year-old Scots Guards officer with five years' army service when he was sent to the Falklands on the *QE2* in April 1982. A few days before his 22nd birthday and $1\frac{1}{2}$ hours before the Argentinian surrender he was shot in the back of the head by a sniper during the assault on Tumbledown Mountain. For his part in the action, he was awarded the Military Cross.
> He says the sniper who hit him was doing his job but believes the military establishment and Civil Service have not done theirs. He was kept out of the way at the St Paul's service of remembrance, had to pay for a 'free car' and was told nothing about how to start a new life.[1]

Charles Wood wanted to meet Robert Lawrence, so Mark Burns drove him over for lunch to the Manor House at Milton, where the Woods lived (an event that was to become the opening scene of the film). Following the meeting, Wood decided to write a script based on Lawrence's experiences and formed a company with Mark Burns to make it as a film. It was to be almost four years before it would be made and shown. Wood took the treatment to his agent, who passed it on to David Puttnam. Puttnam wanted to make it as a television film for Channel 4, with a budget of £400,000. However, Mark Burns in particular wanted it to be a big feature film directed by someone of the stature of John Schlesinger. Puttnam raised a problem: he said he could clearly see what the others would be doing but he couldn't see what Burns's role was going to be. Wood became protective of Burns.

Instead of to Puttnam, Wood and Burns sold the rights to Alan Wright, an independent producer who spent a year trying to set it up as a feature film while Wood wrote and rewrote the script. Simon Relph and the National Film Development Fund gave them help and Rank agreed to put up most of the money providing an American distributor could be found. But the Americans were not interested unless, as Wood said, 'we came up with an overtly anti-war film or a Rambo-style kick-the-spics for-a-shit film'. But Wood was determined 'to please nobody but myself with *Tumbledown*, to get it right for myself and to resist whatever inducements might be offered'.² This desire to keep his script as he had written it made him shy off directors like Richard Lester who were seriously interested in the material. His determination to write the story as a feature film for himself actually ensured it was never made as such: surely only in the realm of television can the writer retain that degree of control. Moreover Wood found out that Wright and Burns were entertaining possible changes – perhaps the addition of a parallel story of a wounded Argentinian soldier – which would make it more interesting to the Americans.

About three months before the end of Alan Wright's option period, Wood's agent, without telling him, had breakfast at the Ritz with Richard Broke, at that time a staff producer at the BBC. Broke expressed interest, so he was given the script, while being sworn to some secrecy. At that time *The Falklands Play* projected by Ian Curteis was also circulating in the BBC and had been read by Broke.

While the agent presided over the demise of Alan Wright's attempts to make the feature film and Charles Wood at last extricated himself from his obligations to Mark Burns, Broke started to move within the BBC. He wanted Roland Joffé to make it but, while Joffé liked it very much, he was pursuing other things and never committed himself. So Broke turned to Richard Eyre, whose last film this was to be before he became the Director of the National Theatre. Broke's main problem was money. He saw its scale would require two BBC budgets. When he had overcome the enormous problems of getting such a sum together the film had to be two hours long to justify the cost; but while he was doing that, Ian Curteis went to the press over the decision to shelve *The Falklands Play*. This ensured that for the next twenty months every aspect of the making of *Tumbledown* would be a matter for public comment.

In 1979 the BBC had broadcast *Suez-1956*, a three-hour play by Curteis which reconstructed the crisis over the canal with Eden, Eisenhower and Nasser in the principal roles.³ In April 1983, at the instigation of the new Director-General, Alasdair Milne, the BBC commissioned Curteis to do the same thing for the Falklands War. After two years of research Curteis wrote a script, delivering the fourth draft to the Director-General and the producer, Cedric Messina, in April 1986. Curteis says it was warmly received and scheduled for recording the following January, with transmission to be on 2 April 1987 – the fifth anniversary of the Argentine invasion. Cedric Messina signed a contract to begin production at the end of September 1986. When Curteis saw the Director-General at the beginning of June, they discussed the possible date of a general election and whether that would affect the transmission date. Milne said, according to Curteis, 'She will hold out as long as she can – probably till 1988. The earliest an election *could* happen, barring some national catastrophe, is Autumn 1987. I don't see that transmission in April represents any problem.'⁴ The BBC Contracts and Copyright Department officially accepted the text, subject only to any comments Cedric Messina might make subsequently. Four days later Messina had a meeting with Michael Grade, then Controller of BBC1, at which the latter gave the go-ahead for the production. Curteis tried unsuccessfully to talk to Bill Cotton, the Managing Director of BBC TV, and wrote to him to find out if he too supported the play. But he never received a reply.

A month later, 7 July, Peter Goodchild, the new Head of Plays, drove down to Gloucestershire to have lunch with Curteis at his house on the banks of the river Coln. According to Curteis's own account, which I summarise below, Goodchild said he felt 'unhappy' about certain parts of the script:

(a) where the Prime Minister exhibited private grief
(b) at speeches which described the Falklands conflict as being fought to resist aggression, and he suggested
(c) that some War Cabinet scenes should be rewritten to include discussion of 'the coming election' and
(d) that more should be written about the opposition to the government's policies regarding the sending of the Task Force and the fighting of the war; and he asked
(e) for some explanation of Galtieri's frequent drunkenness.

Two days after the lunch Goodchild wrote to Curteis saying that the changes were mandatory or the production would not take place. When he published the correspondence three months later, Curteis wrote

I am not an employed scriptwriter. I am a playwright, who owns the copyright in his own work and is responsible legally and morally for what he says... Mr Goodchild's proposals would radically have altered the nature and motives of key decisions of the War Cabinet, and would still have been transmitted as my work and my opinion.⁵

On 17 July, Curteis again tried, unsuccessfully, to talk to Bill Cotton; but he did manage to get hold of Michael Grade. Grade now raised not merely the specific point of the relationship of the sinking of the *Belgrano* and the timing of the Peruvian peace initiative, but also the propriety of writing and producing such a play. Curteis pointed out the play had been commissioned by the Director-General himself. Four days later, on 21 July, the BBC cancelled the production because of 'the next general election'.[6]

By September, Norris McWhirter had got wind of the fate of *The Falklands Play* and on Monday 29 September he published the story on the front page of *Free Nation*, the journal of the Freedom Association. The next day it got front-page treatment from the *Daily Mail* and the *Evening Standard*: it was presented as a blatant case of an attempt at political loading by the BBC hierarchy. But the journalists had also got hold of the fact that *Tumbledown* was in the works, that Michael Grade had approved a budget far in excess of the £390,000 per hour which was the norm at the time, and moreover that this 'left-wing ... subversive ... anti-Establishment' play was scheduled to be made on January 1987 and transmitted the following October: at that time this was a possible date for the general election.

The *Daily Mail* included an interview with Charles Wood:

Is it right to ask people to die, particularly for something like the Falklands? People aren't interested in the Falklands war any more. There was a kind of jingoistic interest at the beginning, then suddenly people began to think about it seriously and felt a bit ashamed about all the flag-waving. Now there's a kind of revulsion against it.[7]

This was too much for the *Daily Mail*'s resident pundit, Paul Johnson, who thundered the next day: 'Whether they like it or not British families are obliged to fork out 58 pounds a year each to subsidize BBC pornography and propaganda.'[8]

Later that week Charles Wood wrote to *The Guardian*, now clearly aware that the long-awaited production of *Tumbledown* might well get blown out of the water by *The Falklands Play*; although presently cancelled, the latter's existence posed a threat. He changed the tone of what he had said to the *Daily Mail*, protesting that in his 'carefully written film' he had

avoided any political stance, concentrating on the courage of Robert Lawrence ... when recovering from his terrible wound ... My own attitudes to war and to the Falklands conflict have been quoted as indicative of the attitude of my script. Nothing could be further from the truth ... There is also, in my opinion, a real danger that the BBC will cancel our film altogether to show its new-broom 'lack of bias'.[9]

Fearing the BBC position that production had simply been delayed because of the impending election would be turned into cancellation, Wood had the script published by Penguin in 1987: it appeared at the same time as the much-discussed election.

Curteis did the same thing at the same time, for the same reason, with

The Falklands Play. When the latter's postponement became public, Bill Cotton issued a statement saying that 'in our professional opinion, it is not a completed commission' and that it would be 'irresponsible of the BBC to embark on a play portraying a Prime Minister in office, other serving ministers and MPs, at a time when the country is leading up to an election'.[10]

During the Tory Party Conference that autumn Peter Ibbotson, Michael Grade's Chief of Staff, told an MP that the reason for cancellation was quite simple: 'It's a terrible play, the characters are two-dimensional...'[11] Michael Grade told journalists on 2 October that the reason for cancellation was the laughably poor quality of the script.[12]

In November the Conservative MP for Langbaurgh, Richard Holt, raised the matter in the House of Commons, first with a question to the Prime Minister, then with a long contribution to the debate on Financing the BBC (Peacock Report). In December Holt asked the Minister of State for the Armed Forces what discussions were recorded between his Department and Curteis concerning the factual accuracy of the play. He was told that the playwright had visited both the Ministry and the Headquarters of Commander-in-Chief Fleet at Northwood. The Minister also mentioned that although the BBC had apparently 'banned this play, Anglia Television has expressed interest in it and many of us will be happy to see the play being made public on Anglia Television'.[13]

Curteis was preparing a dossier on his dealings with the Corporation for the Chairman, Stuart Young, when Young died. After Marmaduke Hussey was appointed as his replacement, Curteis wrote to him, but he only deflected the request to Milne. There were several exchanges between Curteis and Milne, the latter calling 'nonsense' Curteis's insistence that his staff had been guilty of 'dubious political machinations'[14] – until Hussey forced Milne to resign on 29 January 1987. The next week the *Sunday Telegraph* published an abridgement of the introduction to his script that Curteis had prepared for publication.[15] Paul Johnson mounted up again, this time in *The Spectator*:

Curteis's account exposes the shoddy way the BBC is run nowadays: its mendacity, hypocrisy and duplicity, as well as its obvious political bias. Some of the most senior officials at the BBC were involved in this sorry tale.[16]

The BBC asked the *Sunday Telegraph* for a right to reply and by 19 February Peter Goodchild had written 2,000 words. But they were not approved by the powers-that-be, and the next Sunday the paper carried a 400-word letter from Bill Cotton which called Curteis's allegations 'ridiculous'. The *Sunday Telegraph* also printed a long profile on Cotton which contained a quote from a senior colleague saying that Cotton 'was damned if he was going to allow Mrs Thatcher to get the credit for the Falklands all over again'.[17]

The articles provoked another question in the House, with a request that the BBC 'hand over the script to ITV so that it can produce the play to commemorate the successful defence of freedom'.[18]

Richard Broke meanwhile was busy assembling his budget of £1.1 million, which was to rise to £1.2 million by the time it was finished, and the film was finally shot in the autumn of 1987. No publicity material was issued during the production period, but a journalist discovered that the battle scenes were being shot on location in Wales and wrote a story for the *Sunday Express*, in October 1987, which began:

Five months after dropping a TV play about the Falklands which treated Mrs Thatcher sympathetically the BBC is secretly filming a new play by a left-wing author opposed to the Task Force.[19]

Charles Wood complained to the Press Council about this story, saying they had concocted 'a story about Ian Curteis's play being turned down and *Tumbledown* being made in preference. They even printed a photo of me with the single word "Guilt" under it.'[20] The complaint was upheld.

The winter was peaceful; but when the BBC announced the transmission date in April 1988 everyone came out of the woodwork. From April to July 1988 the press had a field day.

The *Daily Express* shouted: SHOCK FILM ON FALKLAND HERO TO BE SCREENED, while *Today* screamed: BBC SHOWS FALKLANDS CHRONICLE OF SHAME. The *Daily Mail* accurately prophesied that BBC TV was SET TO FACE THE STORMS, as leader writers sharpened their pencils, and military and defence correspondents were asked to read scripts and attend drama press conferences.[21]

On 14 April George Younger, the Defence Secretary, said that the Ministry of Defence had suggested major rewriting when it had been shown the script. As this was not done, the Ministry flatly refused any form of assistance to the BBC in the making of the film. The story of its making was rehashed in the papers: the BBC claiming the postponement from the previous year was due to budget reasons, Charles Wood saying it was because of the election.[22]

Richard Eyre gave a much-reported press conference at the National Film Theatre.

I would feel the film a failure if it's not deeply political. I am happy to say I don't think the film *is* balanced, and I hope that's considered one of its ... virtues. *Tumbledown* is meant to be viewed as drama. If it was a feature film people would

understand that you take a real story . . . and you make a piece of drama out of it . . .
Art is trying to give meaning to facts . . . In contemporary British society we have
enjoyed a period of liberal expression. The evidence is mounting that it is coming to
an end.[23]

As the book Robert Lawrence had written with his father, *When the
Fighting is Over*, was published the same day as *Tumbledown* was
transmitted – 31 May 1988 – the previous week the press was filled with
reviews, interviews and much comment. Lawrence told *The Times* on 27
May that he had decided to tell the truth about the Falklands conflict
because the public had been given a sanitised version of events. He also
wanted to show how the wounded had been treated when they returned
home. He said he was angry he had not been allowed to take part in a
victory parade in London.

The Times also interviewed his former CO, Brigadier Mike Scott, who as
a Lieutenant-Colonel led the 2nd Battalion Scots Guards against Argentine troops on Mount Tumbledown in 1982.

The underlying theme of the book is that the regiment failed to look after the
wounded. But I really cannot accept that. It makes me very sad to hear Robert
talking like this. We did all we could for the wounded.[24]

The next day the Scots Guards held a press conference to prove the
regiment had looked after its own. They had a document listing how the
regiment had catered for the needs of the forty-two soldiers wounded in the
assault. Corporals, lance-corporals and colour-sergeants, all with shattered
limbs, were wheeled on to tell their stories of being found jobs and given
loans.[25]

Journalists were busy interviewing all veterans they could trace. *The
Sunday Times* gave the book to the Corporal who was closest to Lawrence
when he was shot. He said, 'It glamourizes war, makes it more dramatic
than it was. He mentions things he could not possibly have seen.'[26]

It emerged on 30 May that the BBC were being asked to cut one scene
from the film before it was transmitted. The scene, which occurred in the
last sequence during the assault on Mt Tumbledown, showed Lawrence
passing a fellow officer: in the published script

PETER FYSHE is sitting behind a rock, shivering, looking incredibly young. He hisses
at ROBERT as he goes past: 'Don't go on, Robert. It's awful. Don't let them make
you. Shoot anyone who tries to make you . . .'
ROBERT glares at PETER FYSHE, who shuts up. ROBERT and his platoon go on.

In the next scene the sergeant explains that

Mr Fyshe back there, sorr, got caught in the back-blast of an 84-mm. Soon be out of
it. He'll be fine.[27]

The same day the BBC issued a statement: 'Our position is that *Tumbledown* is a play which speaks for itself. We have never suggested that it is a documentary or a drama-documentary.'[28]

The next day it was reported that lawyers acting for Captain James Stuart, 24, had taken last-ditch action on the day of transmission to have the scene removed. In the morning, Captain Stuart couldn't comment. 'I have to have someone from the Ministry of Defence here at my side before I can say anything,' he told reporters, but by the afternoon, presumably with a little help from the Ministry, he issued a statement:

I also fought on Tumbledown with many brave guardsmen in my platoon, as we achieved our objectives at the end of a very long and very bitterly fought battle. At no time on Tumbledown, nor at any other stage of the Falklands campaign did I say to Robert Lawrence that we should not go on or that he should shoot anyone who tried to stop him going back.[29]

The BBC said it was decided to remove the scene 'on compassionate grounds' after representations had been made. (Ten days later Lawrence and Stuart 'settled their differences on honourable terms': the 100-word reference to abandoning the assault would be removed from further editions of the best-selling book.)

So, minus twelve seconds and almost four years after its inception, *Tumbledown* was finally shown. Its audience was estimated at 10.55 million, being tenth in the week's ratings, significantly higher than the norm for serious drama. (Alan Bennett's *Talking Heads* had 4 million in the same slot.)

The reaction

Party political comment followed predictable lines: John Stokes (C Halesowen & Stourbridge) could not think why it was written and why the BBC had put it out.

I was wounded in the last war with countless others and we never thought of making a play about our experiences. I can only think that the underlying point is to undermine the sacrifices and heroism which enabled us to repossess the Falkland Islands. It is another example of the BBC stabbing the nation in the back.

Teddy Taylor (C Southend) thought it 'confused, ugly and foul-mouthed and an insult to all those who had been wounded in war and had not complained'.

Robin Corbett, the opposition spokesman on broadcasting, asked:

What is the Prime Minister afraid of? . . . It is only an authoritarian government suffering from political paranoia that is frightened of the healthy political debate this play will cause.

Jack Ashley (L Stoke-on-Trent) asked for an independent inquiry to deal with the questions that the play had raised about the treatment of the Falkland wounded:

It showed the massive gulf between what soldiers expected and what the nation was prepared to give them. There is a need for an Ombudsman to represent the armed forces.

George Foulkes (L Crannock & Doon Valley) thought it 'a very strong indictment of the Government failure to solve a dispute', while Tam Dalyell (L Linlithgow) asked for a right of reply for the services:

The Scots Guards themselves ought to be given time on television to give their side of the story . . . Many of the scenes just reminded us how unpleasant war is, not least Mrs Thatcher's war.[30]

The Times had a leading article which said that

The rest of the nation has an obligation to ensure that those who sacrifice their careers, their health or their lives are cared for as they deserve –[31]

while *The Guardian*, with a quaint idea about the habits of its readers, suggested:

Most ordinary viewers, one guesses, brewing their bedtime cocoa on Tuesday night, will have found the entire fuss incomprehensible, ridiculous.[32]

The Observer felt that

the dirty tricks campaign waged by the Army and the Ministry of Defence against Captain Robert Lawrence for daring to voice his opinions on the treatment he received after the Falklands was sadly only to be expected . . . Has the debate about broadcasting reached such a low point that a programme like this is seen as the edge of what it is politically prudent to show?[33]

The Army was commendably reticent. Journalists discovered that officers of the Scots Guards had held an excited conference afterwards, but were unable to get any juicy quotes. All enquirers were politely referred to 'the adjutant in the morning, if you don't mind, sir'.[34] But a recently retired general pragmatically opined that

We have to shove them (the wounded) into the back of our minds. Soldiers are creatures of the present. They cannot always be reminded of the consequences of war –

adding, in a line worthy of Charles Wood,

There is no such thing as a returning hero, only a returning soldier.[35]

Although *Today* found a guardsman who said Robert Lawrence was a 'good bloke',[36] other journalists talked to the anaesthetist who cared for

Lawrence in the field: he said the film was wrong – 'Five times over';[37] and the Drill Sergeant who pushed Lawrence's wheelchair to St Paul's also said the film was wrong; Lawrence had been in the front row of the transept aisle.[38]

The Vox Pop response was as predictable as that of the parliamentarians. The *Daily Mail* interviewed Mrs Dorothy French, 62, of Gosport, Hampshire, whose son survived the shelling of *HMS Antrim*. She said she was 'disgusted. I feel the whole story was an insult to the brave lads who fought for this country.' The newspaper also spoke to pensioner Mr Fred Berrisford, 69, from Stoke-on-Trent, who lost two limbs fighting in North Africa in 1943. 'The fellow, like me, joined the service to fight. He knew the possible consequences.'[39]

Not only were the 'facts' of the film challenged. To explain away his allegations, medical opinion was mobilised to prove that the present Robert Lawrence was not the man he had been before. Dr Thomas Stuttaford, in *The Times*, suggested:

Robert Lawrence went into action on Tumbledown as a respected platoon commander ... his bravery before he was wounded marked him out as an exceptional soldier. That man was the old Robert Lawrence before an Argentine high velocity bullet remodelled his psyche as thoroughly as a stroke may alter an older man's ... Whether a BBC producer should make a political point based on the memory and feelings of somebody who has suffered such severe brain damage is questionable.[40]

Other neurologists and psychiatrists wrote to *The Times* pointing out it was 'meaningless to "blame" Mr Lawrence' for what he was now saying and that 'survivors feel anger, violence, depression'.[41]

The reviews naturally divided on predictable lines, although sometimes there were differences of opinion within the same paper. The *Evening Standard* editorialised that the film was 'technically superb, harrowing, unsentimental' – while its reviewer found it 'very long and often tedious ... it appeared as if the cast of *Platoon* were lost on a set for *Dr Who*'.[42]

While the *Mail on Sunday* thought the script 'marvellously self-refracting'[43] the *Daily Mail* proclaimed it

A failure, this ghoulish film. It lacked focus and direction and failed to deliver any kind of comprehensible message one way or the other ... Mr Eyre's political message that the war was wrong may have been lost by this ghoulish fascination with the pathology of injuries.[44]

The Times thought it 'fiercely compelling watching and the greatest anti-recruitment commercial since Yorkshire TV's *The Falklands War: The Untold Story*'.[45] The *New Statesman* felt that Charles Wood's 'own knowledge of military matters chimes with what Robert Lawrence reports:

he tells what he has been told, dispassionately but with the enthusiast's eye for an illuminating detail'.⁴⁶ *The Scotsman* called it 'masterly. *Tumbledown* is subversive in the way that Wilfred Owen's trench poetry or Britten's War Requiem or *Journey's End* are subversive. It tells about war and the pity of war.'⁴⁷

The *pièce de résistance* came in the *Daily Telegraph*, who asked their Military Correspondent, John Keegan, to watch it. He soon spotted the reason for Lawrence's behaviour.

The demythologising of the Falklands has begun. The film resembles a string of glossy commercials for sports cars, for Laura Ashley country house living, for Marmite, for the BTA and so on . . . In his book Robert Lawrence reveals attitudes that should have been extirpated in his training as an officer. He shows self-centredness, coarseness of language and manners and contempt for the values of others, which an officer is taught to overcome. As it happens he passed through Sandhurst when its course had been reduced to six months . . . The *Tumbledown* controversy should warn the BBC that the attitudes of its programme makers which they propagate at no risk to themselves in comfortable offices should not lightly be cast into the balance against the legitimate pride of veterans and the grief of the bereaved.⁴⁸

This provoked some fun from Alan Bennett:

I was interested to see that your military correspondent had been put up to review *Tumbledown*. Is this to be a precedent? Can we now expect your architectural correspondent to be reviewing *The Master Builder* and your transport correspondent *A Streetcar Named Desire*?⁴⁹

The correspondence columns of the *Daily Telegraph* were awash with indignation, as personal, political, and practical points were made.

What kind of people made Tumbledown? They must be sick.

Dignity was the one thing conspicuously lacking.

Robert Lawrence suffers from two major drawbacks – a wounded hero complex and self-pity.⁵⁰

Physiotherapists from St Thomas's Hospital were reported as having written directly to Richard Eyre demanding an apology for being portrayed as patronising, abusive, negligent and even sadistic.⁵¹

The Times had the thunderers of the old brigade. General Sir John Hackett, writing from the Cavalry & Guards Club:

A signal disservice is being done to the Scots Guards, one of the British Army's most distinguished regiments, outstanding in performance on the battle field, and, as is common in great fighting regiments, well known for its concern over the well-being of all members of the regimental family. It has been attacked by an ex-officer badly wounded in the Falklands in writings and public utterances which have saddened many by their insensitivity, arrogance and inaccuracy.

This is a good young man gone sour ... Not a few would have been grateful for a small fraction of the 130,000 pounds ... Robert Lawrence was handed out from charity to salve his wounds.[52]

And distraught mothers: Mrs Rosemary Calder-Smith wrote to *The Times*:

As the true-life mother of 'Sophie' portrayed in last night's film of *Tumbledown* I am saddened and disappointed at the exploitation of unquestioned bravery – exploitation solely for the financial benefit of Robert Lawrence himself. Nothing was re-enacted or mentioned of the unfailing support and encouragement which my daughter gave to him during his first months home from the Falklands and which undoubtedly gave him the will and the determination to live and to make the amazing recovery he has since made. The pressures on *her* were enormous and she spent every possible moment of every day at his bedside. She was portrayed as nothing more than a feelingless sex kitten ... I take great exception to this, having seen at first hand the constant support she gave to Robert whilst under a terrible strain in her own life ...
I suggest that the powers that be in future look deeper into the background of potential officers in the Brigade of Guards before recruiting.[53]

The *Sunday Express* was soon onto her daughter, Victoria Calder-Smith, reporting she was

outraged at the way I was presented as an uncaring loose woman ... A lot of it was pure invention. I *was* in bed with Robert as they showed in the play. But they really spiced up the dialogue.[54]

When some weeks later Richard Broke revealed that Miss Calder-Smith had been shown the script by Robert Lawrence before transmission and had approved it, her mother merely said, 'As far as I'm concerned the matter is over.'[55]

In July *The Times* reported a BBC crackdown on TV drama that mixes fact and fiction. Marmaduke Hussey, said to have been 'deeply affected' by Ms Calder-Smith's letter,

has signalled his concern at the hurt and suffering which can be caused to friends and relatives of people portrayed in such programmes, known as faction. *Tumbledown* raised issues about drama based on real life which the BBC will have to consider seriously.[56]

In August *Tumbledown* won the Prix Italia for Drama with Special TV qualities. It went on to win the Best Single Drama award for 1988 from the Royal Television Society, the Broadcasting Press Guild and BAFTA, the latter award being denounced by Ivor Stanbrook, the Tory MP for Orpington, as 'biased and politically motivated'.[57]

Meanwhile *The Falklands Play* remained unproduced. After Anglia it went to HTV who negotiated a detailed contract with Ian Curteis, but failed to sell the idea to the network committee. The rights were then taken by Primetime who offered it to the BBC as part of the 25 per cent quota from independent producers. In 1990 it was turned down without explanation.

Tumbledown: the thing itself

The story of Lawrence's war is told in flashback. The framing device is lunch at George and Helen Stubbs's country house. Robert drives his friend Hugh in a sports car in an opening reminiscent of the opening of *Lawrence of Arabia*. During the lunch we see:

Robert commanding the Tower of London Guard at the Ceremony of the Keys ('Public duties,' he spits out afterwards while enviously watching television news reporting of the Marines and Paras embarking for the Falklands)...

Drilling his squad on the Embankment in American commercial fashion ('Ain't no sense in looking down, Ain't no discharge on the ground')...

Getting drunk in a bar the night before the embarkation: being woken by Hugh early next morning as he oversleeps in bed with Sophie, his girl-friend...

Lying on a stretcher, wounded, with his brain bubbling out of his head ('the buggers think I'm dead')...

Giving the kiss of life to a soldier who collapses from the cold while digging trenches after they have arrived. The soldier vomits. Robert spits it out: 'You rotten bastard, Saltemarsh.'

Complaining while waiting to be operated on ('Look here I've been waiting for four hours... And it's bloody cold waiting out there in the corridor'). The surgeons work on his brain...

Being transported home on a hospital ship, imagining a nurse is an Argentinian soldier trying to strangle him...

His father, John Lawrence, being told at Lord's where he works by a Colonel that his son is seriously ill. Both men are close to tears.

On the ship a violent Ramboesque war film is on the video until a doctor has it turned off. Robert suddenly breaks out laughing: 'Oh, God, watch out. I'm going to have my first shit since Tumbledown.'

His parents get a phone call, via radio, from Robert saying he will be arriving at Brize Norton. On the airfield there is much confusion as to who

7 *Lieutenant Robert Lawrence (L) getting to know Colin Firth who is to play him in the quasi-documentary recreation of an aspect of the Falklands campaign: Charles Wood's* Tumbledown. *BBC 1988*

is on what plane. A wounded officer meets his wife, shouting 'Get the car! Get me away from here!'

John and Jean Lawrence see Robert in hospital. He keeps saying, 'It wasn't worth it.' His father gets the Colour Sergeant to prove to Robert that all his soldiers weren't killed in the battle.

His girl-friend and his brothers visit him.

At the foot of his bed a group of doctors discuss what hit him. They studiously ignore Robert's continued attempts to contribute.
'Bloody doctors! Talk to me!'
The doctor does so: 'Might I remind you, young man, that I am a lieutenant colonel in the RAMC and . . . Queen's Regulations still apply to you, you know, shot or not.'

'You can take your rank and Queen's Regs and you can stuff them up your big fucking arse. Talk to me.'

His father rejoices when Robert starts eating after an operation: 'Double egg and chips ... then another helping. How's that?'

A young doctor tells Robert he will never walk properly again. Robert tells him to piss off! At two physiotherapists trying to teach him to sit in a wheelchair he screams, 'Do you know what it's like to kill someone? Bits come off them! Bits!'

When he can use a wheelchair, with much effort and continual bashing into objects, he leaves the hospital and gets a taxi to the King's Road. A friend finds him and his father takes him back. 'I won't tell your mother.' A woman doctor reads him the riot act. Robert retorts, 'There is no way you are going to tell me off! No way!'

At the memorial service in St Paul's he is sat at the back behind a cameraman. We hear the TV commentary reverentially listing the numbers of soldiers, sailors and airmen killed.

A black physiotherapist gleefully teaches him to use his limbs. 'How would you raise your hat to lady? Now, hands clasped. That's a start. Left foot, right foot ... Oh man, you do look a mess.'

His brothers take him to stay the night with Sophie. Afterwards she tells him, 'Robert, that's the last time.' Robert says, 'Look, I've made a mess in the bed ... Hope you don't expect me to apologise.'

He is taken to a rehabilitation unit who are not expecting him. After a run-in with the first doctor to examine him ('Listen, doctor, test this fist. It's just about to give you your first fucking flying lesson'), he is seen by a Major who asks him, 'What is it like to kill?'
'You push the thing in and nothing happens. Mine broke off. I had to kill him with the broken end of it, stabbing and stabbing at him, and he was shouting at me, talking all the time ... He said "please" in English.'

Robert, wearing a blazer and panama, meets the regiment when it returns to Chelsea barracks. The colonel says he has been recommended for the Military Cross and adds:
'I think the thing that has delighted me most is the fact that you saluted me correctly while wearing a panama.'
'I looked it up, sir.'
The colonel leaves. Some of the soldiers come over. One says, 'Fuck it! Why you? Of all the pricks in this battalion, why you?'

The film ends with a ten-minute sequence showing the assault on Mt Tumbledown. Robert stabs the frightened soldier with his broken bayonet until he is still and picks up his rifle. In silhouette on the top of a hill he brandishes the two rifles – 'Isn't this fun?' – as he is shot.

The final credits come up over the face of Robert wearing the panama.

Of the published screenplay, 20 per cent wasn't filmed. One sequence on board the Queen Elizabeth II as the regiment sailed to the Falklands was cut on grounds of cost. Others, mainly towards the end, appear to have gone on grounds of length or repetition. A speech about the bureaucratic hurdles that had to be overcome so he could drive again was cut.[58] Sally, a therapist who tried to get him to do woodwork, also went (she got the same treatment as the others – 'You silly bitch' – 'You simpering wet cow!'),[59] as did the hospital visit of a beautiful Swedish girl who brings him pornographic magazines and slides her hand under the coverlet.[60]

This fragmented structure enables Wood to gain sympathy for the most unsympathetic of heroes by presenting only the minimum of the pre-battle gung-ho warrior and keeping the most Ramboesque image for the end. First we are confronted with the hard-done-by victim of mindless bureaucracy and inefficiency, guaranteed to get a response from anyone who has had any dealings with an NHS Hospital or Social Security office in Thatcherite Britain. It enables him to have the discussion about the emotional problems of stabbing a man to death before we are shown the butchery. Given the tenacious qualities of Robert Lawrence we would clearly have viewed the ordeal differently had the first 20 minutes simply shown the ruthless young warrior going about his trade with such obvious enjoyment. It also constantly juxtaposes the physically whole body of the youth who went to war with the appalling disablement that followed.

The strength and weakness of *Tumbledown* lie in the character of the protagonist: energetic he may be, but attractive or admirable he is not. The anger which is constantly expressed in Colin Firth's extraordinary performance may be quite justified but it hardly makes for complexity: the action of the film forces us to consider the nature of heroism. It doesn't come from the hero himself, comfortable with military clichés and Sloany friends. The successful soldier in this film is presented as an unthinking trained killer with surface manners and no emotional maturity. What he has to do he clearly does well, and Wood rightly poses the questions about the relationship to society of the men who are paid to protect it and yet are in some ways totally alienated from it by their disruptive behaviour; but does this make for a dramatically complex hero? This man never comes to terms with the fact that he lost almost half his brain for nothing.

In his stage play *Dingo* (1967), which Wood quotes in his introduction, he had for his anti-hero a reluctant soldier, a mere squaddie whose ability to kill went hand in glove with his ability to survive, a man who singularly failed to subscribe to the values of the Establishment, but who was supremely human and asserted this humanity against the world around him. Robert Lawrence, without the doubts and self-awareness even of a Troilus, armed only with the arrogance of Achilles, is ultimately two-dimensional.

What is interesting is what his story throws up about the society in which he lives. Here Wood is masterly. Being anti-war but pro-soldier enables him to write short but sharp scenes from the inside, with many telling details. The quality of the writing gives actors superb opportunities, and under Richard Eyre's direction they are all taken. It is surprising just how little screen time it takes for the cameos to bite. As the parents, David Calder and Barbara Leigh-Hunt reign supreme; they are also given the best single shot of the film: the long walk into camera as they emerge from the first meeting with their wounded son, down a covered corridor between the blocks of the hospital. He is fighting back the tears. She is very quiet. Indeed, it is one of the few shots which has any visual distinction to it at all, where what happens in the frame actually has some correlation with the emotional movement inside the characters. For the rest it is a case of straightforward television shooting of talking heads: except for what appears to be a striving towards the mythic.

There are a couple of shots of Lawrence sitting on the prow of a ship, shot in black and white and looking like the poster for a British 1950s film about the Second World War. These shots relate directly to what Lawrence is thinking (the first comes while he performs the ceremonial duties at the Tower) and appear to express his wish fulfilment: Lawrence as a Boys' Own Paper hero of the 1930s. There is another shot, interposed seven times during the second hour of the film, of a back-lit soldier, wearing his framed back-pack and carrying a rifle, moving slowly as a guitar strums. Unrelated to the visual design of the rest of the film, it seems like a monster cut adrift from arctic lands. The monolithic rhythm contrasts with Lawrence's relentless energy so it appears as an author's comment on his subject: but signifying what?

The received wisdom now is that the BBC did the better play when confronted with a choice in 1986, and that ultimately it became a question of money. As both productions required double budgets the obvious solution (do them both) was not available. Such a view assumes a personification of the BBC as an enlightened individual making artistic judgements. It hides the enormous amount of infighting, for a variety of reasons – many to do with self-interest, protecting one's turf, looking for promotion, etc. – that went on as battle-lines were drawn. There is little doubt that many would have liked to have seen *The Falkland Play* done.

To the BBC it may have been a choice because of the subject-matter, but the plays were hardly equatable (any more than *Tumbledown* was with the documentary on Simon Weston, whose face was savagely burned in the attack on *Sir Galahad*, although it appeared so to one BBC executive who read the script: 'We've done this already'). Curteis was not trying to write the same sort of play as Wood. *The Falklands Play* ends in the House of Commons (the eleventh scene to be set there).

> BENN (*rising*): Will the Prime Minister publish a full analysis of the costs in life, equipment and money of this tragic and unnecessary war?
>
> PM: The Right Honourable gentleman calls it an unnecessary war. Tragic it may have been, but may I point out to him – (*she suddenly flings out her arm and points at him, shouting: it is her true moment of celebration and triumph*) – he would not enjoy the freedom of speech that he puts to such excellent use, unless people had been prepared to fight for it! *The House roars like the sea. Freeze frame on her triumphal gesture.*[61]

Here Curteis is trying to make a dramatic climax using a line he has not written himself, but selected from the acres of material he has meticulously researched. One has some sympathy with him for the laborious dramaturgy he has to employ. He is not a free agent, able to develop his characters at will and construct multi-faceted scenes: he is bound by what happened. So the only interest of such scenes lies in what is said – does the lid come off real garbage? – is some new twist of policy or motive revealed? In *Suez* he had the infamous, and much-denied, meeting of Foreign Ministers in the suburbs of Paris. But *The Falklands Play* has no such nuggets in it.

Charles Wood feels no such constraints in his attitude to character and finding dramatic scenes which will be revealing of the currents beneath the surface. His play could have been written with other names. Where he is limited is only by the broad outline of the story itself and the sensibility of the central character. He writes dialogue that actors can get their teeth into, that does not imprison them into a series of simplistic impulses. Although Curteis says he doesn't want lookalike actors to play the parts, whoever takes them would be severely limited to a recreation of surface reality, which is a severe handicap in drama.

Of course, by using Lawrence Charles Wood attracted a far greater audience for his work than if it had been a totally fictional piece bursting on an unsuspecting viewing public. By this device he entered the market-place and so got a much greater hearing for his work. (Jack Ashley didn't get the inquiry into the treatment of the wounded that he asked for, but without

Tumbledown would he have even asked in the first place?) Unfortunately, as a result, Wood condemned his work to be seen in a highly charged and politicised atmosphere in which many of the onlookers were able comfortably to keep hold of their prejudices. By keeping the names, by appearing to deal with facts, he allowed people to discredit the work. Some of the facts were 'wrong' so the whole thing could be discounted.

It is ironic that one of the most political and Brechtian of modern English playwrights should reach his largest audience with a piece that while exploring his favourite territory – the dichotomy of being pro-soldier and anti-war – would be so compromised by being set in the no man's land of faction.

Tumbledown

Based on the experiences of Lieutenant Robert Lawrence MC

Transmission date: 30 May 1988 (BBC1)   Repeated 8 June 1992 (BBC1)

Cast

Robert Lawrence	Colin Firth
Hugh Mackessac	Paul Rhys
John Lawrence	David Calder
Jean Lawrence	Barbara Leigh-Hunt
Sophie Martin-Wells	Emma Harbour
Nick Lawrence	Rupert Baker
Christopher Lawrence	Jack Fortune
George Stubbs	Roddy Maude-Roxby
Helen Stubbs	Ann Bell
Louise Stubbs	Sophie Thompson
Prothero	Dan Hildebrand
Sgt Brodrick	Tam Dean Burn
Lumpy	Mark Williams
Fraser	Ian Mitchie
Saltemarsh	Paul Higgins
O'Rourke	Stewart Porter
Lieut. Colonel Bill Kirke	Timothy Carlton
Adjutant Stewart Inglis	Mark Wing-Davey
Major Peter Walsh	Robin Daiglish
Major Alistair Tolly	Andrew McCullough
Lt Peter Fyshe	Edward Rawle-Hicks
The Noble Lord	Charles Millham
Harry Hebers	Ben Cole
Terry Knapp	Clive Russell
Surgeon	James Griffiths
Brigade Officer	David Conville

Group Captain	Edwin Richfield
Squadron Leader Wentworth	Brian Hall
Major/Rehabilitation Centre	Peter Postlethwaite
Elderly Man	Charles Lamb
RAF Officer	Richard Owens
Welsh Lady	Arbel Jones
Welshman	Sean Scanlan
Air Commodore	Tony Caunter
Colour Sergeant	Ian McColl
Lt Colonel RAMC	Edward Lyon
Nurse Wendy	Victoria Hasted
Major Newman	Angela Morant
CSM Brown	Murray Ewan
Mrs Prothero	Wendy Nottingham
Young Doctor	Andrew Livingston
1st Night Nurse	Sharon Clarke
2nd Night Nurse	Leila Bertrand
Angie	Lisa Tarbuck
Tricia	Felicity Montagu
Hospital Chaplain	Roy Spencer
Benny	Winston Crooke
Cabby	Steven Law
Yeoman Warder	Alan White
Tug	George Irving
Mandy	Marian McLoughlin
Phyllida	Serena Gordon
Argentinian soldiers	Francisco Morales
	Martin Garfield

Technical and production

Script Editor	Sarah Curtis
Production Manager	Martin Hutchings
Assistant Producer	Tim Ironside-Wood
Designer	Geoff Powell
Costume Designer	Michael Burdle
Make-Up Designer	Shauna Harrison
Medical Adviser	Roger Prior
Sound Recordist	Graham Ross
Stunt Arrangers	Gareth Milne
	Tip Tipping
Continuity	Marissa Cowell
Photography	Andrew Dunn
Editor	Ken Pearce
Dubbing Mixer	Ken Hains
Music	Richard Hartley
Songs by	The Corries
Produced by	Richard Broke
Directed by	Richard Eyre

Notes

1 *The Guardian*, 4 August 1984.
2 Charles Wood, *Introduction to 'Tumbledown'*.
3 *Suez-1956*, BBC1, 25 November 1979: repeated BBC2, 20 and 21 November 1981.
4 Ian Curteis, *Introduction to 'The Falklands Play'* (1987).
5 *Ibid.*
6 *Ibid.*
7 *Daily Mail*, interview with Charles Wood, 30 September 1986.
8 *Daily Mail*, 1 October 1986.
9 *The Guardian*, 4 October 1986.
10 Curteis, *Introduction to 'The Falklands Play'*.
11 *Daily Telegraph*, 16 September 1986.
12 *Ibid.*, 3 October 1986.
13 Hansard, *Report* for 9 December 1986.
14 Curteis, *Introduction to 'The Falklands Play'*.
15 *Sunday Telegraph*, 8 February 1987.
16 *The Spectator*, 13 February 1987.
17 *Sunday Telegraph*, 22 February 1987.
18 Hansard, *Report* for 21 July 1987.
19 *Sunday Express*, 4 October 1987.
20 *TV Today*, 24 March 1988.
21 *Daily Express, Today, Daily Mail*, 13 April 1988.
22 *Sunday Telegraph*, 17 April 1988.
23 *Sunday Times*, 29 May 1988.
24 *The Times*, 27 May 1988.
25 28 May 1988.
26 *Sunday Times*, 29 May 1988.
27 Wood, *Introduction to 'Tumbledown'*, 76.
28 *The Times*, 1 June 1988.
29 *Ibid.*, 2 June 1988.
30 *Ibid.*, 1 June 1988.
31 *Ibid.*, 2 June 1988.
32 *The Guardian*, 2 June 1988.
33 *The Observer*, 5 June 1988.
34 *The Times*, 1 June 1988.
35 *Daily Telegraph*, 4 June 1988.
36 *Today*, 1 June 1988.
37 *Sunday Times*, 29 May 1988.
38 *Daily Express*, 1 June 1988.
39 *Daily Mail*, 2 June 1988.
40 *The Times*, 1 June 1988.
41 *The Times*, 4 June 1988.
42 *Evening Standard*, 2 June 1988.
43 *Mail on Sunday*, 5 June 1988.
44 *Daily Mail*, 1 June 1988.
45 *The Times*, 1 June 1988.
46 *New Statesman*, 10 June 1988.
47 *The Scotsman*, 1 June 1988.

48 *Daily Telegraph*, 1 June 1988.
49 *Ibid.*, 4 June 1988.
50 *Ibid.*, 3 June 1988.
51 *Daily Telegraph*, 6 June 1988.
52 *The Times*, 3 June 1988.
53 *Ibid.*, 4 June 1988.
54 *Sunday Express*, 5 June 1988.
55 *The Times*, 29 August 1988.
56 *Ibid.*, 13 July 1988.
57 *Evening Standard*, 22 March 1989.
58 Wood, *Introduction to 'Tumbledown'*, 71.
59 *Ibid.*, 67.
60 *Ibid.*, 57.
61 Curteis, *Introduction to 'The Falklands Play'*, last scene.

Select bibliography

Books

Curteis, Ian, *The Falklands Play: a Television Play* (London: Hutchinson, 1987)
Lawrence, Robert G, *When the Fighting is Over: A Personal Story of the Battle for Tumbledown Mountain and Its Aftermath* (London: Bloomsbury, 1988)
Wood, Charles, *Tumbledown: a Screenplay* (Harmondsworth: Penguin, 1987)

Reviews/criticisms (other than those quoted in the essay)

Brooks, Richard, 'Writer attacks "Leftist" BBC', *The Observer*, 30 August 1987
Curteis, Ian, 'Play that didn't make the grade' (letter), *The Observer*, 27 December 1987
Eyre, Richard, 'Langham Diary', *The Listener*, 17 September 1987, 12
Fox, Robert, 'Battle for life', *Radio Times*, 28 May–3 June 1988, 10–13
Hebert, Hugh, 'By the left and right to war', *The Guardian*, 4 July 1987
Hislop, Ian, 'I was there', *The Listener*, 9 June 1988
Mackintosh, Gordon, 'Putting a soldier together again', *The Guardian*, 19 May 1988

9 *Four Days in July* (Mike Leigh)

PAUL CLEMENTS

Four Days in July was made for the BBC in 1983–4 and has been shown once on British television. When they were working together on the Hampstead Theatre production of *Ecstasy* in 1979, the Irish actor Stephen Rea suggested to Mike Leigh that he should make a film in Belfast. Four years later the BBC agreed to allow Leigh a one-year schedule for the making of a film set in the city: six months for personal research, and six for production, rehearsal and shooting. The resources and facilities of the BBC in Belfast were made available to him, and he was at liberty to go where he wished. As with all of Leigh's previous projects for the Corporation, there was at this stage no structure, no storyline and no script. It was understood that the substance of the film would grow from Leigh's research and through subsequent improvisation with his actors.

He confesses that his starting-point was ignorance. 'It's not unusual at all, but I do feel the urge to make films about certain things because of a sense of ignorance about them. It's a way of finding out about things, of investigating them, really.'[1] *Four Days in July* is linked generically to the films he made immediately before and after it, *Meantime* (1983), which was made for Channel 4, and *High Hopes* (1988) for the cinema. It would be too much to group them as a trilogy, but they have in common a deep and compassionate concern with the social realities of ordinary experience in the Thatcher era. *Meantime* focuses on the corrosiveness of unemployment and *High Hopes* on the devastation in human terms of the values of the free-rein market economy and the problem of resistance in the moral vacuum which went with it. In this sense the films are overtly political, arising from Leigh's need to define and express his preoccupations during that bleak period. Other than this general sense of his needing to express what he was feeling, he had 'no idea' what the film would be.

Leigh is disposed to say little about his six-month period of research in Northern Ireland.

8 *Mike Leigh directing some members of the cast during the shooting in Belfast of his* Four
Days in July. *BBC 1985*

I didn't only potter around the North, but also the South. I pursued a lot of
contacts. I met a lot of people. I met some very bizarre people, I met some very
dangerous people, I met some very nice people. I did a lot of reading. I watched
everything on tape or on film I could get my hands on, so that I was able to watch the
whole of *The Troubles* series, the whole of *Ireland*, the Jeremy Isaacs series . . ., but
mainly I just spent a lot of time listening to people telling me, from both sides, and
telling me and telling me and arguing.

A sidelight on the research is offered by Antony Sher. He describes a meal
with Leigh, Alison Steadman and John Shrapnel in Rudland and Stubbs
Fish Restaurant, Smithfield, in December 1983.

Mike is just back from Belfast where he's been researching for his latest film. He
looks tired and grey. 'Northern Ireland bears as much relation to life here as
Ancient Tibet.' We all get worked up about the recent attack on a church, where the
congregation were mowed down by machine guns. 'Murder, murder!' cry Ali and I.
'It's not murder, it's war,' says Mike with the weariness of one who's had it
drummed into him for weeks and weeks.[2]

Setting Leigh free to research in Northern Ireland for six months to
produce a film of which no one knew anything, least of all the director, did
of course involve artistic risks, but Leigh had already created an impressive

body of work by the time he began work on *Four Days in July*. Between 1973 and 1982 he had made six full-length films for BBC television – *Hard Labour* (1973), *Nuts in May* (1976), *The Kiss of Death* (1976), *Who's Who* (1978), *Grown-Ups* (1980) and *Home Sweet Home* (1982). He had also made a handful of shorts – *The Five Minute Films* (1975) – as well as two half-hour plays, *The Permissive Society* (1975) and *Knock for Knock* (1976), and a studio version of his 1977 stage hit *Abigail's Party*. It had been widely recognised for some time by BBC producers that Leigh's unconventional method of creating the material for drama through improvisation was in fact a rigorous and disciplined artistic process which had created work of great individuality and distinction.

Nevertheless, it was a courageous decision to support Leigh's intention to make a film set in Ulster. One principal characteristic of his work is the manner in which his characters embody in the actions of their daily lives the quintessential particularities of their social background and class experience – the commonest popular judgement on Leigh's work is that his characters seem to be 'real'. Another primary feature is the way that he sets contrasting groups of characters side by side so that they become known to the audience in parallel tension with each other. This is clearly shown in *Grown-Ups* where Mandy and Dick, the working-class couple, live in a council house next door to the middle-class schoolteachers, Ralph and Christine Butcher. The entanglement of the two worlds of these characters invites the audience constantly to form and modify its opinions and judgements through cross-referral and comparison.

It was therefore predictable that the characters Leigh created for this film would express through their existence the realities of the polarised culture of Ulster. At the time when *Four Days in July* was made, the problem of Ulster was widely covered on British television as a security matter, but rarely as a political issue. Such discussion as there was was conducted in news and current affairs programmes, but hardly at all through the medium of television drama. The prevailing tone of television coverage suggested that a tiny minority of vicious and deranged 'madmen' and 'animals' were conducting a barbaric campaign of terror in a moral and political vacuum while a helpless population stood by, aghast at the atrocities taking place in their midst. With the emphasis on Ulster as a security problem, the broadcast media inevitably projected the government/Unionist viewpoint of the Protestant majority. Nothing in Leigh's previous work would have suggested to the BBC either that he would restrict his investigation to a single perspective or that he would conform to the prevailing tone.

It is helpful to our understanding of how he works to compare Leigh's method with the working process of the solo playwright. Leigh's rehearsal period is divided into two phases: pre-rehearsal and structuring. Pre-rehearsal is roughly equivalent to the stage at which the solo playwright makes notes on subject-matter, character, action and other dramatic elements and begins to clarify his or her dramatic statement. Structuring corresponds roughly to the writing of the first draft of the play and to the subsequent stage at which the dramatist passes the play to the director and actors for its full realisation in rehearsal and production.

The principal difference between Leigh and the solo writer is that Leigh's method involves the actors in the process from the very beginning and that, as the deviser of his works, he combines the roles of writer and director. The collaborative partnership between Leigh and his actors does not, however, imply group authorship. His method, which evolved through a series of stage plays created in the sixties and early seventies and continues to evolve in his current work, is to express himself as a dramatist and film-maker by making rich, creative use of the possibilities of acting.

In pre-rehearsal Leigh creates the world of the play. Beginning with a series of individual meetings with each of his actors he asks them to describe, at leisure, all the people they know. From these lists of 'originals' Leigh will eventually select one person upon whom each actor will base a character. Working alone with each actor, Leigh then sets about bringing the original into existence through the medium of acting.

In a series of what Leigh calls 'figurative' improvisations the actor begins at first to impersonate the original in sequences which unfold in real time and in chronological order. The actor's experience of the original thus accumulates in an orderly way. Through a meticulously detailed process of analysis, during which the actor is required to discriminate between how he is playing the character and the character's own experience of his unfolding life, the reproduction of the original metamorphoses into the creation of an independent character – a free-standing artefact. The distinction between the manner of the acting and the being of the character is crucial. It avoids the possible pitfalls of the actor's over-identification with the character and develops a healthy sense of distance between *what* is being done and *how* it is being done. It also makes it possible for these two activities to be worked at separately. Thus, the manner in which the actor plays the character – the character's external presentation, if you like – can be modified without interfering either with the narrative content of his experience or his inner life.

The transformation from original into character is achieved by means which are analogous to the way in which a piece of sculpture emerges from the raw material of the medium from which it is created. The raw material from which Leigh and the actor begin is a real person: an observable complex of behaviour, experience, feeling, action, thought and motivation.

The actor will, therefore, 'be' that person in a solo sustained improvisation until Leigh asks him to come out of character and to discuss what occurred. How did the character feel about what he read in a newspaper, for example, or what he heard on the radio? Or, why did he do what he did when he angrily threw down a book? By analysing the inner drives and conditions of the character as they become manifest through the acting and by rooting the subsequent improvisations organically in the events and discoveries of those preceding them, Leigh is able to move the actor away from a photographic reproduction of the original. From the material of the original there emerges a new being with its own carefully explored external behaviour and inner life. Leigh is the author of this character.

When Leigh is satisfied that each character is thoroughly grounded and solidly made, he brings the actors together for the first time. A common fiction is agreed upon to gather the group of characters into a feasible shared reality. There then begins a further series of improvisations, which are also conducted within the disciplines of real and chronological time, in which he explores the possibilities of the characters' interactions. This process is multi-layered. The actor is exploring how he plays his character; the character is becoming modified by the accumulation of experience and memory; and the interactions are generating stories and the possibilities for further stories. At no point during pre-rehearsal, however, does Leigh concern himself with the narrative end-product. His focus is on the investigation of the potentialities of relationships: developing the characters; deepening their concrete embodiment of the world which they inhabit; and exploring both their behaviour and its physical expression, in a manner consistent with the emerging stylistic conception of the overall piece.

The end of pre-rehearsal is determined by the production schedule of the work on which he is engaged. In the preparation of a stage play with a thirteen-week schedule, pre-rehearsal might occupy seven weeks followed by a further six weeks of structuring. Structuring is setting out on a fresh set of improvisations following a simple scenario devised by Leigh. The scenario might consist of things which have already happened in previous improvisations, of things which Leigh wants to see happen, or of a combination of both. The events of such scenarios are usually baldly descriptive: A and B are at home; C comes to call; A goes out and so on. The scenario itself is, of course, deeply informed by Leigh's knowledge and understanding of his characters and their world. From the scenario the play is created. The final stage is further improvisation to refine the draft.

In the case of film, pre-rehearsal continues right up to the beginning of shooting. Once shooting begins, Leigh and the actors work on structuring at night, stockpiling material to be shot the following day. In both theatre and film, in these later stages there is as much freedom for new material to be admitted and new insights incorporated as there has been earlier in the process.

A brief, functional description of how Mike Leigh works does not, of course, adequately convey any sense of the meaning and significance of what he does. It is an article of faith that during rehearsals the actors do not discuss their characters with each other. This is in order that the improvisations yield material which is the product only of the characters' experience of each other. As in our own lives, Leigh's characters share their innermost secrets and confess their doubts, uncertainties and hidden fears, their dreams and longings only with those to whom they are close. As a result, for most of their time they struggle with the same imperfections of human communication which beset the rest of us, and share with us the same conditions of frustration, occasional joy and, to borrow Thoreau's phrase, 'quiet desperation'.

By insisting that his actors play within what we might call the broad rules of real life, and through the minute investigation of human behaviour which is rendered accessible through this process, Leigh reproduces the surface texture of real life with uncanny accuracy. Indeed, as has already been noted, the commonest observation on the acting in his plays and films is that the characters seem 'real'. This is not a by-product of the method: it is what the method was evolved to do. For there is in Leigh's work an unmistakable central conviction that the material fabric of daily life is the most fascinating area to explore. This is because what we might rather crudely describe as ordinary or everyday life, in all its detail, is most people's experience of the world. To this instance he brings both a poetic sensibility and an exacting visual sense. The method creates characters in whom the experience of ordinary life is distilled to its essence.

Four Days in July is set in Belfast in 1984. The four days of the title, Tuesday 10 July to Friday 13 July, encompass the action of the film. It concerns two families, one Catholic and the other Protestant, living on either side of the sectarian divide in Northern Ireland. The use of religious labels does not imply that Leigh, any more than the rest of us, sees the conflict in Northern Ireland as a struggle of theology or faith; Catholic is one way of describing the republican standpoint and Protestant, the loyalist view. The Catholic couple, Eugene and his wife Colette, are awaiting the imminent arrival of their first baby. Billy and his wife Lorraine, who are also expecting their first baby any day, are the Protestants. Billy is a soldier in the Ulster Defence Regiment. Eugene is disabled from a wound caused by a stray bullet fired by British troops at joyriders five years before. The film seems simply to observe how these couples pass their time before the birth of their children. Both births occur on 12 July, 'the major feast in the Orange calendar'.[3]

Between conversations at home about family life, domestic arrangements and the troubles, Colette goes out on an (eventful) expedition to buy a second-hand pram, and she and Eugene have their windows cleaned and their lavatory repaired. Between conversations at home about family life, domestic arrangements and the troubles, Billy goes out on (uneventful) patrol, and he and Lorraine attend a street bonfire party on the night of the 11th. Both families entertain friends for a drink; both families sing in their own homes; each of the wives packs a case for her forthcoming confinement and each is fed up with the final stages of pregnancy. Both houses display their partisan icons: above Billy's bed hangs the flag of the red hand of Ulster; at the foot of Eugene's stairs is a photograph of the Pope. The men meet briefly for the first time in the hospital waiting-room. The women, after very similar experiences of labour, find themselves in adjacent beds in the maternity ward. Both babies are born well. Lorraine's son is to be called Billy 'after his daddy'; Colette's daughter will be Magraid, which she explains is 'the Irish for Margaret'.[4]

The intercutting of these parallel narratives forms almost the entire substance of the film. There is a brief sequence before the opening titles in which a group of children is seen in an alleyway. Additionally, there are two characters from outside the families' respective social circles, one of whom appears near the beginning and the other near the end. The domestic scale and low-key narrative will be immediately familiar territory to those who know Leigh's other work. The title of the film is blandly functional. Although it is set in the potentially explosive location of Belfast it contains no intrigue or adventure. There is no on-screen violence. Even the potential resonances of violence are neutralised. When, for example, Billy takes out his revolver after coming home from duty, it is only to tuck it away safely in a homely biscuit tin on the top shelf of a kitchen cupboard. Similarly, when Eugene reveals, almost incidentally, to Dixie, the droll window-cleaner, that he has been seriously wounded as a consequence of political violence on no less than three occasions in eleven years, Colette teasingly accuses him of boasting and Dixie responds to Eugene's account with a wry look and a joke: 'Apart from that you're rightly.'

As well as refusing to exploit the danger and dark fascination of his location, Leigh seems, further, to have eschewed any of those climactic domestic confrontations which in many of his other films have served both to focus and illuminate the drama. One thinks, for example, of the frenetic fight on the stairs in *Grown-Ups* or of the rancorous and bitter birthday party in *High Hopes*. It is hard to identify any full-length work by Leigh in which less of consequence seems to happen.

In the uneventfulness of *Four Days in July* lies its key. In the opening sequence the camera is trained down the length of a scruffy alleyway running between the backs of terraced houses. Three children hurry down the alley, away from the camera. There are some excited dogs about. The scene is instantly familiar and unexceptional; it could be shot in any inner-city residential area in Britain. The children pause at one of several streets which intersect the alley. Suddenly a patrol of two armoured personnel carriers crosses the alley from left to right. The children let it pass and continue on their way, the rhythm of their journey and their sense of purpose unchanged by the violently incongruous appearance of these ominous vehicles. The camera remains steadily fixed on the children. The patrol reappears behind them, this time travelling from right to left along a street parallel to the previous one. It disappears from sight and we are left with the image of the children continuing down the alley while one or two other passers-by casually cross our line of view.

This sequence sets up an immediate tension between the experience of the viewer and the experience of those whose lives are represented in the shot. The familiar urban scene is instantly reassuring: we know where we are and what we are looking at. The armoured patrol disrupts the certainty for us, but not for the children. They accept the military presence totally. Compared with the hours of news and documentary footage we have seen of violence and the consequences of violence in Northern Ireland, the opening of *Four Days in July* is commonplace, even prosaic. But where news footage by definition brings us information about things at boiling-point – and in this respect looks and feels so much like news footage from virtually any other international trouble spot that the images acquire a sort of sameness and predictability – the very coolness of this opening sequence intensifies our sense of the extraordinary thing which is happening in a recognisably British city: these children are completely at home in a state of war.

So, while nothing happens in the way of plot or dramatic action in the opening sequence of *Four Days in July*, it offers an immediately rinsed perspective on what is to follow. The film moves from the alley into a sequence of shots of the patrol vehicles moving against a background of silent industrial premises and what look like pleasant suburban streets. The heavily armed soldiers appear casual, almost bored. There is no tension. This way of life has acquired the quality of routine.

In fact, when the patrol stops to check out a suspicious vehicle, the soldiers explain to the driver that it is 'just routine'. The ramshackle van they stop is driven by the first of the film's two eccentric outsiders, a Mr McCoy, who travels with a rabbit beside him on the passenger seat because 'he goes for the other ones'. McCoy is outraged to be stopped by what we now learn is a UDR patrol.

This country's coming down with people trying to blow our heads off and you're bothering one of your own ... You know what you are, son? ... You are an Ulsterman. Do you know what it means to be an Ulsterman? An Ulster Man? Do you realise that your forefathers ... we, you and me ... are direct descendants of an ancient Ulster people? We have been here in Ulster since before the time of Jesus Christ himself. We heroes of Ulster have been defending ourselves against those so-called Irishmen for a million years. More! They're always telling us about the Plantation, us getting brought here from Scotland. Bollocks! We were here first. We came from here. We went to Scotland, and then we came back again. So it was our country in the first place. Ulster! .. That's how Scotland got its name, you know. Scottie! I don't mean like the wee dogs, now, or the hankies you blow your nose with. We had our own language once. Nothing to do with the Gaelic mumbo-jumbo. It was the language of the people of Ulster ... What about South Africa? The Somme? Where would the British people be without the Ulsterman? Who was it fought the hordes up the Khyber Pass? You see those Fenian bastards? If they don't like it here they can clear off over the border. But you see when they get there, they'll still be Ulstermen. They might not realise it but they will. They're brainwashed you see? Give them two years down there, they'll be crawling back up here, looking for our dole money, what our hard-working taxes is paying for. We're not scroungers, you know, breeding like a bunch of rabbits.

His wild version of Irish history and passages of irrational self-contradiction bring further into focus for us the fact that we are watching a war film, a theme which is sounded again when Billy and his companion, Big Billy, discuss the events of the patrol back at their barracks:

BILLY: I'd rather listen to that bucket head than them Republican shite
           boxes... Calling you Orange bastards all day...
BIG BILLY: Look at us, over trained, underused, babysitting a pack of loonies.

Billy goes on to report a conversation he has had recently with a fellow loyalist, himself an old soldier who 'fought with Monty in North Africa and that':

BILLY: He says to me, he says, how do you boys like it not being able to do
           your business in this here war? I says, what do you mean? He says,
           well, we never see you in any Republican areas. We never see you in
           Andytown, or Bogside or the Falls Road or whatever, you know. I
           said, for God's sake, sure our hands are tied behind our backs, you
           know. He said, not at all, he says, it's the Brits who do all the hard
           work. I says, let me tell you something about the Brits. I says, you get
           a load of wee cubs coming in across the water from Birmingham,
           Manchester or London, right? And they're battering down the Falls
           Road, the best laxative known to man, and they're shiting them-
           selves, they don't know what they're doing. I says, it's like Vietnam,
           you know, there's a load of Americans went to Vietnam, right? And
           they couldn't tell one gook from other. That's like the Brits over here.
           They don't know who's what or anything, you know? He says, how
           would you fancy going into them places, see? I said, bloody magic,
           you know. That's what we're waiting for. Give us a forty-eight hour

blackout, right... Forty-eight hours; no press, no television or anything you know. We'll just get in, root them out and that'll be it, no problem. Oh, he says, you'll lose a brave few men .. Bollocks! ... I told him .. We're soldiers, you know .. You join the UDR you expect to get shot at, you know. I said I didn't take this job on for the money....

BIG BILLY: Anyway, you haven't a hope in hell of getting there... It's the politicians. The sooner they start pulling their finger out of their arseholes and getting their brains out of neutral and start doing something for us, the better.

BILLY: They don't have to do anything. Look, they know fine well as soon as a wee Teig's born, the priest says, 'Go forth and multiply'. Well, in ten years' time they'll have multiplied, you know. So there'll be more of them than us, right? They'll have a head count over here, they'll have a referendum across the water, they'll sell us down the river and they'll be in that Ferry back to Westminster as quick as you like.

BIG BILLY: Sure, let them frigging go. We don't need them anyway. We can do it on our own. Independence! Set up UDI and build a proper defensive border against the Fenian State.

BILLY: Oh aye. Build a Berlin wall, or a mile wide moat, you know.

BIG BILLY: Right. And the first frigger sticks his head over the top of it: zap him!

These exchanges are remarkable for the way in which the authenticity of the acting – characterisation, speech rhythm, dialect and gesture are sharply etched – conveys us into what Leigh obviously regards as the centre of the loyalist psyche. For while Big Billy's verdict on McCoy is 'This bastard's nuts', the three men share a fundamental orientation: they belong to a beleaguered nation at war, facing betrayal on all sides and forced into an aggressively defensive posture against the Republic of Ireland and its agents – the gooks of the North. Billy's use of the analogy of Vietnam is profoundly telling.

There are other chilling indications of the state of war. When, for example, Colette opens her curtains on the morning of 11 July and rearranges a plant on the window-sill, an army foot patrol is framed in the window, and during the social banter with Brendan and Dixie, a helicopter is heard circling overhead.

The parallelism of the central section of the film is its content, contrasting the lives of the two families and their circles. While on the surface nothing happens, through the unfolding of the parallel stories Leigh reveals his perception of the profound differences between the two communities.

Time has a different quality in each of the family circles. This is pointed up by Eugene's slow, difficult movement and by Billy's restless physicality, but each of the characters in Eugene's world embodies a sense of life lived at a more leisurely pace than Billy's. The characters not only talk more, they allow themselves time almost to luxuriate in the possibilities of conversation and relationships. When Colette offers Dixie a cup of tea he protests that he has to get on with his window-cleaning round, but when Eugene, because he enjoys Dixie's company, offers the alternative of a can of Guinness he finds the time to stay and drink it: 'I'll have one while I'm standing here.'

In the given time their conversations acquire great charm and particularity. There is time for passing the time of day, for asking after family and friends, for jokes and riddles and for reminiscences. Dixie and Brendan describe in detail how they constructed a potheen still during their internment in Long Kesh. The conversation has the quality of two old POW's recalling past exploits. In the early morning of 11 July, Eugene and Colette discuss two neighbourhood families, the Devlins and the Currans, who produced forty-six children between them.

EUGENE: You'd wonder how they did it, wouldn't you?
COLETTE: What?
EUGENE: In these wee houses.
COLETTE: Sure they brought up eleven or twelve of a family in these wee houses, but they managed. And they loved them.
EUGENE: Must have been mad in the mornings all the same. For the bathroom and all.
COLETTE: Sure there were no bathrooms!
EUGENE: That's right. *(Pause)*. It's a great day, isn't it?
COLETTE: Aye. *(Pause)*. You should have seen it when the sun come up. It was magic.

Compared with the discursive tempo, languorous melody and occasional lyricism of these and other conversations in Eugene's household, the exchanges between Billy and his wife and friends, often in the same subject areas, appear staccato and often brutal:

LORRAINE: Janet had her case packed for two months before she had her wee Sammy.
BILLY: If Janet told you to jump in the Lagan, you'd jump.
LORRAINE: I can't swim.
BILLY: Well, isn't it about time you learned to swim?
LORRAINE: Well, I've tried, haven't I?
BILLY: Look, how many times have I told you, you hold your breath and you come up. You don't sink.
LORRAINE: Well, it's all right for you.
BILLY: Look, when I learned to swim, if you didn't come up, you drowned.
LORRAINE: Well, no child of mine's going to the swimming pool before the age of five.
BILLY: The bastard is, so he is.
LORRAINE: It's a wee girl, anyway.
BILLY: God forbid!

When the men of Billy's patrol gather in his house for a drink on the night of the 11th, in a scene which parallels the Dixie–Brendan reminiscence, they recall a posting on the border and the slaughter of a bullock.

BILLY: You said to me, I'm pissed off with this shite rations we're getting.
BIG BILLY: That's right. That's right.
BILLY: And then you said to me, if you could kill something you'd have it. And I says, well, you're looking at forty-two sirloin steaks over there.
BIG BILLY: So he says, you kill it, you bugger, and I'll butcher it. You see? So off your man jazz-dances across the field, he says, frig this, I'm not getting my clothes all dirty with blood, he says, so he strips off, right? So he spots a bullock halfway across the field and all I sees is this big white arsehole dancing across the field after the bullock.

The subsequent tale of the butchering of the bullock is unpleasantly told in an atmosphere of macho self-satisfaction.

In the time which the Catholic friends permit themselves, their care for each other becomes manifest. Although Brendan, the plumber, and his wife Carmel are due to be away on holiday on 12 July, Brendan finds time to repair Eugene's blocked lavatory the day before; and on the morning of their departure they will not allow Eugene and Colette to travel to hospital in an ambulance, but take them there in their van. To be fair, Billy's group is equally supportive, rushing him back to the barracks and getting him out of his equipment when the news comes that Lorraine has gone into labour a week early, but this sequence progresses at an accelerated pace and Billy's response is vehement in its expression: 'You would not believe it!' he exclaims, 'you would not believe it!'

The film's treatment of time as a different dimension for each of the two communities reveals Leigh's point of view on the separateness of the cultures which he observes in Northern Ireland. While the companionship of the Catholic group is expressed through neighbourliness and love of the folk, the Protestant group's brotherhood resides in aggression and hatred. This is revealed most clearly in the outsider characters who top and tail the central section of the film. We have already heard from the fantastical Mr McCoy. In the maternity waiting-room, Eugene and Billy encounter Mr Roper, a Protestant loyalist in whom spiritual fury has produced a kind of madness.

EUGENE: Is this your first?
ROPER: My first what?
EUGENE: Child.
ROPER: Aye it is. And it'll be the last. I'm not going through all this again. Drive you round the bend. Years of not getting to sleep at nights ... the screaming. And by the time you do get any peace you're too old to enjoy it. And the cost of raising them. The feeding and the clothing them. And whenever they do grow up, you never know. Get themselves into

> trouble. Disgrace you. What is there for them in this country anyway? Nothing!
>
> BILLY: You want to emigrate, you do.
> ROPER: Emigrate? Where?
> BILLY: Anywhere you like.
> ROPER: Sure, there's nowhere to emigrate to. Everywhere else in the world's as bad as this place.
> BILLY: Is that a fact?
> ROPER: Aye! It is! You're better off never being born at all!

The film is a poetic meditation upon nationality and culture. It draws its vitality from Leigh's perceptions of the essential spirits of the antagonists in Northern Ireland, and its coherence from the symmetry of its form. His sympathy is clearly with the Catholic side. The manner of Eugene's and Colette living embodies a greater richness of warmth and humanity than is the case with Billy and Lorraine. This is nowhere clearer than the film's reflection of the two groups' attitudes to violence. Billy's percussively articulated and aggressive anti-republicanism is contrasted with the melodious lamentation of Eugene and Colette for the maimed victims they have seen in the Musgrave Hospital. Similarly contrasted are Billy's pessimism and sense of betrayal, which finds its most extreme articulation in the reductive negativity of Mr Roper, with the imaginative, life-affirming optimism and simple hope of the Catholic couple.

It must not be inferred, from this description of what Leigh finds in Eugene and Colette, and through them, at the heart of the Catholic spirit, that his view of Eugene and Colette is either sentimental or sentimentalised. Neither the treatment nor the acting attempt to nudge the spectator into a cheaply bought or artificially sympathetic attitude: there are no treacly moments and none of the performances is self-consciously warm-hearted. The structure of the film allows the directness of Leigh's point of view to emerge through the symmetry of its echoes and parallels.

Four Days in July begins and ends with children. Colette and Lorraine lie in the maternity ward in adjacent beds. The spectator might entertain the hope that at last the film is about to offer a unifying event: a spark of a fellowship between the two women, foreshadowing the future reconciliation of the two communities and a bearable future for the babies the two mothers nurse. When Colette and Lorraine tell each other the names they have chosen for their children, however, we see the shutters come down. There will be no bonding and no reconciliation. These babies are named for and inherit inescapable history. It is the sister-midwife's opinion that 'all babies are the same when they start off', but we must assume from what we have seen that these babies will grow to perpetuate the divisions and become like the children in the alleyway, taking the war in which they live completely for granted. If there is any reason for optimism at all it is only that life goes on.

From the perspective of the mainland liberal observer concerned about the problems of Northern Ireland, *Four Days in July* is an extremely uncomfortable film. Leigh's postulate is that there is not a security problem in Ulster but a war. From this fundamental assumption spring a number of challenges. In Eugene's household there is implicit, unspoken support for the republican cause and for those who are, to use Dixie's word, 'operating'. Dixie's explanation to Colette that he was imprisoned because 'they found some gear in our house' passes uncensured. Colette's only comment on him after he has left is that he's 'a tonic'.

Leigh's personal research in 1983–4 convinced him that the Provisional IRA enjoyed much more widespread support among Northern Ireland's Catholics than the mainland government and news media acknowledged, and that a very large number of Catholic people in the province are (or were in 1984) politically active. It's a point of view which is an integral part of the background of the film. If he is correct – and we have no grounds to doubt the principle of Leigh's judgement – the film requires us to attempt to reconcile the apparently irreconcilable: our revulsion at the horrors of political violence with our compassion for Eugene, Colette and their circle.

Four Days in July provides no solution to this dilemma. Leigh says, 'When there's a solution, the audience forgets the film on leaving the cinema. Life goes on. It unfolded before the film and it continues afterwards. People often ask me: what happens afterwards? I haven't got a clue. It's your problem.'

One of the film's achievements is to provide the audience with an intensely close-up view of the experience of the people of Ulster, while simultaneously increasing their sense of distance from it. The urban location generates a feeling of familiarity but the film leaves us in no doubt that we are witnessing events in a foreign country, with its own cultures, values, customs, behaviour and speech, and all of them very different from our own. We are shown what we take for granted as if it were completely unfamiliar, even exotic. If there is a means of escape from the apparently intractable problem of Northern Ireland, Leigh seems only to suggest our acceptance of the otherness of the place as a first step. In order to do this we must dismantle the familiar mental apparatus and acknowledge with full understanding that the Provos represent a legitimate and widely shared political aspiration expressed through military violence and that Unionism is not self-evidently British, nor Loyalism by definition 'right'. We will understand the troubles better if we separate ourselves from the idea that what we face is in any way a domestic problem.

Four Days in July is a radical film by any standards. That it came to be made and broadcast is a significant tribute to the courageous independence of both its maker and of the BBC. At the time the British government's policy on Northern Ireland consisted of increasing the profile of the security forces and of stridently reaffirming its determination not to negotiate with terrorists. It is hard to imagine that the film could be made in the nineties. Leigh again: 'Apart from the fact that I don't think it could have got made at the Beeb more recently ... it certainly couldn't have got made anywhere else at that time ... One of the things overall about this film is that it was never interfered with at any stage, editorially, politically or otherwise and it went out [uncut, even though it ran six minutes over length] ... I think that's terribly important.'

Four Days in July

Transmission date: 29 January 1985 (BBC1)

Cast

Colette	Brid Brennan
Eugene	Des McAleer
Micky	David Coyle
Dixie	Stephen Rea
Carmel	Eileen Pollock
Brendan	Shane Connaughton
Lorraine	Paula Hamilton
Billy	Charles Lawson
Big Billy	Brian Hogg
Little Billy	Adrian Gordon
Mr McCoy	John Keegan
Mr Roper	John Hewitt
Sister-midwife	Ann Hasson

Technical and production

Produced by	Kenith Trodd for the BBC
Devised and directed by	Mike Leigh
Photography	Remi Adefarasin
Sound	John Pritchard
Design	Jim Clay
Music	Rachel Portman
Editing	Robin Sales

Notes

1 All direct quotations of Mike Leigh are from an interview he was kind enough to record with the author in December 1991.
2 Antony Sher, *The Year of the King* (London: Methuen, 1989), 40.
3 Liam de Paor, *Divided Ulster* (Harmondsworth: Penguin, 1973), 16.
4 All quotations from *Four Days in July* are taken from a video recording of the film. The screenplay has not been published.

Select bibliography

Books on drama

Clements, Paul, *The Improvised Play/The Work of Mike Leigh* (London: Methuen, 1984)
Frost, A., and R. Yerrow, *Improvisation in Drama* (London: Macmillan, 1991)
Hunt, Albert, *The Language of Television* (London: Eyre Methuen), esp. 16–24

Books on Ulster

Darby, John, *Northern Ireland/Background to the Conflict* (Belfast: The Appletree Press, 1983)
MacDonald, Michael, *Children of Wrath/Political Violence in Northern Ireland* (Cambridge: Polity Press, 1986)
Ward, Alan J. (ed.), *Northern Ireland/Living With The Crisis* (New York: Praeger, 1987)

Articles

Crowley, Jeananne, 'Leigh's lives' *(Four Days in July)*, *Radio Times*, 26 January–1 February 1985, 8
Hattenstone, Simon, 'The reluctant optimist' (Profile of Mike Leigh), *Guardian*, 14 March 1991

See also:

Hollywood Reporter, 15 March 1985, 22
The Listener, 24 January 1985, 31 (Location report on the making of the film)
Stills 16 (February 1985), 14 (Interview with Leigh)
Variety, 5 December 1984, 20

10   *Tutti Frutti* (John Byrne)

HUGH HEBERT

From its first episode in March 1987, John Byrne's *Tutti Frutti* looked set to break the network audience's resistance to regional drama played in heavy accents. Some other Scottish drama had already dented the defences, but mainly within popular and conventional genres like crime series. The resistance is still there – and was tangible in the reaction to Byrne's subsequent (1990) serial *Your Cheatin' Heart*.

Yet *Tutti Frutti* was significant. For a regional product, it had an unnaturally wide appeal, extended by its use of rock'n'roll. Its critical success was greater than its success in the ratings and encouraged a sheaf of BAFTA awards. But more than most television drama, it was also a highly individual imaginative work that stemmed from, and sometimes subverted, ideas generated at the top of the system. Aside from its patent viewer-appeal, *Tutti Frutti* was invented to answer a felt need to inject a new, strong, popular Scottish/regional presence into BBC network drama.

The basic idea came from Bill Bryden who, in 1984, had been appointed Head of Drama for BBC Scotland while still continuing his work at the National Theatre in London. Bryden asked Norman McCandlish to be his deputy, and they aimed to establish BBC Scotland as a power base for writers, and to win the backing and the funds to make this viable. Their sponsor in this was Michael Grade, then Controller of BBC1. They all wanted a large-scale project for Scotland, a six-hour networked series, not about police or gangsters: the tough Glasgow detective Taggart was already doing well in STV's schedules.

Both Bryden and Byrne had worked at STV during the sixties. After an initial call from McCandlish, Bryden contacted Byrne and asked whether he remembered a Glasgow band called The Poets. They both recalled that this group had had a modest success in the sixties, with one hit record in the charts. Now, twenty years later, they were still doing club gigs, and, as

9 *Robbie Coltrane as Big Jazza in* Tutti Frutti. *BBC 1987*

Bryden expressed it, 'still rocking and rolling in a time warp'.[1]

Bryden's idea was to have a series about such a band, but to develop it by having them move over to Country music, on the grounds that – despite some evidence to the contrary – 'You surely can't go on rocking and rolling at 50.' He even thought the band in the story might have a big success and be welcomed to Nashville. Bryden, in consultation with Grade, also nominated a 'household name' to star in the serial. Both of these last two propositions were rejected by Byrne. He loathed Country music (though it was to become even more central to *Your Cheatin' Heart* than rock'n'roll was to *Tutti Frutti*). And he rejected the household name. Byrne's own nomination was Robbie Coltrane, who was later accepted by Bryden and Grade.

Both Byrne's objections were influential in the making of *Tutti Frutti*.

The Nashville idea, however casually suggested, implied in principle an acceptance of the classic film musical success-and-happiness ending, and there was very little in Byrne's existing work to suggest he would feel easy with that outcome. Robbie Coltrane was not at that time a household name, at least to network audiences, though he had appeared in alternative comedy series like Granada's *Alfresco* and BBC Scotland's *A Kick Up the Eighties*, and had done cameo parts in films. Byrne has said: 'He was, as I read it, on the cusp of becoming a genuine star. I tailored the part of Danny McGlone to his strengths.'[2] Just as important, Coltrane had appeared in the first productions of Byrne's trilogy of stage plays, *The Slab Boys*, at the Traverse Theatre, Edinburgh.

Byrne took away from his initial meeting with Bryden just the idea of the band still playing rock'n'roll, with memories of their hit record many years before, and the title *Tutti Frutti*, one of Little Richard's most famous tracks and a phrase that promises a rich and exotic variety of flavours. Byrne wrote the first draft of all six episodes in eight weeks. They had to be on Michael Grade's desk by 1 October 1985 if the money to make the series the following year was to be released from the BBC coffers. All six were rewritten by Byrne over the next five months, but only to tighten and improve them. In essence they remained as in his first drafts. The very simple idea that Bryden and Byrne discussed developed into a complex structure that was brilliantly realised by the director Tony Smith.[3]

Tutti Frutti begins with the funeral of Big Jazza McGlone, the lead singer of The Majestics, a huge and unforgettable figure who has been killed ramming a car into a Glasgow bus shelter at 70 mph while five times over the alcohol limit and in search of kebabs. It is a Catholic funeral – all the Majestics are Catholic by upbringing, a key fact in the moral framework of the story and the relationships. As the service begins in the ill-kempt cemetery, Jazza's younger brother Danny arrives from the airport dressed in a crumpled powder-blue lightweight suit. From the monochrome flashbacks to the young Majestics in action in their salad days, we see that Danny is as good as an identical twin for his older brother. When the service is over, the band leave in a hired limousine: Danny is left to ride back to town in the battered Majestics transit van driven by Dennis, the roadie, or band factotum.

Cheering himself up in a plasticised wine bar, Danny is recognised by the waitress, Suzi Kettles, as someone she knew at art school. Meanwhile, the members of the band are anxiously discussing how to replace Big Jazza in the line-up for the Majestics' imminent twenty-fifth anniversary tour. Vincent broaches, obliquely, an old proposal: to bring his young girl-friend Glenna into the band. Bomba is fiercely opposed to the co-option of any female singer. In particular he does not want Glenna, because Vincent is married to his sister Noreen. Bomba's tolerance of his brother-in-law's infidelities is being stretched.

The solution to their problem is dreamed up by Eddie Clockerty, the band's sly and conniving manager: Danny is the spitting image of Jazza and has been scraping a living playing keyboard in New York clubs. His presence would be a profound reminder of Jazza's untimely exit and good for publicity. Therefore Danny should replace Jazza.

Danny has just flown in from New York for the funeral and is short of somewhere to stay. Suzi brushes aside his routine advances but allows him to sleep in the one spare berth in her small flat: the bath. In the morning he is hijacked by the band to take on the role of his dead brother for a trial run at a Miners' Hall show.

Glenna arrives and announces to Vincent that she is pregnant. Suzi, against her better judgement, goes along to support her new lodger. The first episode ends on a high note of good humour as the band is taken by surprise when Danny launches into a rumbustious rendering of Jerry Lee Lewis's 'Great Balls of Fire'. They nod approval of Danny as the apathetic audience bursts into sudden applause.

Byrne has, in this opening episode, adopted a parody of the key conventions of the old-style Hollywood musical. Accident, illness, or sudden death spells crisis for a game but ailing act. From sheer urgent necessity, an inexperienced and resented intruder is brought in to substitute for the lost member of the tightly knit group. This leads, through quarrels and tears, to an unexpected triumph and acceptance of the newcomer at curtain fall. Having used that matrix in the first hour, Byrne cheerfully abuses it in the next five.

The band embarks on its jubilee tour disgruntled, disagreeing, and sensing that they are on course for some unspecified disaster. When Dennis and the van cannot be found one morning, they discover he has driven Danny back to Glasgow to take part in a BBC documentary about Big Jazza. Clockerty has not revealed to the rest that the original Majestics will only appear in it as rough archive film, as he explains to his secretary Miss Toner (Katy Murphy). Miss Toner's relationship with Clockerty is ambiguous, but her role is that of the dumb brunette: 'The beef is that while Danny Boy is presenting his kisser in full frontal close-up Technicolor, the Majestics are only appearing in very scratchy eight mil. black and white, shot from the wallbars of the TA Hall in Dalmarnock all of 20 years ago by Mrs Clockerty with a hand-held Brownie, ya stupid girl!'[4]

Suzi, intrigued despite her doubts, joins them on tour, insisting that she is there 'to see that he [Danny] doesn't make a total idiot of himself, not to provide home comforts'.[5] Glenna pursues the band to be with Vincent, and while driving him back from a flying visit to Glasgow, where he has confronted Clockerty over the BBC film and the band's below-the-top billing, she runs the car off the road. Vincent misses that night's show, Suzi is pressganged into the band, and proves she can sing: a repeat of the cliché ending of episode one. Even Bomba is won over.

But the theme of betrayal begins to surface strongly. Clockerty is misleading the band about the BBC documentary. Sheena, the reporter on the documentary (Annie Bruce), is plainly planning a contemptuous attack on Big Jazza: 'one-time amphetamine addict, self-confessed alcoholic . . . a 19-stone delinquent . . . whose carnal excesses won for him a star rating alongside other such celebrated debauchees as Roscoe Arbuckle, Frankie Lymon, and Aleister Crowley'.[6] Vincent feels betrayed by the introduction of Suzi as singer while Glenna is in hospital in danger of losing her child. And Danny has discovered that even the Majestics' one hit record was hyped into the no. 7 position by Clockerty and his shadowy, shady business accomplice Wee Tommy Cairns. He invested several thousand pounds of the band's money in buying the disc wholesale from the shops that provide the chart statistics. It was, Danny says, 'like finding out Hans Christian Andersen was a werewolf or the Pope was a drag queen'. He is not consoled by Dennis the roadie's recollection of what John Lennon once said: 'If it hadna bin for the Majestics, me an' Paul would ha bin quite happy to spend the rest of our lives in a Liverpool drawing office.'[7]

Episode 4 is the turning-point of the series. It brutally undermines the viewer's assumption that *Tutti Frutti* is a comedy with a few dark shadows. The mood turns a deeper shade of black when the tour reaches Buckie, a small fishing town that nearly falls off the northern edge of the map of Scotland. But it also brings Danny to the point of expressing serious feelings about Suzi to her face, instead of his usual mocking pretence of lust.

To a Glasgow or Edinburgh audience Buckie, like Methil, their first tour venue, would seem a remote frontier town. Vincent's wife Noreen arrives to join the tour for a week, discovers the Glenna affair and attempts suicide. Meanwhile, Bomba and Danny take part in an early morning Radio Buckie phone-in, where a young woman calls and accuses an astonished Bomba of being her natural father, and of deserting her mother some twenty years before. Later, in the bar of the hotel, she walks in and addresses Vincent as 'Bomba' before stabbing him. Vincent has betrayed not only the woman's mother, but has betrayed Bomba by using his name to hide his real identity during this long-ago sexual adventure.

In the hotel, Glenna lies sedated after the shock of the stabbing. In the hospital emergency room, the overdosed Noreen lies in the next bed to Vincent, now far down the path of injury – one way or another, always self-inflicted – on which he was launched when he burned his fingers trying to make a lighter work in episode 2: the engraved lighter that Glenna gave him to celebrate the Majestics' twenty-five years. After Glenna crashed the car, and she and Vincent had left the scene, it burst into flames. Fire has pursued Vincent, and is not yet satisfied. Clockerty decides the only way to keep going is for Suzi to go on replacing Vincent. Her duo with Danny at the gig that night is 'Love's Strange'.

This episode crystallises two emergent themes: betrayal first, at the personal level. Eddie Clockerty, its chief practitioner, wants to replace Danny by Suzi to distance the band from the bad publicity he expects of the BBC film. He persuades her that Danny has made offensive passes at both Sheena and Miss Toner: 'Neither young woman is pressing charges, you'll be glad to hear.' So Suzi dumps Danny. Next there is betrayal by the technology of communication. In the editing studio, Sheena is seen sharpening her metaphorical hatchet for use in the documentary form that was invented as a vehicle for truth. Vincent's anonymous daughter/ attacker has turned the DJ phone-in from a form of community entertainment and comfort into an instrument of menace and revenge. We are reminded regularly, with mock-archive film in each episode, of the Majestics in their prime, the centre of adulation, but now betrayed by twenty years of popular neglect. In the recording studio, cutting their celebratory jubilee album, the Majestics find control of their music passes to the recording engineer at his insulated console. The soundproof glass panel and a faulty intercom circuit make it nearly impossible to communicate or expostulate with him.

So gifts, in both senses, also betray and destroy: Glenna's lighter and the woollen jacket she knitted for Vincent give away her affair with him, as perhaps she means them to, as the only way to make him leave his wife. The child Glenna believes she is carrying will destroy her, and finally Vincent's last thread of tattered male self-esteem. She loses the child and commits suicide. For a group of people brought up as Catholics, this is twice a sin and twice a tragedy. Noreen has never conceived, a fact Vincent cruelly blames, to her face, as the cause of his infidelity. But Noreen finally tells him Glenna's pregnancy was a phantom, that Vincent's low sperm count is the reason for her own barrenness. So was he stabbed for and by a child he had not fathered? Or was Noreen's revelation about his infertility a lie, a revenge for all his infidelities? 'Love's Strange' and 'Love Hurts' are the songs that end two episodes. Within the relationships of the Majestics and their women is the implicit painful perception that those who most want children are denied them – Vincent, Noreen, and most tragically Glenna. Those who, on the surface anyway, have least interest in children are entrusted with them – Bomba with four; Frank with seven sons, and no daughter; Suzi, impregnated by a violent husband she has left. In a world of surrogate parenthood and desperately sought abortion, the irony spreads much wider than a television series about ageing rock'n'rollers.

The last episode, like the first, has begun with a funeral, Glenna's. It ends with the Majestics at the Pavilion Theatre, Glasgow, on what was supposed to be their triumphant come-back show. Vincent, grieving and apparently too drunk to perform, is left at home. But dragging himself towards the theatre, he stops outside a television showroom, with a window full of sets all beaming out the documentary about the Majestics, with the archive film of their glory days. As the Pavilion show begins, Vincent finally struggles drunkenly on to the stage where Danny and Suzi, reconciled after Clockerty's trick has been revealed, are in full song. Vincent has soaked himself inside and out with vodka, and is now trying to flick that treacherous lighter into life. As Danny and Suzi get their heads together round the microphone, they are suddenly lit by an orange glow. They stare horrified out of camera shot, and a single scream that mocks those of the teenage fans of their sixties success tells us it is the fire finally engulfing Vincent; in Byrne's words, 'upstaging the parvenu, Danny, and his soul-mate Suzi'.[8] The image slams into the by-now familiar upbeat *Tutti Frutti* title sequence like a rail express into buffers.

Maurice Roëves, who played Vincent, at one point suggested a different end – such as the Majestics' van careering over a clifftop or across a motorway. But this would have been at variance with the laid-back style Byrne and his director Tony Smith had adopted earlier, which often only implies key moments, leaving viewers to make the obvious assumptions about what is happening. And sometimes to enjoy the spectacle when one of the characters makes different assumptions. One wordless example is when Danny wreaks retribution on Suzi's estranged husband Stuart, a dentist. She has kept her married state secret until her husband has forced his way into her flat, beaten her up, and attempted what would clearly be rape within marriage. Danny goes to Stuart's surgery posing as an emergency patient. Once alone with the dentist Danny, who has a massive size and weight advantage, applies the drill on his unanaesthetised victim, though we only hear the screams. The receptionist, affronted by Danny's earlier behaviour, which cleared the waiting-room of patients, smiles with pleasure, thinking it is Danny who is screaming. Later, the dentist is seen at the police station, muffled to the nose, looking through the rogues' gallery. He finally spots the assailant's picture and points to it with speechless certainty. The detective smiles and shakes his head. The file is labelled 'Deceased'. It's Big Jazza, not Danny. (Anyone who watched Byrne's *Your Cheatin' Heart* will see the parallel with McClusky's excruciating encounter with the terrifying tattooist Cherokee George.)

Tutti Frutti's visual narrative devices reflect Byrne's verbal style: which is

punning and allusive. He delights in the comic chain of small misunder-
standings. Dialogue and incident often consist of a series of accidentally or
wilfully missed connections, used as an ironic comic counterpoint in
painful situations.

The point is made best when Noreen visits Glenna and finds her slumped
in despair, crushing out cigarettes on the carpet in Vincent's second home.
Noreen, who does not know about Glenna's pregnancy, has brought cakes.
Glenna makes coffee.

NOREEN: I wasn't sure whether to get a meringue or munchmallows. I hope they
defrost all right ... this'll be tufted, will it?
GLENNA: No, it's instant.
NOREEN: The carpet, I mean.
GLENNA: Aw, that ... who cares? D'you take sugar? We havenae got any ... I
paid for that, by the way, not him, in case you're wonderin' ... same as
I'm payin' for this dump ... out of my trust fund. Did he tell you I lost
it?
NOREEN: Your trust fund we're talking about?
GLENNA: The baby.
NOREEN: Oh, my God! (*She drops her cup of coffee into her lap.*)
GLENNA: Here ... try one of your rock cakes.[9]

In the last episode, Danny has been left to try and cheer Vincent while the
rest go and prepare for the following night's climactic concert at the
Pavilion. But what happens is a new mutual sympathy, eased along with
alcohol, between the bereaved Vincent and Danny. Danny shows the
grieving Vincent the wreath he has bought. It is a Christmas wreath of holly
from which, as he confesses, he has removed the robin on the grounds that
it was perhaps inappropriate. But Glenna, says Vincent, was very fond of
robins. So Danny pulls the plastic bird from his pocket and reinstates it. At
a cathartic moment, Vincent insists that he is known as The Iron Man of
Scottish Rock, and then breaks down completely. By the end of the scene he
is in an alcoholic stupor. Not even the rest of the band singing to him can
bring him round.

This scene shows Byrne up to his favourite narrative trick, the
juxtaposition of acute pain and near-farce, neatly pointed up by Smith's
direction. Vincent's overt grieving is less for his lost girl-friend than for his
spent life and his clothes, which Noreen has burnt after the shock of the
visit to Glenna.

I've had my motor set alight, my skull split open, my entire wardrobe destroyed, not
to mention my marriage. We havenae had a hit record since Nineteen Forget-
about-it and even that was a fix so there's not much likelihood of us ever havin'
another one ... I'm lumbered with two houses to pay ... no offspring that I know
about apart from a big lassie wi' specs that turns out to be The Butcher Queen o'
Buckie and knifes me in the vitals by way of sayin' 'Hello Dad!'[10]

He remains for the rest of the day – the rest of his life – in the tight black leathers that were the uniform of his sixties rock image.

Vincent is the most complex character in *Tutti Frutti*. Intensely conceited, violent, deceiving and dislikeable, yet capable of tenderness and finally cast in a tragic mould, he is also one of the most original creations in television serials of the eighties. Maurice Roëves brought to the part all the essential qualities it needed: lean, saturnine looks, a whiplash voice, and the emotional range from vicious anger to tearful collapse. As one disaster after another hits him, the viewer's sympathies – seriously alienated at first – are gradually won. Glenna's lighter burns his fingers. Headbutting the glass door in Clockerty's office gives him a skullcap bandage. The phone-in girl with the knife reduces him to surgical collar and wheelchair and crutches. No man, you feel, deserves this degree of punishment from a vengeful fate.

By comparison the tasks of the other leading players were relatively easy. As we have seen, Byrne tailored Danny to Coltrane's special talents, 'the fact that he could mimic accents, his ability as a keyboard player (a "keyboard" player in a rock'n'roll band?), his great love of movies, his indefinable "charm" as a performer... It was the first time I'd ever written a part with someone in mind for it.'[11] Another quality, perhaps characteristic of successful stand-up comedians, is Coltrane's ability to deliver comedy lines at speed and make them seem to burst from the character and not from the puppet-master writer.

Emma Thompson as Suzi was both physically and in manner the perfect foil to Coltrane's Danny. She embodied Suzi's essential qualities: elegant, collected, sceptical, unassertive but intrinsically tough. The same qualities were visible in a totally different age and context (and with an equally persuasive accent) in Thompson's performance later the same year as Harriet in the television version of Olivia Manning's *Fortunes of War*.

But the balance of characters and actors in the rest of the band was crucial to their credibility as a group. Bomba the drummer has a strong though slightly unfocused home base. His wife does not appear, she has a full-time job, so he is often seen burdened with the care of twin babies. Frank's wife is also off-screen, looking after their seven sons. Implicitly, and especially in a family group with their religious background, these are all living rebukes to Vincent's childless marriage. Bomba is played by Stuart McGugan as a bossy believer in family life, as long as he can off-load his own responsibilities. Despite the professional ties of the band, he nurses a deep contempt for his brother-in-law's Casanovan antics and his flouting of the conventions of family relationships. He had asked Vincent to be godfather to the twins, 'And yew said ye couldna, because ye had t'buy a pair of shoes!'

At the same time he is a realist in the world of rock. When he hears about Glenna's pregnancy he turns angrily on Vincent: 'A bit on the side is one thing. Two homes ah can turn a blind eye to. But when you do the dirty on ma young sister...'[12] The belief shared by the family is the usual male-protective assumption that it is Noreen who is incapable of having children.

The fourth member of the original band, Frank aka 'Fud', is often in the middle of these in-law affrays. Jake D'Arcy makes Frank a bullied innocent: quiet, even-tempered, unassuming, he is nevertheless – like most straight men in comedy – the unwitting cause of avoidable friction, but also the man who does the chores without complaining. Frank does not see the mischief he is causing when he explains what the others do not know: for instance, that Danny has been called to take part in the BBC documentary while they have not. It never occurs to him that they will be angry, because the fact does not in any way offend his (minimal) personal pride. But this simple passing on of information begins a sequence that cascades towards disaster.

Very few series in the genre-conscious eighties have *Tutti Frutti*'s simultaneous command of comedy and near-tragedy. From the middle of the story onwards they are seamlessly interwoven. Yet the overall effect remains comic. This is partly because of the dominating presence of Danny and the central role given to his pursuit, and final capture, of Suzi. But there are frequent visual allusions to cartoon comedy. Waiting for an errant Danny at various times, Bomba, Vincent or Frank sit watching television or squabbling over the choice of programme: matters not of taste, but of remote-control power. When we glimpse the screen, we see they are wholly absorbed in Postman Pat (or on another occasion, in the olive-oil blandness of a cooking programme). In one scene, we see that Vincent's guitar has been thrown through a window. The hole is guitar-shaped, the guitar is on the ground outside. We don't need to see it flying through. It used to be one of the standard gags of strip cartoons in boys' comics.

Vincent, though the tragic character, is also the nearest to cartoon in his ungovernable anger. In Clockerty's office, Vincent rages and headbutts through the half-glass door behind which he knows the manipulating manager is hiding. ('Oh, was that you knocking, Vincent?') When he goes berserk, which is often, Vincent's classic balloon bellow is 'Ah-h-h-l-l kill 'im!' or just 'A-a-a-r-r-r-g-g-h-h!' And as in cartoons or silent films, injury is presented as comic rather than painful. It expresses the common, if inexcusable, experience of finding the anguish of others funny. But a moral mechanism seems to be at work. The pain is in some way a deserved retribution, and that relieves us of the shame of enjoying the spectacle. Byrne has said there is no intentional parody of comics like *Hotspur*, *Rover*, and *Wizard*, but accepts that they (all, incidentally, published in Dundee) and American comics he also read voraciously in boyhood have been a strong influence on his work.[13]

It is worth comparing the comedy style of *Tutti Frutti* with that of Byrne's 1978 stage play *The Slab Boys*,[14] which he has been [i.e. as at autumn 1991] adapting as a feature film. The slab boys' job is to grind and mix the colours in a carpet factory, but their ambition is to be at least designers, and in Phil's case, a serious painter. Phil's mother suffers from recurrent mental illness (as did Byrne's mother). Phil does not conceal this, he refers to it frequently and makes it the centre of much of his bitter humour. He asks his friend Spanky (later in the trilogy to become a rock musician) whether he thinks 'going off your head's catching'.

SPANKY: 'snot your maw again, is it?
PHIL: Yeh ... they took her away last night ... She wasn't all that bad either ... not for her, that is. All she done was run up the street with her hair on fire and dive through the Co-operative windows.
SPANKY: Thought that was normal down your way?
PHIL: Yeh ... but that's mostly the drink.[15]

In this play, too, Byrne constantly uses disjunctive humour, wilful misinterpretation. *Still Life*, the third play of *The Slab Boys* trilogy (written in 1982) now looks almost to be a dry run for *Tutti Frutti* four years later. Phil's style of jokiness has matured and tightened and is very close in mood to Danny's. There are also common elements. Phil and Spanky meet at the funeral of the third slab boy, Hector. Spanky and his band are appearing at The Barracuda, Herne Bay, and about to acquire a manager.

PHIL: Steeples? Not Big Eddie Steeples from Darkwood Crescent that's mammy used to sell toffee apples through their lavvy window? Jesus ... fingers crossed you don't make the big time, kid ... you'd never clap eyes on a solitary tosser. You haven't signed anything yet, I trust? Aw no ... don't tell me.
SPANKY: It's only a contract ...
PHIL: Listen, son, the only 'contracts' Big Eddie understands is for shooting people ... He's a header, Big Eddie. Used to bite the kneecaps out of whippets for a giggle.[16]

Apart from cartoon-style comedy, another important influence at work in *Tutti Frutti* is, as suggested earlier, the use and subversion of conventions of the American cinema. Funerals as ironic gatherings, especially at the beginning of stories, are a frequent screen-narrative device. The relationship between the exploited band and their rascally manager Eddie Clockerty is another convention of the screen musical. The Majestics cannot function without his entrepreneurial skills, such as they are. And without their skills, such as they are, there is no percentage for Eddie.

In this tradition, Clockerty (played with serpentine evasiveness by Richard Wilson) is in the end the victim of his own manipulations. His plot to replace Danny with Suzi backfires. His scheme to have a new line of Danny T-shirts is sabotaged when he goes to the factory to collect them and finds the shirts have one arm missing. Again, there is a similar joke in *The Slab Boys*, involving Phil's mother's running war with the Co-op: a suit bought for his brother Jim turned out to have only one trouser-leg, and the store refused to exchange it: 'Said it was something to do with the nap of the cloth . . . Jimmucks just had to force both legs down the one trouser . . . gave him a kind of funny mince, that was the only thing.'[17]

The risk *Tutti Frutti*'s music-based structure ran, however, was not comparison with distant American models but with Dennis Potter's *The Singing Detective*, which had been hugely admired when the BBC screened it less than a year before. There is, nevertheless, in one swift sequence, what looks like a passing *hommage* by Byrne and/or Tony Smith: the moment at twilight when we glimpse Glenna leaping to her death from a bridge. It is very close to the recurrent image that puzzles and teases the audience of the Potter serial.

Potter uses music satirically in *Singing Detective*, as distinct from *Pennies from Heaven*, where it is used to express the aspirations and feelings of people gagged by their own inadequacy or by social convention. Since *Tutti Frutti*, in his admired feature film *Distant Voices, Still Lives*, Terence Davies uses songs naturalistically, in the collective singing which was once an essential part of working-class entertainment at home or in the pub.

In *Tutti Frutti* songs are used quite differently, as ironic and sometimes comic comment: Eddie Cochran's 'Three Steps to Heaven' at Jazza's graveside; 'Love's Strange' and 'Love Hurts' reflect the on-off relationship between Danny and Suzi; 'Only the Lonely' the slow mental and physical destruction of Vincent. But *Tutti Frutti* celebrates its chosen musical form even when it makes fun of it. Like one of the wreaths at Jazza's funeral, it declares with affection that rock'n'roll does not die. It survives, despite the sins and shortcomings and absurdities of its celebrants. The title song that enfolds each episode of *Tutti Frutti* tells most of what any viewer needs to know about the excitement that rock'n'roll held for the young of the fifties and early sixties.

Byrne was born in 1940, did art school training and designed many record sleeves for rock'n'roll albums, and all of this has clearly fed into his conception of the serial, for which he also designed the title sequences. (In *Your Cheatin' Heart*, written at the end of the eighties and transmitted in 1990, he had overall control of the series style.) The music and the demands of the commercial system that feeds and feeds on the music fuel *Tutti Frutti*. It summons up a lifestyle which, in the days when the Majestics were the kings of Scottish rock, was relatively new and liable to blow minds as well as fuses, the drum-beat of revolt but definitely not of revolution. Clothes were, as they still are, an integral part of what the music meant to its enthusiasts. The jokes about Jim's one-legged trousers in *Slab Boys*, about Clockerty's one-armed T-shirts, and the destruction wrought by Noreen's anger on Vincent's wardrobe use that obsession with fashion. Clockerty's other business is clothes, the shop under his office is an emporium of what the hip dresser of the year before yesterday was wearing: witness the unnatural assurance that Frank assumes when in the Clockerty store he tries on a bomber jacket that looks like half the back end of a bull.

All of this together emphasises the extent to which in the fifties and sixties the American forces of film/music/dress style colonised popular culture on this side of the Atlantic. In an interview with *The Guardian* at the time of *Your Cheatin' Heart*, Byrne talked about this in the context of Country music. He commented on the number of Glaswegians you could see adopting American Western-style clothes as John Gordon-Sinclair has to in *Cheatin' Heart*. Many Glaswegians, Byrne thinks, 'are cowboys in their heads'. In the specific case of Country music, this illustrates his sense of the two-way influence and exchange between American and Celtic forms. Perhaps there is satisfaction for a people deprived of nationhood to see cultural traditions that travelled West with the nineteenth-century waves of emigrants returned transformed but triumphant in the late twentieth century.

Against that, the first episode establishes a sense of the gap between the myth and the reality of America. Danny, at first claiming he can't wait to get back to the New York loft he shares, reveals to Suzi that he is lying, that his one room is 9 ft square and is shared with a man who makes Spanish-style shoes for a living; Byrne would relish the half-hidden pun on 'cobblers'. Danny tells Suzi this as they are walking round the art gallery in Glasgow, surrounded by the austere elegance of Charles Rennie Mackintosh's architecture and furniture: a hint (four years before Glasgow's enthronement as European City of Culture, 1990) that this was the true Scottish inheritance of style, set against the trashy international eclecticism of the wine bar where Suzi works.

The immediate critical response to *Tutti Frutti* was rapturous and heavily spiked with superlatives. Even reviewers who, risking lynch-letters, made the dangerous admission that they could only understand about one word in three of the dialogue, confessed that it really did not much spoil the pleasure. It mixed a rare blend of distinctive verbal and visual comi-tragedy with nostalgia for the most explosive period of popular music since the twenties and thirties. It won BAFTA awards both in the art and the craft sections. This was a morale-lifter for the Drama Department of BBC

Scotland, and probably for regional studios in general. It extended the reputation of Coltrane and Emma Thompson. But what did it do for the cause of regional television drama, which has always lagged behind the success of regional soap operas and situation comedies?

It brought Scottish screen drama into the mainstream, whereas even outstanding work by Bill Douglas in the cinema and John McGrath on television had remained like strangers dropping in. Bryden's contract as Head of Drama included being able to write and produce one work of his own a year, though he rarely exercised this right. But his *Holy City* (transmitted on Good Friday 1986), for instance, with David Hayman as a Christ-figure visiting Glasgow at Easter, while a striking piece of television, was not in a popular mode. Scottish drama as seen on the network (i.e. outside Scotland) still tended to centre on Glasgow's fearsome reputation as the venue for violent crime and gang warfare – a near-unshakeable reputation pinned on it in the thirties. Hayman (again) as *The Hard Man* was typical – the life and times of Jimmy Boyle, the gang leader taken on by Barlinnie Prison's Special Unit, where he transformed himself into a writer and artist and became a dedicated social campaigner. Other Scottish teleplays kept faith with the stereotypes of a raw, subsistence community in a harsh rural setting.

But Scotland was not alone in trying to develop distinctive, high-quality regional drama that would attract a national audience. Many novelists and poets had found it difficult to deal overtly with the Troubles in Northern Ireland until a full decade after they began, and for the same reasons television usually approached the subject walking on eggshells. And one of the major achievements of the BBC Northern Ireland studios was indeed an oblique view: Graham Reid's outstanding Belfast 'Billy' trilogy (with Kenneth Branagh making his impressive first nationwide mark as the central character). Like some earlier Irish writers, Reid used the strife within an extended working-class family to reflect the unseen mayhem on the streets. Channel 4 produced Peter Ransley's *The Price* (1985), a more direct crime story approach to a terrorist kidnapping. And in a less violent mood S4C, the Welsh equivalent of Channel 4, was also producing some fine one-off plays, reflecting social change. For example, the exposure to the exotic influence of Japanese investment in a society that feared it was in irreversible decline, with the shift of economic power that it brought: from heavy industry to electronics and consumer goods, from men to women.

Yet none of these innovative regional dramas was accepted into the mainstream in the way that *Tutti Frutti* was. Partly timing, perhaps; but one obvious reason was its interconnected central subjects: popular music, always richly evocative of its time, show business with its inbuilt Pagliacci melodramatics, its dubious mores and its life devoted to sham and manipulation, and the Beauty and the Beast aspect of the Danny–Suzi affair. The inherent sexual values are emphasised by the fact that Suzi's husband is a presentable, respectable professional man, who just happens to be not much less than a violent rapist of his wife. The second vital reason is that providing you could catch them on the wing, Byrne had written some of the funniest comedy lines heard in a television drama series for a long time.

Despite its critical acclaim and its admittedly more modest success with viewers, *Tutti Frutti* only partly achieved the strategic purpose implicit in the Bryden–Grade initiative. Byrne has made clear that he did not have this purpose in mind anyway: 'I was aware from the outset that [Bryden] was getting the strongest possible support from Michael Grade but didn't at all see it as a clear opportunity to take a specifically Scottish theme to a wider audience. I just saw it as a wonderful opportunity to write six hours of TV film about a bunch of people of my generation who grew up with rock'n'roll.'[18]

Nevertheless it did make ambitious or possibly foolhardy productions more likely to reach the network: Bryden's *The Ship* (transmitted Boxing Day 1990, BBC2), John McGrath's history of Scotland, *Border Warfare* (first episode transmitted on Channel 4 on 11 February 1990); and at the other end of the spectrum, the Glaswegian low-life drunken comedy series *Rab C. Nesbitt* (BBC2, started on 2 November 1990 by the Comedy, not the Drama, Department of BBC Scotland). But why did others not succeed; for instance, Irish or Welsh dramas that were arguably just as innovative, perhaps just as well written and well made – within their budgets, which were not necessarily as generous in on-screen production values? Why has drama from Scotland, Ireland, and Wales had such a hard time making a United Kingdom impact when English regional soap operas and situation comedies have succeeded in capturing and holding a place in the network schedules over a very long period: from *Coronation Street* to *EastEnders*? The relative strengths of regional ITV companies and of the regional bases of the BBC may partly explain it.

Other contributing factors are pure speculation. Irish drama seems eternally haunted by the long years of violence that the North has suffered. To deal directly with the Troubles is painfully difficult and anyway invites a mass use of remote control switch-off. Not to deal with them at least indirectly is to risk the accusation of ducking out. The Welsh dramatic inheritance seems equally inseparable from rather more natural disasters, and in the context of S4C there is a suspected if not a real language difficulty – some of its innovative work has been in Welsh with subtitles.

But to an observer based in London, part of the reason seems to be the cultural values that are commonly assigned to different regions by people who live in other parts of the country. And these reflect, I suggest, values assigned to those regions in traditional forms like the music hall and carried into television light entertainment – until this internal chauvinism came to be unfashionable and unacceptable. Even then, it continued to enjoy a kind of underground life on the club circuit. Some of these perceived national stereotypes were summed up gently in a different context by Alan Watkins, political columnist in *The Observer*, in commenting on the emphasis on Neil Kinnock's Welshness in a party political broadcast for Labour: an emphasis that Watkins, himself Welsh, did not consider had helped Labour's electoral chances:

> The truth is that the English regard the Scots as industrious and honest, the Irish as charming and feckless, but the Welsh as mendacious and disloyal. No matter that we lost more men proportionately to population than any other part of the United Kingdom; that David Lloyd George saved the nation in the same conflict; that we do not go around killing one another as the Irish do; or that South Wales has absorbed immigrants more peacefully than any other part of the UK. There it is, and we have to make the best of it.[19]

Watkins may think the English regard the Scots and Irish in the kindly way he describes. I suspect a more common, if harsher off-the-cuff character sketch of the Celts presented by an English person would be one of well-slaked and volatile behaviour, combined with intense tribal loyalties and incomprehensible accents. It is difficult, at the moment of writing, to predict the effects on network decisions of the cross-ownership of regional ITV companies that will become possible under the new dispensation; but it looks unlikely to reduce the viewers' reluctance, or increase the television producers' inclination to tune their ears and minds to what are too often regarded as outland cultures.

Tutti Frutti

First episode transmitted on 3 March 1987 on BBC1; the repeat series began on 23 January 1988 on BBC2.

Cast

The Majestics:
Danny McGlone   Robbie Coltrane
Vincent Diver   Maurice Roëves
Bomba McAteer   Stuart McGugan
Fud O'Donnell   Jake D'Arcy

Suzi Kettles   Emma Thompson
Dennis Sproul   Ron Donachie

Eddie Clockerty	Richard Wilson
Janice Toner	Katy Murphy
Glenna McFadden	Fiona Charlmers
Sheena Fisher	Annie Bruce
Noreen Diver	Anne Kidd
Suzi's husband	David Dixon
'Big Jazza'	Robbie Coltrane
'Big Jazza's' vocals	Tam White

Technical and production

Producer	Andy Park
Director	Tony Smith
Script Editor	Peter Broughan
Production Manager	Maryann Wilson
Designer	Bob Smart
Costume Designer	Delphine Roche-Gordon
Make-Up Designer	Lorna Blair
Camera	Norman Shepherd
Sound Recordist	Peter Brill
Film Editor	John MacDonnell
Music Editors	Nigel Read
	Paul Kirkin
Musical Director	Zoot Money
Title sequence	John Byrne

Notes

1 Bill Bryden in conversation with the author, July 1991.
2 Letter from John Byrne to the author, October 1991.
3 In the letter mentioned above, Byrne writes that the decision to cast Coltrane caused some problems, notably the large age-gap with the mid-40s of the band. But he adds, 'If anything, the fact that Coltrane was that fifteen years or so younger than the rest was a godsend. I had to invent a reason why he'd never had any connection with the band and how come they hardly knew him ... his having gone to art school and thereafter to the USA, which also led in turn to Danny having to look again at Glasgow and the other parts of Scotland and admit eventually to himself that mythic America was indeed just that ... a myth ... and that he was much better off embracing his homeland and the problems it threw at him ...'
4 Episode 3.
5 *Ibid.*
6 *Ibid.*
7 *Ibid.*
8 Letter from Byrne to the author, November 1991.
9 Episode 5.
10 Episode 6.

11 Letter from Byrne to the author, November 1991.

12 Episode 2.

13 Letter from Byrne to the author, November 1991.

14 *The Slab Boys Trilogy* consists of *The Slab Boys* (1978), *Cuttin' a Rug* (1979) and *Still Life* (1982). All were first produced at the Traverse Theatre Club, Edinburgh.

15 *The Slab Boys*, 9–10.

16 *Still Life*, 97.

17 *The Slab Boys*, 12.

18 Letter from Byrne to the author, October 1991.

19 *The Observer*, 29 September 1991, 21.

Select bibliography

Books

Byrne, John, *The Slab Boys Trilogy* (Harmondsworth: Penguin Books in association with The Salamander Press, 1987, reprinted 1990)
    Tutti Frutti (London: BBC Books, 1987)
    Your Cheatin' Heart (London: BBC Books, 1990)

Articles

Berry, Simon, 'Blue suede blues', *Radio Times*, 28 February–6 March 1987, 98–101

Young, Douglas, 'Now Mr Tutti Frutti has designs on TV' (John Byrne's *Normal Service* and *Tutti Frutti*), *Radio Times*, 30 January–5 February 1988, 68

See also:

Broadcast, 18 July 1986, 7

City Limits, 26 February–5 March 1987, 21 (Robbie Coltrane about his role in the serial)

The Listener, 26 February 1987, 25

Television Today, 22 October 1987, 17

Time Out, 25 February–4 March 1987, 22 (John Byrne about the serial)

11 *The Jewel in the Crown*
(Paul Scott – Ken Taylor)
The literary serial; or the art of adaptation

GEORGE W. BRANDT

In his James MacTaggart lecture at the Edinburgh International Television Festival 1983, Jonathan Miller 'set some feathers fluttering in a way he evidently enjoyed'.[1] He roundly attacked adaptations of novels for television as 'aerosol versions of great works', suggesting paradoxically that 'as they improve, the failure, the *inevitable* failure of them becomes more apparent...' Novels, he claimed, 'are an absolutely untranslatable art form. Except, that is, in the case of the trivial and the second-rate, when it doesn't matter what happens to them.'[2]

That last barb was not a random one. Granada Television had presented *Brideshead Revisited* in a 13-episode adaptation just two years earlier: this was generally hailed as a hugely successful prestige production. Scripted by John Mortimer, handsomely directed by Charles Sturridge and Michael Lindsay-Hogg, it boasted a number of stellar performances, including those of heavyweights like Sir Lawrence Olivier and Sir John Gielgud. But the acclaim won by this serial does not necessarily invalidate Miller's contention. Is Waugh's novel, for all its wit, stylistic felicities and convincing depiction of period and class, really a work quite of the first order? It could be argued that it is not: the story of Sebastian Flyte and Charles Ryder, satirical in tone to begin with, declines into a religiosity that many find out of key and unconvincing.

Was Miller justified, then, in rejecting all adaptations of *good* novels as inevitably self-defeating? Does his statement stand up as a universal rule?

One naturally wouldn't expect adapters to subscribe to it. According to Tom Stoppard, an adapter may be more of a craftsman than an artist – but it was right to take pride in one's craftsmanship as much as in one's originality.[3] Alan Plater, as prolific an adapter as he is a writer of original stories, is more positive than that: 'There is nothing second-best and certainly nothing easy about dramatising books of real quality.'[4] Fay

Weldon stresses the sheer technical difficulty of the operation: 'The adapter's skill is a learned skill, painfully acquired. It is not a task for beginners, though many think it is ... I have adapted, I have been adapted, I *know* ... A whole scene in a novel may work best, have proper emphasis, as a spoken aside; a single line in a book may need to become a lengthy scene.'[5] Malcolm Bradbury goes still further – he is almost lyrical in praise of dramatisation: 'It is precisely this capacity for powerful retelling that makes me an advocate of television adaptation. I believe that culture has always extended itself by the retelling and remaking of narratives. Shakespeare rewrote Plutarch, opera adapted Shakespeare.'[6]

If we accept (and I admit that this may be contentious) that Paul Scott's *Raj Quartet* is a literary achievement of the first rank (H. R. F. Keating called it 'an immensely rewarding experience')[7]; that it is well crafted, teeming with a life of its own, full of significant insights into Anglo-Indian relations in the last days of the Raj (according to John Bayley, 'Paul Scott's India is entirely believable')[8] – then its transformation into the 14-episode television serial, *The Jewel in the Crown*, makes an interesting laboratory case by which to assess the validity of Jonathan Miller's diagnosis.

The actual success with viewers and critics alike of *The Jewel in the Crown* – a follow-up by Granada of *Brideshead Revisited* in terms of scale and ambition – is not open to question. When first transmitted from 3 January to 3 April 1984, it was instantly recognised and acknowledged as a blockbuster with high claims to quality.[9] Its average viewing figure of 8,050,000 may seem small beer compared to that reached by Granada's evergreen *Coronation Street*, which reached an average viewing figure of 16 million during the eighties, with some peaks greatly in excess of that, as in February 1982 when 29 million tuned in to find out whether Deirdre Barlow would leave her husband Ken to live with Mike Baldwin, and in January 1989 when the Sunday omnibus repeat attracted 22.9 million viewers.[10] Though not remotely comparable, *The Jewel*'s figure was nevertheless highly respectable for a drama which, in contrast to the more relaxed attention span demanded by a continuous serial, required viewers to stay with it religiously for more than three months and to give it their full imaginative co-operation. It may have lost some of its original drawing-power when repeated on Channel 4 in the following year, but it still pulled an average of 1,732,000 viewers. Julian Barnes called it 'one of the best TV dramas ever made',[11] and for Sean Day-Lewis it was 'not just the series of the decade but the richest television drama of all'.[12]

There were bound to be some discordant voices, of course. In a knocking piece entitled, 'This Crown Jewel is only paste', Ferdinand Mount came buzzing in from the ideological right and declared himself 'taken aback by how far the ITV series *The Jewel in the Crown* falls short of the claims made for it ... The production is stilted and jerky, suggesting not so much that the British are out of place in India as that the actors have lost their place in the script.'[13] Irritation with *The Jewel*'s disenchanted picture of British rule in India came in the guise of elegant disdain for the serial's aesthetic qualities – with a neat side-swipe at the BBC. A more surprising thumbs-down came on the BBC discussion programme, *Did You See...?*, chaired by Ludovic Kennedy. The experts on India gathered for the programmes of 12 February and 18 March 1984 to discuss *The Jewel* seemed to be handpicked to utter views unfavourable to any critical depiction whatever of Imperial rule.[14]

There was also a cannonade from the left by Salman Rushdie who dismissed *The Raj Qartet* as an unwarrantedly Anglocentric view of India. He claimed that 'it tells us ... that the history of the end of the Raj was largely composed of the doings of the officer class and its wife. Indians get walk-ons, but remain, for the most part, bit-players in their own history.' He admitted, in contrast to Ferdinand Mount, that there was much brilliant acting in *The Jewel*, but maintained that it was necessary 'to make a fuss about Raj fiction and the zombie-like revival of the defunct Empire'.[15] This would have been justified if the Raj Quartet and *The Jewel in the Crown* had indeed been the story of the end of the Raj as such. However, it is arguably the story not so much of India as of the British officer class of that time, rapidly being thrust to the margin of history but not, for that reason, devoid of interest in themselves.

These contradictory critiques do not exactly cancel each other out (though both Mount and Rushdie agreed in one respect, and that was in taxing Scott with leaning excessively on E. M. Forster's *A Passage to India*). They do, however, prompt the thought that *The Jewel*, leaving partisans on both sides of the fence equally dissatisfied, may well have got the balance about right. The criticisms did little in any case to affect the serial's general success.

Indeed, this success was as wide as it was deep. It strengthened the notion that Britain had the best television in the world, certainly the best television drama. When transmission began in the United States in December 1984 on the PSB network in the Masterpiece Theatre slot sponsored by Mobil, reviews were ecstatic. To the *Boston Globe* it was, appropriately enough, 'a masterpiece', *Vogue Magazine* called it 'superb ... something special', *Variety* spoke of a 'stunning production'. True, it was found necessary to have each episode introduced by Alistair Cooke, perennial interpreter of the Americans and the British to one another; in these chats he not only provided the story links for North American viewers who might have missed the preceding episode, but he also filled them in on the mysteries of the Raj, something alien to their own historical memories. Harry F. Waters in *Newsweek* and Pico Iyer in *Time Magazine* advised their compatriots not to reach for their remote controls too precipitately and to stay with a rewarding viewing experience, unusual though it might be compared to the fast action and genre conventions of American TV drama.

Within a few years, *The Jewel* was to travel around television screens, if not quite of the whole world then certainly of a sizeable chunk of it. Its appreciation in Canada, Australia, New Zealand or Jamaica may not be all that startling; memories of Empire linger. But its acceptance in Europe – in France, Belgium, Italy, Greece, the Netherlands, Finland, Sweden, Iceland and elsewhere – is perhaps more unexpected. Its appearance on the small screen in countries as far apart – mentally as well as geographically – as Argentina, Israel, Morocco, Kenya, Zimbabwe, Brunei and Sri Lanka suggests a cross-cultural appeal almost on a par with that of *Dallas*. Indeed, one wonders what did Mauritius, Angola or Nicaragua make of it? More surprisingly still, *The Jewel* crossed the ideological gulf then still dividing Europe: Hungarian, East German, Polish and Yugoslav viewers all shared this televisual feast with their Western capitalist contemporaries. Perhaps most astonishing of all is the fact that *The Jewel* was televised in India and Bangladesh – astonishing inasmuch as its final episode might be thought to have run the risk of stirring up memories of the intercommunal massacres following Partition in 1947.

The sheer professionalism of the serial was, of course, self-evident. The whole enterprise was the equivalent to making a feature film – correction: to making seven such films, in terms of length at any rate. Its budget of £5,600,000 (modest by later standards) was put up entirely by Granada, who did not wish to be beholden to any co-producers. The venture paid off commercially. By the time episode 8 was transmitted, the sum invested had been recouped from United Kingdom network and foreign sales.

The effort paid off artistically, too. Its producer/director Christopher Morahan, who had a vast amount of stage as well as television experience since the early fifties, left his post as deputy director at the National Theatre in 1981 in order to devote three years of his life to preparing, shooting and completing this telefilm. Some four months of strenuous work at various locations in India – at Udaipur, Mysore, Simla and Kashmir – were followed by many more months of additional filming on location in England and Wales as well as in Granada's Manchester studio. There was an admirably seamless meshing of the work of Christopher Morahan with that of second director Jim O'Brien (who was to achieve even greater prominence in 1986 as the director of Alan Bleasdale's 'controversial' *The Monocled Mutineer*).[16] The fact that Morahan had directed the even-numbered episodes and O'Brien the odd-numbered ones was not apparent to the naked eye. One of the many virtues of their shared style was its lack of pictorial self-indulgence. *The Jewel* was consistently good to look at: Ray Goode, the lighting cameraman, had also been responsible for the glossy appearance of *Brideshead*. But the directors did not give in to the temptation of a picture-book representation of India, unlike some other Western-produced films made in the eighties, such as *Heat and Dust*, *The Far Pavilions* and *A Passage to India*.

The Jewel in the Crown was like a roll-call not only of British but also of Indian and Pakistani acting talent; the latter included such veterans as Saeed Jaffrey, Zia Mohyeddin and Zohra Segal. On the British side, Dame Peggy Ashcroft gave a deeply moving embodiment to Barbie Batchelor, the much put-upon missionary-school teacher – a part she herself had explicitly asked to play; Rachel Kempson, the doyenne of the Redgrave tribe, was a sympathetically statuesque Lady Manners; Fabia Drake brought a lifetime's stage experience to the role of 'Aunt' Mabel Layton. There is no space here to detail all the performances by seasoned as well as by younger players other than to note how much of a career boost this exposure gave to some; thus, Art Malik was elevated to the part of Hari Kumar from an £80-a-week stage role at the Soho Poly in London. Even some of those who were far from being novices were affected by the experience. Thus, Tim Piggott-Smith had years of stage and screen experience behind him; but his sharp portrayal of the sinister battle-scarred soldier-policeman Ronald Merrick made him so highly bankable that he was immediately inundated with offers to play more one-armed sadists.[17] Though Geraldine James had appeared before in Richard Attenborough's *Gandhi*, her performance as Sarah Layton, one of the key characters in *The Jewel*, greatly increased her standing as an actress. Charles Dance, who had been with the RSC for five years without quite achieving star status, overnight turned into what the press called 'the thinking woman's crumpet' as a result of having played Guy Perron.

Honours for such a distinguished production were not slow in coming. Thus, in 1984 the Royal Television Society gave the Writer's Award for an Exceptional Adaptation to Ken Taylor, a Performance Award to Dame Peggy Ashcroft and the Design Award to Vic Symonds and Alan Pickford. In the same year there were BAFTA awards for the best drama serial as well as the best actress (Peggy Ashcroft) and best actor (Tim Piggott-Smith), and an International Emmy Award for the best drama. In 1985 *The Jewel* won the Golden Globe as well as the National Board of Review Award and was voted the programme of the year by the US TV Critics' Association.

But while accepting the quality of *The Jewel* in terms of sheer production values, we may yet ask ourselves whether the whole venture was justified in Jonathan Miller's terms, and specifically what artistic problems were involved in adapting *The Raj Quartet* for the small screen.

When Paul Scott's tetralogy was first published between 1966 and 1975, it was on the whole received respectfully but hardly made him a household name. None of the books sold more than 10,000 copies in hardback during his lifetime.[18] But then his next (and last) book, *Staying On*, won the Booker Prize. Philip Larkin, the chairman of the panel of judges, called it 'simply the most moving novel published in 1977'. Paul Scott unfortunately died in 1978, shortly after this breakthrough into wider recognition. Like *The Raj Quartet*, which is set in the five-year period of 1942 to 1947, *Staying On* looks at the life of the British in India – but twenty-five years later, in the year 1972. Tusker and Lucy Smalley, minor parts in the vast panorama of the *Quartet*, are the main characters of this much more tightly structured story – mere remnants of Empire, stranded in an independent India where they have become the pathetic debris of history.

It was this prize-winning book that attracted the attention of Denis Forman, the Chairman of Granada Television, and led him on to *The Raj Quartet*. Forman, one of the more influential figures in British television who managed to combine managerial flair with a high sense of cultural responsibility, had joined Granada as early as 1955. (Before that he had been the Chief Production Officer of the Central Office of Information and the Director of the British Film Institute.) A hands-on Chairman, he was to take an active interest in programme-making – not, by the way, to the exclusion of other interests, music in particular: in 1971 he published a book on Mozart's piano concertos. Seeing *The Raj Quartet* as a modern epic on the scale of *War and Peace*, he took out an option on it, though he realised how daunting an enterprise adapting it for television would be, logistically as well as aesthetically.

It was decided first to make *Staying On* as a single TV play-on-film in order to test the water for the more large-scale effort. *Staying On*, produced by Irene Shubik and adapted by Julian Mitchell, was directed by Silvio Narizzano, shot on location in Simla in 1980 and transmitted in the same year. Both by virtue of its story and its performers it was genuinely moving – the last time that Trevor Howard (Tusker Smalley) and Celia Johnson (his wife Lucy) were to play together. The fact that they had been the lovers of *Brief Encounter* thirty-five years earlier resonated in the minds of at least the older generation of film-goers. It was to be Celia Johnson's last screen appearance, her death taking place not long afterwards, in 1982. Together Johnson and Howard gave a memorable performance – full of humour, much irritability and disillusionment, brief flashes of tenderness and ultimately deep desolation. The programme was well received, so the decks were cleared for the larger effort of tackling the *Raj Quartet*. From the production point of view valuable lessons had been learnt: that it was possible for a television company to send a large crew to India, do all its own catering, look after its health, and get back first-rate footage. Another important conclusion was to shoot on film rather than video or a mixture of the two.

The adaptation of *The Raj Quartet* was bound to pose major problems apart from purely technical ones. There was the basic question of whether it was feasible to dramatise such a huge and seemingly sprawling work at all.

The quartet's first volume, *The Jewel in the Crown* (after which the entire serial was to be named) opens with the assault by rioters on the Protestant school supervisor Edwina Crane in the period of unrest following the Congress Party's 'Quit India' campaign in 1942. But the book's major concern is with aristocratic Daphne Manners who stays at Mayapore (an invented name meaning City of Illusion). She rejects a proposal of marriage by Ronald Merrick, the local District Superintendent of Police, but forms an intimate friendship with the English-educated Indian Hari Kumar. After Hari and Daphne have made love in the Bibighar Gardens, Daphne is raped by a gang of Indian hooligans: Merrick tries to pin the blame on Kumar together with various political suspects and has them all imprisoned for the duration.

The Day of the Scorpion follows the Kumar case (Daphne having died after giving birth to a daughter), but it concentrates particularly on the life of an Anglo-Indian family, the Laytons. When the younger daughter Susan Layton gets married to Captain Teddie Bingham in the (fictitious) princely state of Mirat, the best man at the wedding is Ronald Merrick, who has meanwhile become a captain in Military Intelligence. Soon after the wedding, Bingham is killed in the Imphal campaign against the Japanese; Merrick loses an arm in trying to save him. Sarah, the elder Layton girl, is seduced by a womanising officer during a one-night stand in Calcutta. The book also deals at length with the Congress politician Mohammed Ali Kassim, who is interned by the British, and his son Ahmed who becomes friendly with Sarah.

The Towers of Silence describes the contrasting lives of the Layton sisters: Susan gives birth to Teddie's son, Sarah has her unwanted child aborted. But the person who now also comes to the fore is the ex-missionary-school teacher Barbie Batchelor, who becomes disillusioned with her Christian and Imperial idealism. Traumatised by a series of shocks, she goes insane. Susan Layton also has a nervous breakdown, albeit only temporarily.

A Division of the Spoils introduces a major new character: the historian Guy Perron. In India as a sergeant in Field Security, he forms a liaison with Sarah Layton. The sinister Merrick, who has risen to the rank of colonel and married the widowed Susan, is assassinated; his sadomasochistic character – linked with repressed homosexuality – has been finally exposed. Hari Kumar is exonerated and released from prison. As Independence comes to India, the departing British are caught up in the upheavals on the eve of Partition: there is a nightmarish journey on a train which is attacked by anti-Muslim fanatics and Ahmed, travelling with the Laytons and others, is murdered in a general massacre.

This absurdly compressed summary of *The Raj Quartet* inevitably fails to do justice to the epic scope of the story with its enormous cast of characters. Could this wealth of material be dramatised at all without falling into the Miller category of 'aerosol versions of great books'? But apart from the question of sheer size, there was also the problem of the 'multiple point of view' – that is, Scott's collage method of telling his story. He called it 'a complex of narratives' himself.[19] This technique is particularly in evidence in the first book of the quartet, where it is linked with the first-person device of a visiting narrator-investigator who collects differing accounts of the Kumar–Manners affair from the various participants and witnesses. These events are viewed retrospectively from the vantage point of 1964 – incidentally the year in which Paul Scott made the first of his three return visits to India after his wartime service there.[20] The same incidents are gone over again and again. Thus, there are as many as thirteen references from different perspectives to the rape of Daphne Manners in the Bibighar Gardens, producing diverse types of statement: direct narrative by Lili Chatterjee, Daphne's upper-class hostess in Mayapore; by the Mother Teresa-like Sister Ludmila; by the lawyer Srinivasan; and other testimony such as letters by Daphne to her mother, Lady Manners; correspondence between Hari Kumar and his English public-school friend Colin Lindsey; an edited extract from the unpublished memoirs of Brigadier Reid; an edited transcript of recorded comments by District Commissioner White; a deposition by Vidyasagar, one of the accused in the Bibighar affair; two letters by Lady Manners to Lili Chatterjee; and Daphne's journal addressed to Lady Manners. The latter at long last clears Hari Kumar of any blame for the assault.

Though the other three volumes of the quartet have a little less of this multi-faceted character, they are not without their own artful literary devices. Time doesn't progress straightforwardly from A to B. Objective events, subjective memories and dreams interpenetrate. Not only does this disjunctive technique give readers a more complex and panoramic view of events; it forces them to think through the motives of actions unfathomable at first, and to work out the wider implications of the whole story.

Having made this project very much his own, Forman decided that only a considerably simplified plotline would serve to make *The Raj Quartet* an acceptable vehicle for television. A linear approach was needed: all the main events were to be arranged in chronological order and secondary episodes were to be excised.

Was this attack, significantly different from the literary original, the right one? According to Jeannette Winterson – 'The first question for anyone transposing a book to the screen, is how to smash up the original and do it justice in a different way. Faithful adaptations make bad television.'[21]

In the cinema we have long been familiar with narrative disjunction: past, present and future chopped up and jumbled about in order to illuminate the inner meaning of events, the credibility of any one version being challenged by alternative versions. *Citizen Kane* and *Rashomon* showed years ago that this was possible. Can't this be done equally well on television? As long ago as 1966, John Hopkins presented a family tragedy from four different points of view in the BBC television quartet, *Talking to a Stranger* (directed, let us recall, by Christopher Morahan). But if time *can* be handled that freely in principle, the decision to opt for a linear approach here was actually the right one. Sustaining interest over fourteen episodes is a difficult enough business anyway. If chronology had been disrupted as well, viewers of this essentially realistic narrative might have found it difficult to keep all its intricacies in mind. *Citizen Kane*, with its running time of a mere 119 minutes, provided no model here. It must be admitted that the simplification of *The Raj Quartet*'s narrative line meant sacrificing some of the story's resonances; but the gain in direct dramatic impact amply made up for this loss.

Given this fundamental choice, that still left open the problem of just how to shape the massive epic into thirteen one-hour episodes (which in the event turned out to be fourteen episodes). The way Forman and Irene Shubik solved this problem – at any rate on the level of mechanics – was to chop up a roll of wallpaper into thirteen pieces about 1 yard square, pin them round the walls of a room, jot down an hour's worth of narrative on each segment and then shift individual incidents to and fro: in other words, do a preliminary story edit until an overall shape emerged. The actual commission to write the script went to Ken Taylor, TV playwright and experienced adapter of plays and novels for the small screen (including works by D. H. Lawrence, Muriel Spark, Rebecca West, Thomas Hardy, Jane Austen and Edith Wharton), who had himself spent some time in India.[22] Even though much of the spadework for the adaptation had already been done, Taylor's handling of *The Raj Quartet* shows a high degree of skill. The narrative is powerfully sustained.[23] While sticking to a linear storyline, he found some sort of an equivalent to Scott's disjunctions in the cinematically quite conventional use of voice-overs and flashbacks.[24] One must admit that it is largely Scott's own world rather than the particular quality of the adaptation, expert though it is, that gives *The*

Jewel in the Crown its driving force and riveting quality. Scott's writing is inherently dramatic and highly gestural, and its dialogue comes off the page (which doesn't mean it can simply be lifted bodily and transposed to a playscript). It is also eminently visual. Perhaps that has something to do with the fact that Scott's father was a commercial artist whose studio he would often visit as a small boy.[25] An equally relevant biographical fact is that between the ages of nine and thirteen he went into 'the film business' together with his brother Peter, strictly for the entertainment of the family. The Scott boys produced, directed, designed and drew pictures on long strips of greaseproof paper – and ended up making 'films' with a running time of up to 60 minutes, some sequences even being in colour.[26] This didn't turn Paul Scott into a film-maker as an adult, but it did give a distinctly cinematic, or rather imagistic, quality to his writing. He himself has stated that for him a novel was in the first place a story-generating sequence of images rather than a story arrived at conceptually with the images, as it were, stuck on afterwards.[27]

But we should not assume that a novel by an author with a vivid pictorial imagination is bound to translate easily into film. There is a fundamental distinction between the ways in which verbal and pictorial images work.

The verbal image readily lends itself to generalisation by fastening on to certain qualities of a given object, to the total exclusion of others. It may open up a poetic dimension; it can readily turn into a symbol. When Shakespeare compares his friend to a summer's day, the comparison holds good in certain respects, but in those respects only: he means the beauty and temperateness of that day, abstracted from any of its other coincidental qualities.[28] Mosquitoes, sunburn and nettle-rash are kept out of the picture.

Now the visual image doesn't take on this selective and metaphorical quality quite so easily, although of course it may do so. Unless handled with skill the photographic image remains stubbornly itself, specific rather than general, with a deal of random noise – fortuitous rather than significant features – tending to blur the intended message.

We shall appreciate some of the problems of transposing *The Raj Quartet* into visual images when we recall the impulse which first gave rise to the entire process that resulted in a work running in the end to over 2,300 pages (in the paperback edition). Paul Scott said this about its genesis, his first spark of inspiration:

My image came . . . in the dark of a restless, sleepless night . . . And there she was, my prime mystery, a girl, in the dark, running, exhausted, hurt in some way, yet strangely of good heart – tough, resilient, her face and figure a sense rather than an observed condition. But she runs.[29]

This vague but crucial image of the running girl, which was to turn into that of Daphne Manners escaping from the Bibighar Gardens after her rape, summoned up in his mind – no doubt unconsciously at first – a cluster of feelings and ideas: mysterious and difficult personal involvements ... the tangled relationship between rulers and ruled in India ... a dim fore-shadowing of the end of the Raj. Actually, this image is stated in verbal, indeed in conceptual terms, in the opening paragraph of the first book of the quartet which is at the same time an appeal for the reader's imaginative co-operation:

> Imagine, then, a flat landscape, dark for the moment, but even so conveying to a girl running in the still deeper shadow cast by the wall of the Bibighar Gardens an idea of immensity, of distance.[30]

This appeal is not paralleled in the TV script. The first episode ('Crossing the River') opens with a wartime newsreel; we then see Sister Ludmila, a Russian expatriate who runs a sanctuary for destitute Indians, finding Hari Kumar as he lies drunk in a wasteland close to the sanctuary. Shortly after he has been taken to the sanctuary, Hari is confronted and threatened by Ronald Merrick. A major theme of *The Jewel*, that of the conflict between the British authorities and at any rate some Indians, has been broached: an appropriately dramatic opening to the serial. The image of the running girl, Scott's original inspiration for the entire work, does not occur until the second episode, 'The Bibighar Gardens'. There it is treated in purely narrative and dramatic, not in poetic (or rather imagistic) terms.

Nevertheless, Taylor's script does retain some of the key images of *The Raj Quartet*, including some with so high a figurative charge as almost to be symbols. Let us look at a few of the more prominent ones.

The image of fire is equally important on the page and on the screen. It is of course highly visual. The school supervisor Edwina Crane experiences fire in its destructive aspect twice: first, her car is burnt by a rioting mob who attack and kill her colleague Mr Chaudhuri; later she commits suicide by shutting herself up in a garden shed and setting fire to it. Fire also engulfs Teddie Bingham's jeep when it is hit by Japanese grenades and bullets – the same fire that is to scar Ronald Merrick for life. The fire image recurs when Susan Layton-Bingham, doubly shocked by her husband's death in action and by the recent death of her father's stepmother, the beloved 'Aunt' Mabel, half-heartedly tries to do away with her baby son Edward: she puts him in a ring of flame, an attempted murder likened to the killing of a scorpion by fire. (This latter image, associated in Scott's mind with the expulsion of the British from India, was sufficiently important to make him call the second volume of the quartet *The Day of the Scorpion*.)

Fire is also implied, though not stated overtly, in the tiffin box of ashes which Susan holds in her lap during the calamitous train journey in the

10 *District Superintendent of Police Ronald Merrick (Tim Piggott-Smith), accompanied on his R by Subinspector Rajendra Singh (Siddarta Kak) and on his L by a Constable, throws his weight around in Episode 1, 'Crossing the River', of* The Jewel in the Crown. *Granada 1984*

serial's final episode. These ashes are the last remains of her second husband Ronald Merrick, who had been cremated after dying in mysterious circumstances. Fire seems to be the element that burns away the Raj. But Scott gives the image yet another, wider meaning when he makes Sister Ludmila refer to Shiva, the dancer in a circle of cosmic fire, a figurine of whom she keeps in her room. We are reminded that the god is implicated in the eternal round of creation, preservation and destruction in which all human affairs, not only Empires but everything else as well, are but transient matters of the moment.[31]

A more overt symbol is the lace christening gown with the butterfly pattern which had been used for Sarah Layton's christening. Sarah asks 'Aunt' Mabel to pass it on to her sister Susan for the christening of little Edward; and it is in this gown that Susan wraps the child when she tries to immolate him. A similar piece of lace, also with a butterfly pattern, is given by Mabel to her companion, the pathetic Barbie Batchelor. Barbie drapes herself in it on the tonga ride which ends with her vehicle turning over and spilling her out – a ride, as it turns out, into insanity. The lace gown makes a clear visual statement as an image of a heritage which has lost its virtue. It does, however, lack the additional literary overtone that Scott gives it in the second volume of the quartet. There we are informed, somewhat romantically, that the lace had been made by a blind Frenchwoman who regarded the butterflies as being imprisoned in the pattern and longing for freedom.

A third image taken over by Taylor from *The Raj Quartet* is the picture of 'The Jewel in Her Crown'. Both Edwina Crane and Barbie Batchelor own a copy of this allegorical print of Queen Victoria, enthroned and surrounded by representative figures of the Indian Empire rendering homage. Scott does not treat this kitsch piece of missionary-school propaganda without a degree of wry sympathy. Its fortunes run in ironic parallel to the actual dissolution of Empire. Barbie gives away her print of 'The Jewel in Her Crown' to Ronald Merrick who doesn't really share the idealism it stands for. He in turn passes it on to his stepson Edward: the grand vision of predestined hierarchical stability has dwindled to the status of a nursery ornament. This particular image, baldly emblematic as it is, perhaps loses least in its transposition to the screen.

A device that could not be taken over direct from the printed page were the excursuses which Scott interpolated in order to supply the necessary social and political background to the story. The solution to this problem was simple and effective. From time to time wartime newsreel clips from Pathé, the Imperial War Museum and the National Film Archive break into the narrative. These chronicle the progress of Allied campaigns in the Far East, celebrate the role of the Indian Army and occasionally bring in events from the European theatre of war. The recurrent use of actuality material was established as a stylistic device from the very beginning of the first episode. Over George Fenton's stirring theme tune we see the opening titles which would be repeated for each succeeding instalment: a sequence of eleven shots from the archives showing the Raj in its days of splendour. One picture in particular stays in the memory – a tiny brown lad eagerly rushing forward to polish the boots of one of a group of enormously tall Indian guardsmen lined up on parade.

Not only do these black-and white newsclips provide a factual background to the story – they also reflect period attitudes in their camerawork, editing style and commentaries. Seen some four decades later, they carry an ironical subtext. Wartime certainties have softened in the light of subsequent history; attitudes natural at the time now seem stilted or patronising.

Even with these aids to understanding, *The Jewel in the Crown* made unusual demands on its viewers. What at first seems the central relationship – that between Hari Kumar and Daphne Manners – flickers out with Daphne's death after the second episode. The Laytons dominate the action after that, Sarah taking over from Daphne as the moral centre of the narrative – but again not to the exclusion of other figures. Ronald Merrick, of course, does provide some sort of a continuing thread, perhaps even more on the screen than on the printed page. But he, too, dies in the last episode but one and appears in the final one only by way of a flashback. Barbie Batchelor, a key figure in that she presents a different perspective on the values of the Raj, vanishes with episode 9. Guy Perron, who comes to play an increasingly prominent role, only makes his appearance in episode 10. The plot constantly reorganises itself around new growing points of interest.

The means by which this wandering storyline is kept on track is by a series of echoes. The reiteration of thematically related events keeps formlessness at bay. This is in line with Scott's notion that the several images making up a novel should be linked by some interesting and meaningful relationship.[32] Let us look at just a few of the many events so related to one another.

The tender love-making of Sarah Layton and Guy Perron recalls that of Hari and Daphne. On the other hand, Sarah's calculated seduction by Jimmy Clark mirrors her mother's coupling with her for-the-duration-only lover, a purely carnal affair which is depicted pretty explicitly for a brief moment. The group assault on Edwina Crane parallels the gang rape of Daphne Manners. The murder of Edwina's colleague Mr Chaudhuri and the killing of Ahmed Kassim are both scenes of Indians being killed by Indians, with Europeans as helpless bystanders. Sarah's visit to Merrick in the military hospital after he has been wounded is counterpointed by her visit to Barbie Batchelor in the mission hospital after the tonga accident. On both occasions she is *sympathique* but ineffectual. It was right to retain these subtle narrative echoes in the adaptation of *The Raj Quartet*.

Another aspect it was wise to borrow from the quartet was a fair amount of Scott's eminently speakable dialogue. *The Jewel in the Crown*, though full of external events, is not primarily an action serial. A great deal of its meaning is carried by the words – precisely the aspect so derided by Frederick Mount.[33]

At the end of the last book of the quartet, Guy Perron – by now, that is, in 1947, merely a visitor to India – flies home again; he has just tried to visit his old schoolfellow Hari Kumar. But Hari was not at home when he called; all Guy could do was to leave a written message. By this near-encounter of two characters from very different parts of the story, the first strand of it fleetingly ties in with much later strands. Up to this point the TV script has been following the novel; if anything it foregrounds the visit more. But in the book, Guy's flight home sets up an echo, absent in the TV drama, with another flight at the end of the first volume of the quartet: that of the narrator figure (who as we have seen has disappeared from the telefilm altogether). The final pages of the fourth volume soar into a literary conceit in mid-air. Guy reads the translation of a poem by a (fictitious) Urdu poet. These lines, which end the tetralogy, reiterate several images that we have encountered before – the prince's court, the hawk, the girl running – and give them a lyrical inflection. The poem places the action of the quartet within the onward flow of time but freezes it in a moment of illumination as the story ends: an entirely literary device.

Television had to follow a different tactic. The scene of Guy's departure begins in colour; then an aerial shot – that is, one taken from Guy's point of view – turns monochrome. This leads us back into the newsreel convention with a brief sequence of black-and-white stock shots of Nehru speaking to a huge crowd. The speech goes on as voice-over as we cut to Guy's calling-card left at Hari's – still in monochrome; the camera pans over to a close-up of a photograph of the late Daphne Manners. We dissolve to a shot of Hari now at his desk, writing, the photograph at his side. As the camera pulls back into freeze-frame, Nehru's voice-over continues announcing his country's independence.

By the change to monochrome, hitherto associated with the old newsreels, Hari is, as it were, reintegrated into his country's history. Hari Kumar has shed the persona of English-educated Harry Coomer. This alienated and persecuted Indian has become – whether happily or not – part of an event larger than his personal fate. At the same time we are shown an abiding bond of affection transcending the racial divide: his love for Daphne. The flow of time, the place of the individual within public events have been asserted as they were in the book, but by visual rather than literary means.

Behind the final credits we see Barbie Batchelor's allegorical picture being consumed by flames and reduced to ashes. Thus two of the key images – fire and the Imperial 'Jewel in Her Crown' – fuse at the conclusion of what is surely one of the most remarkable of all British television serials: a work that does not deny its literary origin but has transmuted words on the page into something wholly visual and wholly dramatic.

The Jewel in the Crown

First episode transmitted on 9 January 1984 on ITV; the repeat series began on 14 January 1985 on Channel 4

For full cast and technical/production credits, see *The Making of The Jewel in the Crown* (Granada, 1983), 131–45

Notes

1 Peter Fiddick, in *The Guardian*, 1 September 1983, 10.
2 'Valete', *Programme of the 1984 Edinburgh International Television Festival*, 85.
3 Quoted by Hugh Whitemore, 'Word into image: reflections on television dramatization', in Frank Pike (ed.), *Ah! Mischief/The Writer and Television* (London: Faber, 1982), 101.
4 'The celluloid collar 1', *The Listener*, 24 March 1988, 17.
5 'A teenager in love (*Northanger Abbey*)', *Radio Times*, 14–20 February 1987, 101.
6 'The celluloid collar 6', *The Listener*, 8 April 1988, 23.
7 'The last days of the Raj', *Country Life*, 1 May 1975.
8 'The matter of India', *London Review of Books*, 19 March 1987, 195.
9 See Introduction, 3–4.
10 Information kindly supplied by Diane Cooke, *Coronation Street* publicist.
11 *The Observer*, 22 January 1984.
12 *Daily Telegraph*, 15 February 1984.
13 *The Times*, 13 February 1984, 12.
14 For protests against the bias shown by these programmes and against the way they were reported in *The Listener*, see the following items in that paper: Christopher Morahan's letter headed 'All the Raj', 29 March 1984, 20, and Denis Forman, 'Langham Diary', 5 April 1984, 19.
15 'Outside the whale', *Granta*, April 1984.
16 See Introduction, 10–11.
17 I am indebted for this (perhaps slightly tongue-in-cheek) piece of information to Mr Piggott-Smith.
18 The first appreciation of *The Raj Quartet*, primarily in terms of its accurate portrayal of the atmosphere of the time, was by Max Beloff: 'The end of the

Raj', *Encounter*, May 1976. For further critical comments, see the following: K. Bhaskara Rao, *Paul Scott* (Boston: Twayne Publishers, 1980); Patrick Swinden, *Paul Scott: Images of India* (London: Macmillan 1980); Robin Moore, *Paul Scott's Raj* (London: Heinemann 1990), as well as the following articles: Francine Weinbaum, 'Paul Scott's India: *The Raj Quartet*', *Critique* 20.1 (1978), and 'Psychological defenses and thwarted union in *The Raj Quartet*', *Literature and Psychology* 31 (1981); M. M. Mahood, 'Paul Scott's guardians', *Journal of English Studies* 13 (1983); Tariq Ali, 'Fiction as history, history as fiction', *Illustrated Weekly of India*, 8 July 1984.

19 From Paul Scott's notebooks, quoted in Moore, *Paul Scott's Raj*, 63; and Alan Boyer, 'Love, sex, and history in *The Raj Quartet*', *Modern Language Quarterly* 46 (1985), 64–80.

20 For a full description of this visit, which provided a crucial inspiration for *The Raj Quartet*, see Hilary Spurling, *Paul Scott: A Life* (London: Heinemann 1990), esp. ch. 11 ('A Passage to India'), 270–305.

21 Jeanette Winterson, 'Adaptation', in Philippa Giles and Vicky Licorish, *Debut on Two* (London: BBC Books, 1990), 59.

22 This description of the genesis of the script follows the account given in the Introduction by Denis Forman to *The Making of the Jewel in the Crown* (London: Granada Publishing Limited, 1983), 7–8.

23 For different views on the status of adapters, see Whitemore, 'Word into Image', in Pike, *Ah! Mischief*, 101–10.

24 For Ken Taylor's own view of his work on the script, see Andrew Robinson, 'The Jewel in the Crown', *Sight and Sound*, 53.1 (1983–4), esp. 48.

25 See Spurling, *Paul Scott: A Life*, 15–17.

26 See 'A writer takes stock (1973)', in Paul Scott, *My Appointment with the Muse/Essays 1961–75*, ed. by Shelley C. Reece (London: Heinemann, 1986), 154–64.

27 See 'Method: the mystery and the mechanics (1967)', in *My Appointment*, 54.

28 Shakespeare, Sonnet 18.

29 Paul Scott, *My Appointment*, 60.

30 *The Jewel in the Crown* (1966), in *The Raj Quartet* (London: Heinemann, 1976), 1.

31 *Ibid.*, 137–8

32 'The architecture of the arts: the novel', in *My Appointment*, 83.

33 See note 13.

Select bibliography

Books by Paul Scott

The Jewel in the Crown (London: Heinemann, 1966)
The Day of the Scorpion (London: Heinemann, 1968)
The Towers of Silence (London: Heinemann, 1971)
A Division of the Spoils (London: Heinemann, 1975)
Staying On (London: Heinemann, 1977)
My Appointment with the Muse: Essays 1961–75, edited with an introduction by Shelley C. Reece (London: Heinemann, 1986)

Books about Paul Scott

Forman, Denis, Bamber Gascoigne *et al.*, *The Making of The Jewel in the Crown*
   (London: Granada Publishing, 1983)
Moore, Robin, *Paul Scott's Raj* (London: Heinemann, 1990)
Rao, K. Bhaskara, *Paul Scott* (Boston: Twayne Publishers, 1980)
Spurling, Hilary, *Paul Scott: A Life* (London: Heinemann, 1990)
Swinden, Patrick, *Paul Scott: Images of India* (London: Macmillan, 1980)

Articles

Fiddick, Peter, 'A master class' (Denis Forman as producer), *The Guardian*, 7
   January 1984
Hoggart, Simon, 'Tales of Empire', *New Society*, 5 April 1984, 19
Keating, H. R. F., 'Last days of the Raj', *Country Life*, 1 May 1975
Robinson, Andrew, 'The Jewel in the Crown', *Sight and Sound*, 53, 1 (1983–4),
   47–50
'Peggy Ashcroft in India', *Sight and Sound*, 53, 3 (summer 1984), 1988–9
Rushdie, Salman, 'Outside the whale', *Granta* (April 1984)
Tariq Ali, 'Fiction as history, history as fiction', in *Illustrated Weekly of India*, 8
   July 1984

There are further articles in the following publications:

American Cinematographer January 1985, 83–4, 86, 88, 90, 92–6 (The music for the
   serial)
Broadcast 9 November 1981, 4 (Details of a dispute holding up the shooting of the
   play)
   13 January 1984, 16–17 (Interview with Christopher Morahan)
   28 September 1984, 40 (TFI buys the serial from Granada)
   21 December 1984, 42 (China buys the serial)
   1 March 1985, 33 (Interview with costume designer Diane Holmes)
   13 September 1985, 4–7 (India buys the serial)
Movie Maker 18, 6 (June 1984), 36–9 (Interview with Christopher Morahan)
Screen International 7–14 January 1984, 28, 37 (Location report)
   29 June–6 July 1985, 32 (Details of the TV Critics' Association Award)
   13–20 April 1985, 1 (Highest ratings ever achieved by a drama serial on US
   Masterpiece Theatre)
Stills February–March 1984, 5 (Appraisal of the serial)
Television Today 21 January 1982, 14 (Detailed cast list and production credits)
   17 June 1982, 23 (Further casting and production details)
TV Times 7–13 January 1984, 4–6, 8 (Production feature)
   14–20 January 1984, 16–17 (Tim Piggott-Smith on his role)
TV Today 12 January 1984, 18 (Editorial comparing *The Far Pavilions* with *The
   Jewel in the Crown*)
Time Out 2–8 February 1984, 5 (An Indian view of *The Far Pavilions* and *The Jewel
   in the Crown*)

12   *The Life and Loves of a She-Devil* (Fay Weldon – Ted Whitehead)

LIZ BIRD AND JO ELIOT

It is twelve years since the publication of *British Television Drama*[1] edited by George Brandt, to which this volume is a successor. *British Television Drama* contained eight essays on the work of individual television dramatists. All of these dramatists were men. Did men still predominate as television dramatists in the 1980s? A glance at the contents list of this volume will show that things do not appear to have changed very much. All the authored texts discussed are written by men, with the exception of this piece on *The Life and Loves of a She-Devil*, which was adapted for television, from the novel by Fay Weldon, by another male dramatist, Ted Whitehead. In what follows we intend, first, to discuss the text, *The Life and Loves of a She-Devil*, in terms of how it was adapted as a script for television and then to consider the position of women writing for television in the 1980s. Thereafter we discuss the genres employed in the making of the TV series and examine both its critical reception and its popularity with audiences. Next we shall ask how the text can be read in the light of psychoanalytic, semiotic and postmodernist critical theory and finally we shall evaluate how far *The Life and Loves of a She-Devil* can be read as a feminist text.

The text – novel into a TV series

The novel, *The Life and Loves of a She-Devil* by Fay Weldon, was first published in 1983 and adapted for television by Ted Whitehead in 1986, produced by Sally Head and directed by Philip Saville. There are a number of differences between the novel and the television series, primarily in terms of emphasis and the inevitable exclusion from the series of certain episodes from the novel. *The Life and Loves of a She-Devil*, like much of Fay Weldon's work, mixes the real and the surreal, domestic and social realism

11 *Julie T. Wallace as Ruth (the 'She-Devil') in episode 2 of the Fay Weldon – Ted Whitehead serial,* The Life and Loves of a She-Devil. *BBC 1986*

are blended and spiced with fantasy and the supernatural.

Ruth (played by Julie T. Wallace, an unknown) is 6 ft 2 inches tall, 15 stone, clumsy, gauche, dressed in crimplene, with moles and facial hair. She is a mother of two, a good wife in a neat suburban house. Her accountant husband Bobbo (played by Denis Waterman) is stolen by Mary Fisher (Patricia Hodge), Romantic Novelist of the Year, 5 ft 4 inches, delicate, fragile, all silks, satins and champagne, an independent and successful dweller in a tall White Tower by the sea. What follows is Ruth's transformation into a She-Devil and her renouncing of the role of 'good soul': she is bent on revenge, power, money and 'to be loved and not love in return'.[2] What drives the plot is Ruth's desire to get even with Mary Fisher. Her consuming envy of Mary makes her want to become Mary. By the end of *The Life and Loves of a She-Devil* Ruth, after a series of agonising operations, *has* become Mary, has stolen her physical appearance, is living in her Tower with her servant and has enthralled and emasculated Bobbo. Mary is dead.

To achieve these ends Ruth assumes a variety of guises. In the novel she first tests her She-Devil powers on Carver, 'over sixty, whiskery and wrinkled, but bright eyed',[3] in his caretaker's hut at the sports ground. Their sexual encounter and Carver's vision of Ruth as a She-Devil ends with him having an epileptic fit. Not surprisingly this sequence was omitted from the TV series. Instead, having burnt down the suburban home, she dumps the children at the Tower with Bobbo and Mary. This concludes the first episode in the TV series, by which point Ruth, having been established initially as a good wife and mother, has become the She-Devil that her faithless husband has named her. The second episode opens with Ruth transformed into Raunchy Rita (see ill. 11) having a week of love with Geoffrey, a travelling salesman, whose eye condition she 'miraculously' cures.

Next she becomes Nurse Lily Latimer, another drastic change of appearance, and gets a job in the old people's home that houses Mary's heavily sedated old mother. Ruth liberates her and sends her off to the Tower, where the romantic idyll is fast becoming a scene of domestic chaos. Having completed the first part of her plan, Ruth now leaves the home and goes to work in a mental hospital where she befriends Nurse Hopkins (played by the inimitable Miriam Margolyes), 4 ft 11 inches and 15 stone. The two have a loving lesbian relationship, understated in the TV series, where they come together through their shared position of being regarded as freaks. In the TV adaptation the two have already become friends at the old people's home and move to the mental hospital together. Ruth now penetrates Bobbo's office, transferring money from his clients' accounts into their still-existing joint account. Episode 2 ends with Ruth 'still with a long long way to go', on course for acquiring the money she needs to achieve power. Once she acquires sufficient funds, Ruth and Nurse Hopkins set up the hugely successful Vesta Rose agency – Vista Rose in the

TV series – an agency which meets all the domestic needs of the women for whom it finds employment. Episode 3 opens with a glossy television advertisement for the agency. Ruth plants employees in Bobbo's office, one of whom, Elsie, sleeps with Bobbo and on telling him she loves him (at Ruth's urging) is hurriedly abandoned. Elsie now becomes the instrument of Ruth's revenge, she writes anonymously to Mary about her affair with Bobbo, thus further disrupting Mary's visions of love, and helps Ruth transfer all Bobbo's deposits to a Swiss bank account. The auditors move in and Bobbo is arrested for embezzlement.

Ruth's next transformation is into Polly Patch, mother's helper to the wife of Judge Bishop, who will be judging Bobbo's case. Here she ensures, by enthusiastically co-operating with the judge's sadistic sexual tastes for bondage and beating, that Bobbo gets a seven-year sentence. She has begun her physiological transformation with extensive work on her teeth and jaw, and for most of episode 3 in the TV series has only stumps for teeth. Mary's downfall is complete, left in the Tower with the children, her crazy mother, short of money, all spent on Bobbo's defence, and her guilt. Even Garcia, her body servant and physical comforter, rejects her.

Ruth leaves the judge's household and, in the novel, lives next with Vickie, single mother of two babies, on welfare. This section is cut from the TV adaptation; instead episode 4 opens with Father Ferguson, a crusading Catholic priest, played with salacious gusto by Tom Baker, employing Ruth – now Molly – as his housekeeper.

Ruth transforms Father Ferguson's life. She initiates him into the joys of sex and convinces him to campaign against romantic fiction, the prime corrupter of women's lives.

In the TV series Mary has already turned to God and worships in Father Ferguson's church, so is ripe for his command to stop writing 'pernicious nonsense'. Father Ferguson has developed a taste, under Ruth's tuition, for wine and women and seduces Mary, who wants to die: she has had carnal knowledge of a priest! At this point in the TV series Mary is visited, as she contemplates the ruin of her life, by a whirlwind, embodying the supernatural shape of Ruth, which literally drives her out through the window of the Tower to her death on the rocks below. (In the novel she dies more mundanely of cancer.)

In episode 3, as well as her dentistry, we have seen Ruth having consultations with Dr Genghis and Dr Black in Harley Street. In the novel she is ordered to lose 3 stone in weight, prior to her major surgery, and she moves into a feminist commune in order to do so. This is omitted from the TV series. Much of episode 4 is set in Genghis's and Black's luxurious Hermione clinic in the Californian desert, where Ruth's physical transformation is completed. The series ends rapidly; when fully transformed Ruth/Mary (now played by Patricia Hodge but with Julie T. Wallace's voice) leaves the Californian clinic, where both doctors have fallen in love with their creation, and returns to England, where she has bought and restored the derelict Tower. We see Ruth/Mary making love with the re-employed Garcia, in the presence of a stupefied Bobbo, now himself transformed into a ponytailed guitar-playing houseboy. Ruth/Mary is now in charge, she has revenge, power, money, and love. Bobbo has become a voyeur.

Both novel and TV series end with Ruth/Mary standing on the balcony of the restored Tower saying, 'I am a lady of six foot two, who had tucks taken in her legs. A comic turn, turned serious.'[4]

Issues of adaptation

Fay Weldon wrote her own adaptation of *The Life and Loves of a She-Devil* but the BBC turned it down: '. . . they said it wasn't true to the spirit of the book . . . thought it was rather cruel and hard and harsh'.[5]

Instead Ted Whitehead, author of *Alpha Beta* (1972) and an established television writer, did the adaptation. He has said[6] that his intention was to make the husband and mistress more realistic. Certainly we feel a far greater sympathy as viewers for Mary and Bobbo as their lives spin out of control than we do for them as characters in the novel. The narrative voice of both novel and television series is that of Ruth, and here Whitehead has stuck closely to the text of the novel. Fay Weldon's acidic tone is clearly heard. Fay Weldon 'enjoyed the series enormously',[7] although she pointed out that her novel emphasised envy, whereas the TV adaptation focused on revenge. Her own adaptation was 'less about the men and more about the women'.[8]

However, in her view, no author can own their work, a story is public property and an adapter will take off in whatever direction he or she wants. She has herself done a number of adaptations of others' work; in the 1980s this included a Penelope Mortimer short story and a five-part serialisation of *Pride and Prejudice*. Fay Weldon finds television 'quite a crude medium, quite limiting, in prose the writer can take longer, be more reflective'.[9]

Her preference is to write for television and then develop the television play/series into a novel. *Heart of the Country* (BBC 1987) and *Growing Rich* (Anglia 1991) both were television first. For Fay Weldon 'To move from television into novel is the perfectly interesting thing to do, to move from your own novel into your own television isn't very interesting . . . you're going to something where you can lose meaning from something where meaning is very precise . . . it's somehow quite disturbing to the spirit to do it'.[10]

Women writing for television

The 1980s was a good decade on television for Fay Weldon's work. She had seven plays transmitted, the two adaptations already referred to and two serials, *The Life and Loves of a She-Devil* and *Heart of the Country*, 1987.

Few other women television writers had such a high profile in the 1980s. Jill Hyem, co-author with Ann Valery of the series *Tenko* (which was highly successful and ran for three series in autumn 1981, 1982 and 1984) explores a number of reasons why women's writing is less often shown in her article, 'Entering the arena: writing for television'.[11] No one expected *Tenko* to be a success: 'The powers-that-be were singularly pessimistic – No-one'll want to know about an all-women cast looking their worst.'[12] She highlights in her account the difficulty women have in 'selling' their ideas for television to predominantly male decision-makers. The woman writer is up against male views of what the audience want.

A survey of the BBC conducted by Monica Simms in 1985[13] found that among the BBC's top grade of personnel there were 159 men and only 6 women, and only 8 per cent of staff in the category which includes heads of department and senior producers were female. The comparatively few women producers and directors make finding a sympathetic 'sponsor' for a project more difficult. It should be noted that 25 per cent of the members of the Writers' Guild are women, but a number of surveys have shown that the percentage of work by women performed on television or in the theatre falls far short of this.

Women have, in the past, predominated in writing for children's television. However, in the 1980s male writers moved into this genre with no concomitant move for women into the male-dominated genres of crime, cops and robbers, thrillers and espionage. Another area where women writers have had a reasonably high profile is in soap opera. A survey by the Women's Committee of the Writers' Guild for February 1985[14] showed that the newer soaps, *Eastenders* and *Brookside*, were employing more women than men writers. But the single-play market was 'becoming increasingly inaccessible to any but top established writers, mainly men'.[15]

Many of the women who write for television, as Hyem suggests, are former actresses who write partly because of the lack of female central characters. An Equity Report for 1985[16] showed that only 14 per cent of mid-evening programmes had female central characters, and most of these were under thirty. Given that figure one might speculate that work submitted by women writers with women central characters, particularly older women, would be looked on less favourably, as 'not what audiences want'. There is a view that discrimination against women writers occurs in the area of budgets rather than the selection of material.

Fay Weldon thinks 'there is reluctance to spend big budgets on women because of a basic assumption that anything done by a woman, that's held by a man's world, is inferior to anything done by a man'.[17] This is perhaps a reason why women's writing is broadcast more often on radio; it's cheaper and less of a risk.

For Fay Weldon 'the problem is writing things ... if you can write something they'll do it'.[18] This seems to contradict the assumption of inferiority referred to above. It only needs a look at the credits for plays and serials broadcast during the 1980s to wonder whether her view of the writer's gift being recognised, regardless of gender, is rather too sanguine.

As Jill Hyem says, 'There are still areas of drama and light entertainment that are virtually inaccessible to women writers. Even allowing for a certain amount of persecution mania, their ideas do tend to be belittled and misunderstood.'[19]

It might be thought that in the 1980s women would have achieved a higher profile as television dramatists, given the rise of feminism and the interest in women writers, clearly reflected in the publishing successes of Virago, the Women's Press and the feminist lists of mainstream publishers.

The genres of *The Life and Loves of a She-Devil*

Philip Saville, the director, has directed other Fay Weldon plays and clearly relished the opportunity to mix genres on television in the way Fay Weldon characteristically mixes styles in her novels. Within the four episodes we can identify the following genres: drama-documentary/faction, advertising, soap opera, social realism, romance, comedy, the supernatural, horror and science fiction.

The opening sequence is shot as a 'real' occasion, reminiscent of a televised Booker Prize Ceremony. Mary Fisher is presented with the Romantic Novelist of the Year award by Edna O'Brien, playing herself, as one who has cultural associations with romance. We see the identical scene in episode 3 two years later as Mary, dishevelled and distraught, watches the scene on television, alone in her Tower, while Bobbo languishes in prison. This time John Mortimer presents the prize, repeating the Booker formula. 'Real' people appear again in the interview that Mary Fisher has with Sue Cook on Breakfast TV, watched by Ruth and Bobbo over breakfast. Television appears within television as Saville establishes his heroine of popular culture using its favourite medium.

Television again appears as itself in the 'realistic' advertisement for the Vista Rose agency. This opens episode 3 and is so convincing that the viewer might be forgiven for thinking they had turned on ITV. However, so wonderful is the product – an agency which takes care of all the domestic chores while you work – one quickly realises that this is fiction. Advertising references appear again in the close-ups on the bubbling chip-pan, the frantic hamster, the smouldering cigarettes, the fire too close to the bed linen at the end of episode 1, when Ruth fires the house, which have strong echoes of public safety commercials.

Soap opera is evoked by Ruth and Bobbo's suburban home, a more upmarket Brookside, a Swindon estate house, with picture windows. Here Ruth is established as a good wife and home-maker with the regulation two children. The house becomes a dolls' house dwarfed by a giantess who seems to grow larger with misery. 'Are you putting on weight?' says Bobbo, as her domestic security crumbles.

Social realism appears in the settings in which Ruth is employed. The old people's home and the mental hospital are hyper-realist; the matron of the old people's home is a Dickensian figure, but the details of both institutions are sharply observed. We are only conscious of a slide into fantasy when we see the old women playing hockey and frisbee, liberated from their sedation by Ruth.

The generic conventions of romance are used for the early Mary Fisher scenes. When Bobbo and Mary first met in episode 1 the camera tracks Mary, swathed in white fur, the soundtrack is 'Some Enchanted Evening', the point of view is first Mary's, then Bobbo's, their eyes meet, they exchange the Look, it is a *coup de foudre*. The scenes at the Tower are invariably introduced by wide-angled shots of the sea and then pan in on the Tower. The Tower interiors are airy, luxurious Hollywood-style settings, in stark contrast to the cluttered and confining suburban interiors inhabited by Ruth.

Comedy is centred primarily in the scenes with old Mrs Fisher, a bravura performance by Liz Smith. Her arrival at the Tower accelerates the disruption begun by the children. In a gloriously anarchic scene in episode 2 she steals Mary's Rolls-Royce and drives crazily around the cliff top, a crate of lager beside her, careering through the dainty picnic Mary has organised on the grass. The children dress up in Mary's clothes, get drunk on her drink, the dogs and cat fight and Mrs Fisher gleefully presides over the chaos.

As the serial develops Saville increasingly uses the genres of the supernatural, horror and science fiction. Episode 1 ends with Ruth's eyes flashing red and then a long shot of her naked body retreating away from the camera, arms elongated to end in power beams, mists swirling around her and discordant music on the sound track. This image is used in different ways through the serial; it appears to Bobbo as he lies remorseful on his prison bed; it haunts Mary. The ultimate scene in this genre is when Mary is hounded to death by supernatural forces, in episode 4. Violent winds buffet her, blood drops from her pen onto the blotter, the sheets of pink paper on which she writes her romances fly up in the air and appear to attack her, the windows burst open and she is forced through them, calling Ruth's name as she falls out onto the rocks below.

Horror and hospital genres mix in the final episode, when Ruth undergoes her revolutionary surgery. There are close-ups of high-tech machinery, incisions, masked and gowned figures. The staff gather around to watch the bandages being peeled from Ruth's face; the face we see is a nightmare, bruised and swollen but recognisably Mary's. Patricia Hodge takes over from Julie T. Wallace at this point, but so distorted is the face that only the eyes reveal the transformation.

Reception

This mixture of genres caused some confusion amongst the critics. *The Life and Loves of a She-Devil* was reviewed in both the tabloid and the quality press, with a mixed response across the sectors. David Taylor of *Today* found it 'coarse, unbridled twaddle ... macabre, melodramatic muck' (12 October 1986), while Paul Donovan, also of *Today*, considered it to be 'polished drama' (9 October 1986). Herbert Kretzmer of the *Daily Mail* was perhaps the most devoted fan, reviewing it three times: 'most startling and original TV drama series of the year' (30 October 1986). Critics saw it as black comedy, fantasy, melodrama, Grand Guignol mixed with social realism, fairy-tale, farce, supernatural horror show.

The Life and Loves of a She-Devil was first transmitted on BBC2, starting on 8 October 1986, on four consecutive weeks from 9.25 p.m. to 10.25 p.m. The very first episode shared first place in the viewing figures for BBC2 at 6.3 million. The third episode achieved the highest viewing figures for the series and for BBC2 at 9.95 million. This may have been in part due to lack of opposition on the other channels; both BBC1 and ITV (Thames) screened documentaries against it. For episode 4 ITV had *The Equalizer* coming in as a new series, which possibly accounts for the fall-off in figures to 8.3 million for that episode. The series was repeated on BBC1 the following year and was also broadcast in the United States. The rise in viewing figures is reflected in the response of British newspaper television critics to its original broadcast as some critics continued to review it right up to the end, unusually for a serial.

Apart from viewing figures it is very hard to know how programmes are received, but it seems that it was a serial which aroused public interest and debate, 'everybody is talking about it', and 'here in our house the women were clapping and cheering as the lads cringed in their seats' (*New Musical Express,* 18 October 1986). The sexual politics of the play were much discussed, from one comment that 'the men were not getting a very good press' (*Daily Telegraph*, 16 October 1986) to debates over whether Ruth was right to exact such revenge. *Today* previewed the serial by an interview with Dennis Waterman (17 May 1986). In this Waterman is quoted as saying that the woman producer felt that Bobbo had been unkind to Ruth, whereas he did not agree at all with this view – 'Look at her, you'd leave her, wouldn't you?' Although, as the *Daily Telegraph* critic stated, there is an 'entirely reasonable and serious question about why we should find one person's body more attractive than another' (9 October 1986), nevertheless the critics overall dwelt on both Ruth's ugliness and her mythic proportions, referring to her as Lilith, Medea, Galatea, Boadicea, Colossus and Lucifer. The sex scenes were not often directly described, although Stanley Eveling of *The Scotsman* argued that viewers were getting their sadomasochistic kicks 'in the best possible taste' (25 October 1986), and one critic wondered why it had not attracted the attention of those wishing to 'clean up the BEEB' (Alan Coren, *Mail on Sunday*, 2 November 1986).

Those critics who had hailed the serial as a 'masterpiece' had their opinions endorsed by the members of the British Academy of Film and Television, who nominated it for the Best Drama Series award. It won this award in a year in which there were five other nominations, including John Mortimer's *Paradise Postponed*, Dennis Potter's *The Singing Detective* and Alan Bleasdale's *The Monocled Mutineer*. The production was co-produced with the Arts and Entertainment American channel and was broadcast in the United States four times. The final showing in the United States was timed to coincide with the release of the film, and the American press was unanimous in considering the television version to be better than the film, both on the grounds of its fidelity to the book and its more assertive sexual politics. *The Life and Loves of a She-Devil* would thus appear to have been popular with both critics and viewers, successful as quality television and in attracting a prime-time mass audience. How can we explain its appeal?

Reading the text

Popular television and other products of the mass media are resistant to aesthetic criticism because they are often classified as debased products. Moreover, the language of aesthetic criticism and its emphasis on value judgements does not come easily to those who wish to suggest that the products of the mass media are valuable in their own right and worthy of serious critical attention. We have ourselves contributed to this debate in an earlier work in which we argued that *Dallas* deserved to be taken seriously.[20] In seeking to provide this serious attention, critics have turned to the theoretical frameworks of psychoanalysis and semiotics as they can provide fruitful ways of understanding popular appeal and deconstructing texts which appear to be simple but are in fact extremely complex. In the following section we have used these frameworks, drawing particularly on those which feminist theory has made use of in its wide-ranging search for explanations of women's oppression.[21]

Woman as myth

Jung suggests that unconscious thought might be structured by myths or archetypes which are themselves framed within oppositions of masculinity and femininity. Ruth becomes the SHE-DEVIL, that is, a gendered embodiment of evil. A she-devil is like a mother-goddess; both are logically impossible if devils and gods are men. Mother goddesses within fertility cults are powerful beings with links to the myths of creation and female archetypes such as Lilith, Pandora and Eve. These can be read as evidence of both the power of women as creators and of men's fear of such power and their need to control female sexuality through the branding of women, all women, as evil and dangerous. As some critics pointed out, Ruth also recalls the Greek myth of Medea. Ruth's revenge is less horrific, but by abandoning her children she, like Medea, offends against the ideal of the good mother. In becoming the She-Devil Ruth becomes unnatural, she is neither womanly nor human, but is supernaturally powerful.

Woman as object

The Oedipal myth was chosen by Freud to explain heterosexual desires, that of the son for his mother, displaced on to a woman who stands for the mother, in a search for the lost unity of the infant with his mother. In the Oedipal myth, women are the objects of male desire, exchanged as objects in marriage, destined to be sought, never the active seekers or the protagonists of the narrative movement.[22] Women are surveyed, the object of the male gaze, passive not active.[23] Their sexuality is thus neither active nor powerful. Clearly there are many ways in which *The Life and Loves of a She-Devil* challenges or transgresses the Oedipal narrative and the concept of the passive woman.

What first disturbs the status quo and sets up the conflict which the narrative then seeks to resolve? While Bobbo's infidelity is the disruptive act, it is clearly initiated by Mary Fisher. She makes the advance and first seduces Bobbo and then entices him to leave Ruth and move into the Tower with her. From the point at which Ruth becomes the She-Devil, all the narrative is in her hands; she is the protagonist and she controls and directs the fortunes of Bobbo and Mary Fisher. By the use of voice-over, we know that Ruth knows exactly what is happening even when she is not there, another example of her magical powers. While the narrative thus places women in the centre, as both Ruth and Mary are powerful subjects and active protagonists rather than passive objects, nevertheless the end of the story is in fact the restoration of the Oedipal myth – Ruth acts in order to make herself into both the object of desire and the rightful wife.

Woman as Other

According to Lacan,[24] the French re-reader of Freud, who has had a great influence on feminist theory, the concept of self is acquired by the infant through a gendered process. The key moment is when the infant first becomes aware of the self, the so-called mirror phase, and sees itself as being separate from the mother. The presence or absence of the phallus determines whether the self is constructed as male or female, and the absence or lack of the phallus means that the female self is constructed as Other, or different from the dominant self. While masculinity is allied to the symbolic, the realm of the ego and of logos or order, femininity is allied to the power of the imaginary, of the id, the realm of libidinal drives and the Other.

In *The Life and Loves of a She-Devil* Ruth can be easily read as the Other. She is already unnatural; even before she becomes a She-Devil she describes herself as a dog, and the powerful sexuality she develops is strongly allied to the libidinal drive of the id. She is also, in some sense, imaginary. Not only is she re-created but her devil-like appearance is often signified by ghost-like hallucinations. She can be in two places at once and her special power frightens the gypsy who begs for money in the street. She challenges the symbolic order of the masculine logos, the world of business through manipulation of the computer, of the courts and of the church through her seduction of the judge and the priest. Her sexuality is able to defeat patriarchy and to overturn the rules of order and logic. She even goes beyond the science of medicine, challenging her doctors to achieve the unachievable in removing 7 inches from her height. Her success satisfies the fantasy of the libidinal drive, that the id can throw off the repressive authority of the ego and superego.

Woman as sign

The idea of signifying systems comes from the theory of semiotics, or the science of signs. This theory depends upon the concept of the signifier/signified split. The signifier stands for the signified, as the word stands for the thing, and together they make up the sign. Thus woman is signified by a number of representations of women which we learn to read as standing for woman/en. We learn to 'read' signs through a series of codes which are absorbed as part of socialisation into a culture.

Some of the most obvious signifiers of woman/en are sexual signifiers, but because the sexual organs are usually hidden in our visual culture, the non-hidden sex-specific signifier of breasts becomes a key signifier, breasts = woman. We can all read this simple code; it will only be subject to misinterpretation if somehow breasts appear in the wrong place, or are counterfeit, as when they are revealed to be false in *Some Like It Hot* or *Tootsie*. Not all signifiers are as sex-specific and some may be subject to misinterpretation or 'slippage': a high voice in a man or a deep voice in a woman, for example.

The Life and Loves of a She-Devil is full of very rich signifying systems, partly because, as we have seen, it draws upon a number of genres all of which contain sets of codes which make up generic conventions. There are also a number of ways in which the serial itself plays with the conventional representations of men and women, or with woman and man as sign. The most obvious play is around the representations of Ruth. Ruth is not conventionally feminine, she can be read as a masculine woman. Not only is she powerful, as described above, she is also tall, has facial hair, a deep voice, and in one early scene, before she has made herself into a She-Devil, she is represented wielding a chain saw. She acts in an unfeminine way, by leaving her children, taking command, having a lesbian relationship in which she is the dominant partner.

Neither is Mary Fisher stereotypically feminine. Although she is pretty and petite, in the beginning she is both rich and powerful and lives in a phallic tower. She becomes more feminine as she loses her power, becoming a mother to Bobbo's children, a daughter caring for a senile mother, and a dutiful and ultimately betrayed wife to Bobbo. If, as Fay Weldon says, Mary becomes good as Ruth becomes evil,[25] then we must also argue that femininity is good and virtuous, masculinity is bad and evil. Mary Fisher becomes feminine by taking on the female roles and their requirement of putting others before oneself, while Ruth becomes more masculine by a ruthless egoism and pursuit of her aims.

Bobbo's gender identity is less defined. In some ways he is a masculine man – ambitious, physically active, driven by lust, running an office and seducing his secretaries. In other ways he is a feminine man, trying to become domesticated, trapped by Mary Fisher, less virile than the Spanish manservant, Garcia, despised by his mother. Finally, on his release from gaol he is represented as totally emasculated, cuckolded by Garcia and wearing his hair in a ponytail. Ruth, meanwhile, has been transformed into the feminine Mary Fisher, having gone through six transformations which draw on an inventory of woman as sign – tart, nurse, businesswoman, nanny, housekeeper, and millionairess, all signified by the appropriate signifiers – blonde wig, coloured nails, uniforms, shoulder-pads, a tailored white suit. With each transformation Ruth acquires a new name and these names are also signifiers – Rita, Lily Latimer, Vista Rose, Polly Patch, Molly and Marlene.

Woman as artefact

When semiotics separated signifiers from the signified it questioned the nature of reality. The signified is that which somehow inhabits the 'real', but once its relationship to the signifier is arbitrary then the existence of the real itself becomes problematic. The cutting-off of signifiers from the signified and thus from the 'real' has given rise to a set of theories which argue that only signifiers have any reality. These theories have clustered together under the umbrella term of postmodernism. In media theory this leads to the proposition that the world is made up of circulating signifiers.[26] Reality can be made/created by the creation of signifiers.

The Life and Loves of a She-Devil can be read as an example of postmodernism, both in its use of different genres, a pastiche of televisual styles, and because Ruth's transformation questions reality. Does she really exist? Or, rather, is she merely a set of circulating signifiers? Her re-making by the Frankenstein-like doctors suggests that she may be a cyborg, that is a human/computer hybrid, such as Arnold Schwarzenegger in *Terminator*. As in *Frankenstein*, she may be a monster, or, as in the myth of Pygmalion and Galatea, she may be a statue which comes to life.

Signifiers belong to different sign systems depending on how they are read by the viewer/spectator. In the most extreme versions of deconstruction, neither authors nor texts have any significance, meaning is constructed by the reader/spectator. The gender of the reader/spectator becomes a crucial question. Do men and women read texts in the same way? Are male and female readers/spectators positioned in relationship to the text in the same way? How are they differently inscribed within the text? (By texts we here mean not just literary texts but also films, television, and paintings.)

What we can say is that however the text is read, gender is crucial. If all signifying systems, not just those of language, are also gendered and gender identity is psychically crucial, then how men and women are represented within those systems is fundamental to the acquisition of gender identity. And finally, if men and women are positioned differently both within signifying systems and in relationship to them, then how they receive and construct meaning will also be different. The theory of the male gaze, that men look while women are looked at, argues that signifying systems have been constructed by and for men. This universalism of the male is challenged by *The Life and Loves of a She-Devil*, but in ways that are by no means simple to read.

Is *The Life and Loves of a She-Devil* a feminist text?

One of the most sustained critical attacks on *The Life and Loves of a She-Devil* came from Melanie Reid, writing on the women's page of *The Scotsman* (27 October 1986). Drawing attention to the way that male critics such as Herbert Kretzmer of the *Daily Mail* had praised the series, Reid accused them of being 'anti-feminist' and of exploiting the opportunities it offered them of 'male delight masquerading as self-pity'. Reid was referring specifically to the voyeuristic appeal of the explicit 'sex scenes', primarily between Ruth and the objects of her sexual power, the judge and the priest. Stanley Eveling, the television critic of *The Scotsman*, fought back the next week arguing that for the first time 'there is a television show which is uncompromisingly feminist and which no man is allowed to praise without being torn asunder' (1 November 1986). Appearing on BBC2's *Did You See?*, Marina Warner also argued that *The Life and Loves of a She-Devil* did nothing to advance the cause of feminism by its surreptitious craving for old female values. Clearly the question of feminism in *The Life and Loves of a She-Devil* is a tricky one.

If we compare the television version with that of the film things become even more complicated. In contrast to the television play, the American film, *She Devil* (1989), was directed by a woman, Susan Seidelman, and starred Meryl Streep as Mary and Roseanne Barr as Ruth. However, the screenplay, adapted by two men, Barry Strugatz and Mark Burns, resulted in a significant watering-down of the original novel. Ruth does not transform herself into Mary, instead she loses weight, has her mole removed and becomes a successful businesswoman, while Mary does not die, instead she becomes a serious postmodern novelist. The conclusion has both women reflecting on the lessons they have learnt from their role-reversal. As one critic pointed out, Roseanne Barr's small stature meant she could not be motivated by Ruth's desire to be able to 'look up to men', but the American press generally panned the film and instead recommended the repeat showing of the television 'mini-series'.

Fay Weldon was obviously unhappy with the film version, but she sees its changed ending as necessary in order to match the correct feminist line in the United States. She feels that her ending in which Ruth wants to be feminine and to have her husband back was unacceptable to Hollywood because it was ideologically unsound. Fay Weldon defends her version: 'It is sad, life is sad'.[27]

Whether *The Life and Loves of a She-Devil* can be read as a feminist text or not involves discussion of two central questions, as indicated above. One concerns the narrative and whether Ruth is right to want to be able to look up to men, the other concerns the representation of women, specifically Ruth's ugliness and her sexuality, and Mary's romantic persona.

In the narrative structure of *The Life and Loves of a She-Devil* Ruth does achieve her ambition of being 'ordinary' and able to 'look up to men', but in between she has shown that women are powerful. She has used her talents to help other women: Nurse Hopkins who takes on the successful Vista Rose agency, Elsie the typist who leaves for a new life in New Zealand, the computer programmer who is given the chance to develop her hacking skills in embezzling Bobbo's accountancy firm's money, and, above all, by running the Vista Rose agency, the answer to every woman's prayer. She has also systematically and ruthlessly exposed the weakness of men by exploiting their vulnerability to the attractions of the flesh. Although the narrative closure could be said to restore patriarchal ideology, between the beginning and the end it has been seriously disturbed.

It is in the representations of that flesh that *The Life and Loves of a She-Devil* is most open to the charge levelled of anti-feminism. The depiction of female sexuality is riven with dangers. Feminists are themselves divided over the question of pornography. Can we distinguish between erotica and pornography? How can libertarianism be reconciled with censorship? Are all depictions of sex potentially pornographic? Two of Ruth's encounters provoke these questions – her seduction of the judge and of the priest. The judge (Bernard Hepton) is especially disturbing. He is a sadomasochist and in one very upsetting scene his meek and cowed wife appears at the breakfast table covered in bruises and barely able to sit or to eat. We never see him beating his wife, we see Ruth hearing her screams through the bedroom door, but we do see him tying up Ruth and beating her with a carpet-beater. The priest (Tom Baker) is initiated into sex by Ruth. In one scene we see what looks like a massive erection under the bedclothes: it turns out to be his crucifix held proudly erect. In another Ruth bears down on the priest as he fondles her breasts, which the camera angle serves to make even larger, erotically covered by a transparent nightgown. Ruth's breasts are large, as is she, and her sexual antics are the reason for Melanie Reid's accusation of 'male delight' and Stanley Eveling's description of the 'huge wobbling lady show' (*The Scotsman*, 1 November 1986).

Undoubtedly some of the male television critics, as no doubt the male viewing public, could be said to have had their voyeuristic sadistic impulses gratified. Yet Ruth's powerful sexuality is also transgressive. She uses it to challenge masculine authority and achieve her own ends. This is in itself threatening, as is the *femme fatale*. What then of Ruth's final transformation into the petite Mary Fisher? Is it an endorsement of the ideals of feminine beauty? Does it mark the reinstatement of the romantic myth which has been systematically demolished in the destruction of its author, Mary Fisher? It is hard to see the final scene of Ruth/Mary having sex with Garcia in front of the emasculated Bobbo as a reinstatement of romance. Yes, conventional female beauty is presented as desirable. It is preferable to being 6 feet 2 inches tall, 15 stone, hairy and covered in facial warts. We live in a culture which endorses these values. The choice of imagery, camera-angle, make-up, *mise-en-scène* in *The Life and Loves of a She-Devil* itself draws on that culture. Ruth has to be ugly, Mary has to be pretty. Without this opposition the serial would lose its purpose. We should not forget that Fay Weldon began her career in advertising. She has herself contributed to the paradigm of femininity while at the same time making a witty and satirical attack on its values. We can conclude by suggesting that while we cannot say that *The Life and Loves of a She-Devil* is a feminist text, it is both possible, rewarding and, we hope, enjoyable, to provide a feminist reading.

The Life and Loves of a She-Devil

First episode transmitted on BBC2 on 8 October 1986

Cast

Bobbo	Dennis Waterman
Mary Fisher	Patricia Hodge
Ruth	Julie T. Wallace
Nurse Hopkins	Miriam Margolyes
Mrs Fisher	Liz Smith
Garcia	Paul Herzberg
Judge Bishop	Bernard Hepton
Father Ferguson	Tom Baker
Sue Cook as herself	
Edna O'Brien as herself	
John Mortimer as himself	

Technical and production

Script Editor	Glenda Bagshaw
Production Manager	Steve Goldie
Location Manager	Simon Moorhead

Designer	Humphrey Jaeger
Lighting Director	John King
Camera	Mike Winser/John Hawes
Video Tape Editor	Malcolm J. Banthorpe
Director	Philip Saville
Producer	Sally Head
Music	Peter Filleul

Title song, 'Warm Love Gone Cold', sung by Christine Collister

Production company: BBC in association with Arts and Entertainment Network and Seven Network Australia

Notes

1 George Brandt (ed.), *British Television Drama* (Cambridge University Press, 1981).
2 Fay Weldon, *The Life and Loves of a She-Devil* (London: Hodder and Stoughton, 1983). All quotations are from the Coronet Paperbacks edition (1984), 43.
3 *Ibid.*, 51.
4 *Ibid.*, 240.
5 Interview with Fay Weldon, October 1991.
6 *Bookmark* (BBC2), October 1986.
7 Interview with Fay Weldon.
8 *Ibid.*
9 *Ibid.*
10 *Ibid.*
11 Jill Hyem, 'Entering the arena: writing for television', in Helen Baehr and Gillian Dyer (eds.), *Boxed In: Women and Television* (London: Pandora, 1987).
12 *Ibid.*, 153.
13 Quoted in Ann Ross Muir, 'The status of women working in film and television', in Lorraine Gamman and Margaret Marshment (eds.), *The Female Gaze: Women as Viewers of Popular Culture* (London: The Women's Press, 1988).
14 Survey by the Women's Committee of the Writers' Guild of Great Britain, quoted in Hyem, 'Entering the arena'.
15 *Ibid.*
16 *Ibid.*
17 Interview with Fay Weldon.
18 *Ibid.*
19 Hyem, 'Entering the arena', 162.
20 Bristol University Extra-Mural Studies Group, '"It's OK to watch Dallas": deconstructing mass-produced fantasies for women', in Helen Taylor (ed.), *Literature Teaching Politics 1985 Conference Papers* (Bristol Polytechnic, 1985).
21 See Mary Ellen Brown, 'Introduction: feminist cultural television criticism – culture, theory and practice', in Mary Ellen Brown (ed.), *Television and Women's Culture: The Politics of the Popular* (London: Sage, 1990), for a good summary of the theoretical approaches.
22 See Elizabeth Cowie, 'Woman as sign', *m/f*, 1, 1, 1978, and Teresa de Lauretis,

Alice Doesn't: Feminism, Semiotics and Cinema (Bloomington: Indiana University Press, 1984) for discussion of these concepts.

23 See John Berger, *Ways of Seeing* (Harmondsworth: Penguin, 1972) for a discussion of how women are surveyed in both Western painting and advertising, and Laura Mulvey, 'Visual pleasure and narrative cinema', *Screen*, 16, 3 (autumn 1975) for Mulvey's influential psychoanalytical reading of dominant cinema and the theory of the male gaze.

24 J. Lacan, *Ecrits: A Selection*, transl. Alan Sheridan (London: Tavistock Press, 1977)

25 Interview with Fay Weldon.

26 It is difficult to give any one reference for postmodernism. The idea of circulating signifiers is most associated with Baudrillard, see J. Baudrillard, *Simulations* (New York: Semiotext(e), 1983). For a good general introduction to the topic, see David Harvey, *The Condition of Postmodernity* (Oxford: Basil Blackwell, 1989).

27 Interview with Fay Weldon.

Select bibliography

Books

Baehr, Helen, and Gillian Dyer (eds.), *Boxed In: Women and Television* (London: Pandora, 1987)

Baudrillard, J., *Simulations* (New York: Semiotext(e), 1983)

Berger, John, *Ways of Seeing* (Harmondsworth: Penguin, 1972)

Bristol University Extra-Mural Studies Group, '"It's OK to watch Dallas": deconstructing mass-produced fantasies for women', in Helen Taylor (ed.), *Literature Teaching Politics 1985 Conference Papers* (Bristol Polytechnic, 1985)

Brown, Mary Ellen (ed.), *Television and Women's Culture: The Politics of the Popular* (London: Sage, 1990)

Cowie, Elizabeth, 'Woman as sign', *m/f*, vol. 1, no. 1, 1978

De Lauretis, Teresa, *Alice Doesn't: Feminism, Semiotics and Cinema* (Bloomington: Indiana University Press, 1984)

Harvey, David, *The Condition of Postmodernity* (Oxford: Basil Blackwell, 1989)

Lacan, J., *Ecrits: A Selection*, transl. Alan Sheridan (London: Tavistock Press, 1977)

Muir, Ann Ross, 'The status of women working in film and television', in Lorraine Gamman and Margaret Marshment (eds.), *The Female Gaze: women as viewers of popular culture* (London: The Women's Press, 1988)

Mulvey, Laura, 'Visual pleasure and narrative cinema', *Screen*, 16, 3 (autumn 1975)

Weldon, Fay, *The Life and Loves of a She-Devil* (London: Hodder and Stoughton, 1983)

Articles

Beauman, Sally, 'Pride in her work' (Fay Weldon on adapting *Pride and Prejudice*), *Radio Times*, 12–18 January 1980, 12–15

Brandmark, Wendy, 'Getting back' (*The Life and Loves of a She-Devil*), *The Listener*, 2 October 1986, 27–8
'Life after mixer taps' (Fay Weldon's *Heart of the Country*), *The Listener*, 19 February 1987, 29–30
Household, Nicki, 'The devil of a time', *Radio Times*, 4–10 October 1986, 4–5

See also:

Broadcast, 30 August 1985, 8 (Problems in casting and producing the serial)
The Listener, 23 October 1986, 39
Television Today, 30 May 1985, 18; 23 January 1986 (Comments from Ted Whitehead); 30 October 1986, 22
Televisual, September 1986, 20 (Notes on the creation of the title sequence)
Time Out, 8–15 October 1986, 43 (Interview with Fay Weldon)

13   *The Singing Detective* (Dennis Potter)
Who done it?

JOOST HUNNINGHER

Dennis Potter dislikes academic critics. In the preface to *Waiting for the Boat: On Television*, he wrote: 'It is no news that there is a contemptuous, hard-eyed hatred of humanistic culture all around us . . . the long, grey, ebb tide of so-named Post-Modernism, pseudo-totalitarian, illiberal and dehumanizing theories and practices lie on top of the cold waters like a huge and especially filthy oil slick . . . The Academic critic reigns, intimidatingly.'[1]

Understandably, I tread cautiously over this bridge shrouded in fog except for an overall hunch, no, conviction, that I should declare now. *The Singing Detective*, expressly conceived for a television mini-series in 1986, is a vision of life, family, love, illness, art and sex that in its form provocatively challenges and uses television and film conventions, and realises in production terms a dazzling and sensitive creative collaboration. This is not to suggest that this process, which lasted well over a year, did not have its share of tensions, insecurity, arguments and, in thriller terms, back-stabbing. Nonetheless, the series reveals a rich process started by the skill and vision of Potter which interacted with the creativity of a production team and an ensemble of actors to produce a unique series which must be the most original British television drama of the decade. My aim is to investigate aspects of this process and find clues as to why *The Singing Detective* is such an inspiring work.

The body

At 9.0 p.m. on 16 November 1986, 8.12 million people turned to BBC1 to watch 'Skin', the first 75-minute episode of *The Singing Detective*. Philip Marlow's 7-hour odyssey had begun and continued its powerful emotional unravelling for six weeks, ending on 21 December with an audience of 6 million. The initial reactions from television critics varied from enthusi-astically cautious to the totally engaged. 'You didn't know where you were with Dennis Potter's *The Singing Detective*: and it made it all the more exciting.'[2] 'Still, this is not the week to linger over the down side of television, for it was the week that launched Dennis Potter's first new work for the BBC for eight years, *The Singing Detective* – an effort as remarkable as most telly presenters are unremarkable. It has been worth the wait.'[3] '...reserve the following five Sundays as well. That way you will be sure to see every moment of *The Singing Detective*, probably the most compelling piece of original television fiction that I have seen in 16 years as a critic.'[4]

What did the audience and these critics react to? Piecing together the construction of the opening episode which starts the manipulation of the multi-layered odyssey of the main character – Philip Marlow – we see how Potter introduces the themes, images and motifs that are to reveal Marlow to us and to himself.

The ingredients seem familiar enough: 'a misty, moody, atmospheric, "thrillerish" winter's evening in London, 1945'; we see a labyrinth of dissolving wet alleyways and pavements, 'a pathetic old busker is playing an achingly melancholy "Peg O' My Heart" on his mouth organ', the well-dressed Binney wearing a trilby and wrapped in an overcoat appears down the 'misty paving stones'; the busker inserts a bar of 'Deutschland über Alles', a coin and a message are exchanged: what is this – treachery? So far the cluster of film noir images seems as familiar as Harry Lime, 'but anyone beguiled into settling down to enjoy a piece of pleasantly stylish pastiche was to be sharply shaken up'.[5] Binney descends into the Skinscape Club, a side-of-the-mouth voice-over, 'it was a rat-hole... Into the rat-hole. Down, down, down. And the one thing you don't do when you find yourself in one of those is to underestimate the rats in residence –'.[6] Suddenly we are in a daytime hospital in a skin-and-cardiac ward – the music changes to 'I have you under my skin'. Mr Hall moans to Reginald about the tea trolley. Reginald pays little attention – he is reading what we later discover to be a copy of *The Singing Detective*. The central character Philip Marlow is being wheeled back to his bed. 'Marlow is glowering morosely, crumpled into himself, and his face badly disfigured with a ragingly acute psoriasis, which looks as though boiling oil has been thrown over him.'[7] The pain is underlined by the black porter who takes Marlow's smock off, 'hoo, man, razz', he stares at Marlow's 'cracked, scabbed, scaled, swollen scarlet and snowy skin'. Marlow is a writer, we have guessed this with his voice-over: 'No, sir. The way those creatures gnaw and nibble can do a lot of damage to your nerves full stop new paragraph...' Cut. Disorienting tilted film-noir shots as 'Binney, now appearing to be a nervous and hesitant businessman not certain that he is going to have a good time, or even that he should' descends into the Skinscape bar. Back to reality, and the hospital, as Marlow in his wheelchair composes the story.

BARMAN   (*voice over*): G'evening, sir. What is your poison? What'll it be, sir? *Ouch-h-!*
Marlow, jolted by a bump on the chair as it trundles along the corridor, winces with pain.
MARLOW   (*to himself, hiss*): Concentrate. Concentrate...

The bar at Skinsrape's reasserts its occupation of the screen . . . Binney looks from side to side, along the empty stools, and empty spaces which fade off into arches of near darkness.
BINNEY: Well. Company for a start.[8]

A big close-up of a bell being pressed and suddenly Amanda, a young hostess in sailor's suit, is sitting next to him.

AMANDA: Hello, sugar.
BINNEY: Hello yourself. Sugar. Would you like a –
AMANDA: Champagne, toots.
BINNEY: Yes. Ah. Of course. Toots.[9]

And so we get clues that Potter is exploring, as in *Double Dare*, the relation between the writer and his creation. Marlow imagines and creates and 'imitates exactly what he mostly cannot possibly have heard'.[10] He is an unlovable, churlish detective writer who, helpless and paralysed by psoriasis, can only escape into the interior landscape of his imagination. As Potter says, 'That's the way you have to deal with physical pain, you know. You have to sort of stand outside it and say, "OK destroy me if you must, but I am going somewhere else."'[11] Marlow, left alone, hums, 'I've got you under my skin', we dissolve to Hammersmith Bridge, a medium close-up of a naked drowned woman as she is pulled from the Thames, Amanda's voice-over says, 'A girl's got to live hasn't she?' On the bridge 'there is but one person, there now, in a trilby, his coat collar turned up, distantly lonely like the man in the old cigarette advertisement. ("You're never alone with a...") It is Marlow, 1945-style, without psoriasis or seized joints. He is watching the recovery of the body with a burning intensity of expression.'[12] Throughout the series, again and again, dead, naked female bodies are pulled from the river. Are they new bodies or repeated memories? The labyrinthine story continues with parallel threads of images that smartly and wryly keep us guessing. Is this a Chandleresque thriller, a psychological drama, a hospital soap? Whatever it is, we are hooked as Potter 'swings with seeming effortlessness through time and space, carrying us repeatedly ... into the condition of a drama, where action and reaction, normal chronology and the shared assumptions of existence, dissolve. Visually everything remains sharp and clear, but a new internal logic dictates the way that the obsessive images come and go.'[13] Back in the hospital, Marlow's relationship with Ali, the cardiac patient in the next bed, is affectionately offensive, Alf-Garnett style.

MARLOW: That's you cardiacs. You heart patients, nig-nog. I'm *skin*, Ali. Skin!

Ali lights Marlow's electronic lighter, the flame shoots out.

MARLOW   I could see the headlines. 'Another Asian Burnt to Death.'[14]

The sexual tension first established in Skinscape is now transferred to the angelic nurse Mills who comes to relieve Marlow's pain by greasing him. The curtains are drawn and erotic polythene gloves massage Marlow's thighs in big close-ups.

Marlow's face fills the screeen with intense concentration...

MARLOW   (*voice over*): Think of something boring – For Christ's sake think of something very very boring – Speech a speech by Ted Heath a sentence long sentence from Bernard Levin a quiz by Christopher Booker a – oh think think think! – Really boring! A Welsh male-voice choir – Everything in *Punch* – Oh! Oh!'[15]

Nurse Mills is suddenly in the Skinscape Club as a singer crooning 'Blues in the Night'. Her singing and the massaging build and when she finally says in her role as the club singer, 'Sorry. But I shall have to lift your penis now to grease around it', all the paunchy middle-age men in Skinscape cheer and bang their palms on the tables as Marlow ejaculates into nurse Mills' plastic glove.

MARLOW   (*off*): I'm – ah – nurse. I'm very sorry. It – that's the one part of me that still sort of functions. I do beg your pardon.[16]

Cut to the Skinscape Club, Binney discovers the busker from the opening sequence murdered and hanging in a cupboard. Lights of a train approach through a tunnel – a woman's voice yells, 'Philip, Philip.' Suddenly with a dynamic fast-moving camera track, the hospital consultants arrive – they hardly hear Marlow's agony, 'God! Talk about the Book of – the Book of Job – I'm a prisoner inside my oooh own skin and bones' – and just as suddenly the consultants burst into Fred Waring's Pennsylvanians' musical number 'Dry Bones'. The number 'transforms the oppressive hospital ward into a hallucinating night club with high-kicking nurses and bossy doctors made into chorus boys'.[17] Big tilted close-ups of Marlow convey his disorientation. Again the train approaches through a tunnel and the consultants' entourage sweeps away. Big close-up of Marlow. On sound-track we hear Marlow's father, Mr Marlow.

MR MARLOW   (*voice over*): Philip! Phil! Philip! Where bist? Philip – Why doesn't thee answer?'

> The Forest forms itself out of Marlow's dead eyes. The small boy is in the treetop, high above the rolling lesser trees.[18]

Unblinking close-ups of Marlow, back at the Skinscape Club Binney speaks Russian, another naked female body is pulled from the river (she seems slightly different from the first one), now all the patients from the hospital ward are standing on Hammersmith Bridge looking down. Back at the ward, the senile Noddy climbs into bed with the paralysed Marlow and starts humping him. Marlow, helpless to push off this sexual attack, yells for help. The amused night nurse brings the situation to order. During the day a registrar probes,

REGISTRAR: It must be hellishly ticklish to work out a plot in a detective story, I should think. I suppose you have to scatter clues all over the place.[19]

And the episode draws to a close with Ali insisting on giving Marlow a sweet. As Ali leans forward, he has a massive heart attack. The bag of sweets, in a big slow-motion close-up, falls from his hand. Emergency! Intercut with big close-ups of Marlow, the medical team assault Ali's body, a fist blow to the chest, electric shocks, mouth-to-mouth resuscitation, an adrenalin injection. The cardioscope shows no pulse. Ali is dead. Marlow reveals no emotion; not until later when he is given one of Ali's sweets. Then suddenly he cries like a child. Back to Philip in the treetop.

PHILIP: I'll find out, I'll find out who done it.[20]

End of episode 1.

'If all this sounds complicated, so it is – but in a wonderfully entertaining way. Here we have not some old novel adapted for television, but an original work created specifically for the electronic medium by a master craftsman who has served a long and productive apprenticeship. Today, Potter uses television with the familiarity and assurance that Dickens brought to the writing of novels.'[21]

The form in all its complexity is stunning, but the Registrar is right. Potter does scatter clues all over the place. There are clues about sex, family, treachery, guilt, illness, creativity, death, and they point to motifs throughout the work. These motifs are not just a fragmented patchwork, but relate to Marlow the patient, to Marlow the imagined detective, to Marlow the boy in the treetop, and reveal the fundamental psychological significance of Marlow as a whole character. These motifs also give a unity to six episodes which becomes increasingly evident to the viewer, and this growing awareness runs parallel with Marlow gaining understanding and self-insight. 'The Singing Detective is an outstanding case in favour of the unique qualities of the TV serial ... The spacing out over time of the serial ... allows the plots and motifs to stay with the viewer and grow in his/her mind.'[22] It also allows for a scale in dramatic complexity which is comparable to the novel, while the structural tightness of a television play or feature film is comparable, in scale, to a short story. As the director Jon Amiel explained to me, *The Singing Detective* 'involves you in a central mystery. Why is this man Marlow the way he is? The series had the faith in its audience to say, this human mystery is of such consummate complexity that you'll want to stay involved and continue to watch. And they did. The lesson I learnt, with great humility, was never ever underestimate your audience.'[23]

The vision and plot

In the *Radio Times*, Dennis Potter said, 'The whole thing began to take shape several years ago when I was feeling rather sad about the death of the studio TV play. It seemed to have gone for ever, but I wrote down some ideas I had, a series of scenes in a hospital ward which I thought were quite promising. I just wanted to make use of some of the comedy that takes place in a hospital.'[24] Potter's first ten plays between 1965 and 1968 were substantially created in the television studio; he knew what was possible there and felt the hermetic artificiality suited his dramatic focus. 'What I liked about the studio was that you could actually get inside people's heads more – if you weren't writing naturalism, that is. And because the temptation for the director was so severely limited, he couldn't embroider and run away with it.'[25] Potter also knew a lot about hospitals. Although he strenuously denies that the events are autobiographical, it is well known that Potter has suffered from severe psoriasis since 1962. The hospital experience and the comic ideas were the starting-points. 'I had no idea what story [the hospital ideas] fitted into, but the ideas stayed with me and much later they fell into place.'[26]

A great deal is revealed about Potter's dramatic construction and use of juxtaposition by the fact that he should decide to develop his 'comic ideas' through a tragic middle-aged detective writer – a character physically paralysed with pain and as mentally shipwrecked as Hamlet.[27] It would be 'a journey in which a man in extreme pain and anguish tries to assemble the bits of his life'.[28] As in much of his previous work, Potter is concerned with 'interior drama' and explores the man's life by juxtaposing complex strands of internal emotion about the present, the past, fantasies, artistic creation, and neurotic insecurity. Rapidly displacing scenes represent his objective and subjective realities. Marlow's development is structured as a psychoanalytical investigation, 'the unearthing of buried memories is consistently linked with the idea of detection in which information blockages have to be overcome. The author's carefully planted narrative blockages (retardations and digressions) are useful not only in sustaining dramatic interest: they mirror Marlow's resistance to analysis and self-insight.'[29]

Potter deliberately avoids the narrative clarity of a chain of events in a cause-and-effect relationship set in chronological order. Yet if we step back from dazzling dramatic and technical innovations in *The Singing Detective*, there is a clear journey. We start with a man who is paralysed, whose body is out of control, who believes in nothing and who, after probing all the elements of his life in seven hours of television time, walks from the hospital having overcome his physical adversities and having found a way through his emotional labyrinth. The illness incites the crisis and starts the complex causal conflicts within Marlow. As Potter said on *Arena*, 'It is the illness which is the crisis. It is the illness which has stripped him ... in dramatic terms it needed exactly that – that starting point of extreme crisis and no belief.'[30]

Throughout the exploration of Marlow's complicated realities and fantasies, 'we alway[s] return to one point of contact,' Potter says, 'the man in a hospital bed... That's what it is really all about.'[31]

The syndicate

In early 1979 Potter and producer Kenith Trodd had a two-year contract with London Weekend Television to produce six television plays. When the director of programmes, Michael Grade, announced in July 1980 that, after having produced three plays, LWT would not proceed with the arrangement because of 'insurmountable difficulties' and 'generous budgets being heavily overspent',[32] Potter hit back in an article in the *Daily Mail* entitled, 'Why British TV is going to the dogs: and I'm going to California'.[33] Potter did go to California to work on rewrites of his script *Pennies from Heaven* for Herbert Ross's film version, released by MGM in 1982. There, other sorts of barriers were up. 'When I was working at MGM in Hollywood I realised that the studio based all narrative forms entirely upon category. At the beginning of a project they would ask what particular bag it was in. Was it a detective story? Was it a musical? Was it a romance? They saw it as a marketing problem, even before the first shot,' says Potter. 'That sort of thinking throws a terrible carapace over the writer and one of the things I want to do in *The Singing Detective* is break up the narrative tyranny.'[34]

Potter has long argued for plays that challenge the viewer's passive consumption of naturalistic television drama. In 1984 he wrote, 'Most television ends up offering its viewers a means of orientating themselves towards the generally received notions of "reality" – that is, the way things are, which is more or less the way things have to be. There is not much space left for what it is that "Art" can do.'[35] Insisting on the artificiality of the television play – 'that a play is a play is a play' – his declared aim is to stimulate and thus 'to disorientate the viewer', to break out of 'the prevailing, unexamined "naturalism" of the medium as a whole ... [which] continually works against the alert attention which any writer wants to evoke in ... his audience'.[36] As early as 1965 he assaulted the naturalistic mode with schoolchildren played by grown-ups in *Stand Up Nigel Barton*, a device which he repeated in *Blue Remembered Hills* (1979). In *Pennies from Heaven* (1978), as in *The Singing Detective* (1986), he threw characters, without warning, into miming songs of original thirties and forties recordings which comment, ironically or ambiguously, even sympathetically, on the dramatic moment.

In *The Singing Detective* Potter uses a growing arsenal of non-naturalistic devices – a range of provocatively integrated stylistic conventions, a range of acting styles and even some actors playing multiple roles, cross-cutting and flash-backs to moments of memory, actuality and fantasy, dancing and singing, etc. 'The advantage of this dramaturgic technique is to energise the viewer – he/she has to put in some effort in order to follow the story.'[37] It is 'creative participation by the audience – they cease to be just spectators "consuming" but are asked to question that very process of consuming by the entertainment of the spectacle itself'.[38]

Jon Amiel says,

The script is written with dazzling confidence and certainty and an extraordinary feel for the power of the cut. Dennis understands how to juxtapose scenes in a way that gives a tremendous sinewy energy to the story. Many writers put in a lot of camera directions, extreme c.u. or cut to w.s.... Dennis never does that, there are never any camera directions at all. However ... when a close-up is necessary he will describe an event in such detail that the only conceivable way to match the intensity of that description is with a close-up.

Referring to the tea scene with the mother and the Gran in the second episode, Amiel gives an example from the shooting script:

'Swot! a gobbet of spit hits the grate and sizzles.' It both graphically describes the smell and event and sound and you have to find a visual way of matching it.... So what Dennis's writing does, rather than insist on or direct you to do something, is to inspire you to do something with the same passion and same specificity. That's what's so remarkable about his script.[39]

The contract

Kenith Trodd is the prolific producer whose first Potter production was *Moonlight on the Highway* (1968) and who then produced most of his television plays up to *The Singing Detective*. He told me that *Pennies from*

Heaven was a clever mixture of video tape and film, while *The Singing Detective* is all film and that was one of the big differences in creative taste between 1976 and 1986.

By 1986, I would not have been able to get a director who was willing to work on a hybrid, even on a play by Dennis Potter. In 1976, it was the norm. Dennis by 1986 had not caught up to changing norms, because he had expected, and indeed wrote, all the hospital scenes, expecting them to be made in the television studio. He wanted to go on the prototypes of the sitcom for those scenes and expected the rest in film.[40]

Trodd had always wanted to shoot on film and he remembers saying to Potter that it was necessary because he couldn't find a good enough director. Trodd feels that directors like Piers Haggard, who in 1976 directed *Pennies from Heaven* and could successfully integrate studio video and location film work, had become in the 1980s almost an 'extinct breed'. He told me that *The Singing Detective* was turned down by

the cream of the British film industry, such as it was, Stephen Frears, Richard Eyre, Malcolm Mowbray, Pat O'Connor – nearly all on the basis that they couldn't interrupt their movie careers to do a Dennis Potter sitcom. So I got turned down by all these names and I then had to start looking, as I've often done, for less tried talents ... Amiel had brought me one or two projects ... but not very much. He'd been a script editor: and unlike some directors, he had an attitude towards the script as well as to the visual realisation ... I thought ... it's probably Jon, and I took a chance ... not knowing if he was going to live up to the job or not ... it was a gamble.[41]

Jon Amiel told me he was surprised to get the job.

I know that the script was offered to five or six people who were more eligible or more distinguished than I was at the time. So Ken Trodd first came in and asked me to read the scripts and said, 'It's not an offer, there are other people, but have a look and see what you think.' I remember clearly reading these scripts, and by the time I was half-way through the first script my hands were shaking as I was turning the pages. I knew for an absolute certainty, because all of my training had been basically in script development [he had been a literary manager in the theatre and a story editor in television], that I was reading a masterpiece. The thought of directing this thing filled me with complete terror and the thought of not being asked to direct it filled me with as much terror. After having read the six episodes, I went to Ken Trodd, and in a surprisingly calm voice I said, 'Look, I think they are wonderful. I think it is a masterpiece, but I think A,B,C,D – all of this work needs doing on the scripts. The sixth episode is not the sum of the five previous ones, the singing detective story needs some detailed work on it, the relationship with Nicola needs looking at – and so on' ... I couldn't believe that I was really saying these things. But the five more distinguished directors had all turned it down and the project evolved to me. And this is often the way things happen. Most people get their breaks that particular way.[42]

After Amiel was appointed to direct in September, he had a series of meetings with Potter. The first two were exceedingly difficult. Amiel felt insecure but 'floundered on'. Then at their third meeting both men seemed to put aside any misgivings and launched into a 'truly joyful' collaboration. They had six further meetings before Amiel received a telephone call from Potter saying he was going to rewrite all the scripts right from the beginning. The pre-production schedule was very tight (two and half months) and Amiel remembers saying, 'Dennis hold on, not the whole script!' Potter insisted and then,

> while under attack from this awful disease psoriasis, he launched into one of the most extraordinary processes I've ever witnessed, he rewrote one episode a week for six weeks. He wrote with the most astonishing and unerring editing instinct I have ever come across in a writer – he rejigged, rebalanced the whole thing and after that even went back to rewrite the sixth episode again.

Amiel found that the more he worked on rewritten scripts the more confident he felt about the production. As he told me, 'my conviction that I was working on a masterpiece only grew'.[43]

Further enquiries
Designs

In *The Singing Detective* the expressive resources of film – decor, costume, make-up, visualisation, lighting, camera and editing rhythms, sound, music, acting – were used very creatively to realise the script and to enhance characters, emotions and the significance of each scene. Considerable creative contributions and collaborations are necessary to achieve such a unity. Besides interviewing the producer and director, I discussed this process with the designer, Jim Clay, and the make-up designer, Frances Hannon.

Jim Clay told me that 'making *The Singing Detective* was a wonderfully uninhibited process'; there was total creative freedom with very little interference from management. After long discussions with Jon Amiel about characters, plots and sub-plots, set designs evolved and models were built. 'Jon's precision is a treasure. He is hard work, but you don't mind it, because he's always pushing you a bit further.' Each set developed a great deal: Amiel never just accepted the first one offered – but this always led to better solutions, Clay says. 'For example, it took a long time to evolve the "Dry Bones" sequence. Dennis had written it in a black void with skeleton costumes ... which we thought was terribly old-fashioned – so we wanted to use some hospital elements and struggled for a long time to find a solution for transforming the hospital into a dance sequence.'[44] He

12 *A break during the shooting of* The Singing Detective. *Seated from L to R: Michael Gambon (Marlow) in the wheelchair, Jon Amiel (director), Ken Westbury (director of photography), Dennis Potter. BBC 1986*

remembers that finally they hit upon the solution as Jon Amiel, Quinny Sacks, the choreographer, and he sat having a cup of tea one afternoon in a hotel room in the Forest of Dean. 'One of us said, "Let's make the hospital into the club", and the three of us yelled, "That's it!".' Suddenly it appeared obvious, and so in episode 1

we were leaping backwards and forwards to the Skinscape Club, we should transform the hospital ward into the Skinscape Club and use neons for bars on the windows; it would become partly a prison, partly a club. The club was his escape, the hospital his prison. So the whole idea then developed into this huge dance routine with nurses dressed as waitresses and so on. We had done a million storyboards and a million sketches on variations, but nothing felt right until we hit on this.[45]

Although people tell Clay that they recognise his design style, he doesn't think of himself as 'having a recognisable style from one film to the next'. However, his background in architecture encourages him to design spaces in terms of how light would affect it – that is 'where I place doors, windows and openings ... I try to make these as realistic as possible – even in a stylised set.' He also is realistic in terms of surfaces and how they are painted and what goes into a set. In his designs he thinks about how the set will help reveal the characters. 'I learnt a lot from working with the director Mike Leigh on how to dress a set for character. For example, he'd come on the set of *Four Days in July* and ask, "Who framed that picture on the wall?" and I'd say, "My assistant, Martin," and he'd say, "No, no, which member of the family?" So I learnt to work closely with actors and to dress a set with characters in mind.'[46]

A set Clay particularly liked in *The Singing Detective* was the scene in the working-men's club. Amiel's brief had been that it should have an overriding sadness about it. They had found a church hall which was a perfect location, but how to make it look sad?

It is easily done when Marlow is sitting there in the derelict club on his own with cobwebs and dust sheets over the piano. But when the whole community is there, it's another matter. I can't tell you how we did it. In the end, I used boring things like texture and colour, shape, placing windows in certain places, one pane of the window broken. They seemed fairly mundane things, but I guess as a whole they come together to make a dramatic space.[47]

Given the effective lighting and camerawork and the strong smoky atmosphere of the scenes in the working-men's club, I was surprised to learn that Jim Clay did not have constant planning meetings with the lighting cameraman, Ken Westbury. Clay felt it was really a matter of Ken Westbury making the most of 'the lighting opportunities' built into the set.

In terms of camera style, Jon Amiel said that he wanted to use a very mobile camera technique, which thematically works effectively to suggest the detection that runs throughout the work. 'For the genre thriller I evolved with Ken Westbury a distinctively old-fashioned style of lighting ... using hard source lights, key lights, pin spots, charley bars to get angles of light, a very distinctive noir lighting style.'[48] To begin with, Amiel had wanted to shoot the detective story in black and white, but Potter persuaded him not to, saying, 'Don't do it in black and white, it gives everybody a very easy signal, when you're in the past and when you're in the present, it breaks the thing into two halves like a walnut.'[49] Amiel also realised that working in short fragmented scenes meant that each scene had to be direct and powerful and graphically almost 'cartoon shots'. 'I knew that each scene had to hit hard, had to say, what's the essence of this scene, what is the emotional centre of it, what does it want to deliver? Then focus everything in delivering that moment as vividly, powerfully and truthfully as I could.'[50]

On the whole, Potter did not get very involved in the production process. He came to the set only a few times and after seeing the rushes on tape would talk to Amiel every four or five days. Amiel took this as a remarkable sign of Potter's confidence in his direction of the script.

Cover-up

In *The Singing Detective*, getting under a character's skin starts with what was put on it. The outer casing of the characters provides clues about the different time periods, the stylistic leaps and the various multiple echoing roles that some actors play. The artistic contribution and skill of a department like Make-Up is of considerable importance. For example, Marlow's physical surface in the hospital appears as painful as the turmoil we discover underneath it. As John Wyver reported in *The Listener*, 'The dominant, almost overwhelming image of the film is of Marlow in a hospital bed, his outer layers scraped away, with raw, exposed tissue fighting across his face and body and the peeling areas of parched, translucent, dead skin.'[51]

Frances Hannon, the make-up designer, told me, 'If you didn't have make-up in *The Singing Detective* it couldn't have worked ... there would be no progression... Make-up is a very good indicator of things happening that people may not lock into but read subconsciously.'[52] Before *The Singing Detective*, Hannon hadn't done 'anything of great standing', but Ken Trodd started sending her scripts as early as six months before the start of production. The greatest challenge for Hannon was the make-up for Marlow in hospital. Believing that make-up should be 'as real as possible', she began by researching the characteristics of psoriasis. She saw the top medical consultants in England and Wales plus a variety of drug companies who were all very helpful, showing her patients, slides and records. She told me that there are hundreds of forms of psoriasis and that, after looking at different forms, she and Jon Amiel agreed that Marlow's form should be arthritic psoriasis – physically the type of psoriatic symptoms that Dennis Potter had suffered from in the sixties until medical advances improved the control of the disease. 'Once I knew what it had to look like, it took me a long time to find out how to make it work. I had to find something which anyone's skin could take every day and not with an allergic reaction... It was a creative process of elimination.'[53] In the end Hannon designed a complicated 'recipe' for

Michael Gambon. She started with a water-based spray to seal the skin and then used six different colours to shade it; that was covered with petroleum jelly, talced, then painted again, sealed, plastics were added to give a three-dimensional look, and she used further sealers and then finished the surface with hot gelatin to give it a crusty finish. The process would take four hours to complete, and Hannon and the make-up team would start on Michael Gambon's make-up at 6.0 a.m. to be ready by 10.0 a.m.

The make-up had to be filmed in the first four hours of the day ... because after some time, due to the heat of the lights and Michael's varying body temperature, the gelatin would not stay hard and crusty, and [would] go soft. We used air-conditioning units around the bed to try to keep the temperature down and took them away just before each take.

Michael Gambon's acting technique added to the heat problem.

Michael has a very expressive and mobile mouth, and with all that shouting and screaming he did, the scabs would be hanging off his mouth at the end of each take. We'd all rush in to repair the make-up. The make-up had its time limit ... Michael Gambon was frequently uncomfortable, but took it all in his stride.[54]

Hannon had plotted the cure element, so that Marlow's skin condition improved over the six episodes. Despite shooting out of sequence, it was scheduled to minimise intermixing Marlow with severe psoriasis and mild psoriasis and as the singing detective. She said that artistic collaboration went on continuously 'and we needed only one meeting in the beginning to know if we were all on the same wavelength'. With Amiel encouraging and co-ordinating decisions, the various departments evolved close working relationships 'to achieve the same mood and look'.[55] For example, Hannon's collaboration with Ken Westbury, the cameraman, was important. Every night Westbury would describe the lighting for the following day and leave a set of the same lighting gels that were being used on the scene. Hannon then lit the make-up room with these gels, so that she could see how the filtered lights would affect her make-up design. 'If I hadn't had this information, Ken could completely destroy my work if he used, let's say, a red light instead of a blue one.' Having agreed on the severity of the make-up on Marlow after some film tests on Gambon, Hannon told me that Amiel had second thoughts. 'The night before we started shooting, we were in the hospital in Tottenham [where the ward sequences were shot] and Jon came up to me and said did I think we should take Marlow's psoriasis down slightly. I think he suddenly had the fear that the audience would be so revolted by the make-up that they wouldn't even look in.'[56] Hannon agreed that slightly less would be enough.

Musical stings

A headline in *The Sun* wittily stressed the musical elements of *The Singing Detective* with 'Marlow's Singing in the Pain'.[57] As in *Pennies from Heaven*, the songs 'distract, tickle, upset',[58] but now they do more than provide an ironic counterpoint to the dramatic action: all relate to the young Marlow's 'troubled childhood' when he heard them 'drifting up the stairs from the crackling wireless'[59] and thus 'connect and underline' different narrative strands in the work.

When, for example, Mr Hall and Noddy mime the words to the Mills Brothers' 'You Always Hurt the One You Love', the associations in Marlow's head lead from memories of a shallow experience with a prostitute, to the working-men's club where his father and Binney (with Mrs Marlow on the piano) are singing the same song, then to the woods where Mrs Marlow is in tears after her adultery with Binney, to Mrs Marlow on Hammersmith Bridge and finally to her naked body pulled from the Thames. The Mills Brothers' song is ironic in its jazzy harmonies, deadly accurate in its 'trite sentiments',[59] and it also effectively binds the narratives.

Even the songs that are not mimed have thematic significance and reveal dramatic contrast. After climbing to the top of his tree in the Forest of Dean, the young Marlow says the Lord's Prayer and on the sound-track Bing Crosby croons 'Don't Fence Me In'. As the camera sweeps back from the forest, we cut to a radio in Gran's house where Bing's song continues and, in contrast to the boy's vision of freedom, we see Mrs Marlow imprisoned by the domestic and social conventions of matrimony. 'Putt thik racket, off!' instructs Gran.

In the final episode, Potter uses the lines from 'The Teddy Bears' Picnic' – 'If you go out in the woods today, you'd better not go alone, It's lovely out in the woods today, but better to stay at home' – as a moment of Marlow's self-recognition. The song binds his memories and fantasies – the fictional detective singing, the mother and Binney on the ground, the young Marlow running away, the loneliness of the father, the hospital experience – and it finally releases 'all of Marlow's fatal traumas... The lyric's power is therapeutic enough to lift the arthritic Marlow to his feet.'[60] Amazed, he stumbles forward and calls out, 'Look, I did it! I walked! I can walk!'

Since the nineteen songs dominate stylistically, Amiel was at first unsure about what music to use for the title theme and dramatic transitions. Eventually he decided that since Potter was playing with derivative styles, he should echo it and turn to an effects disc library. He 'got in over fifty albums of these weird generic titles with short pieces called something like "shock blood corridor" or "stirring chilly crescendo ending in a tympani climax" ... [he] came up with about forty different bits of totally generic music, which was cut together'.[61] The stings and transitions were assembled into a compelling soundtrack which, as in the title sequence, draws the viewer in and underlines the suspense of the investigation.

Casting accomplices

In their themes and explorations, other Potter films, such as *Secret Friends* and *Blackeyes*, explore some of the same territory as *The Singing Detective*, but in emotional terms none achieves the depth of character sustained by Amiel's cast. I was intrigued to find out how Amiel chose and prepared actors. He gave me some clues.

'I didn't find the casting difficult. I found I was like a kid in a sweet-shop, because suddenly I had these absolutely wonderful roles that I could take to actors whom I had admired for many years and finally say, here is a role worthy of you, Bill Paterson, Alison Steadman, Ron Cooke, Michael Gambon.'[62] Amiel relied on instinct, often casting an actor for a very large role 'simply on the basis of a 20-minute conversation'. Sometimes he had a specific idea, 'but many times casting would actually surprise me'. He gave me an example: 'I had no idea what the father should look like, but at the time I was casting for the second of the mysterious men, I had already cast little Ron Cook for the first one, I knew I wanted someone either very tall or fat to play the other one – I wanted them to be a complete odd couple. Michele Guish, a casting director, had said there is this marvellously funny guy who is 6 ft 4 inches tall and was in *Guys and Dolls* playing Big Julie, and in came Jim Carter for the role of the second mysterious man.' Amiel talked to Jim for about 15 minutes: 'I listened to his lovely sad brown voice ... his big earlobes made him look tremendously vulnerable and gentle.' He remembers watching him walk away down the corridor 'with this slightly stooping walk that rather tall men have and feeling an odd mixture of sadness and tenderness and knowing that this was the feeling that I wanted the father to evoke. I had not been able to visualise the father until Jim walked in.'[63]

Amiel believes in the importance of rehearsals with actors before shooting. Many producers balance slipping schedules and financial problems by cutting rehearsal periods. Amiel pushed hard for extra rehearsal time and Kenith Trodd gave it to him. The series was in production for five and half months. Amiel had two weeks of rehearsal at the beginning and a further two in the middle.

In rehearsal period, I used to allow the characters [the actors] to explore the relationship with each other so that a feeling of familiarity that you get within families evolved ... a sense of the things that people express, but don't need to say. We also worked very hard on the text, a great number of alterations were made to the text during the rehearsal period.[64]

Jon told me, 'The great value of rehearsal is that it allows you to make that kind of vulcanised weld between the actors and the text where you can no longer see where the character begins and the actor ends.'

Characters, motives and further evidence

The Marlow family's disintegration sits like a knot in the stomach. The young unblinking Philip, played with an air of inquisitive innocence by Lyndon Davies, takes in the beauty of the forest, but also the human cruelty and treachery around him. His indirect revenge on the son of his mother's lover is chillingly determined. Again, his confused cruelty in abandoning his mother in the underground only surfaces slowly as the guilt for his mother's suicide becomes clear to the older Marlow. We've heard the sound 'motif' of his mother's voice yelling after him, 'Philip, Philip', from the first episode. Associated with that cry are the lights of the train in the underground that, like a hearse, probe Marlow's subconscious again and again. The young Philip's unblinking stare haunts the series. The same stare that watched his mother's infidelity with Binney in the forest in episode 2 also watches his father in the last episode throw back his head and let out 'one long and strange and almost animal-like cry of absolute grief and despair. Philip, in cover, watches this terrible release of anguish with wide eyes, and yet no obvious expression.'[65] It is a riveting mixture of bereavement, guilt, innocence and emotional withdrawal. Earlier, the father, played by Jim Carter, had taken young Philip's hand in the forest,

MR MARLOW   (*suddenly*): I love you, Philip. I love you, o'but. With all my heart.
      PHILIP: Shhh!
MR MARLOW: What –?
      PHILIP: Somebody might hear us![66]

The young Philip holds back and cannot trust himself to feel love ever again. Later we hear the vow that he took then, 'Don't trust anybody again! Don't give your love. Hide in yourself. Or else they'll die ... And they'll hurt you! Hide! Hide!'[67]

As viewers, we long for him to reach out to his vulnerable father. He cannot do it. In the hospital, Michael Gambon as the older Marlow says 'Dad –?' and we remember the echo in the crowded working-men's club in episode 2, where a grown Marlow in his hospital pyjamas appears (at the end of a slow pan) watching his father singing and imitating bird-calls. He says, years later, what he should have said then in the forest as a boy.

MARLOW: That was *my Dad* doing the birds! That's my Dad on the platform – (*shouts*) Dad! Dad! Over here, o'butty! Come over here! Dad! Thee's know how much I'd care about tha –.[68]

But the past and present are not merged and the scene switches quickly to Marlow alone in the empty, poorly lit working-men's club. 'The upright piano on the platform is draped with long, dusty cobwebs.'[69]

Michael Gambon, as Philip Marlow, balances the complexities of the drama of the family's disintegration, the unravelling of his psychological turmoil, the cruelty of his revenges, the sharpness of his wit, the softness of his own human vulnerability with the fictitious wry cynicism of the singing detective. As the detective in episode 3,

MARLOW   (*thinks*): There are songs to sing. There are feelings to feel. There are thoughts to think. That makes three things. And you can't do *three* things at the same time. The singing is easy. Syrup in my mouth. The thinking comes with the tune – so that leaves only the feelings. Am I right? Or am I right? I can sing the singing. I can think the thinking. (*Suddenly savage*) But you're not going to catch me feeling the feeling. No, sir.[70]

His cruelty is sudden and deadly. He turns on the oppressive, revolting George (Charles Simon) for disgusting him with stories of 'shagging Frow Lines' for a few fags. The stories set off Marlow's own memories of his mother's infidelity in the woods, and when George suddenly has a heart attack, the sequence intercuts George's final life struggle with Mrs Marlow and her lover violently 'shagging' in the woods and with Marlow in his hospital bed. And equally cruelly, Marlow claws at Nicola (Janet Suzman), who in his suspicious mind is as unfaithful as his mother and uses sex for money and advancing her career. Gambon gives us much more than just the character's turmoil and revenge and the cool elegance of the detective, he also has us laughing, as is clear in the scene with Ali and the lighter, and sobbing, when suddenly Ali is no longer there. Gambon deserved much critical praise for his performance and he got it. Even the *News of the World* wrote, 'Michael Gambon had me reeling from laughter to tears. That speech of despair, Got under my skin.'[71]

Janet Suzman, the ex-wife Nicola, matches the emotional onslaught with a sad humanity and understandable self-defence. There are obsessive echoes among the ex-wife, the mother and the whores. Women and sex draw Marlow in and, at the same time, push him away. Philip's mother, played by Alison Steadman, is the main cause of the complexity and the play's turmoil, but she is no villain. Her love and concern for Philip are clear. She is a metropolitan character miscast in the Forest of Dean community. In ironic contrast to Philip's father's cuckoo and birdsong imitations, she plays the 'Rite of Spring' on the piano. The powerful tea scene where the dour Gran (Maggie Holland) goes on about a 'lovely bit o' plum' while Grancher (Richard Butler) emphatically spits into the grate has us on the verge of retching with Mrs Marlow. She explodes about 'being squashed up in this poky hole' and accuses her husband of not being 'any sort of a man'. (Philip's vulnerable Dad is not the man to stand up to his mother and wife.) Mrs Marlow's escape from this misery is into the woods with Binney. Alison Steadman's portrait merges with the Lili Marlene character in the fictional story and transfers to the sexual film noir motif of the women's naked bodies being pulled from the river (the mother, Russian Sonia and Nicola are all echoed in that recurring image).

A key role in freeing Marlow's helpless but fertile mind is that of Dr Gibbon, the psychiatrist, cunningly played by Bill Paterson. Dr Gibbon sees that Marlow has a psychosomatic illness caused by repression of painful childhood memories – that his psychological development is reflected in his illness, his writing and his relationship with Nicola and other people. Eventually through the probing and goading of Dr Gibbon, Marlow is able to overcome his paralysis and, in the last episode, he stands for the first time and dances with Dr Gibbon. Potter undercuts the dramatic impact of the moment with an ironic musical number as the two men mime to Ella Fitzgerald and the Inkspots singing, 'Into Each Life Some Rain Must Fall'. It is Dr Gibbon who gets Philip, as Nicola says, to 'come down from his tree'. But walking is not enough, psychologically; Marlow still has one score to settle – that is to resolve the struggle between Marlow the writer and Marlow his creation – the Singing Detective. With typical Potterian irony, the creation – the Singing Detective – tops the creator – Marlow the writer – with a bullet drilled into the forehead.

But these are the heavyweight parts, and in contrast there is much light and amusing comedy acting. The mysterious men, played by Ron Cook and George Rossi, are dressed up to suggest suspense and evil, but in fact add buffoonery to the detective narrative. They are Stoppardian characters looking for roles. As they say in the last episode, 'We're padding. Like a couple of bleed'n sofas',[72] 'Our roles are unclear ... No *names*, even. No bloody handles.'[73] From the beginning we have known that this team was playing at being gangsters and are as innocently dangerous as Wilmer in *The Maltese Falcon*. Mr Hall (David Ryall) and Reginald (Gerald Horan) also continue their endless humorous bickering about tea, bedpans and hospital company. And Reginald, of course, embodies Potter's playful device of reading the book of *The Singing Detective*, which allows him the opportunity of recapping the events for us at the beginning of 'Pitter Patter', episode 5. The relationship Marlow has with nurse Mills is in contrast to the tormented one he has with Nicola. Nurse Mills is never fished from the Thames. Marlow says to her, 'You are the girl in all those songs' – and so she is. Nurse Mills, played by Joanne Whalley, is an uncomplicated, sensuous 'angel of mercy' who delivers mental, physical and sexual comfort. Joanne Whalley's eyes stare down sympathetically at Marlow. She injects a strong life-force into the play. While most of Fleet Street debated the graphic details of the adultery scenes, *The Times* at least recognised the alluring danger of nurse Mills to male middle-aged viewers. 'Joanne Whalley's eyes ought to carry a Government health warning.'[74]

Patrick Malahide plays three characters: Binney the spy in the detective story, Mark Binney who seduces Philip's mother and the modern film producer Finney who steals Marlow's book and wife. We think of him as the slightly pinched evil-hearted catalyst who pushes forward Marlow's real and imagined events. In all three parts, Malahide gives the character the air of predatory treachery suitable for generating injury and neuroses in the young and old Marlow. We never do find out if he smuggled Nazis out of Britain. But does it matter?

There is another kind of treachery in the frightening authoritarian country-school teacher played by Janet Henfrey. As in *Blue Remembered Hills* and *Stand Up Nigel Barton*, Potter shows us 'childhood innocence [as] unspoiled original sin'[75] filled with snivelling, hypocrisy, betrayal and guilt. Janet Henfrey echoes a strong performance in *Stand Up Nigel Barton* and creates an almost religiously fanatical character who will have created traumatic psychic damage in Philip and in generations of her pupils.

The cast of *The Singing Detective* made their own powerful contribution to the play, achieving that invisible seam where the character begins and the actor ends.

Who done it?

The more I investigate clues as to why *The Singing Detective* is such an inspiring work, the more I discover 'further surprising revelations' in the creative journey of making it. The journey certainly seems elliptical, but that undoubtedly is normal in making any television drama involving sixty or more people. Talent does not drop out of the sky, it is fostered and encouraged. Although the series was a relatively low-budget production (about £400,000 per programme), it is not surprising that it was made at the BBC in the mid-eighties when the organisation encouraged confidence in its programme-makers and was comparatively generous in germinating and realising new work.

Potter's script mapped the terrain, but the achievement was the locking together of many artistic instincts. So Who Done It? Well, like Poirot in *Murder on the Orient Express*, I conclude, 'They were all in it ... it was a perfect mosaic, each person playing his or her allocated part.'[76] The process was a creative collaboration which made us sit up and watch television drama, not as an apology for a mini-movie, but as a creative and powerful dramatic medium. *The Singing Detective* was inspiring because it showed us the dynamic possibilities of television drama. Nancy Banks-Smith in *The Guardian* summed it up with, 'If the BBC and its Empire lasts another 50 years, men will still say, "This was one of their finest plays."'[77]

As Poirot would say, 'Having placed my solution before you, I have the honour to retire from the case.'

The Singing Detective

First episode transmitted on BBC1 on 16 November 1986

For cast, technical and production credits, see Dennis Potter, *The Singing Detective* (London: Faber and Faber, 1986)

Notes

1 Dennis Potter, *Waiting for the Boat* (London: Faber & Faber, 1984), 26.
2 Hilary Kingsley, *Daily Mirror*, 17 November 1986, 17.
3 Alan Rusbridger, *The Observer*, 23 November 1986.
4 Christopher Dunkley, *Financial Times*, 12 November 1986, 23.
5 Lucy Hughes-Hallett, *London Standard*, 17 November 1986.
6 Dennis Potter, *The Singing Detective* (London: Faber & Faber, 1986), 2. The book is not exactly the same as the scripts used during the making of the serial: some of the events, dialogue and emphases are different. Potter decided to rework the script so that it would read more like a novel. However, the publication is still a useful reference and I list page numbers when appropriate.
7 *Ibid.*, 3.
8 *Ibid.*, 4.
9 *Ibid.*, 5.
10 *Ibid.*, 6.
11 Dennis Potter, quoted by Richard Corliss, *Time*, 1 August 1988, 42.
12 *The Singing Detective*, 10.
13 Nicholas Shakespeare, *The Times*, 22 December 1986.
14 *The Singing Detective*, 11, 12.
15 *Ibid.*, 18.
16 *Ibid.*, 20.
17 Kenith Trodd, in notes for BBC music cassette of *The Singing Detective* (BBC Enterprises Ltd), 1986.
18 *The Singing Detective*, 30.
19 *Ibid.*, 38.
20 This line ends the first episode entitled 'Skin', but it is not in the published version. The episode headings (1. 'Skin', 2. 'Heat', 3. 'Lovely Days', 4. 'Clues', 5.

'Pitter Patter', 6. 'Who Done It?') are not used in the book either.
21 Christopher Dunkley, *Financial Times*, 23.
22 George Brandt, from unpublished notes for a lecture on *The Singing Detective* delivered at Leeds Polytechnic on 4 June 1991.
23 Jon Amiel interviewed by the author, 4 January 1992.
24 Dennis Potter quoted in *Radio Times*, 15 November 1986, 98.
25 Dennis Potter interviewed by James Seymour, *Stills* 21 (November 1985).
26 Potter, *Radio Times*, 15 November 1986, 98.
27 Nancy Banks-Smith, *The Guardian*, 1 December 1986, 11. Ms Banks-Smith says *The Singing Detective* 'is demonstrably Potter's Hamlet: the wanton mother, the betrayed father, even the built in detective story'.
28 Potter quoted in *Time*, 1 August 1988, 42.
29 Brandt, notes for a lecture.
30 Dennis Potter interviewed by Alan Yentob on *Arena* (BBC2), 30 January 1987.
31 Potter quoted in *Radio Times*, 15 November 1986, 99.
32 Linda Gomez, 'The Subversive Potter', unpublished dissertation BA (Hons) in Film, Video and Photographic Arts, Polytechnic of Central London, 1989, 34.
33 Dennis Potter, *Daily Mail*, 30 July 1980.
34 Dennis Potter quoted in *Radio Times*, 15 November 1986, 98.
35 *Waiting for the Boat*, 30.
36 *Ibid.*
37 Brandt, notes for a lecture.
38 Linda Gomez, 'Subversive Potter', 32.
39 Jon Amiel interview, 4 January 1992.
40 Kenith Trodd interviewed by the author, 5 December 1991.
41 *Ibid.*
42 Jon Amiel interview, 4 January 1992.
43 *Ibid.*
44 Jim Clay interviewed by the author, 8 January 1992.
45 *Ibid.*
46 *Ibid.*
47 *Ibid.*
48 Jon Amiel interview.
49 *Ibid.*
50 *Ibid.*
51 John Wyver, *The Listener*, 13 October 1986, 30–1.
52 Frances Hannon interviewed by the author, 13 January 1992.
53 *Ibid.*
54 *Ibid.*
55 *Ibid.*
56 *Ibid.*
57 Charles Catchpole, *The Sun*, 22 November 1986, 13.
58 Kenith Trodd, in notes for BBC music cassette of *The Singing Detective*.
59 Dennis Potter, in notes for BBC music cassette of *The Singing Detective*.
60 Richard Corliss, *Film Comment* 24, 2 (March–April 1988), 17.
61 Jon Amiel interview.
62 *Ibid.*
63 *Ibid.*
64 *Ibid.*

65 *The Singing Detective*, 233.
66 *Ibid.*, 222.
67 *Ibid.*, 232.
68 *Ibid.*, 79.
69 *Ibid.*
70 *Ibid.*, 86.
71 Nina Myskon, *News of the World*, 23 November 1986, 23.
72 *The Singing Detective*, 231.
73 *Ibid.*, 245.
74 Martin Cropper, *The Times*, 8 December 1986.
75 Philip Purser, *Dennis Potter*, in George Brandt (ed.), *British Television Drama* (Cambridge University Press, 1981), 189.
76 Agatha Christie, *Murder on the Orient Express* (London: Collins, Fontana Books, 1934, 6th impression 1968), 186.
77 Nancy Banks-Smith, *The Guardian*, 11 December 1986, 186.

Select Bibliography

Books

Corrigan, Timothy, *A Cinema Without Walls/Movies and Movie Culture After Vietnam* (London: Routledge, 1992), esp. 179–93
Potter, Dennis, *Pennies from Heaven* (London: Quartet Books, 1981)
   Waiting for the Boat: On Television, also includes *Blue Remembered Hills, Joe's Ark, Cream in my Coffee* (London: Faber, 1984).
   The Singing Detective (London: Faber, 1986)
   Christabel (adapted from Christabel Bielenberg's *The Past is Myself*) (London: Faber, 1988)

Articles (other than those quoted in the notes)

Andrew, Nigel, 'Dark angel' (Dennis Potter directs *Blackeyes*), *Radio Times*, 25 November – 1 December 1989, 4–5
Barker, Adam, 'What the detective saw: family resemblances in the work of Roeg and Potter', *Monthly Film Bulletin*, 55, no. 654, 193–5
Barnett, Anthony, 'Detecting the British disease' (The clues left by *The Singing Detective*), *The Listener*, 1 January 1987, 24
Dunn, Elisabeth, 'Patrick's day' (Patrick Malahide in *The Singing Detective*), *Radio Times*, 6–12 December 1986, 23
Fuller, Graham, 'Dollars from heaven' (*The Singing Detective* and Mike Leigh's *High Hopes* in the USA), *The Listener*, 4 May 1989, 33–4
Hebert, Hugh, 'Singing through the pain', *The Guardian*, 17 November 1986
   'Nobody beats the old conundrum like Potter', *The Guardian*, 20 December 1986, 11
Oakes, Philip, 'A suitable sleuth for treatment', *Radio Times*, 15–21 November 1986, 98–101
Rusbridger, Alan, 'Tune in, turn on, drop out', *The Observer*, 21 December 1986
Wyver, John, 'Fear and . . .', *The Listener*, 13 November 1986, 30–1

See also:

Broadcast, 21 November 1986, 15 (Frances Hannon on her make-up design for the serial)

City Limits, 6–13 November 1986, 21 (Interview with Potter)

Film Comment, 24, 2 (March–April 1988), 13–14, 17

The Listener, 20 November 1986, 38; 11 December 1986, 34; 24 March 1988 (Note about the BBC's reluctance to repeat the serial)

Media Week, 14 November 1986, 12 (Assessment of the serial's ratings potential)

The Observer, 7 December 1986 ('Redemption from under the skin' – profile of Dennis Potter)

Television Today, 27 March 1986, 17; 20 November 1986, 21

Variety, 17 February 1988, 101, 104

Appendix 1: Programmes on Videotape

Some, but unfortunately not all, the productions discussed in this book are available commercially on videotape, either for sale or rental: some outstanding ones among them are unlikely ever to be so, for various reasons.

The list of those currently available has been checked at the time of publication, but it is as well to remember that videotape distribution is a highly fluid area.

BBC Enterprises distribute the following videotapes, either in the UK and/or overseas:

1 'Bed Among the Lentils', one of three monologues from *Talking Heads*, the other two items on the tape being 'A Chip in the Sugar' and 'Her Big Chance'. Total running time: 116 mins. Only available overseas. There is an audio-cassette version of *Talking Heads* available in the UK (Cat. no. AW 85), with a total running time of approximately 195 mins.

2 'The Grand Design' and 'The Ministerial Broadcast', two out of three episodes from *Yes, Prime Minister*, the other item being 'The Smoke Screen' (Cat. no.: BBCV 4410). Total running time: 241 mins. Also available worldwide. Note that other cassettes in the series are also available both in the UK and overseas.

3 *Edge of Darkness* comes in two parts (Cat. nos. BBCV 4169 and BBCV 4170), with respective running times of 150 and 157 mins. These tapes are also available overseas.

4 *Boys from the Blackstuff* also comes in two parts, Cat. nos. BBCV 4217 and BBCV 4218, with respective running times of 172 and 136 mins. These tapes are also available overseas.

(For all further information, contact BBC Video, BBC Enterprises Ltd, 80 Wood Lane, London W12 0TT.)

The Video Collection distributes the following tape:

5 'The Last Enemy', which is on the same *Inspector Morse* tape as 'Deceived by Flight' (Cat. no. VC 6168), with a total running time of 204 mins. This tape is not available outside the UK.

Messrs W. H. Smith distribute the following tapes in the UK:

6 *The Jewel in the Crown*, which comes in a set of three cassettes (Cat. No. CVI 1301), with a total running time of 12 hours. This set of tapes is distributed in the USA by Simon and Schuster (113 Sylvan Ave., Route 9W, Englewood Cliffs, New Jersey 07632).

Appendix 2: IBA/ITC Research Papers

Throughout the eighties, the Research Department of the Independent Broadcasting Authority (now the Independent Television Commission) produced a large number of research papers analysing audience attitudes to various television programmes, including drama. These papers, which contain a wealth of fully evaluated statistical information, have not been distributed to the public at large but are available to interested readers for inspection at the Independent Television Commission, 33 Foley Street, London W1P 7LB.

Relevant papers include the following:

Fiction and depiction: Attitudes to fifteen television series, and the novels from which they were made   April 1980

Brideshead Revisited: A flawed and final masterpiece of major TV series production?   March 1982

The Nation's Health: Viewers' personalities and attitudes to the series
                                                                  February 1984

The Winds of War   April 1984

The Day After and *First Tuesday* (Windscale)   May 1984

Threads and *A Year After*   January 1985

Heroic or humdrum? Some recent characters of the screen
                                                                  February 1989

The Cosby Show: Some black and white audience perceptions and possibilities   November 1989

Select Bibliography

Plays published

(This bibliography, which brings up to date Appendix 1 of G. Brandt's *British Television Drama* (Cambridge University Press, 1981), 239–46, lists – predominantly but not exclusively – TV plays produced during the 1980s.)

Abbreviations

DOT *Debut on Two*, ed. by Phillippa Giles and Vicky Licorish (London: BBC Books, 1990)
IC *Intensive Care and other TV Plays*, by Alan Bennett *et al.* (London: Longman, 1989)

Barker, Howard, *Pity in History*, in *Gambit Magazine*, no. 41 (London: John Calder, 1984)
Batty, Nicola, *Skin*, in *DOT*
Birkin, Andrew, *The Lost Boys* (London: BBC Publications, 1980)
Bleasdale, Alan, *Scully*, ed. by David Self (London: Hutchinson/Studio Scripts, 1984)
  The Monocled Mutineer (London: Hutchinson, 1986)
Bradbury, Malcolm, with Christopher Bigsby, *The After Dinner Game: Four Plays for Television* (London: Arrow Books, 1989). Contents: *The After Dinner Game, Love on a Gunboat, Standing in for Henry* and *The Enigma*
Brenton, Howard, *Dead Head: A Thriller for Television* (London: Methuen, 1987)
Cleese, John, and Connie Booth, *The Complete Fawlty Towers* (London: Methuen, 1988)
Clement, Dick, and Ian La Frenais, *The Complete Porridge* (London: BBC Books, 1990)
Cornell, Paul, *Poppylands*, in *DOT*
Curteis, Ian, *Churchill and the Generals* (London: BBC Publications, 1980)
  Suez (London: BBC Publications, 1980)
Devlin, Anne, *Ourselves Alone* (London: Faber, 1986). Contents: *Ourselves Alone, The Long March, A Woman Calling*
Duggan, Shaun, *You Lucky Swines*, in *DOT*
Evans, Gregory, *Windows of Vulnerability*, in *DOT*
Flynn, Robert, *The Conversion of St Paul*, in *DOT*

Galton, Ray, and Alan Simpson, *Hancock: The Classic Years* (London: BBC Books, 1987)

Giles, Phillippa, and Vicky Licorish (eds.), *Debut on Two*, pt 2: New TV Playwrights (London: BBC Books, 1990)

Glendinning, Robin, and Leonard Kingston, *A Night of the Campaign*, in *IC*

Gray, Simon, *After Pilkington* (London: Methuen, 1987)

Griffiths, Trevor, *Country: A Tory Story* (London: Faber, 1981)
   Sons and Lovers/Screenplay of the Novel by D. H. Lawrence, with an introduction (Nottingham: Spokesman, 1982)
   Oi for England (London: Faber, 1983)
   Judgement over the Dead: The Screenplay of The Last Place on Earth (London: Verso, 1986)
   Collected Plays for Television (London: Faber, 1988). Contents: *All Good Men, Absolute Beginners, Through the Night, Such Impossibilities, Country: A Tory Story, Oi for England*

Hampton, Christopher, *The Ginger Tree/Adapted from the Novel by Oswald Wynd*, with an Introduction (London: Faber, 1989)

Hare, David, *Dreams of Leaving: A Film for Television* (London: Faber, 1980)
   Saigon – Year of the Cat (London Faber, 1983)
   Heading Home (London: Faber, 1991). Contents: *Heading Home, Wetherby, Dreams of Leaving* (London: Faber, 1991)

Haseldon, John, *The Complete 'Allo, 'Allo* (London: BBC Books, 1991)
   Only Fools and Horses: Trotter Way to Millions (London: BBC Books, 1990)

Haseldon, John, David Croft and Jeremy Lloyd, *'Allo, 'Allo 2* (London: BBC Books, 1989)

Hollowood, Jane, *Looking for Vicky*, in *IC*

Hutchinson, Ron, *Bird of Prey* (London: BBC Publications, 1982)

Johnson, Terry, *Tuesday's Child*; with Kate Lock, *The Trouble* (London: Methuen 1987)

Keefe, Barrie, *The Long Good Friday: An original screenplay* (London: Methuen, 1984)

Kureishi, Hanif, *My Beautiful Laundrette* and *The Rainbow Sign*, with an Introduction (London: Faber, 1986)

Lane, Carla, *Bread: The Scripts* (London: BBC Books, 1990)

Leland, David, *Flying in the Wind (Tales out of School 2)*, with an Introduction (Cambridge University Press, 1985)
   Birth of a Nation (Cambridge University Press, 1986)
   Made in Britain (Cambridge University Press, 1986)
   Rhino (Cambridge University Press, 1986)

McEwan, Ian, *The Imitation Game: Three Plays for Television*, with an Introduction (London: Cape, 1981). Contents: *Jack Flea's Birthday Celebration, Solid Geometry* and *The Imitation Game*
   The Ploughman's Lunch: An Original Screenplay (London: Methuen, 1985)

Macgee, Paula, *Breast is Best*, in *DOT*

McLeod, Jenny, *The Wake*, in *DOT*

Mercer, David, *Collected TV Plays*, 2 vols. (London: John Calder, 1981)

Milne, Paula, *Expectations*, in *Juliet Bravo* (London: Longman, 1983)
   Die Kinder (London: BBC Books, 1990)

Monvid, Grazyna, *Choices, 4 Plays for ITV's 'Starting Out' Series Spotlight* (London: Heinemann, 1986)

Mortimer, John, *The Dock Brief* and *The Judge's Elbow* (a Rumpole play), in *John Mortimer Plays* (London: Longman, 1989)

Naughton, Bill, *et al.*, *A Special Occasion: Two TV Plays and One Radio Play* (London: Longman, 1988). Contents: Bill Naughton, *A Special Occasion*; Clive Jermain, *The Best Years of Your Life*; Alma Cullen, *Knowing the Score*

Paul, Jeremy, and Alan Gibson, *The Flipside of Dominick Hide*, in *IC*

Phillips, Caryl, *Playing Away* (London: Faber, 1986)

Pinter, Harold, *The Heat of the Day* (adapted from the novel by Elizabeth Bowen) (London: Faber, 1989)

Poliakoff, Stephen, *Caught on a Train*, in *Favourite Nights and Caught on a Train* (London: Methuen 1982)

Price, Alan David, *A Box of Swan*, in *DOT*

Raphael, Frederic, *Oxbridge Blues*, with an author's Introduction (London: BBC Books, 1984). Contents: *Oxbridge Blues, That was Tory, Similar Triangles, He'll See You Now, The Muse, Cheap Day, Sleeps Six*

Redmond, Phil, *Grange Hill 1: Three Plays Straight from the TV Programmes* (London: Longman, 1985)
  Grange Hill 2: Two Plays from the TV programmes (London: Longman, 1985)
  Grange Hill Scripts (London: Longman, 1985)

Reid, Graham, *Billy: Three Plays for Television* (London: Faber, 1984). Contents: *Too Late to Talk to Billy, A Matter of Choice for Billy, A Coming to Terms for Billy*

Rosenthal, Jack, *P'Tang, Yang and Kipperbang and Other TV Plays* (London: Longman, 1984). Contents: *P'Tang, Yang and Kipperbang, Polly Put the Kettle on, Thank you Thursday, Mr Ellis Versus the People*
  Three Plays (Harmondsworth: Penguin, 1986)
  Three Screenplays (London: Faber, 1986). Contents: *The Chain, The Knowledge, Ready when You are Mr McGill*

Speight, Johnny, *For Richer For Poorer* (London: BBC Books, 1991)

Stoppard, Tom, *Squaring the Circle, Every Good Boy Deserves Favour, Professional Foul* (London: Faber, 1984)

General reference

BBC Handbook (London: BBC, annually 1980–7)

Fulton, Roger, *The Encyclopedia of Science Fiction* (London: Boxtree, 1990)

Halliwell, Leslie, with Philip Purser, *Halliwell's Television Companion* (London: Grafton Books, 3rd edn, 1986)

Hayward, Anthony, *The Who's Who of Soap Opera* (Enfield, Middlesex: Guiness Publishing, 1991)

Kingsley, Hilary, *Soap Box: The Papermac Guide to Soap Opera* (London: Papermac, 1988)

MacDonald, Barrie, *Broadcasting in the United Kingdom: A Guide to Information Sources* (London, New York: Mansell, 1988)

Television and Radio/IBA Yearbook (London: Independent Broadcasting Authority, annually 1980–8)

Tibballs, Geoff, *The Boxtree Encyclopedia of TV Detectives* (London: Boxtree, 1992)

Books

Abbreviations

AM   Pike, Frank (ed.), *Ah! Mischief* (London: Faber, 1982)
BTVD   Brandt, George (ed.), *British Television Drama* (Cambridge University
        Press, 1981)
PTF   Bennett, Tony, *et al.* (eds.), *Popular Television and Film* (BFI, 1981)
TVSC   Cook, Jim (ed.), *Television Sitcom* (BFI, 1982)

Ableman, Paul, *Phil Redmond* (London: BBC, 1982)
    Dad's Army: The Defense of a Front Line English Village, ed. by Arthur Wilson
    (London: BBC Books, 1989)
Alvarado, Manuel, and John Stewart, *Made for Television: Euston Films Limited*
    (London: BFI & Thames TV International, 1985)
Anderson, Lindsay, 'An Introduction: The Old Crowd', in Bennett, Alan, *The
    Writer in Disguise* (London: Faber, 1985), 161–75
Anon., *Coronation Street 2000: Your TV Times Souvenir Album Marking the 2000th
    Episode of Britain's Best Loved Folk Story* (London: Independent Television
    Publications, 1980)
Arrowsmith, S. M. J., 'Peter Watkins', in *BTVD*
Banham, Martin, 'Jeremy Sandford', in *BTVD*
Bazalgette, Caryl, *et al.*, *Teaching Coronation Street* (London: BFI, 1983, 1987)
Bellamy, Frank, *Timeview: The Doctor Who Illustrations* (Bournemouth, Dorset:
    Who Dares, 1985)
Bennett, Tony, Susan Boyd-Bowman, Colin Mercer and Janet Woollacott (eds.),
    Popular Television and Film/A Reader (London: BFI in association with the
    Open University, 1981)
Bennett, Tony, Colin Mercer and Janet Woollacott (eds.), *Popular Culture and
    Social Relations* (Milton Keynes, Open University Press, 1986)
Bentham, Jeremy, *Doctor Who: The Early Years* (London: W. H. Allen, 1986)
Boyd-Bowman, Susan, 'Back to camp', in *TVSC*
Brandt, George (ed.), *British Television Drama* (Cambridge University Press, 1981)
Brunsdon, Charlotte, 'Crossroads', in Kaplan, *Regarding Television*
Buckingham, David, *Public Secrets: EastEnders and Its Audience* (London: BFI,
    1987)
Buckman, Peter, *All for Love: A Study in Soap Opera* (London: Secker & Warburg,
    1984)
Bulman, J. C., and H. R. Coursen, *Shakespeare and Television; An Anthology of
    Essays and Reviews* (University Press of New England, 1988)
Caughie, John, 'Progressive television and documentary drama', in *PTF*
Clarke, Alan, '"This is not the boy scouts": Television police series and definitions
    of law and order', in Bennett, T., *Popular Culture and Social Relations*
Clarke, Mike, *Teaching Popular Television* (London: Heinemann Educational
    Books, in association with the BFI, 1987)
Cook, Jim (ed.), *Television Sitcom* (BFI Dossier 17) (London: BFI 1982, 1984)
    'Narrative, comedy, character and performance', in *TVSC*
Cooke, Brian, *Writing Comedy for Television* (London: Methuen, 1983)
Corner, John (ed.), *Popular Television in Britain: Studies in Cultural History*
    (London: BFI, 1991)
Corrie, Andrew, and John McCready, *Phil Redmond's Grange Hill: The Official*

Companion (London: Weidenfeld & Nicolson, 1988)

Crisp, Mike, *After Tea We'll Do the Fight: Filming Action* (London: BBC Television Training, 1987)

Curran, James, Anthony Smith and Pauline Wingate (eds.), *Impacts and Influences: Essays on Media Power in the Twentieth Century* (London: Methuen, 1987)

Curtis, Barry, 'Aspects of sitcom', in *TVSC*

Davies, Hunter, *The Grades: The First Family of British Entertainment* (London: Weidenfeld & Nicolson, 1981)

Dicks, Terence, *Doctor Who: The Five Doctors* (London: W. H. Allen, 1983)

Dunkley, Christopher, *Television Today and Tomorrow: Wall-to-Wall Dallas?* (Harmondsworth: Penguin, 1985)

Dyer, Richard, Christine Geraghty, Marion Jordan, Terry Lovell, Richard Patterson and John Stewart, *Coronation Street: The Continuous Serial – A Definition* (London: BFI, 1981)

Eagle, Robert, and Herbie Knott, *How They Made Piece of Cake* (London: Boxtree, 1988)

Eaton, Mick, 'Television situation comedy', in Bennett, T., *Popular Television and Film*

Edgar, David, 'On drama documentary', in *AM*

Elder, Michael, *Ten Years of Take the High Road* (London: Boxtree, 1990)

Ellis, John, *Visible Fictions – Cinema: Television: Video* (London: Routledge & Kegan Paul, 1982)

Ferguson, James, *Emmerdale Farm: The Official Companion* (London: Weidenfeld & Nicolson, 1988)

Fiske, John, *Television Cultures: Popular Pleasures and Politics* (London: Methuen, 1987)

Gascoigne, Bamber, *et al.*, *The Making of The Jewel in the Crown* (London: Granada Publishing Ltd., 1983)

Geraghty, Christine, *Women in Soap Opera* (Cambridge: Polity Press, 1988)

Giddings, Robert, Keith Selby and Chris Wensley, *Screening the Novel: The Theory and Practice of Literary Dramatization* (New York: St Martin's Press, 1990)

Giles, Phillippa, and Vicky Licorish, *Debut on Two* (London: BBC Books, 1990)

Glaister, Gerard, and Ray Evans, *Howard's Way* (London: BBC Books, 1988)

Goodwin, Andrew, Paul Kerr and Ian Macdonald (eds.), *Drama Documentary – BFI Dossier 19* (London: BFI, 1983, 1984)

Griffiths, Stuart, *How Plays Are Made: A Guide to the Technique of Play Construction and the Basic Principles of Drama* (London: Heinemann, 1982)

Griffiths, Trevor, 'Countering consent: an interview with John Wyver', in *AM*

Haining, Peter, *The Television Sherlock Holmes* (London: W. H. Allen, publ. in association with Granada Television, 1986)

Doctor Who/A Celebration: Two Decades through Space and Time (London: W. H. Allen, 1983)

Doctor Who/The Key to Time: A Year-by-Year Record (London: W. H. Allen, 1984)

The Doctor Who File (London, W. H. Allen, 1986)

Doctor Who: The Time Traveller's Guide (London: W. H. Allen, by arrangement with BBC Books, 1987)

Doctor Who: 25 Glorious Years (London: W. H. Allen/Planet, by arrangement with BBC Books, 1988)

Agatha Christie – Murder in Four Acts: A Centenary Celebration of 'The Queen of Crime' on Stage, Film, Radio and TV (London: Virgin Books, 1990)

Hare, David, 'Ah! mischief: the role of public broadcasting', in *AM*

Harris, Mark, *The Doctor Who Technical Manual* (London: Severn House, 1983)

Hobson, Dorothy, *Crossroads: The Drama of a Soap Opera* (London: Methuen, 1982)

Hunt, Albert, 'Alan Plater', in *BTVD*
   The Language of Television: Uses and Abuses (London: Eyre Methuen, 1981)

Hurd, Geoffrey, 'The television presentation of the police', in *PTF*

Irvine, Mat, *Doctor Who Special Effects* (London: Hutchinson, 1986)

Jarvis, Peter, *Does the Horse Explode?/Visual Effects for Television* (Elstree: BBC Television, 1989)

Kaplan, E. Ann, *Regarding Television/Critical Approaches: An Anthology* (University Publications of America, Inc., The American Film Institute, 1983)

Kay, Graeme, *Coronation Street: Celebrating 30 Years* (London: Boxtree, 1990)
   Life in the Street: Coronation Street Past and Present (London: Boxtree, 1991)

Kershaw, H. V., *The Street Where I Live* (London: Granada Publishing Ltd., 1981)

Kingsley, Hilary, *EastEnders Handbook* (London: BBC Books, 1991)

Lambert, Stephen, *Channel Four: Television with a Difference?* (London: BFI, 1982)

Lewis, Claire, and Kelly Davis, *35 Up: The Book of the Granada Series* (London: Network Books, 1991)

Lofficier, Jean-Marc, *The Doctor Who Programme Guide*, vol. I (London: W. H. Allen, 1981)

Lovell, Terry, 'A genre of social disruption?', in *TVSC*

Lynch, Tony, *The Bill: The Inside Story of Television's Most Successful Police Series* (London: Boxtree, 1991)

Lynn, Jonathan and Anthony Jay, *The Complete Yes Minister: The Diaries of a Cabinet Minister, by the Right Hon. James Hacker MP* (London: BBC Books, 1989)

Madden, Paul, 'Jim Allen', in *BTVD*

Mechele, Tony, and Dick Fiddy, *The Saint* (London: Boxtree, 1989)

Medhurst, Andy, and Lucy Tuck, 'The gender game', in *TVSC*

Miles, Keith, *The Official Crossroads Special* (London: Grandreams Ltd, 1982)

Miller, Brian, 'Peter Nichols', in *BTVD*

Miller, Jeffrey (compiler), *Street Talk: The Language of Coronation Street*, ed. by Graham Nown (London: Ward Lock, 1986)

Mitchell, Julian, 'Television: an outsider's view', in *AM*

Morley, David, *Family Television: Cultural Power and Domestic Leisure* (London: Comedia, 1986, 1988)

Mustafa, Khalid El Mubarak, 'David Mercer', in *BTVD*

Neale, Steve, and Frank Krutnik, *Popular Film and Television Comedy* (London: Routledge, 1990)

Nown, Graham, *Coronation Street: 25 Years, 1960–1985* (London: Ward Lock, in association with Granada Television, 1985)

Oakley, Giles, 'Yes Minister', in *TVSC*

O'Connor, Alan (ed.), *Raymond Williams on Television/Selected Writings* (London, New York: Routledge, 1989)
   Raymond Williams: Writing, Culture, Politics (Oxford, New York: Blackwell, 1989)

Paget, Derek, *True Stories? Documentary Drama on Radio, Screen and Stage* (Manchester University Press, 1990)

Peel, John, *Doctor Who: Season One: Part One* (Canoga Park, Cal.: Sci Fi Movie Press, 1986)

Doctor Who: The Eleventh Season (Canoga Park, Cal.: Sci Fi Movie Press, 1986)

Peel, John, and Terry Nation, *The Official Doctor Who and the Daleks Book* (New York: St Martin's Press, 1988)

Pertwee, Bill, *Dad's Army: The Making of a Television Legend* (Newton Abbot, London: David & Charles, 1989)

Pike, Frank (ed.), *Ah! Mischief: The Writer and Television* (London: Faber, 1982)

Pilling, Jayne, and Kingsley Canham, *The Screen on the Tube: Filmed TV Drama*, Cine City Dossier no. 1 (Norwich: Cinema City: 1983)

Podmore, Bill, and Peter Reece, *Coronation Street: The Inside Story* (London: Macdonald, 1990)

Poole, Michael, and John Wyver, *Powerplays: Trevor Griffiths in Television* (London: BFI, 1984)

Potter, Dennis, 'Some sort of preface...', in his *Waiting for the Boat* (London: Faber, 1984)

Purser, Philip, 'Dennis Potter', in *BTVD*
Done Viewing (London: Quartet Books, 1992)

Puttnam, David, *Film-Maker in Wonderland*, in Wenham, *The Third Age of Broadcasting*

Pym, John, *Film on Four/A Survey 1982–1991* (London: BFI Publishing, 1992)

Redmond, Phil, *Phil Redmond's Brookside: The Official Companion* (London: Weidenfeld & Nicolson, 1987)

Road, Alan, *Doctor Who – The Making of a Television Series*, with an Introduction by Peter Davison (London: André Deutsch, 1982)

Rogers, Dave, *The Avengers: All 161 Original Episodes – Story, Cast and Pictures* (London: Independent Television Books, in association with Michael Joseph, 1983)

The Avengers Anew, credits and synopses of the 26 episodes of The New Avengers (London: Michael Joseph, 1985)

The Professionals: The Cast, the Characters and the 57 Episodes (London: Queen Anne Press, 1986)

The Complete Avengers (London: Boxtree, 1989)

Danger Man and The Prisoner (London: Boxtree, in association with ITC Entertainment Ltd, 1989)

Rossington, Jane, *The Crossroad Years: The Official Album* (London: Weidenfeld & Nicolson, 1988)

Saunders, David, *Encyclopedia of the Worlds of Doctor Who: A–D* (London: Piccadilly Press, 1988)

Encyclopedia of the Worlds of Doctor Who: E–K (London: Piccadilly Press, 1989)

Encyclopedia of the Worlds of Doctor Who: L–R (London: Piccadilly Press, 1990)

Schumann, Howard, *Video-Mad: An American Writer in British Television*, in *AM*

Self, David, *Television Drama: An Introduction* (London: Macmillan, 1984)

Smith, Julia, and Tony Holland, *EastEnders: The Inside Story* (London: BBC Books, 1987)

Stacey, Chris, and Darcy Sullivan, *Supersoaps* (London: Boxtree, 1988)

Sutton, Shaun, *The Largest Theatre in the World* (London: BBC Publications, 1982)

Swanson, Gillian, *Law and Disorder*, in *TVSC*

Tinkler, Jack, *Coronation Street* (London: Treasure Press, by arrangement with Granada, 1987)

Tulloch, John, *Television Drama: Agency, Audience and Myth* (London: Routledge, 1990)

Tulloch, John, and Manuel Alvarado, *Doctor Who: The Unfolding Text* (London: Macmillan, 1983)

Wenham, Brian (ed.), *The Third Age of Broadcasting* (London: Faber & Faber, 1982)

White, Matthew, and Jaffer Ali, *The Official Prisoner Companion* (London: Sidgwick and Jackson, 1988)

Whitemore, Hugh, *Word into Image: Reflections on Television Drama*, in *AM*

Williams, Raymond, 'Foreword', in John McGrath, *A Good Night Out: Popular Theatre/Audience, Class and Form* (London: Methuen, 1981)

'Foreword', in Hunt, *The Language of Television*

Articles

Abbreviations

MFB	*Monthly Film Bulletin*
NSN	*New Statesman and Nation*
PEITF	*Programme of the Edinburgh International Television Festival*
RT	*Radio Times*
S & S	*Sight and Sound*
TL	*The Listener*

Alvarado, Manuel, 'Who is the Doctor?' (20th anniversary of *Dr Who*), *TL*, 8 December 1983, 39

Anghelides, Peter, 'Dramatic decline' (The decline of the single play), *TL*, 7 February 1980, 174–5

'Griffiths of the Antarctic', *Observer*, 17 February 1985

'EastEnders/One year old this week', *RT*, 22–28 February 1986, 9–20

'Overrated ratings', *TL*, 22 January 1987, 28

Auty, Martyn, 'A Yorkshireman abroad' (Alan Bennett), *Time Out*, 13–19 September 1984, 13

Bailey, Paul, 'Fog over England' (*Bleak House*), *RT*, 6–12 April 1985, 82–5

Ball, Mark, 'Lost in space' (*Doctor Who*), *TL*, 17 October 1988, 18–19

'Heroine dependent' (Feminised dramas), *TL*, 16 February 1989, 29–30

Bati, Anwer, 'East side story' (Farrukh Dhondy's *King of the Ghetto*), *RT*, 26 April–2 May 1986, 82–3

'East side story' (Gareth Jones' *Shalom Salaam*), *RT*, 22–28, April 1989, 10–11

Bellamy, Guy, 'From the horse's mouth' (*Only Fools and Horses*), *RT*, 5–11 November 1983, 4–5

Benedictus, David, 'Precious possessions' (Interview with Jonathan Raban), *RT*, 14–20 May 1983, 14

Bennett, Alan, 'British cinema/Life before death on television', *S & S*, 53, 2 (spring 1984), 121–2

Berry, David, 'The copycat effect – a case to answer?' (Suicides on TV), *TL*, 14 August 1986, 26

Bidmead, Christopher, 'Gene machine' (William Nicholson's *Life Story*, dir. by Mick Jackson), *TL*, 23 April 1987, 30

Billington, Michael, 'Broken rules' (David Hare's *Dreams of Leaving*), *RT*, 12–18 January 1980, 17

'Shooting in the dark' (Peggy Ashcroft in Stephen Poliakoff's *Caught on a Train*), *RT*, 25–31 October 1980, 24–7

Black, Johnny, 'Adventures to cap them all' (John Christopher's *The Tripods*), *RT* 15–21 September 1984, 26

Boyd, William, 'People don't talk like that' (David Mercer's *A Dinner of Herbs*), *TL*, 11 August 1988, 37–8

Bradbury, Malcolm, 'The celluloid collar 6' (University TV dramas), *TL*, 28 April 1988, 22–3

Bragg, Melvyn, 'The celluloid collar 7' (The *Ten Great Writers* series), *TL*, 5 May 1988, 22–3

Brown, Colin, 'Call to arms: Granada film productions', *Producer*, no. 8, 1989, 20–1

Brown, Robert, 'On television ... under drama-documentary: interview with TV producer-director Leslie Woodhead', *MFB*, 50, 593 (June 1983), 154–5

Brunsdon, Charlotte, '"Crossroads" – notes on soap opera', *Screen*, 22, 4 (1981), 32–7

'Problems with quality', *Screen*, 31, 1 (spring 1990), 67–90

Bruxelles, Simon de, 'Cockney soap puts "Street" in a lather' (*Eastenders* and *Coronation Street*), *Observer*, 17 November 1985

Buckman, Peter, 'In praise of the soaps', *TL*, 19 August 1982, 25–6

'Soft soap' (*EastEnders*), *TL*, 28 February 1985, 32

Burn, Gordon, 'Island of adventure' (*Bergerac*), *RT* 8–14, January 1983, 92–5

'Alf's back/For better or for worse' (Warren Mitchell in Johnny Speight's *In Sickness and in Health*), *TL*, 31 August–6 September 1985, 11

Cable, Mike, 'Growing up in the garden of the gods' (Charles Wood's adaptation of Gerald Durrell's autobiography, *My Family and Other Animals*), *RT*, 17–23 October 1987, 102–5

Cadogan, Mary, 'On the trail of the spinster sleuth' (Joan Hickson as Miss Marple), *RT*, 22 December 1984–4 January 1985, 17

Campbell, Jenny, 'On yer bike, Batty' (Roy Clarke's *The First of the Summer Wine*), *RT*, 3–9 September 1988, 11–12

Caughie, John, 'Progressive television and documentary drama', *Screen*, 21, 3 (1980), 9–35

'Rhetoric, pleasure and art television: Dreams of Leaving', *Screen*, vol. 22, no. 4, 9–31

'Television criticism: "A discourse in search of an object"', *Screen*, 25, 4–5 (1984), 109–20

Chapman, Miles, 'Don't laugh at me' (Norman Wisdom in *Going Gently*), *RT*, 30 May–5 June 1981, 6–7

'Changing Lane' (interview with Carla Lane), *RT*, 31 October–6 November 1981, 11–13

'Camp humour' (David Croft & Jimmy Perry's *Hi-De-Hi!*), *RT*, 28 November–4 December 1981, 6–9

Combs, Richard, 'Richard's Things' (Raphael), *S & S*, 49, 3 (summer 1980), 149–51

Connolly, Ray, 'Cheerful echoes' (*Hi-De-Hi!*), *RT*, 21–27 February 1981, 9–11

Cosgrove, Stuart, 'Refusing consent: The "Oi for England" project', *Screen*, 24, 1 (1983), 92–6

Crace, Jim, 'A view of the country' (Trevor Griffiths' *Country*), *RT*, 17–23 October 1981, 11–13

'Cavalier attitudes' (*By the Sword Divided*), *RT*, 15–21 October 1983, 84–91

'Acting Armageddon' (Barry Hines' *Threads*, dir. by Mick Jackson), *RT*,

22–28 September 1984, 17–19

'Breaking the silence' (Anne Devlin's *The Long March*), *RT*, 17–23 November 1984, 21–3

'Comedy of terrors' (Alan Bennett's *The Insurance Man*), *RT*, 22–28 February 1986, 98–101

'Pym's people' (Arthur Hopcraft's adaptation of John le Carré's *A Perfect Spy*), *RT*, 31 October–6 November 1987, 9–16

'Brave new campus' (Andrew Davies's *A Very Peculiar Practice*), *RT*, 20–26 February 1988, 20–2

'Juliet finds a welcome in the hillsides' (Juliet Stevenson in Tom Clarke's *Out of Love*) *RT*, 6–12 August 1988, 9–13

Crowley, Jeananne, 'Belfast revisited' (Stewart Parker's *Iris in the Traffic, Ruby in the Rain*), *RT*, 21–27 November 1981, 13–15

'Home truths' (Mike Leigh's *Home Sweet Home*), *RT*, 13–19 March 1982, 17–18

'Crimes to be committed' (Caryl Churchill's *Crimes*), *RT*, 10–16 April 1982, 14

'School's out!' (*The Burston Rebellion*), *RT*, 23 February–1 March 1985, 4–5

Cunliffe, David, 'That's entertainment', *TL*, 11 August 1983, 29

Cushman, Robert, 'The art of the actress' (Anna Massey in Elaine Morgan's *Journey into the Shadows*), *RT*, 26 May–1 June 1984, 76–80

Dark, Stephen, 'Police tactics' (Cop shows), *TL*, 3 January 1985, 29

Davie, Michael, 'The "truth" of fiction is stranger than facts' (TV biopics), *Observer*, 24 February 1985, 56

Day-Lewis, Sean, 'Not in front of the adults' (Why we need more sex on television), *TL*, 12 November 1987, 34

Donnelly, Frances, 'The farmer's wife' (Cheryl Campbell in *A Winter Harvest*), *RT*, 7–13 July 1984, 72–6

Downing, Taylor, 'Tele-history is bunk – or is it?', *PEITF 1980*, 13–19

Dugan, Sally, 'Dance with a strange one' (Charles Dance in Ted Whitehead's *First Born*), *RT*, 29 October–4 November 1988, 9–13

Dugdale, John, 'Life in the farce lane' (Malcom Bradbury's adaptation of Tom Sharpe's *Blott on the Landscape*), *TL*, 31 January 1985, 27

'Serial polygamy' (Sexualising the British soap opera), *TL*, 9 April 1987, 29

'Comic retainer' (*Porterhouse Blue*), *TL*, 28 May 1987, 30

'TV comedy: who's laughing now?', *TL*, 19 November 1987, 41–2

'Telly classico' (John Mortimer's *Summer's Lease*), *TL*, 7 September 1989, 4–6

Edgar, David, 'Faction plan' (Docu-drama), *TL*, 1 June 1989, 13–14

Eyre, Richard, 'Beating the retreat', *TL*, 1 September 1983, 28

Fenwick, Henry, 'Relatively speaking' (*The Borgias*), *RT*, 10–17 October 1980, 82–9

'First Storey' (David Storey's *Pasmore*), *RT*, 18–24 October 1980, 23–7

'An arresting story' (David Edgar's *The Jail Diary of Albie Sachs*), *RT*, 21–7 February 1981, 16

'Coral Browne as herself' (Alan Bennett's *An Englishman Abroad*), *RT*, 26 November–2 December 1983, 92–7

'Peck's appeal' (Bob Peck in Simon Gray's *After Pilkington*), *RT*, 24–30 January 1987, 82–3

'Frenetic genetics' (*Life Story*), *RT*, 25 April–1 May 1987, 82–4

'The power of love' (Screen Two: *The Temptation of Eileen Hughes*), *RT*, 2–8 April 1988, 15–16

Fiddick, Peter, 'The longest Street on television' (*Coronation Street*), *Guardian*, 4 May 1981

'Heart of drama throbs in Brum' (Central TV), *Guardian*, 9 July 1983, 8
'Squeeze play at the Beeb', *Guardian*, 14 February 1984
'The ratings game', *TL*, 5 January 1989, 4–6
Forbes, Jill, 'Snafu!: *Saigon – Year of the Cat* (David Hare)', *S & S*, 53, 1 (winter 1983–4), 62–3
Fordham, John, 'The swinging detectives' (Plater's *The Beiderbecke Tapes*), *TL*, 10 December 1987, 33
Forman, Denis, 'It is time we came out of our state of technological shock' (The MacTaggart Lecture at the Edinburgh International Television Festival 1984), *TL*, 30 August 1984, 8–12
'British TV – who are the masters now?' (Richard Dimbleby Lecture 1987), *TL*, 16 July 1987, 12–15
Fox, Sue, 'All the fun of the fare' (ScreenPlay: *Shiftwork*), *RT*, 20–28 September 1986, 9
Fuller, Graham, 'Dollars from heaven' (British films and TV programmes in the USA), *TL*, 4 May 1989, 33–4
Gardner, Carl, 'Television's talk shop' (The Edinburgh International Television Festival 1984), *TL*, 6 September 1984, 27
'Do not adjust your set' (John Byrne's *Normal Service*), *TL*, 28 January 1988, 27
Gardner, Carl, and John Wyver, 'The single play: from Reithian reverence to cost-accounting and censorship', *PEITF 1980*, 47–52
'The single play' and 'The single play: an afterword', *Screen*, 24, 4–5 (1983), 114–29
Giddings, Robert, 'Recycling the classics', *TL*, 8 December 1983, 42
Gilbert, W. Stephen, 'Comedy, with chips' (John McGrath's *The Adventures of Frank*), *RT*, 1–7 November 1980, 9–11
'Closed circuits' (Trevor Griffiths' *Country*), *Guardian*, 17 October 1981
Grant, Linda, 'The devil to play' (Robin Chapman's adaptation of A. N. Wilson's *Blore MP*), *RT*, 21–27 October 1989, 16–17
Grant, Steve, 'The quiet man cometh' (Alan Bennett plays), *Time Out*, 5–11 November 1982, 19
'Ah, Mr. Freud!' (Carey Harrison's *Freud*), *Observer*, 9 September 1984
Gregory, Roger, 'The con of social realism', *TL*, 4 August 1983, 28
Griffiths, Katie, 'The vets come marching home' (*All Creatures Great and Small*), *RT*, 17–30 December 1983, 108–9
Griffiths, Trevor, 'A novel Lawrence' (Griffiths' dramatisation of *Sons and Lovers*), *RT*, 10–16 January 1981, 84–6
Grut, Vicky, 'Soap box: writing for television', *Producer*, 9 (autumn 1989)
Hassan, Mamoun, 'British cinema/Life before television', *S & S*, 53, 2 (spring 1984), 116
Heald, Tim, 'Off with his head' (John Hawkesworth's *By the Sword Divided*), *RT*, 12–18 January 1985, 4–5
Hebert, Hugh, 'Blackeyes and red faces' (Dennis Potter directs), *Guardian*, 22 December 1989
Heron, Liz, 'Antiques road show' (Ian McShane in Ian La Frenais's *Lovejoy*), *RT*, 4–10 January 1985, 6–7
'The importance of playing Oscar' (Michael Gambon in John Hawkesworth's *Oscar*), *RT*, 23–29 March 1985, 82–5
'Barker's bite' (Howard Barker's *Pity in History*), *RT*, 29 June–5 July 1985, 8–9
'The short story that became an epic' (Ronald Eyre's *A Crack in the Ice*), *RT*, 3–9 August 1985, 70

'Love on the run' (Alan Plater's adaptation of Olivia Manning's *Fortunes of War*), *RT*, 10–16 October 1987, 98–101

'Women in love with Lawrence' (Anne Devlin's adaptation of *The Rainbow*), *RT*, 3–9 December 1988, 4–10

Hill, Dave, 'Interviews with Carla Lane, Nick Hayes and Phil Redmond', *New Statesman & Society*, 25 August 1989, 35–8

Hobson, Dorothy, 'Slippery soaps', *PEITF 1985*, 55–60

Hodgson, Clive, 'Growing Up' (Jim Allen's *The Gathering Seed*), *RT*, 3–9 September 1983, 8

Horner, Rosalie, 'Jewels in the crown' (Peggy Ashcroft and Geraldine James in Stephen Poliakoff's *She's Been Away*), *RT*, 7–13 October 1989, 14–17

'Ackland's land' (Joss Ackland in Michael Frayn's *First and Last*), *RT*, 9–15 December 1989, 8

Household, Nicki, 'Woman on her own' (Carla Lane's *Solo*), *RT*, 10–16 January 1981, 16–19

'A terminal case' (Ron Hutchinson's *Bird of Prey*), *RT*, 17–23 April 1982, 21–3

'Del keeps it in the family' (*Only Fools and Horses*), *RT*, 2–8 March 1985, 13

'Ode to Joy' (Bill Nicholson's *Shadowlands*), *RT*, 21 December 1985–3 January 1986, 144–5

'Carla takes another dip in the "Pool"' (Carla Lane's *Bread*), *RT*, 26 April–2 May 1986, 4–5

'It all happens on the night shift' (*Casualty*), *RT*, 6–12 September 1986, 4–5

Housham, David, 'Boys from the Front' (Alan Bleasdale's *The Monocled Mutineer*), *TL*, 28 August 1986, 28

Houston, Penelope, 'A house in Ireland: *Reflections*' (Banville), *S & S*, 53, 2 (spring 1984), 149

Hunt, Albert, 'Batty over Nora' (Roy Clarke's *Last of the Summer Wine*), *RT*, 9–15 February 1985, 82–5

'Strife in a northern town' (Barry Collins' Screen Two: *Lovebirds*), *RT*, 5–11 March 1988, 15

Jackson, Michael, 'Cinema versus television', *S & S*, 49, 3 (summer 1980), 178–81

Jones, D. A. N., 'Holy disorders' (Alan Plater's adaptation of Trollope, *The Barchester Chronicles*), *RT*, 6–12 November 1982, 84–90

'Enrolled nurse' (*Angels*), *RT*, 3–9 September 1983, 9

'A new Twist to an old tale' (Alexander Baron's adaptation of *Oliver Twist*), *RT*, 12–18 October 1985, 4–5

'Class war on the Western Front' (*The Monocled Mutineer*), *RT*, 30 August–5 September 1986, 72–3

Kavanaugh, P. J., 'Stock characters' (*The Pickwick Papers*), *RT*, 5–11 January 1985, 4–5

Kemp, Philip, 'On the Black Hill' (Grieve), *S & S*, 56, 4 (autumn 1987), 232

Kennedy, Douglas, 'Ireland of dreams' (Frank McGuiness's *Scout*, Anne Devlin's *The Venus de Milo Instead*, and John McGahern's *The Rockingham Shoot*), *RT*, 5–11 September 1987, 13

Kent, Nicolas, 'Interview with David Rose', *S & S*, 56, 4 (autumn 1987), 260–3

Kerr, Paul, 'London Documentary Drama Group – a response to John Caughie' (with John Caughie's reply), *Screen*, 22, 1 (1981), 101–5

'Classic serials – To be continued', *Screen*, 23, 1 (1982), 6–19

'Situation comedies ... and television situations', *Screen*, 24, 1 (1983), 71–4

'Brit-lit pics' (Films made for television), *TL*, 5 December 1984, 38

'Drama out of a crisis' (*Casualty*), *TL*, 4 September 1986, 26–7

'Series that take drama seriously', *TL*, 12 November 1987, 33–4

'Fitting The Bill' (Revising the format of *The Bill*), *TL*, 28 April 1988, 16

'Quality control', *New Statesman & Society*, 21 July 1989, 36–7

Khan, Naseem, 'Once in David's city' (David Mercer's *A Dinner of Herbs*), *RT*, 30 July–5 August 1988, 9

Kingsley, Madeleine, 'School for scandal?' (Phil Redmond's *Grange Hill*), *RT*, 5–11 January 1980, 84–9

'In deep water' (Jack Pulman's *Private Schultz*), *RT*, 2–8 May 1981, 14–15

'Road to success' (Paula Milne's *Driving Ambition*), *RT*, 3–9 March 1984, 10

Kohler, Renate, 'New Who' (Peter Davison as Doctor Who), *RT*, 2–8 January 1982, 9

'Hospital corner' (*Angels*), *RT*, 4–10 September 1982, 6

Kuehl, Jerry, 'Truths claims' (Drama documentaries), *S & S*, 50, 4 (autumn 1981), 272–4

Kuhn, Annette, 'Women's genres', *Screen*, 25, 1 (1984), 18–29

Lawton, Heather, 'Two sides of Albert Square' (*EastEnders*), *RT*, 1–7 June 1985, 18–19

Lennon, Peter, 'Numero uno' (Profile of Jonathan Powell), *TL*, 21 April 1988, 8–9

Levine, Ian, 'Who's Who's Who' (*Doctor Who*), *RT*, 19–15 November 1983, 84–7

Lewis, Nigel, 'Czech mates' (Screen Two: Tim Rose's *Border*), *RT*, 6–12 February 1988, 8

Lodge, David, 'The celluloid collar 3' (Dramatisation of novels for TV: *Small World*), *TL*, 7 April 1988, 14–15

McArthur, Colin, 'Disabling images' (*Taggart*), *TL*, 4 September 1986, 26

McGrath, John, 'Strike at the fiction-factories', *PEITF 1985*, 53–4

Mackenzie, Suzie, 'Her brilliant career' (Verity Lambert), *Guardian*, 31 October 1990, 19

'A talent to amuse' (Carla Lane), *Guardian*, 10 April 1991, 34

Malik, Rachel, 'Criticising television', *Producer*, 14 (winter 1990), 16–17

Mantle, Jonathan, 'Menace in Venice' (Leslie Megahy's *Cariani and the Courtesans*), *RT*, 1–7 August, 74–7

Martin, Brendan, 'Drinking and drying' (Carla Lane's *I Woke Up One Morning*), *RT*, 16–22 March 1985, 4–5

'Treats in store' (Roy Clarke's *Open All Hours*), *RT*, 31 August–6 September 1985, 15

Mayne, Richard, 'Bad boys/*Another Country* and *An Englishman Abroad*', *S & S*, 53, 2 (spring 1984), 148–9

Medhurst, Andy, 'Move over darling' (Domestic arrangements in the British sitcom), *TL*, 5 November 1987, 34

'Green on the Screen' (*Emmerdale Farm*), *TL*, 19 May 1988, 16–17

Millar, Gavin, 'British cinema/Life before television', *S & S*, 53, 2, 120

Miller, Jonathan, 'Valete' (edited version of his MacTaggart Lecture 1983), *PEITF 1984*, 84–7

Milner, Roger, 'A man of destiny' (*Reith*), *RT*, 12–18 November 1983, 9–13

Morgan, Elaine, 'The hero as hero' (*The Life and Times of David Lloyd George*), *RT*, 28 February–6 March 1981, 74–8

'Spring for all seasons' (The dramatisation of Howard Spring's *Fame is the Spur*), *RT*, 2–8 January 1982, 6–7

'Before the National Health' (Don Shaw's dramatisation of A. J. Cronin's *The Citadel*), *RT*, 15–21 January 1983, 4–5

Mortimer, John, 'The pursuit of love' (*Unity*), *RT*, 14–20 March 1981, 78–81

Moss, Norman, 'Master mind' (Carey Harrison's *Freud*), *RT*, 8–14 September 1984, 11–15

Neve, Brian, '*Fellow Traveller*' (Eaton), *S & S*, 59, 2 (spring 1990), 117–19

Nightingale, Benedict, 'Nasty business' (Alan Clarke directs David Leland's *Beloved Enemy*), *RT*, 7–13 February 1981, 14–15

'Spreading success' (Interview with Alan Bleasdale), *RT*, 9–15 October 1982, 19–22

'Street wisdom' (Nigel Williams' *Johnny Jarvis*), *RT*, 5–11 November 1983, 84–7

Ottaway, Robert, 'Bill joins the Old Bill' (Bill Patterson in Malcolm McKay's *The Interrogation of John*), *RT*, 26 September–2 October 1987, 15

Pannifer, Bill, 'Short and sharp' (*ScreenPlay* firsts), *TL*, 13 August 1987, 25

'Green and unpleasant land' (David Rudkin's *White Lady*), *TL*, 20 August 1987, 25

Park, James, 'Four Films for 4' (Michael Radford's *Another Time, Another Place*, Gavin Millar's *Secrets*, Laura Mulvey and Peter Wollen's *The Bad Sister*, Karl Francis' *Giro City*), *S & S*, 52, 1 (winter 1982–3), 8–12

Paterson, Moira, 'The lady at the lake' (Christopher Hampton's adaptation of Anita Brookner's *Hôtel du Lac*), *RT*, 1–7 March 1986, 8–9

'The lies of the land' (Fay Weldon's *Heart of the Country*), *RT* 21–27 February 1987, 9

Payne, Vicky, 'I felt so at home' (Interview with Rosemary Harris, star of *To the Lighthouse*), *RT*, 19–25 March 1983, 4–5

'Love at loggerheads' (Nigel Williams' *Breaking Up*), *RT*, 15–21 November 1986, 15

Perry, Simon, 'British cinema/Life before television', *S & S*, 53, 2 (spring 1984), 119–20

Petley, Julian, 'The upright houses and the romantic Englishwoman: A guide to the political theatre of David Hare', *MFB*, 52, 614 (March 1985), 71–2

'Millions like her: the career of John McGrath', *MFB*, 53, 635 (December 1986), 360–1

'Over the top' (Reaction to *The Monocled Mutineer*), *S & S*, 56, 2 (spring 1987), 126–31

'Independent access', *S & S*, 56, 4 (autumn 1987), 244–8

'*A Very British Coup*', *S & S*, 57, 2 (spring 1988), 95–7

Phillips, Mike, 'Hartley's heroine' (*Juliet Bravo*), *RT*, 4–9 September 1982, 9

Plater, Alan, 'Langham Diary' (The demise of the single play), *TL*, 17–24 December 1987, 48

'The celluloid collar 1' (Dramatisation of novels for TV), *TL*, 24 March 1988, 16–17

'Write to reply' (The writer's part in the public debate on broadcasting), *TL*, 2 March 1989, 6–7

Poole, Michael, 'TV drama goes live', *TL*, 10 February 1983, 31

'The cult of the generalist: British television criticism 1936–83', *Screen*, 25, 2 (March–April 1984), 41–61

'The state of TV criticism', *TL*, 22 March 1984, 11–13

'Write stuff?' (The London Screenwriters' Workshop), *TL*, 25 October 1984, 31

'The case for the defence: the *Thorn Birds* row', *PEITF 1984*, 12–14

'Follow the leader' (Trevor Griffiths' *The Last Place on Earth*), *TL*, 14 February 1985, 27–8

Pope, Stephen, 'Life with the lads' (Class in popular drama series), *TL*, 3 April 1986, 31

Powell, Jonathan, 'A loss of nerve', *TL*, 28 July 1983, 29

Power, Eithne, 'Michelle – Lofty's wedding belle' (*EastEnders*), *RT*, 20–28 September 1986, 4–5

Pym, John, '*Cream in my Coffee* (Potter)', *S & S*, 49, 3 (summer 1980), 150–1

'Love and property: Andrew Newman's *Mackenzie*', *S & S*, 49, 4 (autumn 1980), 232–6

'Our Alan: *Intensive Care* (Bennett)', *S & S*, 52, 1 (winter 1982–3), 68

'Dole life: *Meantime* (Mike Leigh)', *S & S*, 53, 1 (winter 1983–4), 62

Robinson, Andrew, 'Boys from the currystuff' (Farrukh Dhondy, multicultural programmer at Channel 4), *S & S*, 55, 1 (winter 1985–6), 14–18

Robinson, David, '*My Beautiful Laundrette* (Kureishi)', *S & S*, 55, 1 (winter 1985–6), 67

Roddick, Nick, '*Brideshead Revisited*', *S & S*, 51, 1 (winter 1981–2), 58–60

Rogers, Byron, 'Closing the file' (*Smiley's People*), *RT*, 18–24 September 1982, 88–94

Rosenthal, Jack, 'The celluloid collar 5' (The TV playwright and the director), *TL*, 21 April 1988, 10–11

Russell, David, 'TV drama: a world in action', *S & S*, 59, 3 (summer 1990), 174–9

Saynor, James, 'Black and blue' (Dennis Potter directs *Blackeyes*), *TL*, 1 July 1989, 4–7

'One girl's war' (Dennis Potter's *Christabel*), *TL*, 28 July 1988, 4–6

'Writers' television' (Ten years of *Film on Four*), *S & S*, November 1992, 28–31

Search, Gay, 'Café ooh-la-la!' ('*Allo, 'Allo*), *RT*, 1–7 September 1984, 8

'National Alf Service' (Warren Mitchell as Alf Garnett in *In Sickness and Health*), *RT*, 2–8 September 1989, 6

'Engineering laughter' (David Lodge's *Nice Work*), *RT*, 30 September–6 October 1989, 17

Seymour, Alan, 'This has been the happiest experience of my writing life' (*Frost in May*), *RT*, 15–21 May 1982, 78–84

Shine, Helen, 'Family ties' (ScreenPlay: *Home Front*), *RT*, 20–26 August 1988, 10

Silverton, Pete, 'John and Jersey' (John Nettles in *Bergerac*), *RT*, 3–11 October 1985, 82–3

'Going to the wall?' (ScreenPlay: *Brick is Beautiful*), *RT*, 19–15 June 1986, 16

'They call it yuppie love' (Andrew Payne's *Love after Lunch*), *RT*, 19–25 September 1987, 101

Simpson, Phillip, '"Presentness Precise": Notes on *The History Man*', *Screen*, 23, 1 (1982), 20–30

Smith, Richard, 'You've got to think villain' (*The Chinese Detective*), *RT*, 4–10 September 1982, 8

Smurthwaite, Nick, 'Flying south' (Andy Armitage's ScreenPlay: *Starling*), *RT*, 24–30 September 1988, 114

Strickland, Gillian, 'Novel development' (Joan Lingard's *Maggie*), *RT*, 14–20 February 1981, 16–19

Summers, Sue, 'Return of the prodigal Potter', *Sunday Times*, 15 September 1985

Sussex, Elizabeth, '"Getting it right": Granada's *Strike* and the drama-documentary case', *S & S*, 51, 1 (winter 1981–2), 10–15

Taylor, John Russell, 'Love among the waxworks: *Caravaggio* (Jarman)', *S & S*, 55, 2 (spring 1986), 136–7

Theroux, Paul, 'Schlockwatch: *Coronation Street*', *TL*, 31 March 1988, 50

Thomas, Barry, 'Keep the story moving' (The trials of a TV script editor), *TL*, 18/25 December 1986, 30

Thornton, Lesley, 'Business in great waters' (*Onedin Line*), *RT*, 13–19 September 1980, 82–9

Took, Barry, 'Whatever happened to TV comedy?' *TL*, 5 January 1984, 7–8, and 12 January 1984, 8–9

Totten, Eileen, 'Young wife's tale' (John Harvey's adaptation of Arnold Bennett's *Anna of the Five Towns*), *RT*, 5–11 January 1985, 5–8

Wandor, Micheline, 'Where are the new voices?', *TL*, 25 August 1983, 29

Waterhouse, Keith, 'The celluloid collar 4' (Dramatisation of novels for TV), *TL*, 14 April 1988, 12–13

Weldon, Fay, 'A teenager in love' (Maggie Wadey's adaptation of *Northanger Abbey*), *RT*, 14–20 February 1987, 98–101

    'The celluloid collar 2' (Dramatisation of novels for TV), *TL*, 31 March 1988, 12–13

Wheeler, David, 'Two weeks in winter' (Drama documentary), *RT*, 11–17 December 1982, 79–84

Wheen, Francis, 'The right stuff?' (Malcolm McKay's Play on One: *Airbase*), *RT*, 27 February–4 March 1988, 12–13

Whitehead, Phillip, 'The hidden hand and the mailed fist' (The MacTaggart Lecture at the Edinburgh International Television Festival 1987), *TL*, 3 September 1987, 12–16

Winnert, Derek, 'Heil-de-Heil!' (David Croft and Jeremy Lloyd's *'Allo 'Allo!*), *RT*, 19–25 October 1985, 4–5

Woffinden, Bob, 'Dramatic decline at the Beeb', *Guardian*, 15 May 1987

Woolley, Benjamin, 'Making waves' (The Channel Four 'New Waves' series), *TL*, 14 June 1984, 35

    'Is this guy for real?' (Roy Clarke's *Pulaski*), *RT*, 26 September–2 October 1987, 9–13

    'Nine days that shook north London' (Jack Rosenthal's *The Fools on the Hill*), *RT*, 15–31 October 1987, 95

Wyver, John, 'The delicate art of crowd-pleasing' (The Play for Today slot usurped by an American mini-series), *TL*, 24 February 1983, 32

    'The great authorship mystery', *TL*, 14 April 1983, 36

Wyver, John, and Heather Lawton, 'Heat and lust' (Screen Two: Dennis Potter's *Visitors*), *RT*, 21–27 February 1987, 82–3

Young, Steven, 'Blott on the horizon' (Malcolm Bradbury's adaptation of Tom Sharpe's *Blott on the Landscape*), *RT*, 2–8 February 1985, 82–5

Index